Playful Learning

An Alternate Approach to Preschool

Playful Learning
An Alternate Approach to Preschool

Anne Engelhardt   Cheryl Sullivan

LA LECHE LEAGUE INTERNATIONAL
Schaumburg, Illinois

August 1986

First printing, August 1986, 10,000 copies

Second printing, August 1989, 5,000 copies

Third printing, December 1991, 5,000 copies

Fourth printing, April 1996, 3,000 copies

Book and cover design by Lucy Lesiak

Cover photos by Mary Ellen Anderson and Colleen Weiland

Photos by Mary Ellen Anderson, Lynn Armbruster, Jacie Coryell, Anne Engelhardt,
Kathy Farren, Daniel Gibson, William Gommell, Tom Hack, Reinhold Heinrich,
Becky Hejtmanek, Becky Henderson, Nick Orsini, Cheryl Sullivan, Tommy Tune,
Colleen Weiland.

Photos on pages 54, 63, and 389 courtesy of the Joliet *Herald*.

Sketches by Judy Erwin and Anne Engelhardt

Artwork for parts and chapter titles by Dick Martin

Library of Congress Catalog Card Number 86-082265

ISBN 0-912500-30-1

Every effort has been made to determine proper ownership of copyrighted materials
and obtain permission for their use. Any oversight is unintentional and will be corrected in future printings upon proper notification. Excerpts from the following
sources are reprinted with permission: *Betty Crocker's Cookbook for Boys and
Girls*, © 1975, Golden Press, New York; *The Child under Six* by James L. Hymes,
Jr., © 1963, 1961, Prentice-Hall, New Jersey; *Cooking Up Learning* by Jackie Jundt
and Lucy Rumpf, © 1976, Growing Child Playthings, Indiana; *Creative Parenting* by
William Sears, © 1982, Optimum Press, Montreal, Quebec; *The First Three Years of
Life* by Burton L. White, © 1975, Prentice- Hall, New Jersey; *The Gesell Institute's
Child Behavior* by Frances Ilg and Louise Bates Ames, © 1955, Harper and Row,
New York; *How to Raise a Brighter Child* by Joan Beck, © 1975, Simon and
Schuster, New York; *How to Really Love Your Child* by D. Ross Campbell, © 1980,
Victor Books, Wheaton, Illinois; *Hug a Tree and Other Things to Do Outdoors with
Young Children* by Robert E. Rockwell, Elizabeth A. Sherwood, and Robert A. Wil-
liams, ©1983, Gryphon House, Maryland; *The Hurried Child* by David Elkind, ©
1981, Addison-Wesley, Reading, Massachusetts; *Kinder-Krunchies* by Karen S. Jenkins,
© 1982, Discovery Toys, Pleasant Hills, California; *Learning for Little Kids* by Sandy
Jones, ©1978, Houghton Mifflin, Boston; *Learning through Play* by Joan Marzollo,
© 1972, Harper & Row, New York; *Maria Montessori: Her Life and Work* by E. M.
Standing, © 1957, New American Library, New York; *Mothering Magazine*, "Poetry
for Preschoolers," by Connie Biewald, Volume 24, Summer 1982, © Mothering Publications, Santa Fe, New Mexico, All Rights Reserved; *The Mother's Almanac* by Marguerite Kelly and Elia Parsons, © 1975, Doubleday and Company, New York; *Mister
Rogers Talks with Parents* by Fred Rogers and Barry Head, © 1983, Berkley Publishing Group, New York; *Oneness and Separateness: from Infant to Individual* by
Louise Kaplan, © 1978, Simon and Schuster, New York; *The Read Aloud Handbook*
by Jim Trelease, © 1982, Viking-Penguin Books, New York; *Teaching Math to Young
Children* by Rosalie Jensen and Deborah Spector, © 1984, Prentice-Hall, New Jersey;
Teaching Montessori in the Home: the Preschool Years by Elizabeth Hainstock, ©
1968, Random House, New York; *Your Baby's Mind and How it Grows* by Mary Ann
Spencer Pulaski, © 1978, Harper and Row, New York; *Your Child's Self-Esteem* by
Dorothy Corkille Briggs, © 1970, Doubleday and Company, New York; *Whole Life
Parenting* by James and Mary Kenny, © 1982, Continuum Publishing Company,
New York.

Contents

To our children who gave us inspiration and snatches of time in which to work—

Rachel, Laura, Sarah, Matthew, and Luke; Tara and Darren.

And to our husbands, Jerry and Greg, for their unending faith, support, and encouragement—

In hopes that the benefits of this project will be returned to all of them both directly and indirectly.

Foreword

From the first moment that your baby comes into the world all the way into adulthood, your journey with your child is a journey of love. It doesn't take long to discover that your baby isn't just a passive, quiet being like the pictures you see in magazines. She's a dynamic, unique being who thrives on seeing, touching, tasting, and exploring things. She's an aggressive, small scientist who wants to turn over every rock and know all there is to know in her bright and buzzing world. Loving your child isn't passive. It's being right in there with her, providing her with learning experiences, and offering opportunities for awareness and growth.

Playful Learning is a wonderful sourcebook for sharing learning with your young child. It will help you to set up the kind of environment that enables your child's mind and body to grow to their maximum potential. It gives you all of the hints and tips you need to make learning fun and exciting, enabling you to make your child's life far more interesting than just watching television or riding a tricycle all day long.

Not only will *Playful Learning* help you in teaching your child, but it will also open you up to learning from your child. Ideally it will help you to become an open parent, one who is as ready to grow from her child as to foster her child's growth.

Some lessons your child can teach you will be cherished for the rest of your adulthood—like how soothing and freeing it can be to put your hands in cool, damp sand, how important the snail's path on the sidewalk is, or how glorious splashes of water are. These are the kinds of lessons that you need to tuck away in your heart to remind you to cherish being alive.

There are some deeper lessons you can learn as a parent, too. Patience, for example. You learn how to wait for what seems an eternity while your child masters buttoning and tying. Axioms such as "no use crying over spilled milk," and "don't throw the baby out with the bath water" will become real truths in the day-to-day sharing of new experiences with your child.

If you're lucky, you'll develop a very special kind of compassion that makes you aware of how precious all human beings are and how sad suffering is. You'll learn how to delay your own gratification for the sake of another precious being. And you'll learn how to forgive, knowing that your child's earnestness and sense of his own accomplishments are far more valuable than messed up floors or broken objects.

Parenting isn't easy. In fact, it's just about the hardest job in the world. There are no warranties on children. You hope and pray that they will be safe and protected and that they will turn out to be all that you have dreamed they could be. But the potential for reward is just so super! You get to watch your child grow and expand. All the while you are growing and expanding, too. You get a once in a lifetime chance to go back through the wonder of childhood yourself and to forgive your parents and yourself for the unfinished or unhappy parts of your past. In that way, parenting a child helps to make you more whole.

I'm sure that this book coupled with your desire to do well by your child will make many small, wonderful things happen and maybe even a few big things, too. So, as you use *Playful Learning*, I hope you soon find your house filled with small, bright faces, noise, activities, and laughter. I hope, too, you'll make lots of new friends with other mothers and dads in the process, because they can help to make your life so much more meaningful.

My sense is that whatever you can do to make your experiences with your child happier and more fulfilling is well worth your energy and efforts. Good luck with *Playful Learning*. Make it a part of the rich tapestry of loving your child and being loved by her. (P. S. I believe children deserve both *quality* and *quantity* time, don't you?)

Sandy Jones
Author, Psychologist, and Mother

Preface

A child has a natural desire to learn. He is eager to observe and discover the world around him. With a curious mind, he is excited to explore every offering of life—from the detail of a dandelion seed to the vastness of an ocean wave. With growing body and mind, he runs with open arms to each new adventure. Given the opportunity, a child will embrace every aspect of life and will delight in his play with it.

And as he plays, he learns. Just as he does not have to be taught how to play, he does not have to be taught how to learn. Learning, like playing, happens naturally and spontaneously.

Sown in fertile soil, the seeds of play and learning are so involved with each other that they are inseparable. These seeds, under the best conditions, will become one—playful learning—a superior hybrid. However, like all seeds destined to become lush, full, healthy plants, play and learning need to grow in an environment where they will be nourished for optimal development.

Playful learning will blossom in a child when his basic needs are fulfilled naturally and completely as he is growing in the formative preschool years. The young child will bloom most fully under the nurturing of his parents—his most caring gardeners.

Parents are the most important influence on a young child's growth and development in all areas—physical, mental, social, and emotional. Parents are their child's first and most important teachers. The greatest impact on the early education of a young child is made by his parents. Parents' involvement with their young child's learning provides the best setting in which these young plants will thrive.

Are parents capable of providing the nourishment for their child's growth? Are the seeds planted in the right soil? At the right time? Can parents provide the water? The fertilizer? The sunshine? When the time is right, will these young sprouts survive being transplanted to a larger pot? Do parents want to help their young plants mature? Will they see them blossom? Parents can most significantly affect the early learning of their children. In a cooperative preschool-at-home, parents can be a vital part of their young child's playful learning.

Introduction

How to Use This Book

This book is designed to be a multi-purpose guide for adults working with young children. In Part One, "Seeds of Love," the history and need for preschool are discussed. In Part Two, "Planting the Seeds," specific ideas for organizing an alternative to preschool are given.

In Part Three, "Nurturing Young Sprouts," you will find activities directed to all areas of a young child's growth: physical, mental, emotional, and social. The activities suggested have been specifically selected to offer "hands-on" experiences for children two to five years old. You will not be able to try all of the activities in this section with your children nor should you feel you need to include all the categories of learning in their preschool day. Learning should be playful and fun. By providing you with an overview of the ways a young child learns about his world, we hope to help you better understand how to enrich his time spent with you. Parents who want to organize an at-home cooperative preschool will be able to use this guide for ideas and information.

Parents Who Want an Overview of a Cooperative Preschool-at-Home

You can discover a workable alternative to the traditional preschool in Chapters 3, 4, 5, and 6.

If you want to learn about organizing an at-home cooperative preschool, read Part Two, Chapters 7-11.

If you want to find many detailed examples of activities and projects for a small group of preschool children, read Part Three, Chapters 12-24.

Individual Parents Who Want to Enrich the Time Spent with Their Own Children

You can find ways to appreciate and benefit from the learning opportunities in your home, yard, and community. Your child can experience with you the many activities listed in Chapters 12-24. You can use this

You can discover a workable alternative to the traditional pre-school for your child.

book as a guide for "places to go" and "things to do." You will find a list of easy and close-to-home field trips, detailed descriptions of arts, crafts, and science projects, large and small muscle activities, activities to prepare your child for the later learning of math and reading, suggestions to encourage creative thinking and language skills through pretending, music, fingerplays, story-telling, and simple play, and many more helpful ideas in Part Three, Chapters 12-24.

Parents Questioning the Need for Preschool

Review your relationship with your child and understand his needs from birth to preschool in Chapter 1, "You and Your Child."

If you want to understand the role of traditional preschool in our society, read Chapter 2, "Your Preschool Child."

You can discover a workable alternative to traditional preschool in Chapters 3, 4, 5, and 6.

Teachers and Other Adults Working with Young Children

You will find Part Three a helpful resource guide to a gamut of activities and projects. These are geared to the broad spectrum of developmental areas and differences in ability levels that appear in any group of children. You will notice that most of the suggestions that are directed to the more basic skill levels are simple enough to do with a whole class. Also, many of the things to make and do are low cost using collectible items. Read Part Three, Chapters 12-24.

Part One

Seeds of Love

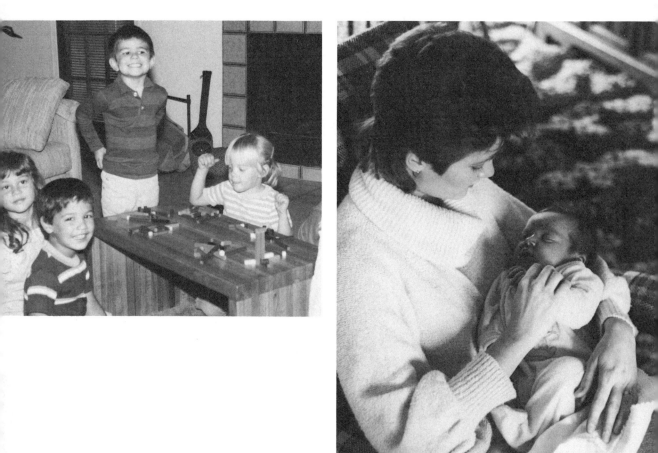

In Part One of *Playful Learning*, we help you explore the relationship you have with your preschool-aged child and evaluate his needs and abilities. We introduce you to the idea of a cooperative preschool-at-home, an alternate approach to preschool that we have enjoyed with our own children. If this idea is new to you, we've tried to answer some of your questions and potential concerns. If you are already familiar with the option of an at-home preschool and want more information on how to do it, you may want to skip Part One and find the details you need to organize an at-home preschool in Part Two.

You and Your Child

Sharing a Special Relationship

To share in the beauty and boundless assimilation of knowledge a two-, three-, or four-year-old goes through is something a mother should never miss. It creates a bond, a deep understanding of the child's mind—you watch it being put together, piece by piece, facet by facet. It's part of our growth as well.

Tamra Hack, mother of Timothy and Dustin

You are a parent of a young child. You picked up this book because you love your child very much and want to give him the very best you can. Every parent wants this.

You might think this book will tell you how to decide which preschool to send your son or daughter to. Perhaps you're wondering if this book might tell you about one type of preschool that is absolutely right for your child. As mothers, we—the authors—believe we have discovered a great preschool option—a cooperative preschool-at-home.

This book is much more than discovering that a cooperative preschool-at-home is a wonderful, workable alternative to the traditional and contemporary preschools available to you today. The preschool-at-home is not one you will find listed in the yellow pages so you can call to enroll your child. Rather, the preschool-at-home is unique because

Your child has a strong need to be with you and you have responded to that need since early infancy.

it is customized to the needs of the parents and children in the group. It is special and strong because it evolves out of the deep relationship you have with your child. This book is really a book about relationships—between you and your child.

Your young child is a very important part of your life. You are his parent. He is yours, forever. The relationship you have with your child is intense, sometimes complicated, and often demanding. You feel the strong need that your son or daughter has for your presence. You know how important you are to him. You are keenly aware that something special is going on between you and your child. You are bonded as only a parent and child can be.

 honestly cannot think of any task more exciting and more valuable that any of us do in our daily work than the task of providing an early education for one's own child under three years of age. The parent who takes the responsibility for structuring the experience of the first three years of his child's life is at the same time taking on an important responsibility for helping to mold that child and helping to give that child's natural tendencies the best possible opportunities to flower. What could be more rewarding than this?

Burton L. White

Evolution of a Parent-Child Relationship

How did this relationship with your child evolve? Well, step back in time just a few short years to the day of your baby's birth. You waited and planned and prepared in every way for this event. Regardless of how the delivery went—whether long or short, difficult or easy—the birth quickly turned into memories of new life. You immediately began to identify your baby's uniqueness. As you fed him cradled in your arms, you began to sense his needs. Your bonding began at this birth (and perhaps even had its roots during pregnancy).

etailed studies of the amazing behavioral capacities of the normal neonate have shown that the infant sees, hears, and moves in rhythm to his mother's voice in the first minutes and hours of life, resulting in a beautiful linking of the reactions of the two and a synchronized "dance" between the mother and the infant.

Marshall Klaus and John Kennel

Your relationship continued to grow. You soon discovered the power of parent-infant bonding. You may be a person unable to hear the alarm clock's early call, but you were able to respond quickly and easily to your baby's first whimpers of hunger in the middle of the night. As the months went by, the relationship between you and your baby deepened. You found your protective instincts awakened when your little one began to grow in awareness as well as size. You carefully selected his toys—giving him ones that were not too heavy, not too sharp, not too tiny. When he was frightened, you were there to comfort him. You shielded him from too friendly and overbearing strangers as he nuzzled his face into your shoulder.

his original mother-infant bond is the wellspring for all the infant's subsequent attachments and is the formative relationship in the course of which the child develops a sense of himself. Throughout his lifetime the strength and character of this attachment will influence the quality of all future bonds to other individuals.

Marshall Klaus and John Kennel

Just yesterday, it seems, your baby pushed himself up on all fours to inch his way across the floor. He found himself in one predicament after another. As he became more mobile, you felt every bump and bruise with him and hugged the tears away. By this time in his life, you knew better than anyone else how your baby would behave in his normal routines and could fairly accurately predict him in unusual situations, too. While he was changing so rapidly you were—and continue to be—his anchor in stormy waters.

ormally an infant learns to use his mother as a "beacon of orientation" during the first five months of life. The mother's presence is like a fixed light that gives the child the security to move out safely to explore the world and then return safely to harbor. . . As the child separates from the state of oneness with his mother, he continues to have an inner experience of a mothering presence which orients him in the world. A child who traverses the symbiotic phase normally has been able to build up an experience of an "inner mother." He therefore is able to take the necessary steps toward personal independence and separate identity.

Louise J. Kaplan

n his first partnership outside the womb, the infant is filled up with the bliss of unconditional love— the bliss of oneness with his mother. This is the basic dialogue of human love.

Louise J. Kaplan

A few months later your creeper became a toddler, testing and trying out every aspect of life around him. You learned to channel his newly acquired skills into constructive activities like building block towers, talking with stuffed animals, and rolling and catching a large ball. Just keeping up with his physical demands at this extremely active stage, you demonstrated your devotion to his needs. He learned he could depend on you for everything from drinks to finding a missing puzzle piece to tying his shoes. You realized that anyone else was capable of doing all these things for him. But you also knew that you didn't want anyone else to take your place. He needed you—not someone else—to be the main person in his life.

Your older toddler with new-found skills became very challenging. The knobs on the television and stereo became the ultimate goal for little hands. Perhaps your toddler looked upon every object or piece of furniture as his personal Mount Everest. Left unsupervised, your toddler might have tried out real wall murals with crayons, pens, or markers. His favorite words were "no" and "me" which reflected his egocentric view of himself in the world, trying to define himself as separate from mother and dad.

Your love and patience were tested in many situations but demonstrated by giving him loving guidelines. Although outwardly your little one seemed quite independent—often daring and sometimes aggressive—he still had very much of "baby" left in him. Only as he became more socially secure with the passing of time would he allow the lead line from mother or dad to be stretched a little farther away with each venture. And you tried to be there for him.

The terrific two's flew by with your involvement in his trials and tribulations. There may have been times you looked at this growing little person and wondered, "Where did my baby go?" He recognized himself most of the time as independent and more capable than he really was. He was determined to try everything all by himself. "No" was still a commonly heard word. But you had to let your fledgling try his wings—watching him pull his wagon for the first time to the corner and back, or go down the slide for the first time.

You have already been a part of your child's earliest learning experiences.

You—as his caring parent—probably had to step in many times to guide him through potentially harmful or uncomfortable situations. You have also had the opportunity to encourage and participate in his rapid growth. Building his self-esteem, you praised his efforts to button his shirt, to say "spaghetti," to hop on one foot, and to share a toy. You looked for age-appropriate playthings and helped him learn how to use them. In your deep caring you wanted to give him each day some undivided one-to-one attention in the same unconditional way that you did when you held him and nursed him for many hours as a baby.

Your soon-to-be three-year-old begins to gain more control of his emotions, his intellect (understanding), and his body skills. He says "yes" more than "no." He tends to cooperate and more readily accepts suggestions and challenges. He is eager to please you and other adults. Compared to a year ago, he seems as different as day is to night. He is growing into a thinking little person with a distinct personality.

By the time your little one reaches the age of three, he loves to play. And he doesn't know it, but as he plays he is working at learning. He is learning everything. He exercises his large muscles as he catches a beachball. With mind-to-hand coordination, he uses his small muscles as he scribbles with crayons and builds block houses. He practices language skills as he "talks" on his play telephone, as he plays dress-ups, or pretends he is a doctor. He enjoys the thrill of singing and dancing. Even as he hears a short story, he is exercising his listening skills. Every waking moment his mind and body are working at his play.

hildren learn best not by being "taught" by parents, but by "doing" and by discovering as they bump through life day in and day out. They learn best with the approval of a caring adult who talks to them about what they are doing.

Elizabeth M. Gregg and Judith D. Knotts

Picture of a Preschooler

If your child is just reaching preschool age, you may want to know more about this delightful stage of growth.* Your three-year-old, you have noticed, is usually pleasant and agreeable. He will easily say "yes" to many things that he so easily used to say "no" to. He has begun to see himself as a part of the larger whole—his family or a group of friends. While he plays, he can share; he is more cooperative and easygoing.

---

*See the Developmental Skills Chart in the Appendix.

Because he has continued to mature and is more secure with himself, your three-year-old likes to venture out more now. He is more confident in making friends and works at keeping them. You might see your little person taking turns or giving up a toy just to maintain a friendship.

 nother aspect of the three-to-six year age range ... is the growth of interest in peer activities.

Burton L. White

The investigative nature of your child comes forward in the three-year-old stage. He has dropped the need for many of the "rituals" of half a year earlier. Now his natural curiosity causes him to ask lots of questions. "Why?" is often heard. He wants to know how everything works and sometimes has fantastic explanations as to his understanding of things.

Your three-year-old also has developed physically enough to be much more self-sufficient. He probably can put on his own elastic-waist pull-on pants and t-shirt. He might even be able to manage to slip on socks and shoes (but no buttoning, tying, or fastening quite yet). He will also be able to handle everyday routines such as brushing his teeth, going to the bathroom, and eating without much help.

Probably the biggest increase in his abilities that shows up by three is his language development. He can use words to communicate to his

Your three- or four-year-old enjoys cooperative play with a small group of friends.

family and his friends. He will use language to entertain himself and others. It can also be used to get what he needs and wants. As parents, you no longer have to guess at what he is asking for. "He loves new words and they often act like magic in influencing him to act as we would wish. Such words as 'new,' 'different,' 'big,' 'surprise,' and 'secret,' all suggest his increased awareness in the excitement of new horizons. Such words as 'help,' 'might,' 'could,' 'guess,' are good motivators to get him to perform necessary tasks" (Francis L. Ilg and Louise Bates Ames). His love of language carries over into an increased enjoyment of books and stories. He will often let you read to him for long periods of time.

The typical three-year-old is in good equilibrium with his world. He can easily conform if needed in a given situation and yet he looks forward positively to new adventures—people, places, and things. He is truly delightful.

y three years, a child will have achieved his initial sense of separateness and identity. However, the reconciliations of oneness and separateness have only begun. The three-year-old has but a small degree of constancy—just enough to allow him to feel safe in the world even though he now recognizes that his self is separate from the self of his mother.

Louise J. Kaplan

At three-and-a-half

But in order to get to four, your little one needs to go through more changes. At around three-and-a-half, his "behavior needs to break up, loosen up, and go through a phase of new integration." This stage may be described as a "period of marked insecurity, disequilibrium, uncoordination" which is to say you will see a lot of emotional ups and downs through this stage of growth. Some children will go through this stage for a very short time without too many difficulties; for others, this disharmony seems to last much longer. You may notice a lack of muscle coordination, such as more stumbling and falling than previously. Or he may be frustrated with paper and pencil tasks as he seems to be taking a step backwards in his drawing. Sometimes stuttering is more noticeable or he seems to increase in thumb-sucking or other habits that seemed to be improved just a few months before.

Even socially, the three-and-a-half-year-old has more difficulties. He might whine or cry more. Or he might be very demanding with adults, saying things like, "Don't do that!" or "Don't talk. Only me!" He would like the exclusive attention of his family and friends.

In this transitional stage, a time when your child may be showing many insecurities that are all normal for growth, you will need to muster up a lot of patience. You will see that things go a little more smoothly if you purposely give him the extra time and attention he needs. Your calm manner and lots of hugs can help keep his disharmony under more control as he grows out of it and into a new stage.

Picture of a Four-Year-Old

Your four-year-old has grown physically and mentally so that he is almost overly self-confident. He kind of explodes in all areas of his life. Physically the four-year-old wants to participate exuberantly in everything, but especially in big muscle activities. And he dearly loves you to participate with him—whether it be roller skating, sledding, swimming, or taking walks. Sometimes he gets carried away with himself as he hits, kicks, and sometimes breaks things. He often talks loudly and likes to use big words or any words with shock value. You will hear him repeat the "in" phrases like "No way!" or "Gross!" or "Hang in there!" even though he may not be sure of their meaning. In his mind he is quite grown up.

In his relationship with others, your four-year-old can get along if he wants to. However, he likes to prove his bigness. You may often hear

Your four-year-old participates exuberantly in everything.

Friendship becomes important to four- and five-year-olds.

him declare that he is "fastest," or "first," or his house is "biggest," and so on. He will exaggerate into tall tales and just plain lies in his attempt to prove something. Generally he longs to play with other children and enjoys his friendships. Very sociable, he shares well and seems to be aware of the attitudes and opinions of others.

 etween the ages of four and seven the child moves from a home-centered existence to the discovery of the world beyond the home ... Children of this age love people, both the important adults in their lives and other children. "I love you, Mommy," is heard frequently. Young children's love for adults makes them eager to copy adults and to please them. Whereas two-year-olds play alone side-by-side, three-year-olds begin to show an interest in other children. Sociability grows. By four, children often want to have friends over to play.

James and Mary Kenny

The imagination of your four-year-old can get quite carried away very easily. He might even believe some of the fantasies which seem real to him. For example, four-year-old Sarah made a flying machine (out of cardboard and paper) and taped it to her head. She went outside to see where it would take her. When she came in, she matter-of-factly said that "the wind wasn't right today. So I'll try it again tomorrow." She really believed that tomorrow she would fly.

A good word to describe a four-year-old is "exuberant." His boundless energy can be overwhelming and even tiring at times. You will find that consistency and firmness on your part will help things go smoothly. You will also discover that meeting the challenges of the new levels of his development will help keep him interested and out of trouble, so to speak. You need to remember that your four-year-old is growing rapidly in body and mind so he will enjoy being given new and different things to do. You can easily direct his exuberance into many projects that he would have been unable to handle at an earlier age.

At four-and-a-half

As the four-year-old begins to approach five, he will gain more control of his "out-of-bounds" kind of behavior. More and more he will try to distinguish between fantasy and reality. He might say something like "Cookie Monster is not real. Bob is real" (Sesame Street). At four-and-a-half though, he is still very good at pretending—putting himself in make-believe play. This is one way he begins to make sense of the world.

P lay is the chief occupation of children. It is just as important to them as a job or a profession is to their parents. In their play, children prepare themselves to cope with the world of reality: practicing motor skills, learning to discipline themselves in accordance with social rules, imitating adult roles, and reconstructing the events of their lives in their imaginations.

Mary Ann Spencer Pulaski

Also at four-and-a-half, your young one can start a job and complete it fairly well. For example, if you observe him playing with blocks, he has an idea in his mind what it will be when it is finished. If he starts out thinking about a town, it will end up a town. Mentally he is beginning to understand the differences from evening to morning and yesterday, today, and tomorrow. He can count to ten. Simple fairy tales are sometimes his favorites.

His physical skills at this age are improving. He can do more and handle more of his self-care if given the chance to be independent. He enjoys practicing skills like throwing and catching balls, as well as drawing. In general, he seems to be gaining more control over all areas of development. He has more refined and precise gestures at this age. He is more clearly focused on what he is and how he is part of his family and his world.

ou can describe these children as searching for a *sense of initiative. A sense of initiative wraps up three-, four-, and five-year-olds, just as a sense of trust beautifully described the overriding concern of infancy, and a sense of autonomy so neatly said the dominant concern of the toddler and the two-year-old.*

James Hymes

A Five-Year-Old

By five years old, he is in a very good stage of equilibrium. You will notice that socially your five-year-old is quite self-assured and will conform to others' expectations of him. In fact, sometimes his overconfidence causes him to act silly and show-off, especially in front of visitors. He, at five, can be cooperative and self-reliant in certain situations. If he has a younger brother or sister, he is capable of being very caring and protective of the younger one.

Mentally, your five-year-old is making great strides. He knows his colors and has a fairly good sense of time. In his language development, he speaks distinctly and with complete sentences. He is very realistic—most of the time—and thinks in concrete terms. For example, he would like to know the exact answer to his questions. Your five-year-old also enjoys humor and can laugh heartily at funny pictures. He even tries his own jokes and riddles, laughing hysterically at the punch line which makes no sense to anyone else.

hrough play three- and four- and five-year-olds use their beginning ability to have an idea, and express their beginning power to plan and organize.

James Hymes

You really appreciate how much your five-year-old is able to do for himself physically. He can dress himself (and perhaps even tie his shoes), brush his teeth, and comb his hair. He has fairly good control over his big muscles—being able to dance, hop, skip, and gallop to rhythm. He can balance, pump a swing, skate, and is able to ride a two-wheel bike usually before turning six years old. His small muscle development has progressed a lot, too. With fairly good control, he manages a pencil, crayons, scissors, stapler, and other tools. His new skills give him a great sense of accomplishment. He feels very good about himself, most of the time.

By five to six years old, your young child is fairly well-adjusted emotionally. Although he cannot understand complex emotions, he is able to communicate many of his feelings and fears. He is learning how to transfer his affection from his mother to his father and to other important adults in his life such as a teacher. He thrives on his achievements and praise can help maintain his good stability for quite some time. Your five-year-old is at a delightful stage—one which is exceptionally pleasant for all around him.

By this time in the discussion of young children and their characteristics at various ages and stages of their life so far, you probably have become aware of some general truths about children. First, you have probably noticed that your child does not fit any description exactly and that tells you that each and every child is unique unto himself. He is highly individual in how he grows, in his interests, and in his personality. Each young person, you have discovered, from infancy on develops in different areas, in different ways, and at his own pace. Your little boy might be particularly good at throwing and catching balls yet struggling with a simple vocabulary. His little friend of almost the same age might be clearly verbal and good at puzzle-making, but not too good at big muscle skills like running or pedaling a tricycle.

By now you are aware that your child's growth is influenced by both his heredity and environment. For example, he might have inherited

You really appreciate how much your five-year-old can do for himself.

a good ear for singing melodies from you and a steady hand from his architect father. And you realize he's good at swimming because you provided him many opportunities from infancy on to be exposed to deep water experience through the environment of your local community swim programs. So, you see, he is a combination of many different influences.

Your Young Child's Most Important Need—You

There is only one thing a child loves more intensely than his playful learning and that is his parents. He looks to you for every opportunity to be with you and to talk to you. Because you have this bond with him, you want to give him what is best to fulfill his needs. His strongest need is to be with you. It is a tightly woven relationship, not yet ready to be broken apart. Therefore, you—as his parent—can enjoy your child's beautiful shining eyes as he beams with pleasure at his new accomplishments. He needs you to be there if he stumbles, to hug his embarrassments, and to kiss his hurts. And you try to be there.

You try to be there when your child needs you.

esponding to your baby and enjoying him create the secure world that allows his body and soul to expand and thrive. Techniques in mothering are useful but secondary to your loving, unfailing concern. Have every confidence in your ability to care for your baby. A mother and father should realize that they are the most important people in their baby's life and the ones who will be best able to meet his needs.

The Womanly Art of Breastfeeding

He counts on you to interpret his newly formed syllables, to practice new words with him, and to carry on lively conversations. When you return after being away from home for a few hours, he can hardly wait to tell you everything that happened. And you listen.

You want to be the first to journey with him into his mind, to see his thoughts unfold as he begins to express all the perceptions he has been storing and sorting out in his little head. And you understand him.

You want to be with him because he is yours—and you are his. The opportunity to capitalize on this preschool relationship will never occur again. You cannot recapture nor reschedule these days of early childhood. They are priceless and precious times—"here today and gone tomorrow" as the old saying goes.

The experiences you have together give you and your child a chance to strengthen the bond between you. It is a bond that began at his birth, was enhanced through breastfeeding and cuddling, deepened in the toddling times, was tested and held true during the terrific two's, and now excitedly waits for the dimensions of the preschool age.

It is this bond between you and your child that will be tested by the demand, and attitude, and decision that your child needs to go to preschool. Please **stop**. Thoughtfully consider the question of preschool for your child.

Your Preschool Child

Learning about His Needs

While my son was in our preschool, I was more aware of his mental and emotional needs. I was able to see him in perspective, working with other children his age.

Judy Erwin, mother of Joshua and Benjamin

About the time your child is two, three, or four years old, you will probably be asked, "Is your child going to preschool? Which one? How many days a week is he going?"

A conversation might go like this. "Brian will soon be three; he needs to become more independent of me. He should be in a preschool situation to enhance his learning. I think I should enroll him in preschool on Tuesday and Thursday mornings. I wonder if I should send him to Jack and Jill Nursery. It's just three blocks away." Or is it really this simple?

The Question of Preschool

Before you answer this question, you would be wise to consider the whole subject of preschool. This is an important question and warrants your careful consideration.

The preschool experience is your child's very first exposure to structured education. It may very well influence his attitude toward learning for many years to come. Will your little one think that learning is some-

Your child's first learning experiences should help him to feel good about himself.

thing you "have to do" or something that you "want to do"? Will his first experience be fun and stimulating and at the right level for him? Or will it be full of rigid rules and regulations and mass produced? Will his first learning allow for his maximum growth, his curiosity, his exploration? Will it be inviting, or repressing? Will it give him encouragement and motivation? Will he feel praised and rewarded for his own particular way of learning? Will his interests be considered or mostly those of his teacher? Will he be able to participate fully without "performing" up to someone else's standards? Even more important—will your little one feel secure and loved and cared for while he is away from his parents, perhaps for the first extended or regularly scheduled time? Will he feel good about himself while he is learning?

These are important questions. Think about them when evaluating your child's preschool situation. The decision may be a difficult one to make.

Being a parent is not always easy. Actually, parenting is (and should be) an enormous responsibility. All along the way you will make choices—decisions that will affect your child's physical being, his personality, his ability to solve problems, and his attitude toward learning. We wrote this book for that very reason. We hope that the fact that you are reading this book is evidence of your questioning attitude. This is good; your questioning and curiosity will benefit your child.

In order to help you in your decision, let's take a look at some of the influences—past and present—which affect your decision-making. How do you finally make the choices you do?

Influences on Parenting

Much of your parenting behavior is based on your background. How you were raised by your parents is a dominant factor in how you relate to your own children. Other informal influences are your friends, neighbors, peers, and doctors.

For you, as well as for many parents, there was probably very little formal training for parenting. An occasional offering through a local school system may have enabled you to take a quick course on being an effective parent. Or you may have read several of the many books written on almost every aspect of parenting. You may find, however, that many of the theories presented in child-care books are conflicting. Due to the ever-changing information and cultural trends, child-care books are constantly being revised and updated. Still another factor that influences parents is what is presented by the media—magazine articles, newspapers, and television.

Much of what you learn about being a parent happens very informally. You have learned not in a classroom, but in the day-to-day experiences of your life. You want to learn out of love and concern for your child.

 n the basis of years of research, I am totally convinced that the first priority with respect to helping each child to reach his maximum level of competence is to do the best possible job of structuring his experience and opportunities during the first three years of his life.

Burton L. White

 t is indeed true that child-rearing involves a lot of hard work and some stress. Let me hasten to assure you, however, that our research has taught us that when the process goes well, it is hugely rewarding and not unduly burdensome.

Burton L. White

Other underlying, yet prevalent, forces creeping into your parenting are cultural pressures and societal expectations. Although you are not strongly aware of these forces, they affect your decisions regarding the preschool issue.

Preschool: How It Evolved

It may be helpful to you to know a little of the history of preschool. When and where did the idea of preschool originate? Why has the preschool experience come to be considered so important during the past generation?

The garden of children

Two educators who greatly influenced the teaching of young children in the late 1800s and early 1900s were Friedrich Froebel and Maria Montessori. Education, at that time, was teacher-directed, allowing for limited movement or verbal interaction in the classroom. Formal education usually began around seven or eight years of age. Montessori and Froebel both recognized the need for a young child to express himself and to explore the environment. Both agreed that instruction should be passive for young children, and stressed the need for guarding and protecting children's spirits rather than prescriptive and categorical instruction which tends to hinder learning.

For this reason, the first kindergartens began. Froebel called them "the gardens of children." However, many persons working with young children—then and now—have difficulty putting their faith in the slow gradual pace of nature which true gardeners must respect in order to reap a rich full harvest.

The work of Maria Montessori

Maria Montessori's initial work in education took place when she was director of the State Orthophrenic School in Rome for deficient children. In 1906, she began working with normal children when she established a school for preschoolers of working parents in a tenement building. This work was undertaken as an experiment. The children were from a situation where both parents were employed outside the home. With mothers away from them daily, these children probably would not have received the same quality and degree of mental stimulation as they did from the Montessori program.

As a result of her work, Montessori contributed some surprising observations about children. Among these, she found that children can

Hand-washing is a specific self-care task recommended by Montessori that can be practiced with children at home.

occupy themselves with intense concentration for long periods of time if the spontaneous interest of the child draws him to the activity. Learning comes from within. She found that children prefer order; they will put things back where they belong if they are shown how and are allowed to do so. These observations apply to children in general and we all know they can occur at home as well as at school. Montessori based much of her method on the materials that children need to experiment with in order to fulfill their developmental stages. Many of the materials and tasks suggested in her prepared environment can be found in the home: pouring, sweeping, polishing, arranging, stacking by size, sorting by various qualities, counting, and learning letter sounds and shapes. Many of these tasks can be experienced with children at home under the caring and patience of a parent. With careful observation, a parent can see what is of interest to her child at any given stage and provide materials for him to explore. (More information on the Montessori method can be found in Chapters 9 and 10.)

Preschools in the United States

Nursery schools, or pre-kindergarten schools, are a relatively modern phenomenon. The preschool has evolved and grown in increasing popularity in the years since 1930 and even more so in the decades of the 1960s and 1970s. The contemporary preschool has its roots in several sources. Preschools have grown and developed out of a rapidly changing history.

Child-development research centers

The first nursery schools were established as child-development research centers in the early 1920s at Teacher's College, Columbia University, and at the Merrill Palmer School of Motherhood and Training, Detroit. Nursery school demonstration centers were opened for student study and practice. The Office of Economic Opportunity—as well as other governmental agencies—also sponsored research to provide information for improving educational practices. The research focused particularly on disadvantaged children. Unfortunately, the research was often short-term, sometimes poorly devised, and used small samples. These preschools began as research projects in order to study how children learn, but they often attempted to claim cure-alls for weaknesses in the entire educational system.

The effect of war times

From 1920 to 1932 the number of nursery schools increased from three to 203 as was reported to the US Office of Education. During the decade of the 1920s, it was reported that the reasons for schools for young children were women seeking employment outside the home because of the war, limited play space for children at home, and needs (perhaps social) of the only child. Schools for young children were in even greater demand after 1920 due to the country's economic depression after the war period. Early childhood schools grew in number due to parental needs, not necessarily children's needs.

Preschool education—catch up in the scientific race

Another social factor entered the historical picture of preschool development in the late 1950s. The United States, feeling a "late start" in the Space Age race, sought to catch up with the Soviet Union. The public became concerned that lack of education before age six might be another late start. A detailed discussion of these factors was presented in the materials for the 1960 White House Conference on Children and Youth. As a result, the US government recommended that free public education be extended downward to include kindergarten. The upper and middle class parents were directed to get their children educated early to catch up with modern times. Ironically, Russian children begin school around the age of seven.

  The same heavy emphasis on increasing the standards of education to keep up with the world powers was made evident again in 1982 in "A Nation At Risk," a report prepared for President Reagan. The report emphasizes a need to focus on the basics of learning, particularly in the areas of mathematics and science. It is being suggested that schools extend their hours. However, more hours at the preschool level may not be in the best interest of our children. On a one-to-one basis at home, parents can create an excitement for investigation and experimentation which will extend long into a child's life. Mathematical and scientific thinking are learned in the day-to-day experiences of life.

Government's "War on Poverty"

In the United States in the 1960s, early childhood education experienced a revival due to the focus on improving the poverty situation and co-existing social problems. Preschools were started through Head Start Child Development Programs—a part of the federal government's War on Poverty.

The Economic Opportunity Act of 1964 authorized the establishment of programs for economically deprived children of preschool age. The purpose was to reach children of low-income families. Children between the ages of three and five were given a preschool education program in order to prepare them to enter public school. Head Start is a total program to meet the underprivileged child's mental and emotional needs. The many competent parts include medical and dental exams, immunization, social services, nutritional care, and psychological services. The parents were involved in all aspects of the program. By participation in activities planned by the center, parents are helped to deal with problems of making a home and bringing up a family.

Parents can provide an excitement for learning in their own homes.

Think about your own child's needs and what you want a preschool to do for him.

Positive effects have been reported in experimental Head Start programs which involved parent participation. "A survey of Head Start parents has found a positive relationship between extensive parent participation and children's scores. The amount of parent participation seemed of far more importance than the kind of model or structure within which participation occurred" *(Parent Involvement in Early Childhood Education* by Alice Honig). The message in this project is special because parents need to realize they make the difference in their child's early learning.

More mothers working

With the feminist movement, more and more mothers of young children entered the labor force during the decade of the 1970s. "According to recent Labor Department statistics, 43.3% of women with children under the age of six are employed, and they comprise the fastest growing segment of the female work force" ("When Maternity Leave Ends" *Parents*, November 1984). Without the daily and constant presence of the mother with her young child(ren), parents often feel compelled to send their child(ren) to school so that they will be ready for kindergarten. In future decades, perhaps the needs of young children will not clash with the economic, emotional, and vocational needs of parents. The concern for more and better part-time jobs, longer maternity leaves, and jobs that can be done in the home should be of national interest.

In summary, preschools in the United States have evolved out of the historical context of national conditions. First, along with the industrial-technological revolution in the 1930s, young children were the subjects of scientific study in group settings. In the Depression and then in the war period of the early 1940s, many children were placed in group care centers so their employed mothers could help the country through the war. In the more affluent 1960s when the disparity of the rich and poor was noticeable, Head Start and other programs were directed toward helping the culturally and socially deprived children become better prepared for school. Middle and upper class families, at this same time, began focusing on the need to give their children an educational background in order to stay competitive with the scientific revolution around them. In the 1970s and early 1980s, the trend to educate and prepare a child as early as possible continued along with the desires of both parents to work outside of the home.

Why Parents Send Children to Preschool

Understanding the evolution of preschool, you may now have thought of questions about preschool and its relevance to your child today. Is preschool really necessary in order for a child to be prepared for school? Is preschool in the traditional sense best for your child? Will a preschool meet the needs of the two- to six-year-old? Why do *you* want your child to attend preschool? What do you think it will do for him?

Now is the time—when your child is very young—to examine and evaluate your ideas and expectations of preschool. What do you think a preschool can or should do for your child?

Preschool to get children educated early

Some parents send their children to preschool because of a not-so-subtle push to get their children prepared or educated early. This seems to fall into the same general category of comparing who walked first, who talked with the longest sentences, and who stayed dry the longest at the earliest age. There is a constant comparison and attempt to prove whose child is the best or earliest or brightest.

Parents may think that when their child is in the best available preschool, he or she will be given the best that society can offer in terms of education. Once the child is in this highly acclaimed preschool, the parents feel assured their child will be given the very best training by the very best teacher, who is a specialist in her field of education. By being prepared academically, his parents believe the child will have an advantage over most of the other children his age. Unfortunately, not all preschool teachers are trained specialists; an objective look at results

*Preschool can provide
a social setting for children to practice getting
along with others.*

will tell you that no preschool can guarantee a child's future success
in school.

In reality, your children will develop to their fullest potential and
be their very best only when their individual needs are met. And this
can be done only on a one-to-one basis.

Preschool to help solve problems

Sometimes parents think that preschool may be the solution needed
to solve their child's budding academic or social problems. They may
think that a preschool experience will help to heal their little one's weak
areas. For example: the parents of Michael—who has not yet shown an
interest in learning his numbers or colors by age three—may think the
preschool teacher can get him to learn them. (Of course, this developmental skill will happen all by itself in due time whether or not he goes
to preschool.) Another child, Rebecca—who was particularly shy and
reserved around strangers—was sent by her parents to a local preschool
so the teacher could draw her out of her shell. (What these parents didn't
realize is that shyness is not always an undesirable quality. And if Rebecca did become more outgoing, it was probably more attributable
to being four than to the particular teacher at the preschool.)

In another situation, four-year-old Ryan's dad traveled a great deal
in his job and spent little time with his son. Ryan's mother thought preschool would straighten out some problems between her and her son.
She thought a preschool might provide more discipline than she was
able to. Some parents put too much emphasis on a preschool's ability
to cure; it cannot be a remedy for deeper problems. In all fairness, preschool cannot be what it is not. Attendance at preschool will not solve
a social or emotional or personality problem.

Children need preschool to develop socially

In a society in which a small family (one or two) children is average, parents feel they must provide an outlet for their child's social needs. He must have an opportunity to learn to communicate, to share, to take turns, to follow directions, and to get along with peers. With few (or no) other siblings close in age, a child must be given a social setting to practice getting along with others. However, parents could—with little effort—set up many shared playtimes with neighborhood children in order to provide a social outlet for their child.

 he child is ready to socialize when he shows confidence and sociability and when he wants to play with other children. The child should have greater opportunities to socialize when he indicates that he is ready for them and wants them. To say that all children should start school at three or four or five does not account for a child's individuality.

James and Mary Kenny

 he young child, on the other hand, while still centered in the home, needs gradually and gently to socialize with persons outside the immediate family. Most children during the period of early childhood will indicate when they are ready to venture out.

James and Mary Kenny

Memories of first-school-day fear

Children may be sent to preschool as a reaction to the parent's own, often deep-seated, remembered feelings toward their own kindergarten experience. Some parents can recall the terror and tears they had when they first attended kindergarten a generation ago. Feelings of being frightened and abandoned by their parents the first days or weeks of kindergarten are remembered. Therefore, in an effort to prevent their child from experiencing these same fears, they want their child to "get used to" school and being separated from them.

In actuality they may be pushing a possibly terrifying—or at least confusing and lonely—experience to an even earlier age. A four- or three-year-old is even less equipped to handle extensive regular separation from the people he needs most. Children are more ready to ease into the school experience at age five or six than at two, three, or four years old. At the age of five, six, or seven, a child will approach school as a new but non-threatening adventure. Even teachers notice the responses of these children. One kindergarten teacher said she could always tell which children had not gone to preschool because they had "stars in their eyes and a look of wonderment about school." Some leading authorities on early childhood education suggest starting a formal education would best be handled when a child is as old as seven or eight. David Elkind in *The Hurried Child* tells parents that their children should be allowed the privilege of growing up slowly to help prevent stress.

A need to be away from the children

Some parents feel they have a need to be away from their child. After all, he does get demanding, loud, rambunctious, and messy. A local preschool may give his parents a break. With their little one out of the house two to five times per week, so much will be accomplished. Perhaps his parents will feel refreshed and eager to see their little one when he returns home each day. In an honest evaluation, however, you will agree that preschool under these conditions is really for his tired and frustrated parents. The need for Susan to be at preschool may really be her mother's need, not necessarily Susan's need.

o matter what philosophy of life we espouse, it is important to see childhood as a stage of life, not just as the anteroom to life. Hurrying children into adulthood violates the sanctity of life by giving one period priority over another. But if we really value human life, we will value each period equally and give unto each stage of life what is appropriate to that stage.

David Elkind

Working mothers

Some working parents feel they have little choice concerning the preschool situation. Often a single mother is trying her hardest to give her best to her preschool-aged son or daughter. Or a working mother believes her income is necessary to meet the family's financial needs. This is always a difficult situation.

Although it may be necessary for a mother to be regularly away from her child while she is working, she will still want to plan a special time

Parental attention is important to a child's self-concept.

with her child. Since she is away many hours, she may benefit from watching him learn and interact with other children his own age. A working mother's time is divided among other things: work, home care, and her children. She will feel better about herself as a person if she can give a higher priority of her time to the little ones she loves than to things and schedules. Time is very special to her and she may be under a lot of stress. Yet, as a human being, she feeds on the "psychological food" of love and belonging.

Dorothy Briggs stresses how important parental attention is to a child's self-concept in her book, *Your Child's Self Esteem*. Children especially need to feel loved and important. Direct involvement with a child tells him that he is worthwhile, that he is important and loved. As a mother trying to meet her family's needs, her own needs must be satisfied. Some of her own needs can be fulfilled simply by being involved with her child. She will also be receiving *his* attention and love. Both mother and her child will nurture each other.

To help children "grow up"

A child is enrolled in a preschool sometimes because his father (or mother) wants him "to get tough" and to "stop being a mamma's baby." Many little ones of any age exhibit clearly and outwardly that they want to be with their mothers. They need to sit on their mother's lap and even hang onto her neck or legs. If she tries to leave, the child becomes emotionally upset and shows it in varying degrees including crying, sulking, shouting angrily, stomping, or thumb-sucking. It may last for a few minutes or as long as mother is away. This emotional attachment, although completely normal, is often viewed by society as being immature.

Fathers and mothers worry about this dependent behavior. They want their child "to be a man" or "to be a big girl." What they are forgetting is that a child cannot be any bigger than he is. He is only as big as a little child—a child with a strong need for the security he can only get from his parents. Once in a preschool screening session (a testing of the child's readiness for kindergarten), a teacher asked a three-and-a-half-year-old to stack ten blocks vertically. The little boy hovered on his mother's shoulder, crying that he didn't want to do it (or anything else related to the testing situation). The gentle-voiced male teacher firmly stated, "I encourage you to send your son to a preschool. He needs to get used to being away from you."

We know of many experts in child psychology who would disagree. They believe that when a need exists, it is like an empty cup waiting to be filled. When it is cold, you do not take a coat away, rather you put one on. To help a child feel secure and confident you cannot take away the very thing that helps him feel secure—you, his parents. If a child has a need for food, you do not withhold it, telling him "to be a man" and do without. When he has a strong need for his parents' presence, you fill up his empty emotional cup by giving him lots of yourself, not less of yourself. Only as he feels his emotional cup is full will he be ready to handle social (and separation) situations with more maturity.

nly if the emotional tank is full, can a child be expected to be at his best or to do his best. And whose responsibility is it to keep that emotional tank full? You guessed it, the parents'.

Ross Campbell

ut remember that eye contact is one of the main sources of a child's emotional nurturing. We all know that children learn by role modeling, that is, patterning themselves after us. Children learn the art and use of eye contact this way also. If we give a child continuous, loving, positive eye contact, he will do the same.

Ross Campbell

Examine Your Attitudes about Preschool and Evaluate Your Child's Needs

Now, when your child is very young, you have the opportunity to examine your attitudes and values regarding your child and his need for preschool. Many preschool-aged children are programmed so extensively that they are spending more time with other adults or teachers than with their own parents. Many of these children experience pressures to achieve and to perform up to the standards set by the programs, which are not necessarily based on the children's needs. In addition, children are often not being allowed to grow up and develop naturally at their own rate.

How can you best meet your child's needs in the way of activities, programs, classes, and so on? Parents need to be and can be more aware regarding their decision to send their child to preschool. Examine your beliefs and your child's needs:

1. Do I really want preschool for me or my child?
2. Does my son or daughter have a real need for a preschool experience?
3. What needs of my son or daughter can be satisfied by a preschool?
4. How much time in preschool is required to satisfy these needs?
5. How will a particular preschool meet these needs? In what ways? To what extent?
6. Is there *another situation* in which my child's needs can be met?
7. As his or her parent, can I provide a situation to meet his needs?
8. Am I **capable** of doing this?
9. Do I want to take the responsibility for filling my child's needs?

 y the age three, most children show a strong desire for companionship as well as a desire to refine the skills they have thus far acquired. Preschools serve both these desires. Whether your child's needs during this stage can be met more effectively at home or at a preschool depends primarily upon your child and the general family situation. Therefore, the decision must be made by you.

William Sears

Probably the best place to start to answer these questions is by looking carefully at your young child. Think over his abilities, his strengths as well as weaknesses, and his personality. Consider how he relates to others, his playmates, his parents, and how he plays when he is alone. Give an honest assessment as you prioritize his needs.

(1) Yes. You most likely want a preschool experience for your child (more than for your own various needs). You may believe that a preschool experience will help get him ready for school. And to give him a preschool background is to give him something very beneficial; not to give him this is to deprive him of the best there is to offer.

(2) Yes. You—and many other parents—think your child has a real **need** for a preschool experience. Certainly between the ages of two and six, approximately, there is rapid brain growth. It seems as though the child of this age is "ripe" for learning. He is full of questions and ready to try anything. However, the need for physical/mental/social stimuli for learning is at a peak in the young child; it is not to be confused with the need for preschool.

(3) A preschool **can** satisfy many needs of the young child. The need to use physical skills, both large and small muscles, is usually satisfied.

A small group of parents can provide a learning environment for their children.

Also a child's need for play, his need for using language skills of listening and talking, his need for free unstructured play, and his need for social interaction are usually considered priorities by a preschool. Also some schools even relate to a child's needs for "hands-on" experience in math, science, and pre-reading activities. One important element that a preschool generally ignores is that *young child still very much needs the continuous interaction, the loving and caring that only his parent can provide.*

(4) It is not a requirement for a child to be in a preschool in order for his needs to be fulfilled. A parent, or a small group of parents, is capable of providing stimulation and direction in fulfilling the needs of young children. They are quite capable of handling some games or exercises for big muscle development. They can provide exciting things for children to do using eye-hand coordination, their enjoyment of music, their interest in making something in arts or crafts, their desire for experimentation—especially in math and science activities. In a small group, children have opportunities for listening and speaking. Together, children can play either spontaneously or in structured ways. The amount of time needed to fulfill the wide variety of needs will, of course, depend upon the child. Each child is so different. How much time is spent on various activities will be relevant only to the degree of a child's motivation to participate. And ideally his need to learn will never be completely filled but will remain strong throughout his life.

(5) Particular preschools put emphasis on different areas. One might stress unstructured (free) play while another might stress pre-reading and pre-math skills. Still another might spend a lot of time "doing crafts." No preschool can really satisfy all the needs of a child all of the time. That would be an unrealistic goal.

To help you decide what preschool might be best for your child, it might be helpful to write a list of his needs and prioritize them according to the most important to him and his development. Many preschools do a fine job of understanding and offering activities directed to the needs of the young child. Yet the traditional preschool overlooks one major need of a child, that is the need for his parent's presence, interaction, and participation with him.

(6) A different situation in which a young child's needs can be stimulated for growth is by a cooperative at-home preschool arrangement. This type of preschool can be planned and run by parents in their own homes where an environment for learning, for social growth, and for emotional security all blend together.

n our studies we were not only impressed by what some children could achieve during the first years, but also by the fact that the child's own family seemed so obviously central to the outcome. Indeed, we came to believe that the informal education that families provide for their children makes more of an impact on a child's total educational development than the formal educational system.

Burton L. White

Considering all of a child's needs, the only need which is nearly impossible for a parent to supply alone is his need to socialize with children his own age. By age four or so when a child's play becomes more interactive rather than side-by-side play, he will express an interest in having his own "friends" to play with. The traditional preschool supplies a group of children of similar ages. A young child, however, will probably handle a group of three or four playmates much better than he will handle being dissolved into a whole class of twelve to twenty-five or so. A small group at home can easily be the source—the setting—to provide for a young child's need for social development. The social growth may even be smoother because of the many advantages of being in his home.

(7) Parents who know their children better than anyone else can very effectively plan, set up, and be the guiding teachers in an at-home preschool. You have the most essential ingredients for carrying this out very well—your child's strong need for you, your genuine and unconditional love for him, and the opportune time of right now.

(8) Yes. You are capable. You are his parents—his "specialist"! Don't underestimate your abilities to guide your child (and a small group of his peers) through his first structured learning activities. You are not delegated only to the role of washer of diapers, dishes, and floors. You are not limited to being taxi driver, housekeeper, and cook. Although these tasks are very much required of a parent, you do not have to stop here. The rewards of parenting can come from being an important part of your child's education, and it can begin at his young preschool age.

(9) You can—if you want to—be a vital part of his first learning experience in a somewhat organized structure. You can be his first teacher (as you have been all along). You can be the provider or source of new information. You can challenge him to new accomplishments. You can have first and direct control over creating a learning environ-

ment that will motivate him, that will be fun and exciting, and that will reach him at his level and interests. You can structure a setting that is free of repressing rules and regulations, but instead encourages hands-on exploration and investigation. You can make it a setting which takes into account his style of learning and his individual characteristics. And most important, you will be offering, simply by being there, an atmosphere grounded in security, in his feeling loved and cared for. You will fill his emotional cup by your presence.

You are vitally important to his first learning experiences

In your careful evaluation of the needs of your little one, you can see that you are right on the top of his list. Next probably is his need for social growth, followed by the gamut of many other needs. But one thing that is not on your list of priorities is that he does not need to grow up too soon. Society often pushes parents into helping along their little ones in ways which are detrimental to their development. Your preschool-aged child is very young and very inexperienced. He is a child. This is his time to be a child, not a miniature adult.

You can, as his parents, make certain that he isn't being pushed too hard, too fast, or too soon. He can only handle so much. He has small-sized limits of how much he can handle in the way of "structured" or "planned" programs or classes. He has limits on how much he is capable of absorbing or learning in a day. He has limits on how many friends (peers or adults) he can handle at one time. And he has limits on how much his emotional system can handle as far as separation from mother and dad. You can be a direct influence on setting the controls to match his limitations. You can take responsibility for his preschool learning experiences.

All you have to do now is to see how you can blend his needs and your caring love into a cooperative preschool-at-home.

Your Child and Preschool

Discovering an Alternative

The kids formed good friendships with other kids in our own neighborhood. They had all the advantages of the formal preschool experience, plus they were in a small group in a home atmosphere where their mothers were constantly involved.

Colleen Weiland, mother of Mike, Eric, Amy, and Matthew

As your child moves out of his baby and toddler years, his mind and body are reaching upward for more and more experiences. Your little person of three or four years old is eager for life. He is curious, imaginative, investigative, and energetic. His very energy alone can sometimes be overwhelming. You may begin to ask, "How can I fill up his cup with all the knowledge he is seeking?" Sometimes you feel drained just watching this bundle of energy burst around you. He has to touch and see and hear and taste all that he can.

You are an experienced parent by the time your baby is a preschool-aged child. You are quite familiar with his routines, his likes and dislikes, and his attitudes toward many different things. By age three or four, he is noticeably a little person, quite capable of handling many physical tasks, managing his thoughts and language fairly well, and always inviting more challenges. Most of the time he is really fun to be with.

On the other hand, you are keenly aware that your preschooler is not yet grown up. He is still very young in many respects. His emotional needs remain strong, whether or not they surface for attention, Your preschool child needs you as much now as when he was an infant, just in different ways. You may not have the physical demands that you had when your child needed ten or more diaper changes a day and a similar number of feedings, yet now that he is three or four years old, your responsibilities toward him do not magically disappear. Just because he is able to dress himself and feed himself, your job is not obsolete.

Conversely, as his physical needs seem to lessen, his mental, social, and emotional needs are begging for satisfaction.

The Child's First Teacher

However large the job of parenting may seem, one thing is certain. You do not have to go outside of the home for your child to learn and grow. In fact, a child's home is the best place for learning to take place. A child's parents are his first and best teachers.

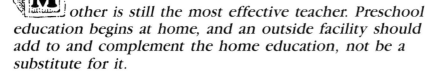 *other is still the most effective teacher. Preschool education begins at home, and an outside facility should add to and complement the home education, not be a substitute for it.*

William Sears

You need only look to yourselves to give your child what he needs. You might think you don't have enough space or materials or knowledge. But you have an abundance of your most valuable resource—genuine, unconditional love. Certainly you can find no one else who has what you have to offer your child, his own parents' love. Only you can demonstrate and communicate this love and caring.

But what about preschool? How can you make your child's strong need for you and your love for him work together to fulfill his other preschool needs? You can do it by giving your child his first preschool experience right at home.

You have all the essential ingredients—your child, his strong need to remain close to you, your genuine love and caring for him, your unique understanding of him, and the opportunity. The opportunity is there for reinforcing the bond between the two of you by planning a preschool-at-home.

t is my belief that parents (with few exceptions) are the very best people to raise their children, and that their parenting styles should be determined by the traditions from which they have come and the people they have grown to be.

Fred Rogers

So, if you want to, you can be a part of your child's first learning experiences in a group or structured setting. You can create an environment to meet the needs of your child in a preschool-at-home.

Preschool-at-Home—an Alternative

A cooperative preschool-at-home under the direction and supervision of parents in a small group, in the relaxed setting of the home, can meet the needs of a small group of young children in effective and positive ways. A child participating in a preschool-at-home can feel loved, secure, and important. He will simultaneously be nurtured in physical and mental development, in creativity, in curiosity, in imagination, in investigation, and in social and emotional development.

You can give your child his first preschool experiences right at home.

45

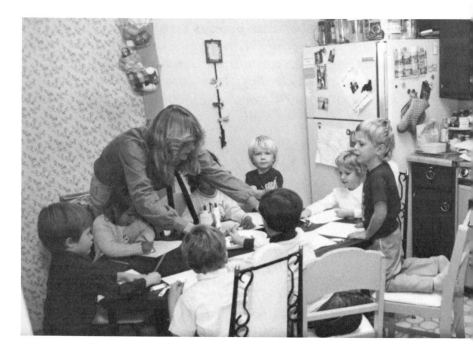

Your little ones have been learning from you all along.

Parents have an advantage

You, as a parent, are the specialist in your child's needs. From the ages of three to six there isn't anything that your child wants to know that you can't help him learn. You can be his guide, his resource, or the catalyst to his own source of knowledge. You can be his "specialist" because you know him better than anyone else. And you care about him more than anyone else.

When he was a baby you trusted yourself to know what to do for him. You knew better than anyone else how to get him to sleep after a fussy spell. You learned how to handle the colds and other childhood illnesses as they came along. You are the one who knows that he likes broccoli but not peas; that he prefers to sleep on his left side hugging his black and white panda bear. You know he cooperates well when you let him make his own decisions. ("Do you want to wear your tennis shoes or the brown ones that tie?") You know that he is good at putting together jigsaw puzzles but he is uncoordinated in large muscle skills like pumping on a swing.

With your understanding of the details of your child's personality and abilities, you have a distinct advantage over others at being his first teacher. You don't have to send him to a traditional preschool; you can make a very good preschool learning situation right in your own home.

Parents combine their efforts

Perhaps a brief look at a typical traditional preschool setting will help assure you that you and your home can offer an equally good environment. Start with play time or free play. A regular preschool has a variety of toys from blocks and trucks to a set of dishes and dress-up clothes.

Many of these can be found in your home and in the homes of a few friends. One of you might have a set of oversized building blocks but not have playdough. Another might have playdough as well as a good collection of children's books and records. A third friend may have a great backyard with play equipment. Among the three of you there may be a better than average setting for a preschool environment. You can combine your facilities and collectibles and talents, so that you are able to draw, paint, read, tell stories, dance, sing, cook and eat, go places and do things—and create exciting adventures for you and your child together with a small group of other parents and their children.

As your child's parent, you can be the one to offer him a place and time to let his natural drive for learning take off. You can continue to be there to appreciate all the "firsts." You can see the delight in his face as he watches the zinnia seeds sprout and grow, inch by inch, and finally bloom. As he learns how to trace a circle and cut a straight line, you can guide his little hands. You can be his partner to "The Hokey Pokey."

You can continue to be the "specialist" in meeting your child's needs while providing a learning environment.

You can be happy with him in his first adventures on a commuter train, or holding a one-day-old piglet on a farm, or tasting fresh-baked doughnuts at the local bakery. You and your child have so much to share with each other, so much to learn from each other.

Parents are teachers

You need not be afraid to be your child's teacher, you already are. Your little one has been learning from you all along; perhaps you haven't even noticed how much day-to-day teaching you already have been doing. For example, if your daughter sees you hammering nails into a picnic bench you're making for the backyard, she might pester you until she can do it, too. So you find a small hammer for her and scraps of wood, start the nail for her, and let her build "boats" or "airplanes." It's so easy, so natural, and you are an important part of her learning about building.

Parents, of course, always teach their children. From the first baby talk to the first rattle placed in the crib, to the encouragement of walking, bowel and bladder training, self-care, and awareness of household dangers such as poisons, electric sockets, and so on, parents teach their children a wide range of concepts and skills. Parents also teach their children manners, as well as motor skills such as riding a tricycle, wagon, or bicycle. In the ordinary course of parenting, mothers and fathers do a great deal of teaching in the many domains where children will eventually have to function independently.

David Elkind

Another example of your ongoing teaching could take place when you and your children go to a wedding reception. Your four-year-old probably wants to do the polka with you. You take him to the edge of the dance floor and lead him through the steps. He doesn't need to go to dancing class; he picks it up—a little at a time or all at once—because he wants to. He is motivated.

Or, you might be humming a melody that you sang to him when he was a baby. If he asks, "What you are singing, Mommy?" You don't say, "I'd better send you to singing class for music lessons." You spontaneously begin to teach him "It's a world of laughter, a world of tears" one phrase at a time. In a few minutes he's singing it with you. He doesn't

In the shared experience of a preschool-at-home, children and their parents blossom.

know or care if you are singing off-key or have good pitch. He's learning melody and rhythm and words, because he wants to and because you want to teach him.

When he was a baby you gave generously to him. Think back to the hours you held him, rocked him, and cuddled him. His eyes held you entranced even as the phone rang and the dust deepened on the end tables. He was your priority, first in your life. When he was a toddler, your hours of time were spent less in cuddling, more perhaps in keeping up with his energetic little body. Every room, every cupboard and cabinet, everything in the house was a new frontier to be explored. He had so much to learn. Although the days were long and often physically tiring, you gave so that he would be protected and entertained and challenged. You kept his curiosity satisfied with new and different things to do while answering his endless questions.

Even though his energy alone is sometimes a lot to handle, you wouldn't want to trade the tiredness or the precious moments. Do you remember when his little legs finally mastered the rhythm of tricycle pedals? Or the time when he snipped confetti-sized pieces out of an old newspaper, amazed that he was able to cut? Or when he brushed his own teeth?

You were there to read to him and play games. You sang his first song with him. You showed him how to measure flour, crack eggs, and wash his hands. You guided his paintbrush on paper, demonstrated a forward roll, and pronounced "yogurt" and "electric" when he faltered.

Do you really want to pass up the opportunity to be your child's teacher now that he is a preschooler? As his parent, you can be the one to enjoy the smiles, the discoveries, and the new skills practiced in every adventure.

As his young mind and body continue to grow, you can be the one to answer his questions. Most of the time you will find that all he needs is a simple answer. But when a more detailed answer is required, you can both learn something new—together.

In your preschool-at-home you will play, talk, read, hop, skip, jump, cook, eat, draw, cut, paste, sing, and dance together with your child and with other parents and their children. The synergism—where one and one and one are more than three—that comes from the vitality of the preschool-at-home makes the child's first learning experiences rich and fun.

As Parents—You Can Do It!

As parents, you are better than anyone else at nurturing your child. Anyone can prepare your child's lunch, wash his jeans, and tie his shoes. But no one else can read his emotions the way his parents can. No one except you can wrap him in the security he needs in order to venture forth confidently into a waiting world.

 hat's why a child's closest caregivers—the people I think of as parents—are very, very special. They are the people who are best able to provide that security, sense of worth, and belief that life is worth the effort to live.

Fred Rogers

Parents can feed their child's desire to learn and to play. Under the age of six or so your child's needs are fundamentally and extensively intertwined with the relationship he has with you. Parents can water his insatiable curiosity with opportunities to experience with all of his senses. You can fertilize his desires to discover and explore by providing a variety of things to do and places to go. You can give the sunshine to warm him emotionally. You can, as parents, fulfill your young child's needs in all areas of his life.

Once you become a parent you will always be your child's parent. You are his first teacher. You can choose to remain his teacher, to nourish your child as he grows through his preschool years.

An Invitation to Parents

You are invited to look at an alternative to the traditional preschool—the alternative of organizing and participating in your own preschool-at-home.

This book explains why a preschool-at-home is a valid choice and for many, a preferred choice. It gives suggestions on how to go about it, from finding other parents with whom to share this experience, to organizing and scheduling, to samples of daily lesson plans. You will find samples of activities that can be included in a preschool day or used individually with your own child.

Now, if you find a few other parents who have the same deep commitment to their children as you have, you are on your way. A small group of parents has so much to offer to a small group of preschoolers. Highly motivated to give their best to the children, the parents will draw from their interests and talents. The children will learn to adapt to different people and different situations. Spreading the responsibilities among the entire group lightens the load for parents who establish a high level of one-to-one interaction within the very small group of children. The many positive responses between parent and child and among other parents and other children help to maintain a high level of interest and enthusiasm.

When your seedlings are watered, fertilized, and given the sunshine of a loving environment, the synergistic effect takes over; one and one do not equal two, rather one and one make twelve or twenty or one hundred! Ready for their next learning experiences, young sprouts are allowed to flower in any season and in any color. Happy and secure, a child who participates in his own preschool-at-home takes with him some basic tools for problem solving, a zeal for learning as large as an ocean wave, an insatiable curiosity, and a zest for the adventure of life. In this shared experience of preschool-aged children and their parents, rich relationships blossom through playful learning.

Preschool-at-Home

What It Is

Real school, i.e., kindergarten, seemed like the logical consequence of a playgroup/preschool experience. My child had the opportunity to function among peers with Mom close enough "to touch base" and then gradually and with love graduated to the separation that kindergarten entails.

Colette Henley, mother of Debbie, Peter, Ben, and David

What Is a Cooperative Preschool-at-Home?

A preschool-at-home is simply a small group of preschool children who are brought together to share the experience of playful learning under the cooperative guidance of their parents. Any parent, mother or father, or even a close relative or friend, may want to share in the preschool-at-home experience. Because mothers have been most often involved in the preschool situations we have observed, we will generally refer to the parent as a female. This is not meant to exclude fathers who can play an equally important role in a preschool-at-home.

A child's home provides a relaxed, informal setting for his learning experiences. It is warm, comfortable, and inviting. He is used to being in a home. Under the love and care of a parent who knows him well, the child participating in a preschool-at-home receives much focused attention and consequently feels loved and secure and important. As his individual needs are recognized and focused upon, he will learn and grow and develop in many ways. He can gradually become accustomed to interacting with a group of his peers, responding to an adult other

The children's natural curiosity together with the enthusiasm of the parents provides the framework for learning to take place.

than his parents, and learning within the guidelines of simple routines and a simple yet flexible structure.

The most important of the materials needed are already present—the child's natural curiosity, lust for adventure, and desire for playful experiences. The other materials and tools can be found in almost any home and yard. Add to this the enthusiasm and genuine caring of parents and you have all the ingredients for some fantastic learning to take place.

The ages of the children to which this type of preschool applies are three, four, and five years old—the one or two years before beginning school. Some parents feel that the group will function better if the children are within a year's age range. However, this is not a requirement.

The size of the group may vary from three to eight participating children. If younger children are involved, a smaller group may be preferred. It is not necessary to have an even number nor to have even numbers of boys and girls.

The children may be from your immediate neighborhood or town or from a slightly larger area. Yet, they should live close enough to each other so that the distance and time involved in travel will not be a discouraging factor to the parents.

ursery school is pleasant but not essential. If money or distance make it difficult, parents can still arrange play situations for their outgoing four-year-old. Parents might even begin their own cooperative nursery school. Two or three mothers of preschoolers can agree to take turns having the children over. Fathers might take turns with the preschoolers for a couple of hours on the weekend. Parents do not need a degree in preschool education for such activity. Merely set aside two hours exclusively for children, plan some activities, provide some toys and a play space, and feed them a nutritious snack when they get hungry.

James and Mary Kenny

The preschool may meet as often as the parents wish. They may want to meet every other week, once a week, or even as often as three times a week. This will depend on what the parents feel are the needs of their children. The parents cooperatively will decide how often to meet, which day(s) of the week, and the time of day best suited for all. They can be as flexible as their schedules allow.

Cooperatively, each parent takes a turn being the leader, each in her own home, while the children rotate from home to home on a planned schedule. Some groups, particularly with younger children, prefer to have another parent as helper, or assistant, to the parent in charge. The responsibility for the plans and supervision of the preschool is shared among all those involved. They determine the goals and the activities around the various needs of the children. The variety of backgrounds and interests of the parents lends itself to the best feature of the team approach. The small group with many interested and available helpers gives opportunities for many different field trips into the community. The children will learn within a wide range of experiences.

Comparison with Other Types of Preschools

The preschool-at-home may be set up in many different ways. Why is the preschool-at-home different from other preschools? To better understand the type of preschool that we describe in this book, we must take a look at other preschools—some similar, some very different from the preschool-at-home.

Children feel secure in a home setting with a parent nearby.

Playgroup of preschool children, mixed ages

This nonstructured playgroup may include children of different ages. It may meet regularly or irregularly, rotating homes. For younger children, this seems to work well as a first experience of interacting with children other than siblings. Staying with their children, the parents also have an opportunity for socializing while maintaining a secure environment for their little ones. Although there is no structure, the parents have the freedom to spontaneously include a story, song, fingerplay, game, or simple project. To make this beneficial for the children, parents must think of their little one's needs and not let their personal interests predominate. This simple playgroup can offer enriching social experiences, for mothers as well as children.

Playgroup of preschool children, close ages

This playgroup involves children of similar ages (usually less than a one-year age range). With one or two parents as hostess, the children meet regularly without the other parents present.

Some young children may not be ready to be separated from their parents. If you have a child who is *not* ready to be separated from his parents and gets upset or worried, his mother or dad should be encouraged to stay. He will gradually gain confidence as his parent sits back and interacts less and less with the group. When he is secure and comfortable, his parent may choose to disappear into another room. Or she can step out of the house for a short time. If handled gradually, there will be no trauma, no fear of being left behind, but rather a warm feeling of sharing new experiences with new friends.

This playgroup's primary goal may be to provide the children with time for socializing away from parents for short periods of time. A simple daily plan may include an art or craft project, a song, story, game, or fingerplay. The bulk of the time will be spent playing with the parent-leader providing guidance. The group may take field trips together if they wish. The parents are responsible for the planning, and should be cautious that the playgroup time does not revert into a babysitting arrangement.

Preschool that meets in a non-home building

This variation of the at-home preschool may be established in a building other than the children's homes such as a church nursery. The parent-leaders are supervisors and establish the daily routines and schedules cooperatively. The major advantages are that there will be more consistency in the environment and that there will probably be space for storage of materials. The disadvantages of this plan are the possible costs of rent, insurance, and shared equipment—as well as the probability of a more formal setting which may distract from spontaneity.

Preschool run by parents with non-parent teacher

This preschool is run by parents who serve as the board of directors and financially support their preschool, but they hire a certified teacher. The parents may donate time assisting with fund-raising, secretarial or bookkeeping duties, grounds-keeping, and may occasionally aid the teacher with the classroom activities. The major advantages are that the parents determine the standards of education and care they want. The most obvious differences from the preschool-at-home are that (1) the parent is not the teacher and (2) it is not held in a home.

Preschool in a day-care setting

In a day-care setting several children, usually of mixed ages, are brought together for the purpose of being looked after by a babysitter. Their parents pay another adult who is licensed or registered by the state to give basic physical care to their children for a certain number of hours. The cost depends on how many children, how many hours, additional programs, etc.

A wide range of preschool experiences may be found in day-care settings from no structured learning to a full, traditional preschool program during a specified time of day.

The day-care preschool differs even more from the at-home preschool. The obvious differences are (1) it is not at home, (2) the parents have a minimal part in their children's education, and (3) the parents pay for the cost of the caretaker.

The traditional preschool

In the traditional preschool a certified teacher is paid to teach a group of children, usually ten to twenty-five in a class, in a building other than a home. The teacher determines the program, usually geared to the average needs and abilities of the children of that age range. The teacher, the environment, the day, and the times are firmly established. Field trips are usually limited due to lack of enough adult supervision and other factors.

Traditional preschools vary from each other in their areas of emphasis. One preschool's goal may be academic preparation, stressing recognition of the alphabet, printing, and use of numbers. Another preschool may focus on scientific exploration and discovery. Still another may emphasize free play and social cooperation. A few very good preschools balance the areas of learning and are directed toward the needs of the child rather than simply filling the objectives of the chosen program.

Again, the differences in the traditional preschool as compared with the preschool-at-home are many. The major differences are (1) the preschool setting is not at home, (2) the days and time are locked into a schedule, (3) programs are directed to the "average" child, statistically, (4) limited "playful" experiences, (5) few, if any, field trips, and (6) minimal involvement of parents.

Preschool-at-Home Is Special

We believe from our experiences that the preschool-at-home provides the best possible environment that motivates a child to learn. It offers the setting and tools needed to help a child develop in all areas. The preschool-at-home meets and goes beyond the requirements of the best of society's preschools. The preschool-at-home is special!

1. Due to its small group, it accepts and focuses upon the needs of the child on an individual basis most of the time. It is not directed to the statistically "average" child. It is flexible enough to plan projects according to the areas of need and the appropriate levels of ability.

2. Due to its smaller number of children, it fosters many positive interactions with other children and several adults.

3. Due to its home setting, it provides an environment in which the child feels secure a great majority of the time. With caring and kind parent-leaders, he feels that he belongs to a close-knit group. He feels liked and capable—a great foundation he will use as he ventures into learning experiences.

4. Due to the energy and interest of several parent-leaders and the different home settings, it offers a great variety of learning activities that are interesting, motivating, stimulating, and fun for the child.

5. Due to parent availability for transportation and assistance, it allows more freedom for the group to go on field trips wherever and whenever the group desires.

6. Due to the parents' intimate involvement, it stimulates a closeness, or bond, between parent and child which cannot be duplicated in any other setting. The specialness of the relationship, often an extension of an earlier bond, is certainly a foundation for the future of parent and child. Most parents who participate in the preschool-at-home say that the best thing that happened to them was the special feeling of closeness they (re)discover for their own little person.

 ontinuum parenting is an uninterrupted, nurturing relationship, specifically attuned to a child's needs as he passes from one developmental stage to the next. The two principles of continuum parenting ... are "immersion" mothering and "involved" fathering. Immersion mothers and involved fathers convey such a deep love to their child that he feels right, which naturally brings forth a desirable behavior and sends a message of love to the parents.

William Sears

 timulated by their child's reactions, continuum parents also feel right and consequently increase their immersion mothering and involved fathering. This mutual giving raises the entire parent-child relationship to a higher level.

William Sears

Preschool-at-Home

Its Many Advantages

When the school bus came and took the second two girls to school for "kindergarten," school was a new, exciting, fresh experience. They were very, very happy to go! They were not two five-year-olds "burned out" with the thought of "school"! They were ready, willing, and able and they still are!

Chris Matheis, mother of Julie, Amy, and Lisa

The preschool-at-home gives the best preparation for a child's future education. The advantages of the preschool-at-home as a child's first learning experience are inherent in the overall structure. Each preschool-at-home will be different and unique. Each one may highlight certain specific characteristics more than others. However varied these preschools may appear, the common denominators of parents and homes are the basis of the playful learning of the preschool child. Here we list the major advantages of the preschool-at-home.

How the Child Will Benefit

High interest level

Because the preschool-at-home is far from static, it maintains a high level of interest on the part of the children (and parents). Constantly changing, the group makes new plans frequently. The child participating at home is not heavily exposed to "school" and therefore is not showing signs of being "burned-out" by having it too much or for too long a time.

Variety of learning experiences

Each home is unique in its learning environment. Each home has different playthings, toys, books, and so on. In the home environment a young child feels more comfortable than in a large, strange room in a building away from home.

In the various homes, a child develops a good understanding and respect for other people's property, furniture, and things. Here, the toys are not owned by an institution. It is obvious that they belong to another child—a friend in his preschool. The children soon learn to be careful and responsible for the things they use.

Gentle guidance

Disciplinary measures are practically unnecessary in an at-home preschool. Instead, gentle and sometimes firm guidance provides boundaries for the behavior of the children. The children's enthusiasm is high and the motivation is excellent due to several factors:

1. The learning activities are varied, interesting, at the appropriate level.

2. The parent has a great interest and cares deeply about what is happening in her preschool. She has a big investment in it—her time spent "teaching" and her child's time "learning."

3. The child's self-esteem is high because he feels good—secure and pleased with himself.

 f the most crucial ingredient of mental health is high self-esteem, where does it come from? ... It comes from the quality of the relationships that exist between the child and those who play a significant role in his life.

Dorothy Corkille Briggs

No pressure to achieve

The preschool-at-home does not place pressure on a child to perform or achieve. The parents do not put their children in competition with society's current requirements of academic and/or social standards. The underlying attitude toward the child's development is to accept him where he is developmentally, simply encouraging him to try, and praising him for his efforts. We enjoy his childness.

aluing childhood does not mean seeing it as a happy innocent period but, rather, as an important period of life to which children are entitled. It is children's right to be children, to enjoy the pleasures, and not to suffer the pains of a childhood that is infringed by hurrying. In the end, a childhood is the most basic human right of children.

David Elkind

One-to-one interaction

The one-to-one interaction between parent and child is greater in a small group than it can be with a teacher and a whole class. There will be more eye contact, more physical contact, and more focused attention. This is due to the ratio of one or two adults to three to eight children.

In an at-home preschool, parents can spend more time helping each child feel special.

Individualized program

In a small group it is easier to individualize the program to the abilities, weaknesses, or interests of the children. The adults in charge can give more time to helping each child feel special.

hysical and eye contact are to be incorporated in all our everyday dealings with our children. They should be natural, comfortable, and not showy or overdone. A child growing up in a home where parents use eye and physical contact will be comfortable with himself and other people. He will have an easy time communicating with others, and consequently be well liked and have good self-esteem. Appropriate and frequent eye and physical contact are two of the most precious gifts we can give our child. Eye and physical contact (along with focused attention) are the most effective ways to fill a child's emotional tank and enable him to do his best.

Ross Campbell

ut one of the most important gifts a parent can give a child is the gift of that child's uniqueness.

Fred Rogers

Security in being with parents

Because a parent is present at all times, the child can feel "mothered" by his various parent-leaders. The need to be mothered is real and strong in the three-, four-, and five-year-old.

Feeling secure in the presence of his own mother, the child can extend his secure feelings to the other parents in the group. His fears and anxieties will be reduced as he *gradually* allows himself to build relationships with the other parents. Often his worry about being separated from his mother is lessened because he is being cared for by other mothers. If the child shows a need to have his parent with him, the opportunity is present for his mother (or father) to stay for as many days as needed. Gradually the young child will be more and more ready for the parent/child separation that he will be required to make as he goes to traditional school. Also, the child frequently "touches base" with his own mother as the group rotates homes.

Teaching versus learning

The child is not "taught" in a preschool-at-home but rather is given many opportunities to "learn." His learning comes from within, growing and developing at his own pace, in different areas, and in his own way. The parent simply provides her presence, a few materials, and a variety of experiences. The child does all the rest.

Opportunity for play

When children participate in a cooperative at-home preschool they may be allowed and even encouraged to "play" more than in other school settings. That is, they can have more time to play socially with their peers, to play with toys and/or learning materials, and to play out their thoughts, fears, beliefs, and so on through pretending and fantasy. Joseph Pearce who wrote *Magical Child* believes in the value of play for mental growth and development. It is widely accepted that for young children, they work and learn as they play—these are inseparable. In the at-home preschool with more flexibility, schedules are secondary to the children's involvement in an activity. If the children, for example, get caught up in the presentation of a puppet show and want to continue, the parent in charge can easily let this "play" activity go on and cancel out other parts of the plans for the day. Since she realizes the importance of spontaneity and understands that children's interest is a motivating force behind learning, the parent will let the children "go for it" when the desire is there.

Children need the opportunity to play with toys and learning materials.

Parents are there to soothe hurt feelings or settle a dispute in a peaceful way.

How Parents Will Benefit

Financial savings

There may be a financial savings of up to hundreds of dollars. The parents will not be paying tuition for the traditional or private preschool. One mother, Kathy Hoag, writes, "I am so happy about the money I am saving by having an at-home preschool vs. a public preschool. My son is gone two and a half hours on two days a week and in return I am responsible one week out of six. But that one week when it's at my home is so enjoyable, it's more than worth the effort!"

Better understanding of your child

Due to the parent's close involvement with her child's preschool learning, the parent gains a better understanding of her child's unique characteristics. A parent learns directly what her child's strengths and weaknesses are and can become prepared to accept and deal with these qualities.

Self-worth

The parent's involvement in her child's learning is greater. She has assumed more responsibility in being a part of the cooperative team of teachers. Her efforts give her a feeling of self-worth when she gives of herself in a significant, tangible way. This all reinforces her parenting abilities.

Bonding strengthened

The parent-child bond is extended from infancy and toddlerhood into the preschool-at-home setting. The parent fills the emotional needs of her preschoolers who are the recipients of her love and caring in a relaxed setting. The special attachment between parent and child is reinforced through frequent interactions.

Team teaching

Parents are a team of teachers. Each can apply her interests, abilities, hobbies, and talents to the preschool-at-home. As a result, children are exposed to a broad range of experiences.

Influencing children's values

Another advantage in the cooperative preschool-at-home is that parents have another means by which to influence their children's values. When they are involved in their child's preschool experiences, they have additional opportunities to guide their children's attitudes and emerging concepts of life. For example, when a conflict comes up over sharing a certain desired toy, parents will have a hand in how to solve the problem in a peaceful way, agreeable to all. Or, if a toy is accidentally broken the parent may use this situation to demonstrate being accountable for one's actions. Many other situations will present themselves for discussion and problem-solving. Parents can be the guide.

Time invested; time saved

The time that the parent spends on her sessions is minimal compared with the returns of her happy, well-adjusted, learning child. The time is invested in her own child's future.

With cooperative driving, planning, and teaching, there is a savings of time. For example, when four mothers are teaching together, one will have only twenty-five percent of the total teaching sessions. The responsibilities are shared equally among the parents.

 he preschool should be an extension of the home and, therefore, the facility you select should have the same child-rearing values and priorities as you.

William Sears

Good communication

The communication between the parents is strong due to working cooperatively on their preschool. They have opportunities for increased communication during the planning and evaluating sessions, field trips together, car-pooling, and so on.

Support group

The parents can talk over how their children are doing in all areas of development. What is said can be put in a kind and supportive way. A genuine concern for each other's children naturally occurs as the parents work together.

The Children Love It

The children's enthusiasm for their preschool pervades the atmosphere. The high level of interest and excitement is constant throughout the year.

Six children (about three and a half years old) participating in a preschool-at-home were interviewed for a feature story for a local newspaper (*Joliet Herald News*, February 1983). They were clearly expressive as they responded to the question "What do you like about preschool?"

Adam: "You get to make neat things and play with new toys."

Crystal: "I like it because I always get to go to somebody's home."

Lisa: "I like to play and do different things."

Julie S: "I like it because I always get a good snack."

Ryan: "I like to share my toys at share time."

Julie M: "I like it because all my friends get to come over."

Preschool-at-Home

Some Questions and Answers

In a playgroup or preschool, I can be sure our Lizzy is exposed to what skills I feel are necessary before kindergarten. It is true I now have more responsibility, but I also am a part of my child's education. My children are not in the genius category, and that's fine with me, but I do want the best education that I can give them.

Jacie Coryell, mother of Lizzy, Will, Kit, and Amy

In this chapter we'll try to answer some of the common questions we have been asked about preschool-at-home. If you have any questions or concerns that are not answered here, we'd be glad to try to help you. Just write to the authors, Anne and Cheryl, c/o La Leche League International, P O Box 1209, Franklin Park IL 60131-8209.

Q: Will my child be ready for kindergarten after experiencing this type of preschool?

A: The preschool-at-home, or any other type of preschool, is not a guarantee of a child's readiness for school. No preschool experience can predict a child's level of achievement in school. No clear-cut evidence even points to the necessity of a preschool experience.

The more important factors in preparing a young child for his school years are: (1) his normal physical/mental/emotional/social development which occurs naturally at its own pace for each child individually; (2) his good self-concept or high self-esteem which can be fostered by the praise and encouragement of his parents and other significant adults in his life; and (3) the positive, strong relationship he has with his family and, specifically, the amount of affection and attention he receives from the primary adults in his life.

A study by Edward Zigler (1970) stresses the importance of parents in influencing a child's motivation for learning. He analyzed how important familial-cultural experiences are to a child's educational achievement motivation.

 irst, a well-documented phenomenon is that children who do not receive enough affection and attention from the important adults in their life suffer in later years from an atypically high need for such attention and affection. When faced with cognitive tasks, such children do not appear highly motivated to solve the intellectual problems confronting them but rather employ their interactions with adults to satisfy hunger for attention, affection, and yes, as unscientific as it may be, their need for love. We have conducted longitudinal studies of children who were socially deprived in the first few years of life and we still find the effects of early deprivation experiences some ten years later.

Edward Zigler

More than any other factor, parents' involvement in their children's education is "more crucial to successful educational outcomes for young children." The family is the most effective system for fostering and sustaining the development of a child.

Q: If there is no guarantee that any preschool will help my child be ready for school when he is five or six, why should I have a cooperative preschool-at-home?

A: There are several reasons to choose to have a preschool-at-home.

1. I want to continue to support and strengthen the bond between my children and me, a bond started at birth, and continued through our breastfeeding relationship. I believe that the parent-child relationship, if solidified in the preschool years, will carry over into the elementary years,

adolescence, and the teenage years—a time when trust, openness, and communication are vital.

2. I want to enjoy the quantity of time, not just the quality of time, I have with my young children. The total time that we have our children under our guidance is very short. Once they begin school, parents gradually, and all too soon, become the secondary influence in their lives. School and related activities, as well as peer groups, soon have a primary emphasis in our children's lives.

   Even the daily time we have with our children is significantly lessened to only a couple of hours a day at most when we elect to send our children to schools outside our homes. So the time of the preschool years becomes very valuable. In their preschool years, the time we can spend with our children is still available. And their desire to be with their parents is still at a peak. I want to take full advantage of this precious time with them.

3. I want to continue to select and emphasize certain morals and beliefs and attitudes towards life during these formidable, impressionable years. (Note: Most leading authorities on child development contend that the most formative years in terms of value systems and attitudes toward himself and others are the ages of birth to five or six.) I want to be the most important factor in influencing my child's values.

4. I want to enjoy and be a part of their playfulness as my children learn and grow. I want them to be a part of my life.

For all these reasons, I believe we can interact in a significant way in the lives of our young children. The preschool-at-home offers the best opportunity for us to stay critically involved with our young children while offering them the many other aspects of their first group structured learning experience.

Q: Why would you choose this type of preschool-at-home rather than another type of preschool?

A: The preschool at home gives us the opportunity for

1. excellent parent involvement in their children's learning;

2. enhancement of each child's self-esteem, a basic necessity for learning to take place;

3. the gradual preparation for separation of parent and child.

In a small group, your child can learn at his own pace with lots of encouragement and reinforcement.

Q: Can my preschool child really learn at home?

A: First of all, his learning comes from within himself—not from another person. The preschool-at-home provides an environment rich in qualities for learning to take place:

- high percentage of one-to-one interactions, due to small group;

- much focused attention due to low ratio of child to leader (three to one or two up to eight to one or two);

- the parent-leader, because of her personal interest, can focus on specific areas of development;

- the many "hands on" experiences help keep motivatation high;

- the frequency of school days is limited enough to keep the child interested;

- at the three- to five-year-old level, the parents can easily handle the information and ideas presented;

- most importantly, the child who feels emotionally secure is open to spend his time and energy on learning (and not coping with his anxieties).

Q: What will this cost me in terms of time and money?

A: It will cost you as much as you want to put into it. Your amount of time spent being "teacher" depends upon how many parents are in your group. For example, if there are five, you will be in charge about twenty percent of your planned sessions. If your group has "helpers," you will probably be directly involved another twenty percent of the time. And you must consider a few planning meetings and the field trips, too.

Very little, if any, money needs to be spent. You may want to purchase a good book with lots of ideas for preschool (see additional suggested titles listed in Appendix). And you may want to spend a couple of dollars once in a while for a few project supplies.

We would rather look at our time spent as an investment in the future of our child not as a sacrifice. Even more valuable is the irreplaceable time you spend with (and for) your child. Most of us want to give whatever we can for our children. The preschool-at-home is a great opportunity to give of ourselves.

Q: If I have a full-time job, how can I help with an at-home preschool? How can I fit it into my schedule?

A: Find a time slot convenient to you and the other mothers. You may have to juggle dates once in a while, but flexibility is one big advantage in the preschool-at-home. For example, Kathy—who was a full-time working mother as editor of our local paper—was "parent-leader" on Friday, her day off. But all the other four moms in the group were parent-leaders on Wednesdays. All were pleased with the schedule. If preschool-at-home is what you want, you'll find a way to fit a couple of hours once in a while into your schedule. The time invested will be special for you and your little one.

Q: How can my child learn to be independent of me if he's with me constantly? Won't he become even more clingy, more dependent?

A: Becoming independent is a gradual process just as weaning and learning how to walk. Independence is directly related to a person's feeling secure and adequate. A three- to five-year-old will show varying degrees of independence, related to his background experience, his age, who he's with, and where he is. He may behave very independent of his parents while he's in the home of a good friend. But he may show much more dependence if taking a train ride for the first time; yet a year later he may be much more confident—even sitting alone on the upper deck while his parent sits below.

It is helpful to remember that to fill the need to become independent is like filling an empty container. You must put something in—not take it out. A child must be "filled" with lots of mother and dad before he will be "full" enough to act independent of them. An example of this is on a below-freezing day you would warm the child by putting on his coat, hat, and mittens, not taking them off. In the same way, to help a child become independent, you must allow him to be "full" of his dependence on mom and dad.

Q: Will my child be cheated if he does not go to a regular preschool?

A: No. He'll not be cheated of anything. He can get all the various components of early learning experiences in his small group setting at home. He will have opportunities for activities in all areas—big and small muscles, mental, social, etc. One of our goals is to introduce a wide variety of ideas about our world; we do not attempt mastery or achievement of anything at this level.

Parents who have participated in at-home preschools agree that a child will not be cheated of anything. Rather, they agree that he will receive more of a good emotional foundation—the main requirement for further development in all areas. A child who feels secure and likes himself is not afraid to try, usually doesn't give up easily, and genuinely likes new things. His eagerness and curiosity and imagination are not stifled but rather stimulated.

Q: Our public school system is very competitive. Will our child have the skills needed to keep up with the best students academically?

A: We feel that although the push to achieve academically is strong in our society, it is in the best interest of our little ones to allow them to learn at their own pace. At the age of three or four or five, the child should not be programmed into academics. We believe a general exposure to many concepts through the experiential (hands-on) approach is the best foundation for the learning of academics when the child is developmentally ready to do so.

Q: What is the most important thing he will get out of a preschool-at-home?

A: While he will receive a good general background in every major area—-physical, mental, social, and emotional—the best thing he will receive is a very positive attitude about himself. He knows he not only is "okay," but he's better than okay; he's terrific and special. He will have a good self-esteem—giving him a solid foundation on which to build his education in the future.

Children love to have their friends come over to their house.

Q: What do I do with the younger brother at home?

A: Many of us had a preschool child and another younger child (or children) You have several options as to how to handle this.

1. We felt strongly about keeping the youngest ones with us. So, generally, if they were under two, two-and-a-half, or sometimes three years old, they stayed with us. In a small group (five or less) of preschoolers, usually the baby just fit in. The older child, say two or three years old, often joined in where he could at his own level.

2. Another solution is to have an "assisting" mother, especially with a larger group or with younger children. Then if the parent-teacher in charge needs a break to nurse the baby or tend to a toddler, the helping mother simply takes over.

3. A third choice which works well with mature two-and-a-half or three-year-olds, is to have another "playgroup" going on in another home. This is especially nice for two or more three-year-olds who might feel left out of their older brother's and sister's preschool. This can be a very happy, playful social experience and needs almost no preparation. Talk with the other parents in your group to see if they might be interested.

Q: What can my child get out of this at-home preschool that he cannot get anywhere else?

A: Only in the at-home preschool will a child have the presence of his parent(s) who take an active part in his learning. There will be a strengthening of the parent-child bond while giving him a very gradual introduction to the more formal learning he will encounter in the school system.

Q: Will my child be confused by going from place to place with more than one teacher?

A: The children may be unsure of the rotation from home to home as it takes place the first time around. If a child's parent explains to him a day or two ahead of preschool, he will be prepared to make the changes. A three- or four-year old usually doesn't think ahead to next week or next month—he is more concerned with today (and sometimes tomorrow). If the parent-teachers understand clearly, the children will operate under their self-confidence. Even though the place will change, the underlying structure is carried through in the daily plan which is similar from one time to the next.

Several advantages become apparent with the cooperative quality of the preschool-at-home. The child begins to make several friendships with the other children in the group. He also learns to accept and to like more than one teacher. He begins to make more than one attachment to other adults while keeping the most special place for his mother and father.

Q: I don't think we have the right house for an at-home preschool. We don't have the kind of educational things that kids need. How can I do this without the materials and supplies needed for a preschool?

A: Any home and yard will be fine. Things are not as important as people—the feelings shared among parents and children are the basis for a good environment. It's easy to find something fun and meaningful for the children in your home. An old magazine can be cut up for pictures of different transportation. Pots and pans and wood blocks can start off a rhythm band. Empty and full and one-half can be discovered in measuring out the ingredients for cut-out shape cookies. A box of old hats, gloves, and shoes are good for pretending. Whatever you have for your own child to use and to play with will come alive and be transformed into new learning experiences when used with the group of preschool children.

Q: Won't my child be cheated of a group experience? Is there a disadvantage in being in a small group of five or six rather than, say, of twenty to twenty-five?

A: The same opportunities for social experiences exist in a group of four to eight as in a class size of twenty or more. In the preschool-at-home, the child has a chance to practice language skills, to learn to get along in a group, and to practice other social skills.

Generally, too, the smaller group allows the child more opportunities for self-expression. He has more and longer chances for verbalizing his thoughts. And he can concentrate on a few (rather than many) other boys and girls with whom to develop friendships.

At the preschool level, learning takes place when children can experience things firsthand.

Many kindergartens stress working in small groups of four to six children for the main reason, perhaps, of keeping control of the class as a whole.

Q: I don't know the facts. How can I tell them about such things as "How cocoons are made by caterpillars"?

A: First, it is helpful to remember that preschool children are much more emotional than cognitive (factual).

One of the most effective approaches in learning something new is to allow the child to "experience" it firsthand. At the preschool level, you can answer many of their questions from your general knowledge. And when they occasionally throw you a curve, you need only to be honest and say, "I don't know. But let's find out." Then look it up together, if possible. Perhaps you can even plan a session around the curious question using a book, a song, and a project to help the children learn the answer.

Q: Isn't an at-home preschool a lot of work? It sounds as though it might be very time-consuming.

A: It will probably depend upon your attitude toward it. We looked upon it as a fun thing to do with our children. Even though we had some concerns about it, once the preschool got started we found it exciting! We actually looked forward to our turn at being parent-leader much the same way we'd look forward to putting on a birthday party (with less work).

Remember, too, that the preschool at home is shared by all the parents involved. We cooperate on planning and scheduling. You should be able to plan ahead after the schedule is set up so that you will have plenty of time to get yourself prepared. You can make use of your "time off" as teacher thinking of new ideas and gathering any materials needed.

Q: What about discipline problems? I'm not sure I can handle several rowdy three- and four-year-olds. I can hardly handle my own all by myself.

A: We think you'll be surprised how little disciplining is ever called for. Children, when they're busy playfully learning, don't get into situations that need heavy disciplining. Occasionally you may need to step in and do some directing, explaining, or gentle (but firm) guidance to help solve a problem.

With the other parents during a planning session, you will want to discuss your attitudes about disciplining or guidance, and then establish some guidelines that all will be comfortable using.

Q: Will I favor or protect my own child more than the others?

A: Yes, you probably will to a certain extent. This is all right because it is truthful. It is natural that your feelings toward your own child are much stronger than toward the others. It may keep your child from feeling jealous if you can give him an extra hug or sometimes call on him first to do something. He will be sure he is special to his mother.

Should you notice yourself becoming too overprotective or showing too much favoritism—in your judgment—try to put things in a little better balance. Make an effort to exhibit fairness and equality when possible, such as when giving praise. Be sure to say something positive to every person in the group, including your own.

And remember, since the parents take turns, the situation changes as the parent-leader changes.

Q: What if my child gets sick on the day that I'm in charge of the group?

A: You have several options.

You can quickly call the parents and cancel. (Use the plans next time.)

You can call the parents and reschedule for a few days later.

You can ask another parent to take over for you in her home, giving her anything you have prepared (such as a book, craft materials, special snack, game, etc.).

A box of wigs, hats, and gloves can provide the basis for make-believe.

Q: What about distance from home to home? How far is too far?

A: You can have your group spread out as many miles as the parents are comfortable driving. Keep in mind, though, the length of time your young children will ride happily. Perhaps fifteen to twenty minutes' ride may be a good outer limit as a guideline.

An advantage to having a preschool with more distant children is that their social world is pleasantly expanded to beyond their immediate family and neighborhood. Children they play with less frequently offer them fresh experiences.

Q: Why should I organize a preschool-at-home when I can send my child to a very good traditional preschool with a caring, kind teacher just a short distance from our home?

A: We hope you'll organize your own preschool-at-home for the same reason(s) we did—because we wanted to. We wanted to be close to our child and give him the best emotional foundation on which to grow. We feel that very early education should be a natural and gradual process and that we, as parents, have the ability to have a direct part and control in this happening. Our total commitment to our parenting led us to consciously choose this type of preschool in which we are accountable and responsible.

Soon into the preschool-at-home, you will be pleased to discover the rewards as you observe firsthand your child's developing mind and body. You may see him learn one-to-one number correspondence, how to balance as he walks the length of a log, how to manage a scissors as he cuts a straight line. These moments are just as thrilling as watching him take his first steps. Furthermore, you will have many precious memories of fun (and worthwhile) times that you spent together.

Part Two

Planting the Seeds

In Part Two of *Playful Learning*, we'll give you an overview of what's involved in organizing an at-home preschool. Since we hope this project will be an enjoyable experience for you and your child, we recommend keeping the organizational details to a minimum. You will need to find enthusiastic parents, plan your goals, and provide a learning environment for the children. These chapters tell you how to do just that without becoming overwhelmed.

Finding Parents for Your Preschool-at-Home

The Search Is On

As far as I'm concerned, we both benefited from our at-home preschool. My son was able to do something fun and I was able to be a part of it. What happy memories!

Colleen Weiland, mother of Mike, Eric, Amy, and Matthew

By now you may be wondering how and when to begin creating a playgroup or preschool. What are the first steps needed in order to initiate this group experience? To take on the responsibility of learning along with your young child, you have two options. First, you can start a small group with other parents cooperatively working together or, second, you can create a family preschool with only your own children.

The advantage of a small group experience is that your child will enjoy a social situation in a home under the guidance of a parent or parents. The disadvantage will be the need to find several other parents who are willing to participate in this type of education rather than sending their children to an established preschool. In this day and age when day care and preschool are big business, you may need to convince other parents of the advantages of an at-home preschool. One of the best ways to help parents feel at ease about working with their own children is to have them talk to kindergarten teachers. Ask them if they have seen a difference between children who have attended preschool and those whose parents worked with them at home instead. The answer should be reassuring.

n seven years of teaching kindergarten I have observed that children who have had preschool experience have a little easier time coming to school the first few days. By October it is often difficult to spot children who have been to preschool because those who have not catch up very quickly.

We try very hard to teach the "whole" child. In pushing academic skills only we create a child who is unable to make independent decisions or cope with others. The happy, well-adjusted student seems to learn eagerly and is able to assimilate his information into all sorts of everyday situations. A child who is "pressured" too early is sometimes frustrated easily. The child who has had the opportunity to explore the world, to experiment with materials, and to have lots of interactions with the environment and other people is much better prepared to start school.

Vickie Shoemaker, kindergarten teacher

Comments from kindergarten teachers in general support the idea that preschool is not essential. They emphasize that children who have parents who either organized home preschool groups or provided their own children with lots of experiential learning opportunities come to school more excited about learning in a group. Often the children are more interested in the activities and group participation than children who have several years of traditional preschool.

If you choose to begin a preschool-at-home with just your own children, you will not need to find a group of parents to work with you. You will simply need to find activities and opportunities to make learning fun. Some background and preschool learning activities you can use are suggested in Part Three. One problem is that you will be on your own; when you lack ideas or enthusiasm you will not have other parents to encourage your efforts or to fall back on. Your children will not have the opportunity to socialize routinely with a small group of friends in a playful home environment.

Whichever preschool method you decide to use, both mothers and fathers can participate. Today, both parents are becoming actively involved with their children. Your children will learn and enjoy new experiences with either parent. We encourage fathers as well as mothers to share in this as their time permits.

We will, however, be inclined to use the word "mothers" when referring to parents simply because—in our experience—playgroups are usually started by mothers. We hope the fathers who wish to get involved will understand.

Finding Parents

One method of finding parents for your preschool-at-home is to simply tell other parents about what you would like to do. Share the idea with neighbors, friends, and relatives if they have children the same ages as your own. It is not too early to begin looking for other mothers with a similar feel for parenting, even if your child is not old enough for a playgroup. Children who are from around two-and-a-half to five years old can benefit from this experience. Before two-and-a-half years old, a child is not ready for a playgroup unless the parents simply use the time to get together informally.

Become familiar with another mother's way of dealing with her children by informally getting together, along with your toddlers or young children, to chat, work on a project of mutual interest, or just go to the park. It will become fairly evident if a parent does not have the desire or patience—or whatever—to become a part of a playgroup situation.

Providing lots of learning opportunities at home helps prepare a child for kindergarten.

It is not necessary to have exactly the same ideas about raising children; you should, however, mutually agree on the important things you value highly such as using an understanding method of dealing with conflicts and frustrations or believing that people are more important than things.

Where to look

Begin looking for other parents at least several months ahead of the time you wish to start meeting on a formal basis. If it's nice outside, try discussing the preschool or playgroup idea with parents you meet at the park or while out walking with their children. You may want to try contacting parents at local child-oriented organizations such as the YMCA children's programs. Another source is to contact parents through your local elementary school or PTA. Often parents who have children in kindergarten also have young children at home. Babysitting co-ops, church functions, and La Leche League meetings provide other sources to meet mothers who are interested in working and learning with their little ones. Many parents are receptive to the idea when they learn some of the advantages. This is a good time to invite them to a get-together to discuss the playgroup idea.

Parents who enjoy children

Look for parents who are concerned about their relationship with their children. These parents will enjoy working with their children, especially during learning and play activities. Often parents concerned about the early mother-child separation that preschool assumes to be necessary are interested in an at-home experience.

Some parents may not be totally confident with an at-home group. They may need to get their feet wet. They may choose a traditional preschool situation several days a week (as insurance for them that their child will not miss anything important) and then participate in the preschool-at-home on alternate days. Often this parent, with the support of the other mothers, eventually feels confident that the at-home preschool is a wonderful alternative to the traditional preschool.

 ost mothers and fathers can provide deeper security, closeness, sharper instincts, longer continuity, warmer responses, more logical control, and more natural examples than the staff of the best care center or kindergarten.

Raymond and Dorothy Moore

It may be wise to suggest some books for parents to read on the subject of learning with young children. *Home Grown Kids: A Practical Handbook for Teaching Your Children at Home* by Raymond and Dorothy Moore has some very encouraging advice. Sandy Jones, author of *Learning for Little Kids*, has put together a wonderful sourcebook for parents. *Teach Your Own* by John Holt is an excellent book on home schooling. Many more books supporting the idea that parents make the best first teachers can be found at the library or bookstore.

Flyers and newspaper ads

A few other ideas for getting parents interested in the at-home preschool may be helpful. Post a handout with a brief description of a cooperative preschool at the supermarket, pediatrician's office, the library, children's bookstore, or at church. An interesting idea is to list yourself in the "wanted" section of your local newspaper. An example for a newspaper ad is:

WANTED...

Enthusiastic parent with eager preschool-aged child to participate in a home cooperative playgroup; only experience necessary is a love of learning with your child.
Want more info...
call 555-4567.

Meeting other parents in a new community

Another situation worth mentioning at this point is meeting other parents after recently moving to a new city or town. It can be discouraging to try to set up a preschool in a new area. Yet, when you do get started you will not only enhance your child's excitement for learning, but also acquaint yourself with a few other parents with similar ideas. First, begin looking for mothers everywhere within reason. Second, you will need to accept other mothers' backgrounds and ideas. Remember, share your thoughts enthusiastically, but remain open to each new parent's comments.

One mother, Starr Shillington, has this to say about the experience:

"Being new to the area, I felt it was important for my son to meet some children his age to help him adjust to our move. He was still quite lonesome for his old friends, one in particular, but the playgroup was really helpful in helping him make new friends."

After having moved to a new city and sharing the playgroup concept with several mothers, Cheryl Sullivan discovered some new ideas.

I was intent on starting a playgroup for my three-year-old son as I had with my older daughter back in our home town. But now, in a new area with few friends to gather for a playgroup, I found my ideas being questioned. I discovered that the playgroup concept means different things to different people. Some mothers considered it an extension of preschool; they wanted to meet on a day that children did not attend preschool. Others felt quite strongly that the group must meet in the same environment, such as a church nursery, rather than in one another's homes. Besides these differing ideas, I discovered a preschool and/or day-care center around every corner that I turned. I began to lose faith.

By expanding on my ideas and remaining flexible, I was able to generate a fair amount of interest. I found three other mothers by September (I had begun my search in May). By November, one of them had moved out of state. By January, another mother moved across town. In February we had two devoted mothers and a few others remotely interested in joining us. Even though the age range of our group widened, we continued to meet and enjoy field trips with our group of six children.

In May, I had only myself and one other mother. I almost gave up. Then a new idea came my way. As part of a parent-participation early-childhood program at my older daughter's elementary school, I was given permission to pass out a questionnaire concerning parents' interest in a playgroup experience. I received a number of very positive replies from other parents. My faith in the playgroup concept was renewed. It turned out to be much different than my first experience. A group of parents with a wide range of preschoolers was given permission by the school principal to use the kindergarten room when it was available. Each parent participated on a rotating basis by sharing a craft, an art project, movement activities, cooking, or a musical game or song. Two parents were in charge for each meeting; all the parents participated at each meeting. Free time to play and socialize was a top priority. This experience was exciting for my son, even though it was not exactly what I had hoped we would have.

The happy ending to this story is that through the experience of meeting more parents with preschoolers, we were able to form a cooperative at-home preschool for our four-year-olds. The motto: Keep the faith.

Where to find parents
parks & playgrounds
YMCA & YWCA
elementary school
park district
PTA
babysitting Co-ops
La Leche League
pediatrician's office
Mothers at Home
use newspaper ad
& flyers

True education does not come packaged or sequenced. Much of it is spontaneous, an outgrowth of openness and curiosity. It is this attitude toward learning, this openness to questioning and curiosity that parents need to impart to their children.

David Elkind

Who Can Do This

Experience has shown that any parent interested and enthusiastic about working in a playgroup or preschool-at-home can do so. One advantage to learning from parents is the diversified backgrounds and experiences the parents have to offer and share. Often what one person lacks another excels; everyone has strengths and weaknesses. The care and concern of a parent for his or her child is the basic requirement. The only degree required is the attainment of an M.O.M. or D.A.D. degree.

Playful Learning Association

The Board of Trustees on the recommendation of the faculty and administration has conferred upon

Mary Ellen Anderson

the degree of

M. O. M.

together with the rights and privileges as well as the responsibilities of that degree.

Time is the greatest investment necessary and it is very flexible for each particular group. The rewards from this investment will far exceed the time and effort you have put into it.

A Get-Together

Once you have contacted a group of interested parents and children, the next step would be to have a get-together—a gathering of parents and children who are interested in getting a preschool-at-home started. Parents should not feel committed to the group at this time, but rather be interested in getting to know the other mothers and allowing the children to play together.

You will begin to get an impression of the attitudes the parents have about children. You will need to discuss what each of the parents values in working with children. Parents may emphasize certain qualities they wish to maintain in the preschool group. For example, some parents feel strongly about the way the children will address the adults, that is, preferring parents to be called Mrs. Smith or Miss Nancy. Other parents will not be concerned with this. Parents may have very definite feelings about dealing with disruptive behavior. You will need to address this concern and discuss, as a group, how to handle a problem if it should occur. Parents will also begin to realize that this is not simply a babysitting arrangement created so mothers will have some free time, but rather a group devoted to allowing children to learn, experiment, and play together.

If this is the first time several parents and children have met, try to focus on general topics. There will be time at your next meeting to discuss the details of the group such as group size, scheduling, what to include in your preschool day, and any other details. More details can be found in Chapters 8 and 9. Encourage the other parents toward understanding that it's all right to teach young children at home and that they need not feel guilty about choosing not to send their child to a traditional preschool or worry that their child is being cheated.

 hile a good preschool program can offer numerous opportunities to a child, plus the chance to socialize with other children, such programs do not come cheaply. And, mothers writing to us stress, an interested mother or group of mothers armed with some good books on the subject and a few craft materials can be every bit as effective in providing a child with a stimulating environment.

Mary Ann Cahill

There is no disadvantage to not having teaching experience or a background in education. As a parent you are continuously teaching your young child. You teach him about the seasons when you talk about snowflakes in the winter, about the autumn leaves, and about the flowers that bloom in spring. You give him his first crayons or scissors and watch him color and cut with pride. Being a parent involved with your child's excitement for learning is all that is needed.

Feeling unsure

Any parent who feels unsure of her ability to work with a group of young children may want to observe the group in action before taking her turn. You can then discover how the parent-leader makes her plans for the group and prepares her home. Or, instead of having one parent lead the group, several parents can participate in the planning which will allow you to ease into the role of leader. For the first several meetings of your playgroup, several or all of the parents may want to stay and work with the group in various degrees. For example, one parent may choose to read a story and talk about it afterwards. Another may choose to stand back and observe for a while. One of your group's aims should be to focus on the happiness of both the children and parents involved. Chapter 8 has more details on parent-child separation.

Importance of the get-together

Once you have found several other interested parents—from four to six depending on the children's ages—you will begin getting to know one another better in terms of your expectations, needs, and interests. It is of great importance that the parents get to know each other in the early stages of planning if possible.

One at-home preschool had a difficult situation in which one of the five mothers in the group had an extremely different attitude toward children. This mother had joined the group about a month after it had started and, consequently, had not been a part of any of the discussions or preliminary planning. The differences in philosophy came out when the children came home very upset after preschool had been held at her house. It was soon learned that the mother had teased the thumbsuckers, yelled corrections at the children, threatened to lock them outside, or to spank them and send them home. The children, usually exuberant about preschool, were frightened and upset. Immediate and open dialogue with this mother resulted in her recognizing that she really did not wish to be involved (for various reasons). As soon as she dropped out of the group, everything went smoothly again.

Another solution to this problem might have been to ask the new mother to join the group as an assistant to one of the other mothers. In this way, she would have gradually become acquainted with the manner in which the other mothers handled the children. She may have needed an assistant to help her ease into the role of parent-leader. She may not have been comfortable handling the group alone. We learn through imitation, whether we are children or adults. By having a mother ease into leading the children by observing another using loving guidance, she learns how to deal with her own child and the group in a more relaxed manner. One of the advantages of the group situation is that learning is shared by all. If you or your child are uncomfortable at a particular parent's home, remain with your child. Use your best judgment in terms of your child's needs.

After this unfortunate experience, the mothers in this group realized the importance of the initial get-togethers as a time to become familiar with each other's attitudes, ideas, and needs. The problem might have been completely avoided if handled in the early stages of planning.

A situation occurred with a happier result when another new mother joined an existing group. She had telephone conversations with several parents in the group and expressed her desire to join after hearing about the group's goals. She had similar feelings about these goals and about the parents' attitudes. She fit in beautifully, having observed and assisted before her turn. To ensure your group's success, use a get-together to verify your similar attitudes about your children and your goals.

Now you can consider what kind of playgroup you want for your children. By the time you have met informally, you should be familiar with the attitudes of the other mothers toward children and their expectations of the group. You have discussed any unsure feelings about working with a group of children. You are now ready to talk in more detail about what kind of program you think will be the best.

 aking the time to talk to children, to answer their questions is an important form of intellectual stimulation; reading to your child is another. Going on trips to the park, the zoo, the museum, and the country are important learning experiences for young children, the best education parents can provide is to acquaint them with that world through language, shared activities, and trips in the context of love and protection.

David Elkind

The Preliminaries of Your Preschool Day

All the Little Details

I feel that it's important for children to know that you care. Being involved with the transition phase from the home environment to the neighborhood environment makes it more gentle and easier to handle.

Starr Shillington, mother of Shawn and Mark

Now you are ready to begin planning for your preschool day. You have a group of interested and enthusiastic parents willing to participate in learning with their preschoolers. You will need to hold a planning meeting to decide on the specifics of your cooperative at-home preschool. The following considerations can be discussed formally or informally among the parents, depending on the make-up of your particular group.

Remember to be flexible with your group. If you had hoped to have a group with similar-aged children but could only generate interest in parents with children of several different ages, do not despair. Some wonderful playgroup experiences can be offered to your children when flexibility is allowed in your day.

How Old? How Many?

After you have found several interested parents and children, decide on the ages and size of the group that will work best for you. Remember, children learn best in a small group. Intimacy is very important to preschoolers.

Three-year-olds

Mixed age groups and those younger than three and a half need a less structured situation. A "playgroup" program would be a suggestion for these younger children. Playgroups stress more playtime than planned activity time. Three-year-olds do best in a group of four children or fewer. Parents should remain until their children are comfortable with the group.

hree is an age period when the mother-child relationship is smooth and satisfactory. It is for many children a "we" age, and for many, mother is the especially favored companion.

Frances Ilg and Louise Bates Ames

 three-year-old's ability with and interest in language help him to be a delightful companion, an interesting group member. Three goes forward positively to meet each new adventure.

Frances Ilg and Louise Bates Ames

t three-and-a-half there comes, in many, a tremendous change ... a period of marked insecurity, disequilibrium, incoordination.

Frances Ilg and Louise Bates Ames

Four-year-olds

A good rule-of-thumb for planning your group size is to have one more child than the children's age. If your group consists of four-year-olds, then a group of five to six children is ideal. This rule has been applied to guests at a child's birthday party, too.

As the number of children in the group increases, the number of parents who will be present to assist can also be increased. Some groups may choose to have more parents stay and participate with a younger group or a large group. This is a choice your group needs to think about. When deciding on the number of parents who will remain, consider the needs of the children. If parents wish to participate on a rotating schedule, a good ratio of adults to children would be three to four children for each adult. Therefore, a group of four children will work nicely with one parent, but as the group size increases to six, two parents may need to be participating. It is helpful if an assisting parent will be taking the group at her house the next time.

There are several ways to group the children:

1. Similar ages—Some parents feel comfortable keeping the children within a four to six month age range. A year age difference, as children encounter in school, seems much greater for young children in terms of maturity and developmental skills. Even if you are able to form a group having very similar ages, you must still allow for differing levels of abilities, maturity, strengths, and weaknesses when planning group activities. One reason parents might prefer this plan is that their children may all enter school in the same grade level.

2. Similar ability—Children who enjoy being together, regardless of age, may demonstrate some similar abilities. For instance, Sara and Kristen enjoyed each other's company while in a neighborhood babysitting co-op even though they will be a year apart in school. Their mothers have similar attitudes about children and would enjoy working together in a playgroup situation. Different ages need not be a factor as long as there are other common bonds.

3. Different ages, different abilities—Older children can be grouped with younger children effectively. Older children often serve as a model for younger ones. At the same time, the younger children may learn simply from observation. When younger children are ready, they will actively join in the group activities. In this grouping, involving several different ages, an environment emphasizing a "child's choice" might be needed. (See Chapter 8.)

 very child has an inner timetable for growth—a pattern unique to him. And his particular way must be respected.

Dorothy Corkille Briggs

Other Children at Home

Other children at home can create a challenge for the hosting parent. She has several alternatives. She may choose to let her younger child remain with her, especially if the child is small enough to be content in a baby carrier. Or, the baby may be happy playing or napping nearby.

It is somewhat more challenging to have a toddler underfoot during your preschool session. This is a time when an assistant may come in handy. The helper parent can either entertain the toddler or take over the preschool group while the host parent meets her little one's needs. Experience has shown that younger children do very well participating with the group if given the opportunity. You may want to have your little one participate by modifying the activity to his level. Provide paper and crayons if the group is doing artwork; he may enjoy cutting or coloring from his high chair for quite some time.

Another alternative is to provide a playgroup experience for the younger children such as a special storytime or a walk to the park. Another parent with a young child may be available to help out with this small group or a babysitter may be hired. The main consideration here is that these younger children are content and comfortable with this alternative.

One parent, Kathy Hoag, makes this comment: "Having two children in two different playgroups is interesting. My two-year-old's group is strictly 'play' and my four-year-old is in a preschool playgroup. They are almost possessive of their own group, calling it 'my' playgroup."

A younger sister or brother may join in the preschool activities at a simpler level.

Mother-Child Separation

The question of mother-child separation should not be taken lightly. A three-year-old has difficulty in understanding that his mother will return in a short while. The playgroup experience should be an enjoyable adventure, not a stressful one. Until a child is accustomed to the group, the parent-leader, and the home, he should not be left alone.

 ntellectual growth does not occur apart from emotional growth; the two are intertwined. The child whose emotional needs are unmet is less likely to do well academically.

Dorothy Corkille Briggs

One mother was asked by her three-year-old to stay with the group. When it became another mother's turn to be the parent-leader, the child became quite concerned. His mother chose to remain in the new home but not participate with the group. She quietly sat on the couch and figured out her checkbook while her son enjoyed his time with the other children. An hour into this playgroup session, her son went over to her saying, "Okay, Mom, you can go now for a little while, but come back soon!" The mother took a walk to the park and arrived back before the playgroup was over to see her son confidently playing out in the backyard with the "gang." One mother, Karen Leon, tells of her experience:

> *It's halfway through our year, and my girls are still not comfortable with my leaving. For the most part, they need me to stay and this is no problem for me as I always enjoy the activities. I'm not going to force them to be "big girls" but I see their confidence growing with each session.*

In contrast to the above situation, another chose to leave her very upset child. He remained upset for a short while. Even though he calmed down, it was apparent he was concerned about when she would return and he had difficulty relaxing with the group. Eventually he came to understand that his mother would return and he would not be left alone. Children have very real fears of being left alone and we need to be sensitive to their feelings.

Many children who attend traditional preschools experience similar fears. Their parents are reassured after several sessions that their children have adjusted to their absence. It is, however, interesting to note that the children who are not secure with leaving their mothers often build a strong relationship with the caretaker, which is often at the expense of forming new friends. Be sensitive to your child's need for you to be near. Rather than be embarrassed by your child's dependency, accept the special loving bond that only a parent and child can have. In time your child will become more independent. This is one of the many reasons that some parents want to have a preschool-at-home: to be able to gradually fulfill their child's emotional needs.

How Often Do We Meet?

How many times per week or month will you meet? What time of day and what day of the week fits everyone's schedule? Three-year-olds seem comfortable meeting for about two hours or less. Four-year-olds may be comfortable for a little longer before getting tired. You may need to experiment for a while to see what hours work best for your children. Mornings tend to be better than afternoons for many children because they are fresher and well-rested.

Next you must decide how often to rotate houses. Younger children do well meeting at least two times at the same home in order to become familiar with the hosting parent. (See sample rotation schedules later in this chapter.)

Other things to consider

In groups where children feel comfortable without their mothers, you will want to discuss car-pooling if the homes are spread out. An assistant parent may be the driver and then stay with the group to help the host-parent. It works nicely if the assistant drives and/or helps out just before it is her turn to host the group. She can become reacquainted with each child while the children again become familiar with her. It is a good transition from home to home and also enhances the communication between parents and children.

You'll need to discuss what materials each child should have. Decide if each child should carry his own supplies to each meeting or if the supplies should be stored in a supply box which a parent rotates from home to home. Chapter 10 addresses this question more specifically.

You will also need to talk about snacks and any special diets the children may be on. Any allergies can be noted at this time. Most mothers prefer that snacks be nutritious and simple. For a variety of nutritious and simple snack ideas see Chapter 17. Snack time can also be a time to stress self-help skills such as setting the table, passing out treats, or pouring juice.

Rotation Schedules

Rotation Schedule			
Host	Helper	Day	Date

Several home rotation samples may be helpful for you to see.

SAMPLE #1
(Six children—six parents)

The following group met once a week, staying at the hosting parent's home two times before rotating. They used a helping mother who was available for assistance with the group or to help with younger children. The helping mother was scheduled to host next. This provided a nice transition for the children. Each parent was involved for four Wednesdays—twice as an assistant and twice as a host; she then had eight Wednesdays free. Field trips were scheduled in between the regular sessions when desired. There were six children in the group and they were all turning four years old between March and May.

Host	Assistant	Day	Date
Cheryl	Janine	Wednesday	February 25
"	"	"	March 4
Janine	Chris	"	March 11
"	"	"	March 18
Chris	Tammy	"	March 25
"	"	"	April 1
Tammy	Connie	"	April 8
"	"	"	April 15
Connie	Marlene	"	April 22
"	"	"	April 29
Marlene	Cheryl	"	May 6
"	"	"	May 13

In addition to the fact that children do not learn positive socialization by being exposed to large groups of children such as in a nursery school, there is strong evidence that they lose initiative and creativity.... Many children become emotionally upset in various ways by such separation from their parents.

Raymond and Dorothy Moore

SAMPLE #2
(Six children—five parents)

A second group met once a week on Wednesdays for two weeks before rotating. They felt comfortable without an assistant parent. The children were all turning four years old within the session. The parent who would host next was to pick up the children and take them home. They had one working parent and adjusted the schedule to meet her needs. The mothers were involved for two Wednesdays each and had eight free Wednesdays. As before, field trips were scheduled when possible.

Host	*Helper/Driver*	*Day*	*Date*
Georgette*	Connie	Wednesday	September 16
"	"	"	September 23
Connie	Kathy	"	September 30
"	"	"	October 7
Kathy**	Anne	Friday	October 17
"	"	"	October 24
Anne	Kelly	Wednesday	October 28
"	"	"	November 4
Kelly	Georgette	"	November 11
"	"	"	November 18

---

*Had twins in the group
**Working parent

SAMPLE #3
(Seven children—seven parents)

A third group tried something different: they met for three Tuesdays at one home. Before she was host, a mother took her turn helping. However, the helper did not necessarily work with the group the entire three times before her turn. The hosting parent was involved for six Tuesdays—though not always consecutively—and free for fifteen Tuesdays. Each mother decided to help on two other Tuesdays scattered in the next several sessions. Parents touched base with the children more often this way. There were seven mothers in the group. The children were three-and-a-half to four years old.

Host	Helper	Day	Date
Chris	Cathy	Tuesday	September 25
"	Anne	"	October 2
"	Cathy	"	October 9
Cathy	Ginny	"	October 16
"	Darlene	"	October 23
"	Dede	"	October 30
Dede	Chris	"	November 6
"	Karen	"	November 13
"	Darlene	"	November 20
Darlene	Chris	"	December 4
"	Chris	"	December 11
"	Ginny	"	December 18
Christmas get-together			December 21
Ginny	Dede	"	January 8
"	Anne	"	January 15
"	Karen	"	January 22
Karen	Dede	"	January 29
"	Darlene	"	February 5
"	Anne	"	February 12
Anne	Karen	"	February 19
"	Ginny	"	February 26
"	Cathy	"	March 5

SAMPLE #4
(Five children—four parents)

Another way of rotating homes is to meet twice a week for two weeks. No mother assistant was required as the five children had been with the group for over a year and worked well together. Often they added a field trip on Fridays. The children were all turning five years old during this session. One parent had two children in the group but only hosted once. The parents were involved for four days and had twelve days free.

Host	*Day*	*Date*
Judy	Monday	February 24
"	Wednesday	February 26
"	Monday	March 3
"	Wednesday	March 5
Colette	Monday	March 10
"	Wednesday	March 12
"	Monday	March 17
"	Wednesday	March 19
Paula	Monday	March 24
"	Wednesday	March 26
"	Monday	March 31
"	Wednesday	April 2
Easter Break		
Anne	Monday	April 21
"	Wednesday	April 23
"	Monday	April 28
"	Wednesday	April 30

SAMPLE #5
(Seven mothers—seven children, four and five years old)

This is a sample of one group's rotation schedule including their field trips and study units. This group really liked going on field trips and planned them on a routine basis. They also wanted to introduce the children to math concepts as a study unit. This way, the children were introduced to activities in a sequence of easier to increasingly more detailed study. They had concentrated on introducing letters in the previous sessions. The children continue to talk about letters but not in a formal way. It is a good idea to list your objectives and any field trips or themes you want to plan. This gives parents a sense of commitment to the group and also allows for any readiness activities to have some consistency. Four- and five-year-olds enjoy this study. It would be too structured to do this with younger children. Chapter 9 has more information on what to include in your preschool day.

DATE	*NAME*	*THEME*	*STUDY UNIT*	*FIELD TRIP*
February 4, 6, 8	Nancy	Earth	Shapes-Basic	State Park
February 11, 13, 14	Becky	Valentine's Day	Numbers 1-5	Florist
February 18, 20, 22	Karen	President's Day	Numbers 1-5	Downtown Library
February 25, 27 March 1	Kathie	Handicaps	Comparison words	Handicapped School
March 4, 6, 8	Cheryl	Transportation	Numbers 1-10	International Airport
March 11, 13, 15	Becky D.	Emergencies	Numbers 1-10	Ranger station
March 18, 20, 22	Nancy	Space	Numbers 1-20	Planetarium
March 25, 27, 29	Marty	Gardening	Comparison words	Plant a garden
April 8, 10, 12	Becky H.	Nature	Numbers 1-20	Nature Center
April 15, 17, 19	Karen	Domestic animals	Polygons	Dairy farm
April 22, 24, 26	Kathie	Wild animals	Patterns	Zoo
April 29 May 1, 3	Cheryl	Elementary School	Simple addition	Kindergarten classroom
May 6, 8, 10	Becky D.	Mothers and babies	Puzzles	Farm
May 13, 15, 17	Marty	Outdoor fun	Farewell Party	Picnic/Hike

The above samples provide some idea of the different schedules a group can work out. Working parents, parents with twins, or any other unique situation you may encounter can usually be worked out to the group's satisfaction.

Rotation schedules will be much the same for younger playgroups and groups where the mothers all stay. As a group, decide how often you want to meet per week or month. Then decide how many sessions you will have at each person's home.

Planning Your Preschool Program

We're Ready to Go!

I loved almost every aspect of the playgroup. The best part for me was that it got my creative juices flowing. The ideas used in the group carried over to everyday mothering. I am a more exciting and creative mother when there is a playgroup in progress.

Judy Erwin, mother of Joshua and Benjamin

What do you wish to accomplish during your preschool day? What is the purpose of the group? What do I want my children to get out of the preschool experience? These questions should be addressed by parents no matter what type of playgroup or preschool they are planning for their child. Before exposing children to a group learning situation, parents should form an idea of what they expect their children to gain from the experience.

For example, in a gym and swim class for tots, parents may expect that their children will learn to swim independently. They are disappointed if their children are unable to learn to swim on their own, yet, the goal of the group may have been to teach water safety and enjoyment of the water. Parents need to have a clear idea of their goals and what kinds of experience they want for their children. And they need to accept each child's individual learning style.

Establishing the Goals

At your preschool planning meeting, ask yourselves, "What can this pre-school situation do for my child?" When parents respond to this question, their answers will vary. The following responses are typical when a group of parents discuss an at-home preschool:

> "I want my son to be able to express himself better with his friends and with other adults."

> "Laura doesn't do well with paper and pencil. She needs practice with writing and drawing."

> "Tara needs to become more comfortable with big muscle movements."

> "I'd like Timmy to learn the importance of caring for himself and his belongings when I am not with him."

> "I'm concerned about how Ellen will be able to share and get along with friends her own age."

> "I want Darren to get a good start in school. I would like to have him exposed to following directions and playing and learning in a group."

> "Joel is interested in letters and numbers. I would like for him to be able to learn in a fun situation and yet still get a good foundation for school."

> "Tina is very creative and imaginative. I feel she needs an opportunity to foster these traits with a few close friends."

Following this discussion, you will be able to form a list of goals for your group. From the responses above, a list of goals might look like this:

- communication experiences
- paper and pencil and art experiences
- big muscle games
- independent self-care
- sharing and cooperative play
- following directions
- pre-reading, pre-math, readiness activities
- creative exploration

Activity Outlines

With input from the other parents, a list of activities you would like to include in your preschool day can be formulated. By considering the children's interests, strengths, and weaknesses, you will begin to focus in on what your preschool day will be like.

A sample Activity Outline may include:

- reading a story: listening and discussion (communication)

- snack/self-care: pouring, clean up, etc.

- art, craft, or cooking: creativity and drawing skills

- simple big muscle game: cooperative play and big movement

- song or fingerplay: small muscle coordination and memory

- playtime

The above sample may work well with a group of three-year-olds if a large chunk of time can be devoted to the free play. When working on your plans, remember children have very short attention spans when doing group work. The sample may be too much, at first, for your group. You may want to begin with play only and gradually add the other activities. Then, at the next meeting, read a story and discuss it. At the next meeting, include storytime and a snack. The group can be exposed to various learning materials during their playtime.

 hildren need time to explore in a responsive environment in order to acquire a healthy sense of initiative. When children are hurried from one day care center or caretaker to another, there is no time to explore.

David Elkind

 In one playgroup, the children began their day with free play. The wooden blocks were set out. The children began using the blocks in different ways. The parent hosting the group sat on the floor nearby and began to discuss each child's block structure with him. She commented on Joel's tall structure and Darren's long road. She was able to draw the children's attention to the size relationships of the blocks and their shapes. When putting the blocks away, she was able to guide them in putting the largest blocks in the box first, then the half-size blocks, and so on. There was order to the clean-up; it became a learning proj-

Planning your preschool day involves looking at the needs and interests of the children.

ect as well. The next time the children had the opportunity to choose blocks for playtime, they were aware of the sizes and shapes and the order for putting the blocks away.

The activities can be adjusted as you observe the children to ensure that the routine is comfortable to all. The children will soon become used to changing from one activity to another and feel a sense of order to their preschool day. One mother, Karen Leon, learned, "In retrospect, I realize I overplanned on activities and did not give the children enough free time. They let me know by the second session."

Another sample Activity Outline includes more structured activities with more time for mental concentration. It may look like this:

storytime (stress listening and group discussion)

art/craft/cooking project (stress creativity or small muscle dexterity)

big muscle movement (stress coordination, balance)

snack (stress self-help)

sitting game (pre-math, pre-science, or pre-reading)

fingerplay or song

playtime

 hildren not only need an atmosphere that encourages curiosity and exploration, they need rich exposures to a wide variety of experiences.

Dorothy Corkille Briggs

Each of the activities listed in the previous samples are discussed in Part Three. More ideas can be found in specific book references found in the Bibliography. In considering the needs of the children, you may want to look through the Developmental Skills Scale in the Appendix.

The activities you decide to include in your preschool day and the length of your day will depend on many different factors:

- needs of the children
  "What do the children need practice with?"

- interests and abilities of the children
  "How long can they pay attention?"
  "What can they do with some success?"
  "What do they enjoy?"

- parent interests
  "What is the parent good at?"

- time of day
  "Do the children need a nap?"

- length of preschool day

- number of children in the group

Finding Teaching Themes

Another consideration in each parent's planning will be the parent's strengths, background experiences, vocations, and any other enrichment they can offer to the preschool experience. It may be useful to establish some teaching themes. Each parent may want to specialize in a particular interest area and use it as a springboard to teach certain skills.

Themes for new learning experiences can be found in everyday occurrences. For example, in early fall, Judy was working in her garden when she came across a beautiful whole web with a black and yellow spider. She pointed it out to her three-year-old son, Josh. When Josh showed an interest, she thought this would be a good topic for her playgroup session. She remembered a song on one of her children's records called "Creeping Critters," which she used. The children pretended to be bugs, moving along to the words of the song. Then the children, with small jars, collected bugs outdoors. Then they looked at them through a magnifying glass. Their small muscle skill involved making a butterfly out of construction paper wings glued on a clothespin body. They sang the song "Itsy Bitsy Spider." Their snack was "ants-on-a-log." Starting from her son's spark of curiosity, Judy fit all the activities into their general preschool plan.

*C*hildren need vital contact with real people, not masked robots acting off borrowed blueprints.

Dorothy Corkille Briggs

Parents come to the preschool group with a variety of backgrounds, interests, and ideas to share. Some even surprise themselves with their creativity. When Tammy joined the group, she expressed a desire to work with the children on creative movement due to her background in dance.

Anne is talented with art and craft creativity; she chose to weave these talents into her preschool day by providing an endless array of materials for the children to experiment with. Colette has a science and biology background and used the animal world as her springboard. Cheryl was able to touch on the weather and transportation because her husband, who is a pilot, added some excitement to these subjects. Darlene had experience waitressing. She included cooking and a pretend restaurant in her preschool plan. The children were thrilled. Every parent is an individual just as each child is. You bring much of your personality and interests into your preschool ideas. Find the areas that excite you and the children and make the most of them.

Field trips—adventures outside the home—enrich understanding from the smallest "trip" into the backyard to the bus trip across town wherever opportunity suggests. Children learn best from doing, seeing, touching, and, in general, experiencing with all their senses. Now you can begin your preschool adventure by scheduling each parent and her theme. Plan for any assistants needed and discuss future field trips to be taken by the group.

Planning Your Preschool Day

You, as parents, are in charge. Plan activities to meet your children's needs and yet allow enough flexibility to adjust for "off" days. A routine will aid parents in planning their scheduled days. An established routine provides an order to the flow of activities, similar to what the children would experience in a school setting; it also maintains a consistency from week to week. The children will experience making transitions from one activity to another.

Some form of "plan book," or traveling notebook in which your Activity Outlines can be kept, along with other pertinent details, will be handy to have. By keeping a record of your plans, it is possible for the other mothers to review what has been done by the group already, which activities worked especially well, and those that were a flop. And you may choose to evaluate your preschool day by commenting on the children's level of interest, abilities, enthusiasm, or difficulties they may have experienced. Any hints you may have about stimulating interest, curiosity, or cooperation can be shared.

Some parents feel strongly about establishing a structured routine while others seem comfortable with leaving the plans rather loose. Another alternative is to provide a "child's choice" environment. We do this by preparing our home with a variety of materials for the children to explore as their interest draws them to the materials. These options will be explored in more detail later in this chapter. Regardless of whether you choose a tight or loose routine you must remain flexible, observing the children's attitudes and making adjustments in your day when necessary.

Here are a few tips to consider when planning your day:

1. Keep activities short and simple.

2. Plan a moving activity, then a sitting activity; try to alternate them.

3. Plan a big movement activity when the group first comes in as they are usually very excited; then follow this with small movement activities. (Your group may have different needs though, so remain flexible.)

4. Plan a time for children to choose freely from a variety of discovery-oriented activities.

5. Plan a quiet time before the end of your day (story, quiet playtime, etc.) so the children are relaxed before leaving the playgroup.

6. Be sure any preparations are completed and materials you will be using are set out before the children arrive.

7. Have a special place for the children's belongings.

s much as possible the ideal program and activities should resemble a good mother's home program—involvement in homemaking activities, including gardening and other useful work, nature experiences, rest, and freedom from academic pressures.

Raymond and Dorothy Moore

Parent-directed plans

Two plans that work especially well with younger children:

Example I "Parent-Leader Directed"

Approximate Time Span	Activity
15 minutes	Show & Tell (speaking & listening)
10 minutes	Read aloud & discuss a short story
15 minutes	Big muscle movement
15 minutes	Snack
15 minutes	Craft, cooking, or art
20 minutes	Playtime
10 minutes	Song or fingerplay

TOTAL: 1 hour and 40 minutes

Example II "Parent-Leader Directed"

Approximate Time Span	Activity
30 minutes	Playtime (dress-ups, pretend play) Discovery time: puzzles, counting games, pouring, tying experiences
15 minutes	Snack/cooking time
10 minutes	Story
10 minutes	Big movement
10 minutes	Song or fingerplay

TOTAL: 1 hour and 15 minutes

These routines are flexible enough to allow for more or less time for each activity depending on the children. You might find it easier to think of your preschool day in 10 or 15 minute segments rather than a "two-hour" day.

The child should be permitted to choose what he *wants to work with and to repeat or stop as he pleases. However, each task must be completed before the material is returned to its place. He must not be allowed to stop simply because he has lost interest.*

Elizabeth Hainstock

Child's choice plans

Wishing to provide for free choice of activities, you may want to allow thirty to forty minutes for children to move at their own pace exploring prepared interest areas. This is loosely based on Montessori's philosophy.

 he Montessori method is based fairly and squarely on the spontaneous activity of the intellect....the child is by nature an explorer of his environment.

E.M. Standing

You may choose to establish several areas of interest such as: an art project, exploring a musical instrument, cooking in the kitchen, working with manipulatives (blocks, legos, puzzles), working with numbers, measuring or shape and size materials, working with colors (matching or grading color intensity), matching letters or pictures, or exploring water (test for floating objects, pouring, measuring, etc.). More ideas for materials to use in this type of day will be found in Chapter 10. Let the children explore the different materials. The parent-leader or any helping parents can work with small groups or on a one-to-one basis. Guidelines can be established as needed to ensure that children do not disrupt one another or that children respect the proper use of materials such as putting away materials as they move on to a new interest.

From home to home, interest areas will fluctuate. Materials can either travel in a large box from home to home or change completely. The parent-leader needs to prepare her home before the group arrives. She may choose to take the children on a tour of the various interest areas and demonstrate the use of the materials the first several times the children are exposed to them. She may individually work with the children explaining how to use each material the child chooses to work with. Some children may simply observe other children, others may choose to explore several interest areas, while other children may spend the entire time at one activity. A sample of a prepared home may be set up as follows:

Have the following interest areas set up:

> KITCHEN: Ingredients to mix a simple recipe to share at snack time such as "counting muffins." Children can pour, measure, sift, and decorate.

KITCHEN SINK: Warm sudsy water for washing utensils; sponges for wiping up spills, artwork areas, cooking surfaces or dishes.

KITCHEN TABLE: A simple craft finished on display with all materials needed to make it OR various art materials such as crayons, scissors, blank paper, watercolors (allow for creative artwork to just happen).

DINING ROOM TABLE: Imaginary play prop box (store: play money, items to sell).

LIVING ROOM: Use rug mats to display various materials such as blocks, sorting games, cards, puzzles, a shoe to tie, pre-math, pre-reading, pre-writing, or science experiments (magnet, floating vs. non-floating experiment).

LIBRARY AREA (an end table): Have several books on display for browsing.

Example III "Child's-Choice Prepared Home"

Approximate Time Span	Activity
10 minutes	Good morning song, calendar discussion
15 minutes	Tour various interest areas; demonstrate use of materials
30-45 minutes	Allow children to explore interest areas choosing to do whatever interests them; provide guidance if needed
10 minutes	Signal time for clean-up
10 minutes	Group snack
15 minutes	Group circle: sing, do a fingerplay, do big muscle exercise
10 minutes	Read a story and discuss

TOTAL: 2 hours

Three important guidelines for having a successful child's choice day are:

1. Children must not disrupt another's work;

2. Materials must be used as demonstrated;

3. Materials must be put away before beginning a new activity.

This type of playgroup works well for children who have a need to work independently, or for children of different ages. The role of the parent-leader will be to move from child to child as children request assistance or recognition for some work well done. As a parent-leader you may need to stand back and simply observe busy minds at work. There are times when adult direction is necessary. However, there are times when adult interference can backfire and distract a child rather than stimulate learning.

Sample Plans

By reading the following sample plans, you can see that each parent varies a little in her planning to suit her abilities and interests.

SAMPLE I—TAMMY'S DAY
(A parent-directed plan)

Big Muscle Movement (approximately 15 minutes)
Simple stretching, toe touching, twists, etc.

Give an example of mime

Let the children try to mime—a dog, a baseball player, brushing teeth, going to bed, eating, etc., and create some of their own mimes

Speaking and Listening (approximately 15 minutes)
Discuss calendar

Review five senses

Use sense of touch to describe an object

Small Muscle Skill—Art (approximately 20 minutes)
(Alternate two small groups)

Helper: guide the children with painting a large refrigerator box to make a puppet theater box

Host: use magnetic letters to spell their names on the refrigerator using a "feely" bag to select correct letters

(Trade groups)

Free Play (approximately 20 minutes)
Allow free play with puppets and music to dance to

Snack (approximately 15 minutes)

    Fruit slices, juice (let children pour)

    Round-robin prayer on being thankful

Craft Project (approximately 20 minutes)

    Discuss mimes and their makeup

    Draw a face—paint it white—color in the features (happy, sad, surprise, etc.) for his expression

Song and Fingerplay (approximately 15 minutes)

    "Itsy Bitsy Spider"

    "He's Got the Whole World in His Hands" (use mime actions)

Tammy followed up this day with a field trip later in the week to see a mime at the children's theater. She knew about going to see the mime and planned her day around that theme. Tammy's background included dance; she enjoys children's imaginative spirit.

SAMPLE II—CHRIS'S DAY
(A parent-directed plan)

Big Muscle Movement (approximately 15 minutes)

    Let children each choose an exercise

    Play "Simon Says"

    Play "Hokey Pokey"

Speaking and Listening (approximately 20 minutes)

    Discuss special people (blind, deaf, wheelchairs, etc.)

    Show sign language book such as the one from Sesame Street

    Practice "signing" each of their names

    Pretend game: let each child experience being blind, unable to walk, etc.

Small Muscle Skills and Math (approximately 10 minutes)

    Make a number (1-5) collage with fabric cuttings (comment on different patterns and textures)

    Let children glue in the correct number of fabric cuttings for each numeral

Free Play (approximately 20 minutes)

> Weather permitting, go outside for a ("S") swing on the tire swing and a ("S") slide down the slide

Art/Reading Experience (approximately 10 minutes)

> Use string and tempera paints to make "S" actions and sounds

Snack and Cooking (approximately 15 minutes)

> Fresh fruit ("S") salad, say grace, all serve, and all clean up after each other
>
> Let children mix their own salads

Story (approximately 15 minutes)

> Read *Clyde Monster*, a story of a monster afraid of people at bedtime

Chris followed up this day with a trip to a bakery run by handicapped persons and later in the week, took the children to a classroom for the hearing-impaired. Chris is a high school graduate and has worked as a florist. She prides herself on being a loving mother.

SAMPLE III—CHERYL'S DAY
(A child's-choice plan)

Thirty minutes before the children arrive: Set up

1. Put out ingredients for making the snack: Dandy Candy

2. Prepare sink with warm sudsy water for washing dishes

3. Put out materials to explore:

water colors, cup with water to rinse brushes, blank paper (put on kitchen table)

3 wooden puzzles (in living room)

tray with 1 to 10 counting cards

lacing and typing board

button sorting tray with muffin tin for sorting

magnifying glass with leaf, penny, flower, bug

noodles for stringing with string (put in a bowl)

blank paper, colored pencils, templates for tracing

Listening (approximately 15 minutes)

Read the *Story of Ping*, allow time for discussion of being lost and frightened

Activity Work Time (approximately 40 minutes)

Show children materials they may choose to explore; have assistant mother help those who wish to make Dandy Candy and wash dishes

Move around guiding children in exploration of materials

Snack (approximately 15 minutes)

Allow children to pour their own juice, pass out napkins, etc.

Let children who helped make Dandy Candy pass it out

Big Muscle Movement (approximately 25 minutes)

Have children come outside to play catch using: beach ball, sand-filled sock, frisbee

Allow for free play on climber, in sand box or with outdoor playthings

Music (approx. 15 minutes)

Allow for free movement and dance with scarves to the music of "Nadia's Theme"

Cheryl had been impressed with a Montessori school she had recently observed. She enjoyed the children's freedom to choose "work" which they were interested in. She was easily able to incorporate many of the activities into her preschool day. Cheryl had previous experience working with learning-disability children and enjoyed working with the children individually.

Defining Your Goals

As you can see from the previous samples, each parent had an idea of what she wanted to share with the children. Your group should discuss whether they want to use "parent-directed" or "child's choice" and how important a "routine" will be to you. Sometimes the main goal for the day would be surrounding the senses, sometimes around emotions, or possibly a letter sound.

As a group, it is often helpful to decide on specific readiness goals ahead of time. Parents can introduce skills in a progressive manner as the group rotates. It is important to remember that children learn at their own pace. We will need to respect individual abilities whenever introducing skills in a progressive manner.

One group decided they would discuss shapes, beginning with three simple shapes for the first two meetings. Then progressively adding two more shapes at each meeting until all of the shapes the parents wanted to expose the children to were introduced. No child was expected to learn them all.

 very child needs to feel both loved and worthwhile. But lovability must not be tied to worthwhile performance.

Dorothy Corkille Briggs

Another skill some groups choose to introduce progressively is numerical values. In one preschool group, each parent worked on three numbers. When they had worked with the numbers 1 to 10, they incorporated learning materials using the numbers such as puzzles, card games, and games involving numbers.

The introduction of letters can be done progressively, too. The chapter on reading discusses some of the methods of introducing letters.

Movement skills can also be introduced progressively. You can incorporate such skills as balance, strength, body awareness, and coordination into the preschool day as much as possible.

It is helpful to write down any specific skills that you wish to stress at each playgroup meeting. Establish which parents will introduce which

The children will let you know when they become bored with an activity.

skills and how the skills will progress, allowing for children's ability and interest. List the parent's date for hosting the group, any themes she may want to use in leading her playgroup, along with any skills she will introduce to the children. Have this list kept in the plan book for easy reference. By writing down your goals you provide a sense of order to your preschool, you have a direction to move in, and you will see the progress as you go. Some groups will choose specific skills as goals while groups with younger children should stress playful skills. Always use the children as your guide when deciding if you should add more progressive skills. Some children will be ripe for learning certain skills, others may need more time.

Checklist for Your Preschool Day (four- to five-year-olds)

(Try to include as many of these as you can as you plan ahead for several weeks of preschool sessions.)

Did we include ....

1. play or pretending time

2. big muscle activities (any of these)
   balance
   strength
   body awareness

3. creative time
   music
   art

4. language experiences
   time for using senses
   time for language development

5. listening/speaking time

6. observation time
   math
   science

7. investigation projects
   crafts
   foods

Preschool-at-Home

Sample Planning Sheet

Parent Host

Assistant

Date

Purpose/Emphasis

Activity/Project	**Approximate Time**	**Materials Needed**
1.		
2.		
3.		
4.		
5.		

Evaluation/comments

Providing the Environment

Home Is Where the Heart Is

I sent my three-year-old son to a private preschool. I stayed with him fifteen to thirty minutes every morning until he felt comfortable. I thought two days a week for two hours each day was a good introduction. Some days my son really liked school and some days I couldn't get him to go out the front door. I finally withdrew him, feeling he wasn't quite ready for this.

During the time I stayed with my son, I'd watch what would take place in the preschool. It was a very good experience—very loosely structured, lots of activities to choose from, nice facilities, very friendly, good teacher-child ratio. But I kept thinking, I do all these activities with Allan now. The only benefit is socialization (at a considerable price). Why am I paying someone else to do the same activities with Allan that we do with each other already? And believe it or not—I missed doing those things with him. I felt that I was cheating both of us out of some fun times—fun times that help build our close relationship.

Alison Cooke, mother of Allan

An important ingredient in creating a learning environment for your young child is your home. Some parents may base their opinion of a certain preschool primarily on its environment, its playground, its equipment, or its cleanliness. Many preschools and day-care centers are "borrowing" a homelike environment which will appeal to both parents and children. With a touch of imagination and thought, your home can become a stimulating learning environment for your preschool-at-home.

Every Home Is Unique

You may become overwhelmed at the prospect of converting your home into a preschool. Yet, the most vital ingredient is already present. A young child lives in your home. Due to the cooperative sharing in a playgroup, children are assured of having a variety of stimulating learning opportunities. It is not necessary to have every piece of equipment, toy, or learning material suggested. If one child's home has no swing set, it may have a sandbox. If a home has no yard, it may have a park nearby. The children are exposed to a variety of outdoor equipment.

Indoors, much the same happens. One home may have a wonderful pretend play area, equipped with play sink, stove, and refrigerator—yet it may lack an area to provide large muscle movement. This parent will compensate for what she lacks: she may choose to do large movement outside or she may choose to push some furniture aside creating more room. Another home may lack in manipulative toys such as Tinker Toys, puzzles, and blocks. The parent may choose to provide a basket (laundry baskets work well) with donations from persons having a greater supply of these materials. Parents have created stimulating learning environments under a variety of circumstances. They share the common enthusiasm of working, playing, and watching young children in action. This is where the similarities may stop.

Consider the following examples. Each one shows how the hosting parent was able to make the best of her situation.

One hosting mother lived on a farm in a tidy, yet compact, farmhouse. She had turned a pantry into a playroom for her own children

Every home will have something unique to offer in the way of learning opportunities; a backyard with a large sandbox is just one example.

and was able to utilize this room on her playgroup days. She used what she had to her advantage. Her large kitchen table was great for crafts and cooking. Outside, her swing set and tire swing provided an area for large movement which her small living room did not. She tried to choose planting and harvest times of year to host the playgroup so that the children could experience these activities more fully while on the farm.

Another parent lived in a subdivision with a deck in her backyard. It was an ideal place for warm weather playgroup meetings. Crafts and nature-centered activities were adapted to this area easily. During free play the outdoor deck provided a variety of imaginative props, from a pirate-ship deck to Cinderella's ballroom. The children enjoyed being outdoors; it was an exciting change from being inside most of the winter. This mother lacked backyard play equipment, but the children never seemed to notice.

If your home seems an unlikely place to have a small group of young children, don't be frightened; instead use your imagination in planning. One hosting mother was very concerned about her small, very urban townhome: her kitchen table had seating for only three people, her living room lacked space, and her backyard had only a sandbox. She chose to push her couch aside on her playgroup meeting day to provide more room in her living room for exercise and dance movements. She had the children come outside to play catch and several running games. For free time, the children used the front walk and several big wheels and a wagon she had collected. For snacktime, she provided an "indoor" picnic by laying a dropcloth over the living room carpet. For playtime, toys and prop boxes were provided in several mini-baskets. By strategically placing these toys in the living room, she was able to provide free play even on rainy days. This small home had what it takes after all: a creative parent and a small group of enthusiastic children.

Creating a Child's Environment

When creating an environment for young children, try unleashing childhood memories. Children are not as big as adults and therefore their world seems so much greater in terms of space. Children enjoy being at eye-level to their friends—both playmates and adults, so creating an environment geared to the child's size is important. Maria Montessori, noted educator and observer of young children, found that young children need materials fitted to their size in order to work to their maximum ability. A child-size spoon for spooning wheat germ from one dish to another brings more accurate results than using a large over-sized spoon. A small pitcher with a handle and spout for pouring is easier to handle for pouring juice from than a cumbersome carton.

hile adults meet eye to eye, children must meet adults from way down below. The overall effect of the giant world and tall people robs the child of a sense of mastery over her world.

Sandy Jones

Children enjoy nooks and crannies suited to their size. Coffee tables make great work tables for young children to gather around since they are closer to the ground. Kitchen tables can be converted to "child-size" by booster chairs or by allowing children to sit on their knees. Child-size table and chair sets are excellent work areas, too.

Cleanliness is next to ...

As with any meeting you have at your house, you will want to make a good impression. Before the group arrives, you may think you need to clean thoroughly. But that's not necessary for this group! Children will leave fingerprints, spots to mop, scraps to sweep, and crumbs to wipe. The children don't care how clean the carpet or floor may be. However, they do care about putting their "all" into a project—including the clean-up. One of the best ways to develop a child's self-esteem is to let him clean up himself. If you provide a wastepaper basket or garbage bag, children can take care of these messes. Let the children wipe up any spills and they will feel less clumsy about spilling in the first place. Let them sweep up the flour on the floor and they develop good coordination. The clean-up process may not meet your standards, but the pride and cooperative effort the children experience far exceeds the energy you will put into cleaning up after your playgroup session is finished.

A spotless house will only lead to frustration on playgroup days. Of course, an orderly house is nice. Young children do respect and respond to some sense of order. Playthings need special places to be returned to as do art materials, cooking supplies, etc. You may be able to provide boxes, baskets, or bins to sort playtime toys or you may have a room with shelves or special spaces to which the children will return playthings. Young children do possess a strong tendency for order when given the direction and time.

Your indoor area

The main area of your playgroup home environment will be indoors. You need not open up your entire home to the group; in fact, children function much better when given limits. Establish some rules as the group enters each new home.

A home tour can be your first order of the day. Begin where the children will hang their coats or put their supplies and belongings. Show the children around, having your own child lead the group into each area if he wants to. Next, tour the kitchen and play areas that the children will be using.

It is a good idea to visit the bathroom as a group, too. You may want to discuss flushing the toilet and wiping any water splashes. Have a hand towel near the sink and a stool to reach the sink. You will want to demonstrate how to wash and dry hands properly and then show them how your faucet works to avoid confusion.

Tour any "off-limits" areas of the house, if warranted. Give a short explanation of why this area is not for children during the playgroup session. Talk about proper use of furniture and materials if you feel the need. One advantage to having the children meet in several different homes is that they quickly learn to respect another's property. The hosting child learns to share his home and toys with his friends. Before your turn as host parent, you may need to discuss with your child that he will be sharing his things. If there are any really special belongings he does not wish to share with the others, you will want to keep them off limits in another room.

Artwork areas

Provide an area of your house for artwork, craft projects, or cooking. Logically the kitchen is the first choice, though some parents' dining room tables afford more space. Consider basements, garages, backyards, or porches as alternatives to unsuitable kitchen areas. Provide a receptacle for trash, a sponge, and a whisk broom for spills. Cover any table tops with newspaper or a plastic tablecloth if you are concerned about glue or markings.

Any painting or messy work can be left to dry on the floor, counter top, or table. Some parents have wooden clothes-drying racks which work well as drying racks for paintings, too. Clothespins can be used to attach artwork to the drying rack. Otherwise, a string or cord stretched across two chairs will also work well for drying paintings.

If the weather is nice enough, artwork can be done outside. Paintings can be left to dry outdoors.

Cooking areas

A cooking area can be set up in several ways. You may choose to do mixing at the table, then move to the stovetop or oven area for cooking or baking. Dishes can be washed by one child and dried by another.

When planning these kitchen-oriented activities, it works best to have all of your ingredients or materials set out ahead of time so that little time is wasted gathering supplies. Chapter 17 has some other tips for cooking with children.

Movement space

The other main area you will need to provide in your home is a movement area or a central gathering area. If you choose to use indoor space rather than outdoor space, you may need to do some rearranging of furniture. Movement for children requires a safe open area free from sharp corners, glass tables, or precious knick-knacks. Be aware that such things as brick fireplace hearths can cause injury if a child falls against them. Sometimes simply pushing back the furniture opens up the room enough for free movement. Look around your home; decide which area of your house will best suit the movement needs of your group.

Circle time

A circle time for stories, discussions, and music can also occur in a more open area of your home. Some playgroups find it advantageous to provide each child with a rug or mat to mark each child's space. Hand towels will serve the same purpose and are less difficult to purchase and store. A record player or tape player may also be nice to have in this area. Puppet boxes and props for simple skits should also be accessible to this area of the house if needed.

Coffee tables are low enough to provide a nice work area for children.

Some indoor rules may be discussed during circle time. The following can serve as guidelines you may wish to stress with your group.

Indoor Rules

1. Children are responsible for hanging up their own coats and supplies or putting them in the appropriate places. Adults will be available for help.
2. Everyone speaks in "indoor" voices.
3. Everyone is expected to walk inside the house unless the group is working on movements.
4. Children will not disrupt another's work or play.
5. Children are expected to put away materials they take out. Parents may need to pitch in and help the children pick up. This can be an opportunity for children to learn about group rules.

Supplies to Consider

Your home will provide much of your group's needs. Many groups also have each individual child bring supplies—a special box or bag can be the container. Any teaching aids or group supplies can be contained in a rotating playgroup box.

The child's own supplies

Each group will make its own decisions as to what the child will need. Some groups choose to have children take their own supplies to each session. The advantage to this method is that each child is responsible for remembering his own supplies. Other groups, especially those with younger children, keep each child's supplies in a box that rotates from home to home. Children's supplies will vary.

A suggested starting list might include:

crayons	paint shirt
pencil	sponge (for spills)
glue	watercolor paints
rounded scissors	

A playgroup box

Parents may also choose to create a playgroup box which contains supplies needed by each parent. Borrowing and sharing among the participants is common.

Borrowing and sharing materials

Some groups create a common box of materials which is rotated from home to home. You should discuss the kinds of items you have that the group may be interested in having on hand for each meeting. One group's box contained such items as:

> 2 Ella Jenkins record albums
> 1 Hap Palmer album
> 6 tempera paint containers
> 3 colors of powdered tempera paint
> computer paper
> glue, scissors, etc.
> 1 set of graduated rods (from a school supply store)
> colored construction paper
> magic markers
> rug squares (samples from carpet store) to provide a personal
>   space for children to sit

Another group felt it would be worthwhile to make a list of materials that they could purchase. They obtained a school supply catalog from a local store and held a special meeting to discuss their wants and needs. It was decided that they would share the expense of the new materials. If a parent chooses to keep a certain item after the playgroup disbands, it will be her responsibility to reimburse the group. Any items remaining could be sold or donated to a local preschool or sold at a garage sale. These parents compared the cost of monthly preschool tuition to

A laundry basket provides a handy place to store preschool materials that are moved from home to home.

the cost of purchasing materials that their group wanted and found that the cost was certainly less than preschool tuition and well worth the effort and expense involved.

Keeping a record

As parents, you will want to have a "plan book"—a traveling notebook in which plans and comments concerning your playgroup can be kept. Important phone numbers should also be listed in this notebook.

1. Emergency phone numbers for each child

   home
   father's work
   neighbor or relative
   doctor*
2. Poison control center
3. Police
4. Any allergies a child has
5. Any other phone numbers you feel are important

Another nice addition might be a first aid book such as *A Sigh of Relief— The First Aid Handbook for Childhood Emergencies*. It is always wise to be prepared. Emergencies do happen from bloody noses to sand in the eye. If a trip to the doctor seems necessary, it is helpful to have another parent on call for emergencies.

Collectibles

It is wise to begin gathering collectibles and ideas that you will want to explore with the children. In Part Three of this book, "Nurturing Young Sprouts," many suggestions are given for teaching aids and materials to use for your preschool. Most of the materials suggested are found at home; some can be found at toy stores, school supply stores, or even yard or garage sales.

Usually a parent will gather her supplies for her preschool session as she decides what she will be doing with the children. She may need to ask the other parents to help with some of the items. Some items frequently in demand are:

---

*Most doctors will give first aid treatment, but will not perform procedures without the parent's consent. A form requesting care may be signed by each parent in the event that the parent is unavailable. However, to avoid this unlikely event, it is better that parents notify the hosting parent where they can be reached during the playgroup session in case they would be needed.

empty paper towel rolls
empty egg cartons
styrofoam meat trays
empty cornmeal boxes or oatmeal boxes
empty milk cartons
empty spice jars
empty cigar boxes
empty plastic cigar tubes
yarn, string, wire
big and little boxes
paper of all sorts
pine cones, shells, nuts, seeds
fabric scraps
rubberbands, brads, paper clips
buttons, coins, nuts, screws, and bolts (for sorting)
muffin tins (for sorting or to hold paints)
paint sample strips (for matching or grading colors)
wood scraps (for building or for making collages)

These items are simply ideas for collectibles that are often needed when working with art, crafts, matching or sorting activities with young children. Specific uses for these materials can be found in later chapters or in books designed for working with young children.

Child's Choice

A child's choice environment is discussed in Chapter 9 in detail. This program is dependent on a number of materials being readily available for the children to explore and work with. The concept for this style of program comes directly from a Montessori classroom and requires more explanation.

In the 1900s Maria Montessori recognized the potential of young children and developed a method of teaching that used children's natural interest in exploring the world through their senses. The main difference between a Montessori classroom and a more traditional preschool or kindergarten is in the role of the "teacher." The "directress," as a teacher is referred to in a Montessori classroom, has the function of helping individual children or small groups of children work with the materials they are drawn to. The class does not all work on one activity together but rather each child decides which area of learning he wishes to work in. There is a great respect for the child's natural need to work with materials that suit his developmental needs. Children put forth a tremendous effort to—for example—tie their shoes, if they are in the sensitive period for this type of activity. The teacher does not always know which sensitive period a child is in until she observes that child choosing the activities that interest him.

If you are interested in some of Montessori's methods of teaching and philosophy, your local bookstore or library will have reference literature for your use.

In a Montessori classroom, children are exposed to four areas of learning activities to explore. You may want to set up your house with all four areas or you may want to choose just one or two. The role of the adult is to direct children to activities suited to their interests and demonstrate the proper use of the materials. The adult's main purpose is to simply stand back and observe the children's minds at work. This method depends heavily on the materials available for the children to explore.

ontessori felt that in these early years a child has what she referred to as "sensitive periods," during which time he is particularly receptive to certain stimuli. A particular sensitivity toward something lasts only until a necessary need is fulfilled.

Elizabeth Hainstock

Practical life area

The first area that Montessori suggests children need exposure to is that of "practical life" skills. These include exercises in the care of ourselves and our environments. As playgroup parents, you can incorporate many of these exercises. The home is the most natural place for the child to learn them. Remember: process is more important than an end product to a child.

1. Care of the person

    dressing skills: buttons, zippers, buckles, snaps, ties
    brushing hair
    washing hands (washing slowly, soaping each individual finger, the palms, and the back of the hand and drying each of these)
    brushing teeth

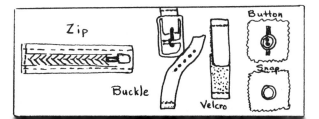

2. Care of the environment

sweeping activity (provide wood chips to be swept up from a marked-off area on the floor with a child-sized broom or a whisk broom)

dusting

washing dishes

pouring activities (have children practice pouring solids such as rice, sand, or wheat germ from a small pitcher to another pitcher; have them progress to pouring colored water from pitcher to pitcher)

spooning (same as pouring: use solids, progress to liquids, provide a spoon that is child-sized)

folding (napkins, socks, washcloths, etc.)

sifting flour

squeezing oranges

measuring

using an eye dropper to transfer small amount of liquid from cup to cup

cleaning vegetables

sponging up liquids from one bowl to another

Sensorial area

The second area of teaching a child in this method is called the "sensorial" exercises. The child's hand becomes the instrument of his mind as he uses his senses to sort out his world. Sensorial materials try to isolate individual qualities such as size, shape, or color. When stacking a tower, the cubes will only differ in size—not color or shape; when grading color, intensities of the colors differ only—not shape or size. Activities you can incorporate into your program in the sensorial area include:

- stacking activities (a "pink tower" consisting of cubes 1 centimeter to 10 centimeters square is typically used for this activity; sometimes school supply stores carry them)

- matching color squares (begin using primary colors and gradually add more colors)

- grading color squares by intensity of color (paint store color samples work well for this)

- matching shapes: begin by having children match circles, triangles, and squares; lead up to matching various sided polygons (make certain the shapes are of the same paper and color)

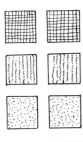

- learning names of shapes

- pairing sound containers: use opaque containers such as cigar tubes which contain sand, rice, macaroni noodles; let children shake the containers trying to listen for two that are the same (try putting more difficult substances to distinguish such as cornmeal from salt or flour)

- grading the sound tubes from loudest to softest

- matching grades of sandpaper; cut into squares and glue them onto cardboard to make them sturdier; (mark the backside with color circles so children can check to see if they are matched correctly)

- matching fabric squares: try blindfolding a child to see if he can pair the fabrics by touch

More activities can be found in Chapter 19 and in the book *Teaching Montessori in the Home*.

Language area

In the "language" area of learning, children are exposed to matching cards such as those used in commercial memory games, looking at books, tracing sandpaper letters, and learning initial letter sounds. Chapter 21, which discusses reading and the preschooler, has specific tips on introducing reading. Montessori also stresses pre-writing skills such as tracing shapes in metal templates and forming letters in a tray of cornmeal. Chapters 14 and 16 have other good pre-writing and drawing activities. Listening to stories and participating in discussions and singing songs are also stressed for language development. Chapter 18 has some favorite song ideas and Chapter 20 has tips on encouraging communication.

Math area

The last area found in a Montessori classroom exposes the children to math concepts. This is a natural transition from the sensorial area of learning. The children learn to recognize the numerals 1 to 10 by matching the number of objects to the numeral. Begin by having numbers placed in the correct numerical order and asking the child to put objects in the correct number of holes that correspond with the numeral. An activity to demonstrate this would be a number puzzle that requires the child to put one peg in one hole under the numeral one, two pegs into the two holes under number two, and so on. Another example would be to print the number on a blank index card and use a hole punch to show how many objects are to be placed over each hole to represent the number. When the children are required to sequence the numerals first, the task gets harder. Try putting numbers on containers such as baby food jars and ask the children to put the proper number of checkers into each jar. The task should be self-correcting in that the exact number of checkers that are needed to complete the task correctly are provided.

In order to learn more about this method of working with your young child, you may desire to observe a Montessori class in action. Montessori's method of teaching is ideal for some children and will appeal to some parents. It is not, however, the only way to approach it. There are many other ways of exposing children to learning.

The Waldorf Schools

In other early childhood schools such as the Waldorf schools, the emphasis is on the child's creative processes. Direct experience of the natural world helps children learn through observation and imitation. The approach is somewhat different from Montessori schools; the children are exposed to life with story-telling, creative dramatics, singing, dancing, gardening, creative expression, play, and the caring for animals and plants. The school is an extension of the home—the playgroup is a perfect setting for this kind of learning.

There are many schools of thought on educating the young child, some new, some quite old. No one way is best for every child. In spite of the method, children grow and learn. Watch your child sprout in his own rhythm; he will let you know the way he enjoys learning best. Just as adults learn at different rates and embrace life in many ways, so do our children.

The Outdoor Environment

When hosting a preschool in your home, you will also want to consider your outside environment. Regardless of the climate, season, or weather, children thrive out-of-doors. Outside time is well spent; children develop large muscle coordination on play yard equipment. Small hand and finger movements are practiced when playing in a sandbox or gardening. Cooperation and sharing take place.

Playing peacefully

Adult supervision is necessary, though interference is not. You will need to be there when the inevitable squabble over the dump truck erupts. Rules will need to be established. As a parent, you may need to referee by providing a similar toy for an unhappy child or you may need to ask the child in possession of the toy to find "his friend" another toy. Or use a wind-up toy for a timer. When the wind-up toy stops, it is the next person's turn to use the toy in demand. Before playtime, take some time with the children to discuss sharing and the consequences of fighting over a toy. One Montessori class in New Jersey established this list of rights and responsibilities which may be useful to your group.

A Child's Right—A Parent's Responsibility

1. The child has a right to use any of the equipment provided for the children as long as he uses it respectfully.

   The parent's responsibility is to see that each child is guided toward equipment and materials that he can use effectively, giving assistance if called upon.

2. The child has a right to play alone if he so desires or he may share his play.

   The parent's responsibility is to know the children and their individual needs for quiet contemplative play or group play.

3. The child has a right to stand as an observer of group activities.

   The parent's responsibility is to wait for the appropriate moment when the child will feel he can become a group member.

4. The child is free to do "nothing" as long as he is not destructive.

   The parent will explain to children that we can't hurt things and we can't hurt people.

Play equipment

Large movement play equipment takes a variety of forms. Many parents have a climber or swing set in their yard. These can range from tire swings in a tree to sets with swings, see-saws, slides, forts, and on and on. The sturdiness of these sets is worth careful scrutiny before allowing a group of children to play freely on them. Consider the following:

Is the set well anchored?

Do your swings fit snugly around children?

Have you repaired any rusty edges, exposed screws, or bolts that could scratch or otherwise hurt a child?

Check to be sure that backyard swings are in good repair and sturdy enough for a whole group of children.

Are broken parts repaired properly?

Are ladders, forts, or platforms sturdy?

If the set is wooden, are splinters sanded?

Is the surface below the set soft enough to absorb shock from falls?

There is a variety of large muscle play equipment to consider should you be concerned about your lack of yard equipment. Consider collecting: tires, hoola hoops, jump ropes, walking or balance boards, ladders, or logs. These items can be used for balance and coordination or for whatever a child's mind desires them to be.

Another outdoor item you may include in your yard is a tent or a fort. A tent can be erected from an old sheet draped over a table or chairs or a clothesline. It may be that old backpacking tent or a child's tent or that big refrigerator box you weren't sure why you were saving. Tents can be props for learning. Ideas include pretend mountain climbing excursions when discussing the earth or weather. Another might be an African hunting adventure when you are studying animals or countries.

A special area for woodworking is an excellent idea. Provide light hammers, nails, and boards to nail together. Dads can be a real help in this area. Large screws and wrenches are great fun to work with. Add a tool apron, a ruler, a pencil, and some sandpaper to create a real-life experience in carpentry.

Skating and sledding

Depending on your climate and area, you may want to consider a roller skating area such as a driveway or patio. In the winter, an ice pond provides much excitement with or without skates. A sloping hill in winter provides a sledding area just right for sliding, rolling, jumping, or romping about in the snow.

Bats, balls, and beanbags

Large balls and batting equipment provide much-needed eye-hand coordination exercises. A simple game of catch, either rolling or tossing balls, is great fun. Beanbags have numerous uses such as tossing them into a basket, walking with one on your head, or tossing one into the air and trying to catch it.

Batting utensils are an extension of a child's arm and present an exercise in spatial discrimination—where his arm ends and the bat begins. It also demands good eye-hand coordination. Big balls and oversized bats increase the likelihood of making a hit. Using a batting "tee" is somewhat difficult for the young child because the area on a child's body that the ball must rest between is often too low for the batting tee to adjust to. Preschoolers, however, are wonderful golfers. You may choose a plastic bat for putting practice, or use miniature golf clubs or cricket mallets. Under good direction, these can create an exciting game of golf. There are more ideas in Chapter 13.

Mud, water, and sand

Not to be forgotten—and the children certainly won't—are sand, water, or mud. An area outside (unless you have a special area such as a garage or basement inside) can be provided during free time for such play. Sand utensils range from trucks to dishes and sand shovels or buckets. Children can experiment with sifting, pouring, digging, and molding. Mud from the garden or wherever has an unending appeal to young children. Add water to sand or mud and the fun begins. For more ideas on sand, water, and mud play see Chapter 12 and Chapter 23.

Gardens and greens

Your garden, should you have one, can provide a place for bug catching, weed picking, and fruit or vegetable gathering. Children can see where the foods they eat come from while enjoying the fresh air outside.

Fresh air, be it cool and crisp or hot and sticky, is always cherished

A garden can provide many opportunities for learning experiences.

by our young sprouts. The outside is a land of enchantment for children not to be overlooked when planning your preschool day.

Every playgroup is unique as is every preschool child. Children enjoy learning in an intimate atmosphere—in a home shared by a close group of playmates and interested adults. Your home is the best place for learning to take place.

Evaluating Your At-Home Preschool

We Live, We Learn, We Love

I feel much closer to this child than the one I sent to preschool outside the home. Instead of asking the teacher how the day went, I can see how it went firsthand.

Carolyn Fischer, mother of Brad, Heidi, and Darcy

Creating a successful preschool for your children will require some group evaluation. As parents you will periodically need to look at your progress. Are you achieving what you set out to achieve? Have your goals for the program changed? Discuss the needs of the parents. Are they comfortable with the program? An evaluation meeting is an ideal opportunity to deal with specific problems that may have come up. The key to a successful preschool program includes good communication and adaptability.

A Plan Book

A plan book that moves from one parent to another can include each parent's plans and reports. A simple spiral notebook will serve the purpose. Parents can read the previous plans to see what has already been covered. You may want to keep a comment area in your plan book so that parents can evaluate their own day. For example, when Cheryl had a group do animal walks as the very first activity instead of a sitting/discussion type activity, she discovered a nice change. The children used up some of their energy and seemed more relaxed for the next activity. She commented that Tara still seems to need work on balance but really tries hard. She also noted that Tim tends to get silly but when complimented, he will work hard, too. The comments are intended to provide constructive self-criticism and a record of what activities and abilities the children need and enjoy.

Parent Communication

Sometimes a hosting parent may be stumped as to how to deal with another child's weak area. A friendly phone call to his parents may provide the best insight. The child's parent may have some hints as to how to solve the problem. A suggestion from the parent often provides the hosting parent with background information. We all have different expectations of children. Be sensitive to each other's parenting styles and each child's style of learning.

An Evaluation Meeting

A meeting to evaluate your program helps to ensure a successful program. Parents will need to discuss their own strengths, what they especially enjoyed, and what excited the children. They will need to comment on their concerns. Some parents are more creative than others and may want to share some ideas. Sometimes you may be concerned about keeping up the enthusiasm among the children; this can be discussed at a group evaluation meeting. One parent at an evaluation meeting commented: "The children seemed bored with exercises this time." Another added, "Wouldn't it be fun if we incorporated yoga instead of just exercises to add some creativity? The book *Be a Bird, Be a Frog, Be a Tree* gives some nice illustrations." Cooperation is what a cooperative preschool depends on.

You might find this checklist helpful at your evaluation meeting:

Discuss what goals you achieved and if any were unrealistic
Discuss new goals
Reconsider the children's interests
Reconsider the children's abilities
Discuss any need for schedule changes
Consider any new approaches to your group

An evaluation checklist

Some groups use a developmental checklist for parents to check off after hosting the group. It may include specific goals that the parents feel the children need to be pursuing in areas such as: Large muscle movement, small movement, communication, and social areas (see Appendix). The purpose of a checklist is not to evaluate the children's progress. Its purpose should be to remind parents of the goals for the group. The checklist encourages each parent to include the types of activity the group might want to stress.

If you choose to do a checklist for individual children, you will need to remember that it is not a progress report but rather a guide to keeping your preschool on target. Using a check, a plus, or minus after each skill for each child after a parent hosts the group can get tedious. If you use a progress checklist, do so in a general manner. In general, each child will have strengths and weaknesses that need to be focused on individually. You are not grading the children but simply introducing them to the skills. Some children will be more ready than others to learn new skills. Instead of grading the children, take some time to comment on ways to simplify certain skills for children having difficulty or ways to add more challenging skills for children who have mastered the basics. Comments will often stress a child's effort and attitude which checks and minuses cannot. Many groups will feel a checklist is not necessary if comments in the plan book are sufficient.

 use the words "growing on the inside" when I talk with children about such things as learning to wait, learning to keep on trying, being able to talk about their feelings, and to express those feelings in constructive ways. These signs of growth need at least as much notice and applause as the outward kind, and children need to feel proud of them.

Fred Rogers

 think it helps little children feel good about who they are when we adults put value on the many things children can do.

Fred Rogers

Common Problems and Solutions

An evaluation meeting will aid in preventing some problems simply because it provides for communication among the parents in the group. Problems may occur between parents, children, or a number of other factors. Friendly phone calls among the parents may be useful in some circumstances to understand why a child may be acting out of sorts or excitable. When problems with the children occur, it is very important to discuss your feelings and the child's feelings with his parent. If you are concerned about how a parent who is hosting the group deals with your child, you may wish to stay and observe, help out, or you may need to discuss some of your concerns with this parent. Your attitudes are reflected by the children.

Plenty of warranted praise, physical pats, winks, and eye contact can show children we care. Most often, children will be self-motivated and happy if allowed to move at their own pace. Guard against criticism and creating a competitive atmosphere.

 ncouragement is more important than any other aspect of child raising. It is so important that the lack of it can be considered the basic cause for misbehavior.

Rudolph Dreikurs

 ore and more, I have come to feel that listening is one of the most important things that we can do for another person, whether that someone is an adult or a child. Our commitment to listen to who that person is can often be our greatest gift to that person.

Fred Rogers

The essence of encouragement is to increase the child's confidence in himself and to convey to him that he is good enough as he is, not just as he might be.

Tips on dealing with problems:

1. Do not let the problem grow; if it bothers you, discuss it.
2. Address the problem—state it clearly.
3. Be sure all agree—that they see it the same way.
4. Be open—be honest.
5. List the alternatives—ask the other for ideas.

During an evaluation meeting or a discussion of your preschool, various problem areas can come up. The following concerns are somewhat common from group to group. It would be interesting for you to first read the problem, then try to think how your group would handle it before reading the various solutions others have used.

When the children seem bored, how can I create enthusiasm?

SOLUTION: Very often boredom comes from an activity being too difficult or too easy. This is why flexibility is so important in your day. Spice up the activity if it seems too simple. Sometimes when a project is too difficult, the children begin acting up when success doesn't come quickly enough. Alter the project. If necessary, let the children choose what they feel they can cope with. This may be a situation when you will need to provide individual discovery time. Provide several options for children to choose from. This way children are in more control of their abilities. The Child's Choice Plan discussed in Chapters 9 and 10 covers this option.

What can we do if the children become too excited and wild?

SOLUTION: You will need to establish some guidelines before attempting a potentially explosive activity. Let the children come up with some rules on their own. Provide an area such as a couch for quiet time if one or several children are finding it difficult to settle down. Quietly ask the disruptive child to leave the group and watch from the couch and then when he is ready to cooperate, to come back and join the group. You may need to praise the children who are cooperating. Think about the activity—are most of the children getting out of hand or just one or two? You may need to alter your plan and do something different for a few minutes.

You may need to praise some aspect of what the children are doing even though they are getting wild. Then lead the group quickly into a more relaxed activity. "I'm really pleased with your enthusiasm but we must move on now. Let's all lie on our bellies and imagine we're clouds." This is a nice time for some deep breathing exercises. A game can be created. Tell them to lie down and sleep; after a few moments, ring the alarm and have them jump up and down; then tell them to go back to sleep and repeat.

I'm not sure what to do if one child seems to be having a bad day and finds it difficult to cooperate during all of the activities.

SOLUTION: Put yourself in the child's shoes and try to feel what he is experiencing. Evaluate the activity from his eyes. If it seems he is frustrated or embarrassed, alter the task. Praise each child's effort, not just success. If it seems he is insecure and not ready to participate, socially he may need to "just watch" for a while until he wishes to join in again.

Be sensitive to the child's reason for misbehavior and make changes if necessary, but also explain to the child how the group feels about his disruption. Never make him feel like an outcast; there will always be room for praise.

Often guidelines or—at the most—a time out, are all that is needed. The group enthusiasm and sensitivity of the parents ensure success.

Be aware of a child's physical state when he is having an "off" day. When Tara was having the preschool session at her own house, she remained uninterested and unenthusiastic about participating. Her mother felt disappointed in her behavior. Later that day her mother discovered she had a fever.

We have experienced some uncooperative and show-off behavior in our own children when hosting or helping with the group. What can we do?

SOLUTION: First, bear in mind that the ultimate joy for a preschooler seems to be having friends come over to "my" house to share in "my" life. A birthday party, Christmas, family get-togethers, all create a similar mood. It is very helpful to have your young child help his friends hang up their coats or show them where to put their belongings. He can show them the bathroom and the room they will gather in or where the playthings will be. He may want to choose some toys for free play and explain a few of the family rules such as no jumping on the couch or not going upstairs to play. He is very proud, a little

A parent may need to intervene and set limits when a child's behavior is out of control.

silly, and very excited. Don't despair; he will settle down after the excitement wears off.

As the group's host, you will always remain a parent first. Your child must share his toys, his room, and his parent with his friends. He may need to let the others know that this is his home and his parent. It may be necessary for him to re-establish his limits within his own home. You may want to discuss beforehand his desire to do things his own way rather than with the group.

any three-and-a-half-year-old children go briefly through a stage when not only are they uncertain and badly coordinated in motor ways—that is, they stutter and stumble—but they are uncertain and insecure in their emotions as well. They fear that people do not love them. They demand extra attention and reassurance. They are excessively demanding of their parents' love and attention.

Frances Ilg and Louise Bates Ames

Darren was quite uncooperative when having the group at his house the first time. He cried if he did not go first, insisted on a special treat other than what the group was having, and, in general, made his first preschool day miserable for both his mother and himself. The situation was handled carefully. He was not allowed a special treat. So instead, he cried on the couch. While the group was eating, his mother had time to talk to him. She explained that he was feeling sad and left out and that made her sad. They talked about the snack and in the discussion, his mother realized he was bored with the same banana bread that they had had for the previous two days. His mother discussed his feelings of jealousy and promised him a special story when the group left. He soon joined the group feeling much happier. His attitude was much improved the next time he had preschool at his house.

On the day before you will host the preschool, you will want to explain to your child that there will be a need to do some things a little differently. Let him help you make your plans; contributing ideas will make him feel needed and important. During the preschool session, remind your child that he is special to you by some pats or winks or cuddles, but explain that during the preschool session, you will share your time together with the group, too.

How do I deal with children commenting about one another or their projects in a critical way?

SOLUTION: You will need to be sensitive to each child's feelings. When one child seems to be critical of another, he may be trying to prove that his own work is adequate. Help the critical child feel comfortable with his own work. Try individualizing the project so each child is doing his own thing.

Help the children comment on their own work in a nice way while explaining that each child is trying hard and likes to hear nice things about his work.

If a child seems to be put down by the others due to a speech difficulty, a physical problem, or whatever, you may try explaining to the children that each of them should be proud of his own uniqueness.

During free play the children seem to have difficulty sharing certain toys. What can we do?

SOLUTION: One of the reasons you decided to get together was to provide social opportunities for learning. Several routes can be taken to aid the children in sharing. You may need to take the item away until the children decide to use it together or alternately. You may need to set a time limit on the play time with the item in demand. A fun way to do this is to use a wind-up toy which the other child gets to wind. When the wind-up toy stops, it is the next person's turn. Another alternative is to try to get the children interested in something different while the toy in demand is put out of circulation. These suggestions require adult intervention.

Sometimes minor disputes would be solved best if left alone. Let the children decide who will play with the item among themselves. Often a conflict arises between two children who want your attention; they need to learn that they can solve the problem themselves. However, it is nice to be close by at those times. If two or more children disagree and begin hitting or physically hurting one another, quickly separate them—one on each side of you. Ask them to tell you about the disagreement one at a time without interruption. Very often once the stories have been told and the children have cooled off, they can come up with their own solution to the problem or accept one from you more readily. Remind them of your rules: we don't hurt people and we don't hurt things. By giving them your time, attention, and a hug for support, they learn an important concept in the art of sharing and problem-solving. Sometimes a sandwich hug is called for to seal the agreement: you all hug and depart. Try having them "sign": "I'm (point to self) sorry (use flat hand to rub each other's heart) I struggled (clasp each other's fingers and pull back and forth) with you (point to other person)."

What can we do for a child who doesn't want to try; he just says, "I can't do this" and gives up?

SOLUTION: Look at the activity from the child's point of view. You will gain some insight by watching him during various activities. If he gives up mostly at paper and drawing projects but loves movement time and stories, he may be insecure with small motor abilities. Discuss the project with him; make changes if warranted. Provide several options for the group to choose from.

If he shows this attitude in every area of your day while the other children seem content, it is time to discuss his discontentment with his mother for advice. Insecurity with the group or even with himself may warrant some extra effort. Often a ''show and tell'' time gives us a clue as to a certain child's interests and we can follow up on them with special projects. Try to be especially aware of that spark of excitement he may have during some part of your day. When it occurs, make the most of it!

What if one of the parents is using a discipline method that is not acceptable to the other parents?

SOLUTION: Establish guidelines before the group begins to meet in order to find parents who have similar attitudes to those of the others who will be in the group. A parent who has a totally different belief regarding children will probably stand out in the first get-together. It is essential that these differences be discussed so the entire group can

A squabble may develop if one child tries to show off in order to get attention.

decide if such a parent should participate. If the group is worried, she needs to be confronted with your concerns. She may choose to stay or leave.

If the other mothers feel all right about her attitude but you are still uncomfortable, tell her you want to be her helper, that your child is more comfortable when you stay. She may be more relaxed with a helper.

If this comes up in an established group, hold a special parents' meeting to discuss feelings the parents have about the group. Are they enjoying the group? Does it seem too time-consuming right now? Are the children happy? Are there special concerns anyone might have?

You must be sensitive to the other parents' needs and the stresses they are under—but not at the expense of the children.

We have one parent in our group who seems to lack interest; she doesn't seem to provide a very stimulating day for the children. What can we do?

SOLUTION: As with the children, you must be sensitive to this parent's situation and background. Step back and examine her situation. Lack of interest or enthusiasm may stem from a variety of outside influences. A mother may be dealing with other young children at home during her turn and become overwhelmed; she may need an assistant. Other problems ranging from economical or family stress to personal feelings may be influencing the parent's attitude toward the group. Discuss schedules; maybe a parent would be better off switching days for a while until she feels more interested.

You can offer ideas to the parent who seems to lack initiative and creativity. As a group, discuss ideas to spice up a daily plan. Providing a checklist or comment sheet to ensure that all areas agreed upon are being covered by each parent is useful, too.

A parent may lack enthusiasm due to apprehension. Never having worked with a group of children before may cause uncertainty. You can let each parent in the group know that his or her opinions are valuable and that idea sharing makes a cooperative preschool work. Go over a daily activity plan with the group for a parent feeling uncertain about her day with the children. Or she may choose to observe several days before her turn, or she may choose to help but not host. She may feel most comfortable only doing one activity with the group such as a read-aloud story and a discussion while assisting another mother.

Another consideration is that this parent does not have the same goals in mind for the group. She may feel that the preschool session should be a time for her to rest, shop, exercise, or otherwise be on her own with one less child. When it is her turn to host, she may lack enthusiasm because her goals for the group are different. This needs to be discussed. Ask your group what they like best about the preschool

The enthusiasm and excitement you and your child will share with friends make it well worth your while to organize an at-home preschool.

for themselves. Responses will vary but many will highlight the relationship of the parent to the child and the playful learning excitement. Then ask in what ways do you feel the experience is good for your child or if the parents have learned anything about their child. This experience should be enhancing your parent-child bond and give insight about how your child will enjoy school later on. You should feel good about yourself and your child.

Through communication, cooperation, and flexibility, your group will flourish. The special caring and sensitivity that parents have for their own children and their children's needs provide the foundation for your program. The enthusiasm and excitement you and your child will share with friends provide the motivation for your program. Finally, the continued cooperation and communication between parents and children allow for continual evaluation and a maintenance of high standards. The investment you make in terms of time and effort will reap many rewards for you and your child in terms of love and understanding.

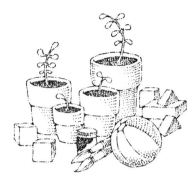

Part Three

Nurturing Young Sprouts

For most of you, Part Three of *Playful Learning* will be an exciting introduction to many areas of learning experiences for young children. It will help you understand how children learn and provide you with creative approaches that will stimulate children's natural curiosity about the world we live in. By including a wide variety of activities from which to choose, these chapters can be used in many different situations and circumstances. In selecting projects for your group of young children, be sure to focus on their interests, needs, and capabilities. Their enthusiastic responses will tell you when your planning has been right on target.

Imagination: Play and Pretending

I Am What I Am, Except When I'm Not

In a playgroup, my daughter learned early how to cooperate and play well with others. Watching my daughter interact with her peers showed me some different aspects of her personality that I had not seen before.

Becky Hejtmanek, mother of Kristen and Lindsay

Children like to play. Children like to play because it's fun. But play is so much more than fun. A child learns through play. It is his way of thinking, remembering, trying out, testing, proving, creating, absorbing—making sense of the world around him and how he fits in it.

Learning through Play

Play is an inborn and vital part of a young life. It is natural—it happens spontaneously in a growing child. If a child's basic needs are satisfied, he will express himself through play. This is good because play serves many purposes.

Through play, a child can exercise his large and small muscles. In a game of "Shadow Tag" for instance, arms, legs, and the whole body are involved. Playing "doctor" may involve finer, smaller movements as a stethoscope is used, pills are given, or bandages are put on.

or many children, dramatic play is one of their most important tools for dealing with everyday problems.

Fred Rogers

Play can allow a child to channel his energies and emotions. Play provides a controlled emotional outlet. A child can vent his frustrations, anger, fear, or excitement in his play activities. Rachel, for example, may not be able to tell her mother how upset she is over her sister's interference in her things, but behind the little cardboard stage, using some stick puppets, Rachel is able to vent her anger and express her emotions in an acceptable way. Fears, too, may be played out. By putting on some dress-ups—a long dark sheet, a pointed hat, and a broom—Laura can play out her fear of witches (or monsters, tigers, trolls, or other frightening creatures). This imaginative play is a safe context in which she can express her fears. Play also can be a means by which a child can be in control of others or gain a sense of power. This can be seen as the preschoolers play "Star Wars" when they imagine they become the powerful Darth Vader or Princess Lea. In their play, they model and become someone larger than life and, in a sense, control their imaginative world.

Play offers children the opportunity to learn cooperation and social interaction.

Communication is strengthened during play activities. Vocabulary is practiced. New words are tried out in playing out situations such as restaurant or doctor. Many opportunities for one-to-one interactions are available in play situations. A preschooler's talk with his playmates may range from silly to serious.

Opportunities to grow in social understanding and in cooperation are provided through play. Very young children up to about two and a half to three years of age will play with things in "parallel play." That is, two children will play in the same setting at the same time but independently, side-by-side. As they get a little older, children will begin to interact in their play—giving and taking toys, asking and answering questions. Trading and sharing desired toys become more evident. Taking on leadership roles in the small group is a developing social skill. Taking turns may happen when there is just one of something such as only one swing. In the at-home preschool setting during a time for free play (nonstructured, nondirected), the children will try out social exchanges which are early understandings of the adult society which they will someday be a part of. They will play at being "mommy" and "daddy" and soon expand to being other adults like "mail carrier," "teacher," "doctor," etc.

think play is an expression of our creativity; and creativity, I believe, is at the very root of our ability to learn, to cope, and to become whatever we may be.

Fred Rogers

Play gives preschoolers a chance to exercise their developing minds by encouraging their imaginations. Pretending allows them to experiment with new concepts and to represent many different things, persons, and events in their lives. Dawn may not be able to be Cinderella, but she can pretend to be. Or Steve in real life may or may not have seen a death, but in his play he will explore the idea of death and dying by pretending to shoot and kill or pretending to die and to be dead. He is trying to understand the happenings in the real world.

Another real-life situation that most children play out, at one time or another, is a "visit to the doctor." In this acceptable play setting, children can learn about their bodies. They also can release fears of doctors, injections, x-rays, and so on. This kind of play is valuable in rehearsing real-life experiences.

Through your child's play you can observe him as he moves through many developmental stages. You cannot push a child into growing up

in his play activities. He needs to take his time in each level of play development. Your role is to encourage and provide opportunities for him to experiment.

You can give him various objects or props to stimulate his growing imagination. For example, a large cardboard box can be a house, a boat, the engine of a train, a fort, a baby basket, a pet's house, a cave for trolls, a puppet theater, and many other things.

Using a large box you might say, "Can you make a cage for your lion?" or "Let's turn the box this way for a little store." Then we might, if needed, show a few things to do with the stuffed lion or play foods. Usually just a few hints can activate creative play. Our job as parents is easy and fun to do—simply encouraging play. But the most important thing is that our children have many and different opportunities to express themselves through play. The real world will be so much easier for a child to accept and to understand when he plays with it first.

Stages of Play

Play can take form in many different ways. Children will experiment with many forms of play—some simple, some complex.

Free play

In its simplest form, "free play" is spontaneous and has little or no structure. For example, a very young child in the sandbox will play with sand by digging, pushing, filling a pail and dumping it, sifting it through his fingers and even blowing, tossing, or throwing it. He is playing, but he is doing more than that. He is experimenting with all his senses and is acquiring information about his world.

Imitative play

The next stage of play in the developing child is "imitative play." This involves the child in a make-believe role in which he participates in the activity. He expresses himself in copying actions or words of people, things, or situations. In the sandbox, Lisa may use the sand toys to set a table and imitate a birthday party. She may be the hostess, putting sand "cakes" on the plates and pouring sand "drinks." By allowing herself to directly enter the action, she is imitating the real world as she sees it.

Imaginative play

In the following stage of "imaginative play," the child plays make-believe in regard to objects and/or situations. He uses his mind or imagination for various objects or words to symbolize something real. Sometimes he will substitute a toy for the real thing he is copying. Again using sand-

box play as an illustration, we can observe three-year-old David playing with a wooden block as a race car. (A child with a lesser developed imagination will need a more real object, such as a toy car.) He pushes his "car" around the sand track. He is outside the action, yet his imagination tells him where to push the car and how to make the correct racing noise. He combines his understanding of an adult world with his imagination in order to symbolize his knowledge. A child's imagination enables him to broaden the limits of his world and generally is used to make the play more realistic than it would otherwise be. The more advanced a child's imagination, the fewer and less realistic objects he will need to assist him in his play. His imagination does more of the work.

Socio-dramatic play

The next step in play happens when another person is added to the play. Now the verbal interaction between the two can imitate children and adults and can coordinate the actions of all the players. This is where a child has the possibility of practicing social skills, especially cooperation. Playing "birthday party" in the sandbox is more enriching when a real guest participates. Now she can ask, "Pass me the sugar" and say "You can pour the coffee." Verbal exchanges are included in this more advanced socio-dramatic play. When children participate successfully in more advanced play, they develop patterns of behavior necessary for full cooperation in the "school game." For example, in school a child will have to visualize people in other lands or imagine a story to write. These require make-believe because the child has not had these real experiences.

In your preschool group, the children come with varying degrees of skills in imaginative play. To increase the quality and variety of play, you have the opportunity to stimulate them in their play. You can challenge their imitations and imaginations. How can you do this?

One technique is for the parent to make a suggestion to the child in order to lead him toward developing a specific skill. The parent is not a player herself but can guide the child from outside the play situation. You might suggest "Could you sit your children (dolls) around the table and make some oatmeal for them?"

Another thing you can do is to demonstrate to the child the play skills as another player might. Children readily accept a parent as a role-player for brief periods. You only hope to guide them in their play; you do not want to influence the content of the play. "I'm hungry. Could you please make me a hamburger and some French fries?" This is an example of a parent as an active role-player.

In his imitative play, a child needs two main ingredients. He needs to acquire information about his world. Some ways to gain information are through stories, discussion, and field trips. Also, to imitate successfully, a young player will do well with props or objects that can be identified as relevant to the play. The combination of information and appropriate props is generally enough to stimulate his mind.

Let's see how this works using "doctor play" as an example. Start with a discussion of your four-year-old's own experiences going to the doctor—for check-ups or during an illness. Then you might read a book on the subject such as:

Betsy, Back in Bed by Janice May Udry

Elsa's Bears Need the Doctor by Anna Virin

Gregory's Stitches by by Judith Vigno

Betsy and the Chicken Pox by Gunilla Wolde

After talking briefly about the book, you may assign roles to each of the children. Here are some suggestions, along with prop ideas.

- Nurse-receptionist: telephone, pencil, pad of paper
- Nurse: blood pressure cuff, tongue depressor, cotton balls, and bandages
- Doctor: stethoscope, otoscope, reflex hammer, white shirt
- Boy (or girl): security blanket or teddy bear
- Mother (or father): purse, keys, money, etc.

f "play" still seems like a confusing word for summing up the significant activity of three to six, call these years of peak imagination. They become good years if children have the time, the freedom, the materials, and the companionship, the support from adults to be what they are not, to do what they cannot.

James Hymes

Role-playing a visit to the doctor can help children overcome their fears.

Next, offer a situation and setting for role-playing. A simple suggestion for encouragement might be, "Brett was climbing up into the backyard fort and injured his foot. His mother thinks he should see the doctor." Usually the play just takes off. Just sit back and observe their working minds. (If the children have difficulty at first, give a few more verbal suggestions or play one part yourself for a minute or two.) This enhances their imitations and imaginations. It works on small muscle development. Cooperation is practiced, as well as vocabulary and speech. Learning certainly happens through play.

In summary, play is important for children. Imagination is that intermediary step between the world of things directly experienced and the world of thought. Imaginative play helps children explore different possibilities, exercise muscles, endure boredom, control emotional impulses, and increase language skills.

If you notice a child in your preschool group who seems to be bored in his play, it may be that one (or more) of his basic needs are not fully satisfied. At this point, you might look for symptoms to identify the problem area(s). Ask yourself:

1. Is he tired?
2. Is he hungry or thirsty?
3. Is he experiencing an emotional upset? (death, moving, parents divorcing, etc.)
4. Has he had enough variety in his play activities?
5. Has he had a good balance between large and small muscle activities?

When these basic needs of the child are satisfied, you will notice healthy, constructive play. Imaginative play, at its best, is a creative mental ability which makes life richer for us all.

Types of Play

Children use everything from their senses and their imagination to props and toys when acting out their play. Playful learning happens in a variety of ways.

Sensory Play

Sensory play is free-flowing, non-structured play. Using some or all of the senses, it is simple experimentation with part of the world. During sensory play a child acquires and sorts out information about the world.

At the preschool level, a child will mostly use his hands to perceive size, shape, textures, hardness, wetness, temperature, and so on. Some things to give your preschool child for sensory play might include:

> sand/mud
> rice, popcorn, or seeds
> flour
> fingerpaints/pudding/shaving cream
> clay
> playdough (see homemade recipe in Chapter 16)
> water tub
> leaves

Any substance that can be made into a mess is probably good for sensory play. With a little supervision, however, preschool children can have a wonderfully playful learning experience. (See Chapter 19 for more ideas.)

Building a city with blocks is one step in the development of creative expression.

Construction play

Another type of universal play is constructing, that is, putting together pieces of a similar building material. Some building materials for preschoolers might include:

cardboard box blocks (shaped like bricks)
Tinkertoys
Bristle Blocks
Lincoln Logs
Cuisennaire Rods
Legos
Duplo Blocks
wood blocks
Popoids

Probably the oldest, simplest, and best-liked are the wooden blocks. Children of all ages—from one through old-age—can play with blocks. In the preschool years, block play offers opportunities for growing and learning. Beginning with stacking two, three, four, and then many more blocks together, your young child begins to understand the concept that many parts make a whole.

A child will use blocks to "imitate" real things. He may make simple objects out of just a few blocks such as cameras, guns, airplanes, and telephones. Another stage of block building is "pattern" building. A child might make platforms, roads, and streets which require patterns of blocks.

As a child matures, he will use his imagination in block play to form many structures. At first they will be random structures that will have a name or meaning only after they are completed. Then a little later in his development, he will begin building with an idea. That is, if he starts with the idea that he is building a spaceship, that is what it will be when he is finished. Using his imagination to construct farms, a village, a circus, or a playground, he is constructing "symbolically." His forms symbolize the real world as he sees it.

Blocks offer opportunities for a wide range of social interaction. Children of many ages or stages of development can play side by side, each in his own way, with a pile of blocks. A very young child might simply stack or make rows by himself. A slightly older child might "trade" or "divide" blocks so each has what he wants. A child who is a little more socially mature will be able to construct something with someone, both working on the same building together, showing real cooperative play.

When a child can interact with another person, blocks can be a material for additional learning. Two or more can play "copy cat," a simple copying game. Both people take an equal number of the same shape and size blocks. A beginner may start with four or five blocks; an advanced builder may use up to twenty or so. One person builds a structure or pattern, then the second person copies it with his blocks. They check it together. Then reverse the procedure so the second person builds first. This game requires concentration and the mental ability to discriminate front/back, up/down, straight/angular, and many other fine perceptions—all needed for readiness for reading.

Blocks may also be used for sorting games. A child may sort them by shape, size, or color (if they are painted). They may be used for counting, too. Regardless of how they are used, blocks are a means to creative expression through play.

Dolls

Dolls have long been a part of the play activities of children. Dolls can serve as a stimulant for a child's imagining an interaction between himself and someone else. Dolls can represent the child in imaginary play. They are also valuable in that they provide a means to practice nurturing.

Dolls which are soft, pliable, and pleasing to the touch are likely to be much more attractive to young children—both boys and girls. Witness their genuine liking of the Cabbage Patch Kids in the early 1980s. Furthermore, in order for a doll to stimulate a child's best imagination it does not have "to do" anything. The doll only has to be there; the child does all of the play.

Many types of dolls are attractive to the preschooler:

a. Dolls that represent a super hero, such as Wonder Woman or Superman;

b. Dolls that represent a monster or strange creature such as Cookie Monster, E.T., or Gremlins;

c. Dolls that represent family members, especially brothers and/or sisters, the baby doll, and grandparents;

d. Dolls that represent the adult world such as athletes, police, doctors, nurses, etc.;

e. Dolls that represent a make-believe world such as Star Wars characters, or Care Bears, etc.;

f. Stuffed animals that are simply for cuddling and talking to.

Dolls and doll play can be used in the preschool setting during free play. If they are always made available, dolls will frequently be chosen for play. You can observe many interesting conversations which often reveal the children's relationships, feelings, and desires. Their play with dolls can often give you clues as to their difficulties in social settings as well as other problem areas. More than any other reason however, doll play is valuable in that it delightfully demonstrates the growth of the child's mind and emotions.

Puppetry

Puppetry is a semi-structured form of play in which the player cannot be seen, but can be heard. He talks for the puppet and gives it life. What a sense of control! Behind a simple puppet theater with his hand covered by a puppet, the young actor can feel secure enough to allow himself to be released in drama. Preschool-aged children often bubble over with language when given the opportunity to speak for the puppets. Colleen, four and a half, very quiet and reserved in the preschool setting, was transformed—as if by magic—into a chatterbox as she played the part of "Goldilocks" behind the cardboard theater.

Puppets can be made in a wide range of sizes and materials. Many types of puppets are simple enough for young children to make themselves as we describe in Chapter 15. Puppets may be made from paper bags, old socks, sticks, paper, felt pieces, fabric scraps, an old glove or mitten, drawing on fingers or hand, balloons, paper plates, Indian corn, rubber balls, and vegetables.

A puppet theater can be very simple, too. A kitchen table with a blanket draped over the front, with children kneeling behind it, can serve as a theater. A large cardboard box with the back cut out and front flaps open also works well. A large appliance box with a door cut in

Expressing thoughts through puppets can transform a quiet child into a chatterbox.

the back and a window cut in upper front makes a very good puppet theater.

Whatever puppets your children use, they will delight in performing for each other or their parents. A few ideas to implement the use of puppets are:

1. Try out different voices, expressions, new words.

2. Use puppets to act out a story that the children are very familiar with.

3. Let children make up a story as their puppets act it out.

4. The children can play the part of parent(s), friends, movie or cartoon characters.

Mime

Mime uses the dramatic art of communicating with physical movement without any words. The mime attempts to move people by their emotions or their minds.

A mimic usually has a painted face. If parents are willing, the preschooler will enjoy having a white face. Dimestore makeup or white base makeup can be used. The painted face gives the young actor a disguise to play behind. The transformation of the painted face helps the player feel safe to release his feelings and actions. Add some white gloves or mittens and the effect is complete.

Mime suggestions for young children may include:

- Brushing teeth—add: a tooth falls out, or toothbrush falls down the drain, or toothpaste tastes like lemons.

- Going to bed—add: saying goodnight to dolls or stuffed animal, or pulling down the shade and seeing a friendly monster, or falling out of bed.

- Making a cake—add: cracking eggs and shells drop in the batter, or spoon gets stuck in the mixer, or cat jumps on counter and gets a lick of the batter.

- Learning to ride a bicycle—add: being chased by a dinosaur, or bike flies like a bird, or a tire falls off.

- Building a playhouse—add: painting it, or a king comes to live in it, or smashing a finger under the hammer.

- Show a single feeling: happy, sad, lonely, frustrated, excited, disappointed, angry.

Drama

Drama, which can be informal or formal, is self-expression in more structured play. It takes much experience in thinking, remembering, and acting before an audience. An actor expresses himself in language and movement, fearlessly, with self-confidence. Drama is usually rehearsed and has as its end product a specific performance. Drama has a goal which is to entertain or to move the emotions of the audience.

Most preschoolers are not ready for—nor do they need—formal drama. Only if there is real keen interest by the whole group should you consider extending some of their simpler play activities into a formal dramatic presentation. Usually, it is more advantageous for three- to five-year-olds to experience less structured play activities.

However, if the parent and/or children desire, they might be able to do a very simple presentation of a well-known or classical children's story such as *Goldilocks and the Three Bears, Hansel and Gretel, Rudolph, the Red-Nosed Reindeer, Frosty the Snowman, The Three Little Pigs.*

If presenting a mini-play becomes the goal of the preschool group, then follow a few simple suggestions.

1. The children should be thoroughly familiar with the story. Let them listen to a record or tape of it. Read it and read it again. Let them retell it in their own words.

2. Let the children select or assign the roles of the characters.

3. Let the children decide on costumes and props.

4. Give them time to practice their play.

5. Be sure to have them present it at least one time for an audience. A good time to do this for the parents might be at the end of the day.

6. Let them do it ... it's theirs. And praise them for their efforts. It's a great support to their developing self-esteem!

 ut children need to be given opportunity for pure play as well as for work. If adults feel that each spontaneous interest of a child is an opportunity for a lesson, the child's opportunities for pure play are foreclosed. At all levels of development, whether at home or at school, children need the opportunity to play for play's sake.

David Elkind

Pretending

Pretending is imagining something real or unreal. Children do this very naturally. In pretending, a child can use words and/or actions. But he does not have the help of dolls or costumes (like dress-up), or props (as in prop boxes). The young player, therefore, needs to use more of his imagination. He must rely on his own ability to convey feelings, actions, or a whole situation.

Here are some suggestions for "pretending" situations for the children in the preschool group.

Pretend feelings:
happy, sad, lonely, jealous, excitement, angry, impatient, hurt.

Describe a situation for children to pretend:
going to grandparents
new bike run over by a car
baby sister got a new toy for
    her birthday, but you
    didn't get any

Pretend real-life situations:
planting a garden
shopping with mother
going to school on the bus
getting a haircut
eating out
washing car

Pretend to be animals:
spider making a web
frog on a lily pad
dog on a leash
elephant in a circus
kittens chasing a ball of yarn
bear in a cave

Pretend to be scary things:
witches
monsters
trolls
ghosts
skeletons

Pretend the ending of a story:
once upon a time ...
when I was ...
what would happen if ...
how I escaped ...

Pretend to be other people:
circus performers like clown or
    tight rope walker
ballerina
pro football player
motorcyclist
secretary
pop singer
teacher

Dress-ups

Dress-up is simply clothing and accessories of all kinds for spontaneous free play. It gives a child an opportunity to try out what it feels like to be in the role of other people and other things. Dress-up is a type of dramatic play which helps a child understand his environment and identify with people. When two or more children are together, dress-up gives them an ideal setting for more social interaction.

A large laundry basket, a box, or wicker basket might include:

a. clothing: dresses, shirts, vests, scarves, jackets, pajamas, etc.

b. hats: fireman's, baker's, party hat, baseball cap, racing hat, ski cap, bridal veil, nurse's cap, etc.

c. shoes: boots, high heels, slippers, etc.

d. accessories: flashlights, purses, play money, jewelry, etc.

Prop boxes

Prop boxes can be an extension of spontaneous play which gives a child freedom to be in control and to experience power or bigness. With the assistance of the props, the child feels a sense of accomplishment and awareness of what he wants to live, act out, be.

Prop boxes work very well in the home setting. Most items can be found in your home. A small cardboard box keeps materials organized and ready. A box is flexible and easy to carry so it can be used both inside and outside. This activity provides for both sex roles. Also, the use of prop boxes encourages the child to assign his own roles as he views the occupation. Furthermore, prop boxes stimulate his curiosity for new ideas and concepts.

Prop box suggestions:

Auto Repair

Tools
Auto parts
Wires
Flashlights
Rope
Empty oil cans
Air pump
Small tires
Keys
Rags, old shirts
Gloves
Trucks and cars

Beautician/Barbershop

Mirrors
Curlers, clips
Dryer
Aprons, bibs
Combs, brushes
Towels
Shampoo bottles
Emery boards
Wigs
Make-up
Shaver
Fake scissors
Comb
Shaving cream
After-shave

Astronaut/Pilot-Airport

Instrument panel
Food containers
Camera
Pilot's hat
Airplane radio
Microphones
Radio speakers
Earphones
Stewardess outfit, hat

Shoe Store

Shoe store stool
Various styles of shoes
(include men's and
women's shoes that re-
present different cultures
and careers)
Shoe laces
Shoe horn
Shoe boxes
Shoe measurer
Shoe shining kit
Sales slips
Cash register

Plumber

Piping, all lengths widths,
joints
Spigots
Old faucets
Plumbing parts
Hard hats
Shirts
Plunger
Wrenches
(Mount a base on large
piece of plywood so pip-
ing and joints can be
screwed on and sculp-
tures created.)

Doctor-Nurse/Veterinarian

Bag
Stethoscope
Bandages
Surgical masks
Gowns, hat, gloves
Instruments
Syringes
Plastic bottles
Watch
Doctor and nurse coats,
uniforms
Baby dolls
Stuffed animals
Cots
Prescription pads

Ballerina

Leotards
Tutus
Scarves
Full skirts
Ballet slippers
Record player (all different
mood music)

Birthday Box

(for individuals to create
on their special day)
Styrofoam square or shoe
box lid or tray
Colored glue
Junk items
Plastic flowers
Broken pieces of toys
Collage items

Ophthalmologist

Many shapes and sizes of
glasses
Glass cases
Reading charts

Hat Store

Mirrors
All styles of hats (men's
and women's—different
occupations)
Cash box
Sales slips
Hat boxes

Electrician

Wire-cord
Small spools
Clock parts
Old plugs and sockets
Interesting switches
Flashlight
Timer
Electrical junk parts
Pliers

Business Office

Old typewriter
Old hand calculator
Microphone
Punch
Stamp pads
Stamped letters
Office supplies
Paper

Restaurant

Menus
Centerpiece
Tables
Tablecloths
Aprons
Fake or real food
Dishes, silverware
Pads to write on
Cash register
Small carts
Trays

Movement: Big Muscles

Hop like a Bunny

My involvement gave me greater awareness of a child's development and interaction with other children. It gave me more sensitivity to all children's needs.

Karen Leon, mother of Anthony, Lynda, Lisa, and Tina

Big muscle play is often thought of as the fun part of a child's day. Yet it is a very necessary part of a child's learning process. Most people know that big muscle movement is a basic physical need in order to build strength and control one's body. That's right. But if you look at why children need and love to move, it will help you encourage this type of activity during your preschool day. Big muscle movement is the basis for later learning tasks.

Children learn first in a self-centered manner, then they begin to incorporate more of the world outside their body. They learn big movements before they master refined movement. Young children begin rolling a large ball, for example, before they can toss a smaller ball with control. Bouncing a large ball involves coordinating what he sees (where the ball is in space) and what his hands are doing. When a young child has had enough experiences with his own body movements in relation to non-moving objects, he will be able to attempt catching and bouncing. Once a child can coordinate his hands and his eyes to catch a large ball, then he will be able to move on to smaller "eye-hand" skills. Children should have many opportunities in eye-hand coordination before they are required to grasp a pencil and copy a design.

Catching a large ball requires that a child coordinate what he sees with what his hands are doing.

A child's movement explorations are some of his beginning learnings about himself and his world. Newell Kephart, author of *The Slow Learner in the Classroom*, explains that a child begins to find out about himself and his world through movement experimentation. This movement knowledge is the foundation upon which most of his higher learning will be based. Babies spend most of their energy exploring with movement. Later in a child's toddlerhood he puts this knowledge together with his sensory explorations and builds upon his experiences. Once he has had lots of these experiences he will begin using words to describe them such as right, left, up, and down, etc.

Labeling Body Parts

In learning about their bodies and how they move, children first become aware of how to move each body part separately, along with learning its proper name. Then they begin to put this knowledge to work when they begin to coordinate their body parts in controlled movement.

Children learn to use their bodies as a reference point so it is very important that they have a clear picture of their body and its position in space. Children learn through imitation—through mirroring others. Good body image is important for the imitation of movement. "Follow the Leader" and "Simon Says" are good examples of games that stress body image through imitation. Through imitation a child learns to picture his body in his mind.

Helping children learn to label their body parts gives them a more complete understanding. Children should show an understanding of where the following body parts are:

eyes	ears	knees	waist
neck	shoulders	heels	hips
elbows	wrists	ankles	

Some ways to enhance body imagery is through following direction games. Ask children to close their eyes and then demonstrate their knowledge of their body parts by following your commands. For example:

move your hands up
shake your head
lie down on your back
lie down on your back and slide your legs from side to side
move an arm and a leg from the same side

In this way children can show that they have internalized a good body awareness. Make a game of this exercise using "Simon Says" format—you'll all have fun! Once children can move their body parts separately, have them move in relation to other objects. For example:

touch your shoulder to the wall
touch your knee to your elbow
put your head on the table
stand with your hands and feet on the floor
put your back against the wall

You can use a hoop or a rope to help children learn the names of body parts; an elastic rope works exceptionally well. Have the children sit in a circle and have each take hold of the "magic rope" with both hands. Then ask them to hold the rope to their knees, nose, eyebrows, ankles, thighs, etc. You can get as technical as you like in naming their anatomy—they love it. Have the children lay the rope on their knees and clap hands as you gather up the rope to put it away.

Another way to encourage a good awareness of body parts and spontaneous movement is through relaxation and tension of muscles. Let the children experience "stiff" legs or "floppy" arms. Have them experiment while lying down, during quiet time, by tensing body parts and then "letting go," and relaxing those parts. Once a child acquires the ability to make a mental picture of his body as it moves in space, he will be more ready to relate this to the shape of a letter before he prints it.

Laterality: Sorting Body Sides

Newell Kephart explains that the development of laterality (sidedness awareness) is extremely important since it permits us to keep things straight in the world around us. A child first learns the concept of sidedness from within, using his own body as a reference before he can use this awareness with other objects around him. **Sidedness is the only difference between a "b" and a "d."** Until a child is internally aware of his body symmetry he is not ready and should not be expected to print letters or words.

Babies and children learn about where their body is in space. They begin to move feet and arms first at random, later with purpose. They become aware of the difference between one side of the body and the other—that they can move these together or alternately. This does not mean they will be able to correctly label their right and left sides, but rather they learn that they can move either side of the body to solve a movement problem. This is called laterality.

In sorting one side of the body from the other, children go through various stages. If a child is asked to hold up his right arm, touch his right ear, or hop on his right foot, he will consistently use one side of his body, either left or right. He understands he has the ability to move one side or the other; he does not move a left arm and a right foot. He is aware of his body symmetry. Children can be helped to experience body symmetry. While children are lying down, gently squeeze an arm or leg on one side of the body and then ask the child to move them on his own. This is similar to making angels in the snow.

Learning about sides of the body should be distinguished from handedness. Handedness—having a dominant right or left hand, foot, or eye—develops at about two years old. Children will consistently use one hand to feed themselves, grasp a crayon, or point. This does not mean they should not do things with the non-dominant side but rather that they tend to use one side as a control. When children develop a leading side, it helps them in sorting out their sides. By placing objects in the middle of a child's body rather than always putting the spoon, pencil, or whatever in his right (or left) hand, you let him naturally use his leading side. Don't try to tamper with a child's handedness. If a young child is still using both hands and doesn't seem to have developed a strong leading side, it's best to continue to give him the choice. Sidedness awareness will be more difficult for this child, but with lots of experiences in movement he will become more comfortable.

Labeling left and right is more difficult. This concept may begin developing around the age of four, but may not become internalized for several more years.

The stages young children go through in learning about their body symmetry might be explained by the game "Hokey Pokey." The youngest children need help with each part used: "Put your right arm in, put your right arm out." They will need to be shown "in" and "out." At this point you are not concerned with right or left, but since you are showing them the proper movement anyway you can demonstrate with the correct arm; when they perform on their own don't correct right and left. Later, when you tell them to move their right leg in and out, make sure they are consistent with the same side as the arm.

Balance: Coordinating Sides

You can provide many variations in body symmetry experimentation. When children crawl or climb they are automatically sorting out which side to move. Experimenting with balance is really experimenting with "sidedness awareness." Children learn which side to move in order to catch their balance when walking a board or running between obstacles. Have children balance on a board about six inches off the ground, three to four inches wide and six to eight feet long. Encourage them to be independent; let them jump off if they think they will fall. Have them try:

walking forward (one foot in front of the other, eyes on feet)

walking forward with eyes looking ahead

walking sideways with eyes ahead

walking with eyes closed

walking while balancing a beanbag (try this on the floor first)

Balance is a way of controlling movement; it is a way of using one's body symmetry to keep movement in control.

Controlling Movement and Direction

Once children begin to use their sidedness skills they can begin solving more complicated directional problems with their body, coordinating both their bodies and the space around them in a controlled movement. As he practices moving through space, a child develops a sense of direction. He learns about up and down, forward and backward, in and out while using his body as a reference point.

You can aid children in their understanding of where their body is in space by playing "listening" games. For example, have them use various body parts to describe spatial words such as:

above—below	apart—together
around	open—closed
between	high—low
far—near	inside—outside
in back of—in front of	off—on

Some other examples of using these spatial words might be to tell the children to demonstrate "open" with a part of their body, then "closed." Let the children decide which part can perform the function. Have them put their arm above their head or put their back up high. See if they can move around down low; then ask them to move stretched up high.

When children begin moving through space they are learning how to slow and stop, to judge when to avoid obstacles, and which parts of the body to move. For example, have them run across the floor to a wall and touch it, gently, with one finger. Next have them run and stop just before they get to the wall. Play "run and freeze." Try this with various movements such as:

walking	jumping	tiptoeing
hopping	skipping	sliding

You can enhance a child's concept of space by providing an obstacle course for children to move, crawl, climb, or jump around. Another example would be to use a rope laid in a circle as an obstacle. Have children walk on the rope (stressing balance), walk inside it, outside it, with right foot out and left foot in, with both feet out and hands inside, and any other contortion you or they may come up with.

Another way to use the rope: With a helper hold the rope just off the floor and ask the children to go to the other side in whatever way they choose without touching the rope. They may leap on one foot, jump, hop, etc. Vary the height of the rope so they can crawl or belly-creep under it. Call it a "squiggly snake" or a "floppy fish" as you add movement to the rope. By adding movement, children gain a sense of timing.

Now think of the relationship of moving in, around, and on that rope to the task of printing on a line. Children must experience starting and stopping with large movement before attempting more refined hand movements required in paper and pencil tasks. Think about the relationship to the line that a "v" or a "y" creates. They must relate to the line on the paper as they did to the rope, deciding whether to stop above or below the line.

s children mature they gradually develop concepts concerning spatial relationships, which are eventually formalized and applied in mathematical situations.

Rosalie Jensen and Deborah Spector

When you create a good body awareness in space by using lots of directional words, children begin to internalize the meaning of the words and are then able to transfer this knowledge into math, reading, writing, and many other areas of learning.

Enhancing Flexibility and Strength

We are living in an age of great awareness of physical well-being. The media bombard us with health and exercise tips. By understanding that good body awareness can create a happier person, we can then feel good about stressing positive movement experiences with our little ones. By heightening total body awareness and by providing positive movement experiences, we enhance our children's self-confidence and provide a foundation for further learning.

Flexibility is the ability to move without restriction—"bendability." Have children warm up for a movement session by playing some bending exercises. Begin with some upper body warm-ups: look left, look right, look up, look down; now moving slowly, twist around. Warm up shoulders by imagining a see-saw with Mickey Mouse on one side and Donald Duck on the other. Raise the right shoulder up and drop it down, then the left. Don't let Mickey Mouse or Donald Duck fall off!

While sitting down, stretch out your feet in front of you. Now wiggle your "spidery" fingers to your toes. Now straddle your feet and walk your "spiders" down the left leg and then the right. Touch your toes if you can. By stimulating their imaginations, we can help the children stretch without getting bored.

Now have them get a partner and sit opposite each other, feet to feet and holding hands. Have one child rock back and pull up, then the other. This can be great fun!

Experience different body positions. Have children hug their knees, tuck in their legs, then extend them. Now arch, push up on your arms lifting your upper body with the legs pointed out in front. Now squat, jump up, and stretch—"jack-in-the-boxes!"

By using your imagination you can create lots of fun with movement experiences that enhance the children's flexibility. Don't force it;

it should not hurt—just stretch gently, reaching as far as it's comfortable. Try not to compare each one's accomplishments, but rather stress the good feeling they all get from stretching.

Building strong muscles enhances a child's ability to control his movement. What child is not impressed with strength? Take advantage of this obsession. By doing some fun strengthening exercises you will further enhance a child's body awareness. Use your imagination in creating the exercises. Some fun creations are listed later in this chapter. Include some tumbling "tricks," too.

Coordinating Eyes and Ears with Movements

When children learn about the movement of their own body in relation to another moving object such as rolling, catching, or throwing a ball, we call it eye-hand coordination. By using their eyes, they coordinate their movement and the movement of another object. Catching, tossing, or bouncing a ball involves the coordination of hand and eye movements. Providing practice in "eye-hand" coordination using big muscle movements is a prerequisite to asking a child to perform refined eye-hand coordination tasks such as writing his name or coloring in the lines.

Children can also begin coordinating what they hear to how they move. As they learn about rhythm, they move through space at a specific pace, to a beat. They can learn to march, clap, or bounce to a rhythm from a piano, a drum, or a clap. They can move various body parts such as head, knees, feet, or arms to the beat.

Later on when children begin to make one-to-one relationships, in order to count a specific number of objects they will use a form of "ear-hand" coordination. They will coordinate the sequential number they say to the objects they are counting. A good sense of ear-hand coordination will aid in this mathematical skill.

Still another form of eye-hand coordination can be encouraged in a silent game of "follow my directions." The leader faces the standing group and by using hand motions, leads the group. The trick is to keep your eyes on the leader and follow his directions. Start with pointing left and the group moves sideways in that direction, then point right and they switch. Then add a forward and backward hand signal. This helps the children gain movement control by using their eyes. As they become more skilled, they master control during even more rapid movement changes while having fun and gaining confidence.

There are other ideas to make eye-hand and ear-hand control rewarding and fun later in this chapter. Chapter 14 on small muscle movements includes some ideas for more refined eye-hand coordination.

Creating Movement

When they play outside, children can experiment even more to learn what their bodies are capable of doing. Very naturally they explore more challenging activities outdoors. Being present to watch and provide assistance when asked for, parents enhance movement exploration. Provide ideas for the children to practice such as front and back rolls, jumping tricks, hanging tricks, or creative balancing tricks. If an imaginary story is created during this play it provides added motivation. Try going on an exploration up a mountain or in a jungle, or pretend to be circus performers.

Inside, children can also be allowed to experiment with movement abilities. Children will delight in being able to move freely with music. No formal dance style is needed; free movement to the music will allow for many creative moments. Try varied music ranging from classical to pop, soft to loud, fast to slow—let the beat move them. Encourage experimentation with arm, head, leg, and finger movements. Join them in their dance and let yourself go. It's great fun!

Children may even try dancing with their eyes closed so their movements are uninhibited by those around them, though this is more necessary as they grow older and become more self-conscious. You want to end a free movement session by having the children move while lying down, slowly unwinding until they are relaxed. Have them breathe deeply, stretch, and relax. As with other activities, set limits of space before you begin this movement session.

Without music you can encourage creative movement through imagination. Animals and emotions are easy to imitate and mime. Some animals children enjoy miming include:

lions	eagles
elephants	snakes
horses	cats

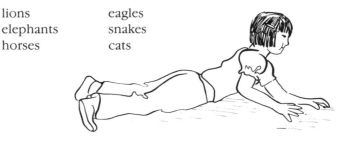

Try letting the children explore movement by suggesting they become:

elves	Smurfs
giants	tin soldiers
puppets	rag dolls

*When they play out-
doors, children can ex-
periment with
movement to learn
more about their
body's capabilities.*

Try exploring feelings while moving:

   a very sad girl

   a frightened little boy

   an angry man

   a surprised woman

   an excited child

Some other suggestions might be more elusive such as:

| the wind | a camp fire |
| rain | flowers |

Using props such as long silky scarves, hoops, or pompons adds another dimension to the movement.

Creative movement exploration will enhance self-discovery, self- expression, and self-esteem—a "free to be me" time. This kind of movement is similar to art as the process is more important than the product.
It leaves no permanent record to be evaluated later. It does encourage
concentration; the mind and the body become one for the moment.

As a young child's parents, you can provide a good movement foundation through a variety of different activities. A child's play is really
important work; he enjoys while he is learning, experimenting with his
capabilities, coordinating his body parts, and relating to the outside
world.

Ideas—Big Muscle Movement

Movement helps children gain strength and control of their bodies. Through big muscle movements a child learns about total body awareness. Experience is the best teacher; self-confidence is the result of positive experiences. Big muscle movement should stress: balance, strength, flexibility, eye-hand and ear-hand coordination, two-sided movements (left-right), social rules, total body awareness and—most important—fun. Sources for additional creative movement ideas can be found in the Appendix.

 eing involved in physical activities with the children indicates graphically that you think physical activity and play are important. For the child who feels very comfortable in active play this means, "The teacher appreciates what I'm doing." For the child who feels more comfortable with sedentary activities, this means, "The teacher thinks physical activity is fun. Maybe I'll give it a try."

Molly Sullivan

TIPS FOR LEARNING NAMES OF BODY PARTS

- **"Put Your Finger on Your Nose"**: touch finger to nose, then nose to knees, then elbows to toes, and take it from there!

- **Be a Mirror**: the children reflect your movement; start by touching body parts, then try to jog in place, stretch high then low, fat then thin, tall then short.

- **Simon Says**: (have children touch or move various body parts, then add another object)—"touch your nose to a chair"; "touch your shoulder to the floor"; "touch your foot to your elbow."

- **Twister**: Use the commercial game or draw large circles on an old sheet or tablecloth. Use 4 colors of permanent markers for circles and 3 x 5 cards for instructions.

- **Magic Rope**: have children sit in a circle; each holds rope and follows directions: "touch the rope ... to your nose ... to your ankle ... to your hip ... to your toes ... now clap your hands loudly (as they drop the rope, you can gather it up), now clap your hands softly."

The "magic rope" can help children learn the names of body parts.

CREATIVE BALANCING IDEAS

- **Follow the Yellow Brick Road:** spread out yarn or rope on the floor, zig-zag it, have the children walk with the yarn winding through the house or outside.

- **Walk the Plank:** (use a ladder, a long board, or tape to outline the plank) "pretend the pirates have captured us and we must walk the plank" (don't fall in the water!) Have them walk forward, sidewards, backwards and with their eyes closed or blindfolded, walk with hands on hips, knees, or shoulders.

- **Balance Board Ideas:**

walk forward	walk sideways
walk backward	eyes closed
balance a beanbag on head	hands on hips
arms out in front/to the side	turn a circle
tiptoes	crawl across

- **Slanted Balance Board:**

climb up	climb down
crawl up	climb up backwards

- **Vault the Fence:** having hands on the balance board and feet in back on the floor, lift hips (weight on arms) and jump feet to other side of the board.

- **Climb the Fire Escape:** prop a ladder so it is slanted and have child climb up using alternative foot-hand movements.

- **Cross the River:** prop a ladder between two chairs; have children crawl across.

- **Stepping Stones:** use bricks or blocks to create stepping stones.

GAMES TO AID IN SIDEDNESS AWARENESS

- **Hokey Pokey:** follow traditional song while standing in a circle. Put right hand in, left hand in, and so on.

- **Yoga:** be a tree (very still), a cobra (lying down, push upper torso up with arms, and stretch head way back), a frog (squat with arms on head and hold that position); do each slowly and hold. *Be a Frog, Be a Bird or a Tree* is an excellent source by Rachel Carr.

- **Mirroring:** (first have the group sitting in a line until control is gained, progress to standing) try varied simultaneous arm movements; try varied alternate arm movements; add leg movements when standing.

- **Jumping Jacks:** (begin with legs only) jump together, jump apart; add arms as they gain control.

- **Ladder Walks:** Put ladder on floor; walk in spaces, then on rungs. Ladder slanted onto chair; crawl up. Ladder between two chairs; crawl across.

- **"Hop like a Bunny":** hop with two feet together, hop one-footed, left foot twice, right foot twice, change the rhythm—have children create new patterns (hop over obstacles).

IDEAS TO COORDINATE EYES AND EARS

- **Jumping Rope:** begin with rope on ground swinging slightly; if children are ready, try twirling over head. (eye-hand)

- **Basketball (Bozo's Pockets):** use beanbags to toss in a bucket, then try a large ball. (eye-hand)

- **Marching Band:** children march with invisible instruments to a beat.

- **Circus Lions:** child tosses ball through a hoop; then he jumps through it to get the ball and hands it to the next child.

- **Ball Tricks:** (using a large ball) drop it and catch it with two hands; when expert, then drop, clap, and catch. Toss it up and catch it with two hands; when expert, toss and clap before you catch it.

- **Racket Ball:** (shape a coat hanger into a square, round the hook and cover with tape, pull a nylon over the hanger for your racket) play racket ball with balloons—hit it high, low; hit it and turn around; play with a partner.

IDEAS TO ENHANCE MOVEMENT CONTROL

- **An Adventure Trip**: make an obstacle course (use chairs, tables, ladders, or beds), make up an adventure story for each peril they will encounter: "crawl through the cave," "climb the mountain," "jump the river," "walk the cliff," or "creep under the fence."

- **Leap the River**: use two parallel ropes to create a river, have the children run and leap the river (you may want to widen it by degrees), or try using a tire (now it turns into a deep pit); have them walk around it, walk the rim, jump over it, or climb through.

- **Jack Be Nimble**: choose an object for the candlestick, say the rhyme while acting it out, try jumping backwards or sideways (be creative). Put it all together: Jack (jump forward) be nimble (jump backward) Jack be quick (jump forward) Jack jump over (jump backward) the candlestick.

- **Statues**: "When I say go, begin to move (hop, run, tiptoe, gallop, skip), but when I say stop, you all stay still while I count to ten." Try to guess what each "statue" is. Let the children take turns telling when to go or stop.

- **Listen and Do**:

   climb over a chair
   walk around the couch
   climb under a chair
   stand in front of the door

EXERCISES FOR MUSCLE STRENGTH

- **Exercise**: touch toes, sit-ups (knees bent), jumping jacks, hip twists, arm circles, etc. (Children love to be the leader during exercises.)

- **Animal Walks**: use animals to stimulate movement exploration:

   ducks: squat on heels, tuck hands under arms for wings, and
      swing one foot out at a time to walk (don't forget to quack!)

   crab: sit on the floor, bend your knees, place your hands behind
      you, and lift up. Walk like a crab—sideways!
   seal: lie face down, raise up you hands, and pull yourself forward
      Have the children make up their own animals to try.

- **Mule Kicks**: put hands down in front, lift hips, and kick up

- **Roll-ups**: squat and tuck, roll back and up again

Experimenting with animal walks can provide creative movements to strengthen muscles.

■ Tumbling Tricks:

forward rolls—tell them, "put you hands down in front, bend knees, tuck head (look at your belly button)."

backward rolls (much harder)—tell children, "squat down, roll on back, put hands on shoulders palms up and push with hands to get over, keep knees bent." To finish: "have feet come to floor as your arms reach forward, stand, and stretch."

straddle rolls—"start in a standing straddle, tuck head, and roll over, keep feet apart, put hands between legs, and roll again."

airplane rolls—"do a forward roll keeping arms out (wings)."

wheelbarrows—hold child's upper leg as he walks on his hands across the floor.

head stands—"place head on floor (use a mat if possible, place hands to right and left in front of face, push on hands"; parent helps him hold his feet up.

bridge—"lay on back, put hands palms-up near ears, feet on floor with knees bent; lift elbows and slide palms under shoulders as you push body up with hands and legs." Experts can try to walk forward or backward.

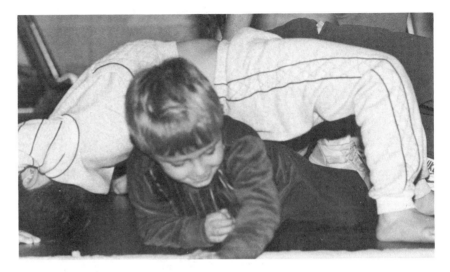

One child is a bridge that the other one crawls under in an exercise to enhance flexibility.

CREATIVE MOVEMENT IDEAS

- **Move to Music**: dance or march to music.

- **Pantomime**: "trees in the wind," swimming, running, flying.

- **Baby Bird**: have children squat down (in their eggs), then slowly pick out of the shell, roll over to dry off, and then slowly try their wings while flapping and falling until they fly.

- **Some other ideas**: Caterpiller to Butterfly — Baby to Grandparent

- **Alphabet Jump**: print several letters on blank paper or tiles; let children jump or hop on the letter you call.

ENHANCING FLEXIBILITY

- **Imitate Imaginary Characters**:

  Scarecrows: loose and floppy muscles.
  Strong Men: tense muscles and move slow and powerfully.
  Rag Dolls: relax muscles, "wet spaghetti noodles." Have children tense body parts starting with feet and move up their bodies naming the parts they will tense to their faces, then relax.

- **Twist Me, Turn Me**: while sitting, have children look left, look right (slowly), look up, look down now slowly twist your head around.

- **Spider Web Walks**: while sitting with legs stretched out in front, walk your fingers to your toes; now legs apart, walk right, then left (stress a slow stretch within comfort).

Coordination: Small Muscles

Snip It, Snap It

I'm so grateful for this experience with my children because a playgroup is an excellent way to share the joy and excitement of learning.

Becky Henderson, mother of Maren, Dustin, and Kirsten

As parents you want your children to be ready for small eye-hand coordination activities that involve paper and pencil skills. If you encourage big movement experiences that develop eye-hand coordination your children will, when ready, apply these skills to paper and pencil tasks. Writing will come easily and naturally when their small muscles are ready. They will begin experimenting with writing in their own time.

A child learning to manipulate his environment with his fingers and hands experiments in many ways. He matches information he gets from his eyes to what his hand is doing. For example, when Darren was a toddler he first learned to eat soup with a spoon by carefully watching the spoon and guiding his hand to his mouth. He was experimenting with this eye-hand activity. He was sufficiently reinforced by the soup reaching his mouth and with practice he soon become a proficient "soup sipper"—well, as neat as a mother can hope for.

When children practice and experiment with eye-hand coordination, they must be motivated by some degree of success. Before you ask a child to copy a shape or color in the lines, be sure he is developmentally ready to be motivated by success. If a child is not ready, if he has not had enough experimentation, he may experience failure instead of success. His desire to continue the task will quickly fade.

Small Muscle Experimentation

You need to challenge your preschoolers and encourage their desire to learn by providing them with small muscle experimentation. Many areas of your preschool day will provide eye-hand coordination tasks. The following are the general areas that will provide small muscle exercise; in later chapters more specific activities will be provided.

Music

During music activities a child learns about rhythm using small hand movements. He may have to clap, snap, or tap his fingers to a song. Using musical instruments he experiments with small finger movements: playing the drum, piano, flute, tambourine, or guitar. Whether these instruments are real instruments, toys, or handmade is not significant. Teaching fingerplays to enhance small finger dexterity adds a new dimension to some songs.

Arts and crafts

During art and craft projects children experiment with many craft materials through hand movements. They should be exposed to clay, scissors, paints (especially fingerpaint), paper folding, crayons, sand, mud, glue, glitter, lacing, and stringing objects.

Cooking

When cooking, children use lots of small hand movements as they use utensils in preparation tasks such as mixing, kneading, measuring, pouring, or decorating. And don't forget the serving and clean-up tasks of setting the table, washing the dishes, and sweeping the floor.

Self-care

Self-help skills almost always stress refined hand and finger movements. When dressing themselves children are exposed to buttoning, snapping, tying, lacing, buckling, and zippering. When caring for their surroundings children gain skills when folding clothes, making their bed, picking up toys, watering plants, or dusting furniture.

Some practical life skills for eye-hand coordination include:

pouring cornmeal from cup to cup
liquids (use colored water)
using tweezers to pick up cotton, buttons, etc.
slicing fruit (a good "pre" cutting exercise)
spooning cereal from cup to cup
tying practice
zippering practice
sewing cards

Play

Last—but far from least—children experience small muscle movement when playing. Toys found on the market that require manipulation are abundant. A few toys to expose the children to include:

blocks	pick-up sticks
stacking toys	tools
shape sorters	dolls for dressing
Tinker Toys	pretend dishes
Legos	Lincoln Logs
bead stringing	pounding boards
puzzles	dress-up clothes
sewing cards	puppets
pegboards	jacks
card games	color forms

These experiences can be accomplished at home. Each of the activities listed has the advantage of providing small muscle experience while stressing another stimulating area of learning. Music, arts, crafts, cooking, self-care, and play are ways to stimulate the development of small eye-hand coordination.

Only a small part of your older preschoolers' day needs to be devoted to paper and pencil tasks because eye-hand coordination is stressed in so many other ways. Remember that children usually become proficient in skills that are reinforcing and motivating.

Refining Eye-hand Skills

Parents can tell when children should begin using their crayons or pencils by exposing them to some simple paper and pencil or crayon experiences. If certain children seem disinterested, it may mean they are not ready for these skills. Try to direct their attention to eye-hand experimentation using the other activities previously mentioned.

Children develop at very different rates; sometimes they plateau and need more experimentation in one area before moving on to another. Other times they may have a learning spurt and need to be challenged by exposure to new skills. By watching their level of enthusiasm and their successful attempts in a skill area, a parent can tell how much each child should be challenged. Poor cooperation, angry outbursts, or just giving up may indicate that a task is too frustrating and should be altered or dropped until a later time.

Sometimes boys (and some girls, too) tend to prefer large muscle movements more than "sit-down" activities. This doesn't mean they will lag in small muscle skills—just that they are more content to practice large movements for the moment. They will come along when they are ready.

Grouping children into groups of two or three or treating each one individually during some eye-hand activities can be helpful. Due to the large variation of abilities in three-, four-, and five-year-olds, it is one way to cope with different skill levels. Using a "Child's Choice" set-up as discussed in Chapters 9 and 10 is another good individual method. Remember to be flexible—we are all individuals and learn at our own pace in our own way.

Some eye-hand coordination games:

Have children follow their thumbs with just their eyes to develop eye-hand coordination.

- **Follow Your Thumb**: While sitting, have children hold thumbs out in front of them (at arm's reach), move arm left then right while they use their eyes to follow their thumb. Move arm up, then down, in a circle and near, then far again. You may make this more fun by drawing a face on the thumbs or by using finger puppets to follow. You may want to have them follow your thumb or a flashlight, too. Do not let them move their heads though—just their eyes!

- **Catching and Tossing**: Begin with large ball tossing and catching. You can reduce the ball size gradually.

- **Bouncing**: Have children hold the ball with two hands and "drop it," then catch it again. Try bouncing it to each other or off a wall.

- **Ball Catching**: To provide practice in listening, call a child's name and bounce it to him, then assign each child a code name and toss the ball while calling the name or code name.

- **Ball Bouncing**: To provide practice in learning numeral names, hold up a number, have the child show understanding by bouncing the ball the appropriate number of times.

- **Balloon Punch**: Attach a balloon to a string and "punch" it; this helps develop timing and rhythm.

Coloring and Drawing

Before beginning paper and pencil exercises, children should experiment with colorful markings. When children grasp their crayons, be sure they use the two first fingers of the hand on top of the crayon and the thumb as an anchor behind the crayon. If a child is still using all of his fingers to hold the crayon, have him practice outlining shapes in cornmeal or sand using his first two fingers to draw. Fingerpaints work well for exercising finger movements.

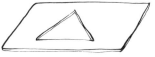

If coloring is difficult for a child, try using a template—a piece of cardboard or posterboard with a circle or square or triangle cut out of it to help him feel the turns. Have him trace it first with his two fingers, then have him use a crayon, marker or colored pencil. Let children experiment with overlapping shapes and changing colors.

Provide plenty of blank paper, crayons, markers, paints, and chalk for early drawing experimentation. Let the children design their own pictures; they may not label the drawing until it's finished, so ask them to tell you about the picture rather than asking them what it is. A wrong guess can cause hurt feelings whereas a comment about the color choice or style of drawing will elicit some dialogue.

Cutting Practice

When introducing cutting skills, let the child decide the hand in which to hold the scissors. Hopefully it will be with his dominant hand, the one he will eventually use for writing. If a child has difficulty with the finger placement, use a large-handled pair of scissors in which you can both place your fingers. You will guide his hand through the movement. Lots of tweezer and tong practice helps aid in developing this skill. (See Chapter 15 for craft projects.)

Put the child's tall finger and thumb in the holes, pointer finger "goes along for the ride." Try these practice skills for beginning cutters:

1. open and shut scissors (cut the air)

2. have narrow strip of paper for children to cut (it is the process, not the product, that is important)

3. have them cut slits in a paper

4. have them try a straight line

5. have them try to cut a corner like a square

6. now they may try to tackle a curve or a circle (this is difficult so don't expect too much)

Help the child learn cutting skills by guiding his hand in the correct movement.

Paper and Pencil Ideas

If you think the children are ready to begin some paper and pencil tasks, the following hints will be helpful. When you begin paper and pencil or crayon activities, you may want to begin with simple tracing. Let the children use jumbo crayons until they gain more skill in using a small crayon or a pencil. Try drawing a vertical line first—about 12 to 18 inches long. Begin with large shapes and gradually use smaller ones. You can use old newsprint to draw on if you use a heavy dark line for the children to trace. You may need to guide their hands from the top of the vertical line to the bottom, stressing when to start and stop. When they are ready, they can trace the line without guidance and then attempt to make one of their own. Here are some basic drawings to use as the children progress.

1. VERTICAL LINE

2. HORIZONTAL LINE

3. CROSS

4. CIRCLE

5. SLANT LINE

6. "T"

Remember to begin with large heavy dark markings, having the children first trace your mark before copying it on their own. Use word cues to help the children learn when to start and stop their crayons or pencils. A green "X" is a good visual cue to show where to start. Some children will have success when they use visual cues such as a green "X" to begin with and a red "O" for stop. (Using roads to draw between and dots to connect are also visual cues for reinforcing the direction to go.)

Other children will do better with word cues, listening for you to tell them when to start and stop. From the six drawings above you can make variations using ovals, squares, or rectangles. A rectangle or square involves a change of direction several times; at first you may need to let children *feel* where to move their hands. To do this, use a ruler to provide a stop for his crayon and guide him to a 90-degree turn.

This method is rather structured and may not appeal to some preschool groups. It is good to remember that children learn naturally when they are ready and when opportunities are provided. If your group tends to enjoy more creative methods of beginning eye-hand skills, by all means provide opportunities. Put out markers, crayons, chalk, and paint. Let the children experiment with tracing your lines or their own on blank paper. Sometimes just providing a set of circle templates is enough to excite them into working with that shape.

Other means to reinforce these beginning tracings:

trace it in the air
draw it with "worms" of clay
draw it in wet sand
draw it on the sidewalk with chalk
draw it in a tray of rice
make it with a rope or string and then have them walk it

Reinforce the shape or the form children will make using small movements with large movement variations as much as possible. For example, use a rope to make lines on the floor or draw on the sidewalk with chalk. Let the children walk their lines, before trying to draw them. A good body awareness is essential before a child can orient the direction his hand must go when tracing or copying on paper.

Printing Letters

You can see that forming letters is still in the future of our preschoolers' development, but the basics are coming. Forming letters involves a series of and/or combination of straight lines, circles, slant-lines, and crosses.

It is a lot to ask of a three-year-old to print his name before mastering some of these other drawings. Rather than dwell on printing an entire first name, try teaching children to print just the first capital letter proficiently and then slowly add a letter at a time (lower case) as they seem ready. Spend that valuable time in some area more motivating to a preschooler and you will soon be surprised that printing will come easily in its own time with very little effort.

One group of parents learned a valuable lesson about too much too soon when it comes to printing. The parents attempted to have the children print both their first and last names, along with their addresses. They soon realized this was not an appropriate expectation. The letters were sloppily written and frequently reversed. The task would have been left incomplete without parent prodding. Clearly the children's faces and moaning showed that they were not happy. The parents asked themselves the important question: "Is this the attitude we want our children to have about an academic-oriented task?" These parents soon revised their expectations of their preschoolers' printing.

It is important to also be aware of children being critical of one another during a printing task. Because a permanent record is made of each child's attempt at writing his name, the evidence cannot be destroyed. The more-ready children will often make comments about their peers' work and compare it to their own. This can be avoided by having these children print on paper—if they want to—while allowing other children to practice in a cornmeal tray or on the chalkboard.

Children will naturally take an interest in printing letters when they are ready. This should be on an individual basis for several reasons. First, natural curiosity comes at odd moments, not necessarily on a designated day or at a certain time. Second, small muscles of the hand develop at much different rates. Children can become very discouraged if they cannot keep up with their friends. You want to stress cooperation—not competition—in your preschool activities. Third, children can sense when they are given busywork to pass the time. Use spare time to foster creativity and spontaneity in language or listening, rather than in tedious exercises.

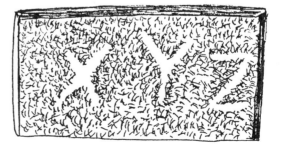

Productivity: Crafts

Color It Rainbow

I liked all three playgroups I have been involved in—I know the children do more activities than I could ever think of. I have enjoyed home preschool so much that my third child is involved now. I feel that each playgroup has been geared for the individual children, and I have seen moms and children learning a lot.

Anne Lotarski, mother of Mary Beth, J. P., and Tommy

A craft project is not the same as an art project. The distinction between these two kinds of project needs to be made clear. As a preschool parent, your purposes and goals for crafts and art will be very different, so the differences between these two need to be explained.

Differences between Arts and Crafts

Art is the means to release creativity in a developing person. An art project is the medium—or way—to express an organizing, developing, and growing mind. It is a process, not a product. The artist is completely open to create; that is, he will be directed and structured internally, not externally. What he makes, or builds, or draws, or paints, will be his own—not someone else's.

For example, an art project may follow an excursion to a dairy farm. The parent involved will give each child a large blank sheet of paper. She will then allow them to choose any drawing or coloring tools they want such as crayons, chalk, paint, etc. She might get the children started by saying, "Can you make a picture of something you experienced on

your trip to the dairy farm?'' (It is preferable to not even suggest something they *saw*—for they also hear and smell and feel.) The children use their own imaginations to create something meaningful to them. The end is not predicted; even the child might not know how it will turn out.

A craft, on the other hand, is externally directed. The mother will usually have some—or all—of it planned. Parts of the project may already be prepared for the children. (A craft doesn't allow as much room for imagination or creative expression.) The end product is usually predicted and making it has a specific, planned purpose. Sometimes there is even a model—or sample—to copy. The craftmaker usually just follows the directions given to him by someone else, perhaps his teacher who might have followed the directions out of a book.

Why do crafts?

Why then do we even suggest including craft projects for the preschool child? Is there any purpose or good that comes from a craft? Yes, definitely yes.

ince crafts are once again a part of our culture, every child deserves the chance to become adept at them. While young children can't have the ability of an artisan, each of his attempts makes him appreciate the value of handwork. A child is never too young to learn that everything in life doesn't come from a department store.

Marguerite Kelly and Elia Parsons

A craft is simply a way to reach another goal. A craft project is a means—or tool—that can be used for many purposes related to a preschooler's learning. It can be very instrumental in introducing new ideas, in using new or different materials or tools, in practicing many different small-muscle skills, and in reinforcing social behaviors.

Introducing basic concepts

A craft project can be used to help the children learn many **basic concepts**. Simple projects will introduce and illustrate basic shapes such as circle, square, triangle, rectangle, and oval. Some projects will lend themselves to discussing sizes and size relationships. Most projects will

Selecting shapes for a craft project uses small muscles and helps prepare children for math.

involve colors. Amounts, numbers, and letters may be incorporated occasionally. Spatial relationships and position of objects will be learned simply through imitating or copying. And, of course, simple drawings are the precursor of being able to print.

Practicing small-muscle skills

The craft session provides many opportunities to learn different **small-muscle skills**. By using tools like crayons, markers, glue, scissors, stapler, etc., a child practices with his small muscles. He gains control, strength, and coordination. For example, eye-hand coordination is exercised by cutting with scissors. The simple action of manipulating scissors is a beginning step. The many small muscles of his hand will be strengthened by the opening and closing motion. He will like to practice by cutting many slits on the edge of a sheet of paper. Then he will cut off long sections and pieces. Later on, he will be able to roughly—then more precisely—follow lines as he is cutting. Some children are so thrilled over this new mastery that they will cut for long periods of time. And sometimes they will cut anything, including books, magazines, clothing, their favorite blanket, their hair, or their doll's hair. (However, if you can provide them with lots of suitable paper, such as old newspapers, and monitor this activity, they'll have fun cutting without the problems.) When this new-found skill is applied to a craft project, a child enjoys his accomplishment of actually making something such as paper chains. (In Chapter 14, there are more comments on learning the use of scissors.)

Craft projects often require cutting, gluing, coloring, matching, listening, and following instructions.

Exploring different materials

Over several months' time, the preschool children will be exploring **many different materials**, some of which may be unfamiliar to them. Depending on the different things planned, they may use many different types of paper, wood scraps, plastics or metals, fabric pieces, cotton, glitter, objects from nature, pipe cleaners, yarn, string, and many other media for creating.

 hildren especially love craftwork, and should at least be given the chance to create and use handmade games, toys, and things of beauty.

Phyllis Fiarotta

Using different tools

The child will get a chance to see and use **many different tools** such as crayons, chalk, markers, ruler, paste or glue, paper hole punch, stapler, and scissors. There is much value in just being introduced to various materials and tools. A child's natural curiosity will invite him to try these out, either with or without supervision. If he has a small goal to accomplish, he can direct his energy and interest. And he will come away with something he made so he can be proud of his efforts.

Practicing social interactions

The craft session also provides an ideal opportunity to **practice social interactions**. Listening skills are acquired since the children will need to listen carefully and attentively to be able to make the craft project. If a child doesn't listen well, his craft may be left unfinished or mixed up. Also, the children will be reinforcing their ability to follow directions in the proper order. They will also have the opportunity to be responsible for their supplies and tools. At the same time, they will be learning how to clean up after themselves.

Making a craft project can be both enjoyable and valuable to the preschool child. The serious business of experimenting with new tools and materials is itself motivating. In addition, the children have the opportunity to practice small muscle skills and eye-hand coordination. They will be able to apply their understanding of basic perceptions of circle, square, triangle, and other shapes. Fun is spontaneous in this social activity. If handled carefully, a craft session can help build a child's self-esteem.

 nd if, by chance, you find yourself the recipient of one of the beautiful, handmade craft objects, consider yourself lucky indeed. Your reward is a gift from the heart—your child's special sense of accomplishment.

Phyllis Fiarotta

Choosing a Craft Project

1. The more the parent has to do ahead of time or during the project, the less the child will get out of it. A good craft will allow maximum participation by the children. Therefore, it must fit their level of ability.

2. Parents need to look at the craft project and evaluate the skill level and the attention span of the children in the group. First gather the materials and decide what you need to do ahead of time. For example, a group of three-year-olds may not be able to trace and cut out a shape. But given the pieces already cut out, they may be able to assemble and glue it. A few months later, the same children may be able to copy a very simple cardboard stencil and cut around it.

3. Ask yourself—how much can the children do? Can they copy or trace? Hold a pencil, crayon, or paintbrush? Can they snip or cut paper? Are they able to glue? Assemble parts? Try not to do too much for them. Let them try a new skill; that's how they learn. But be ready to give them lots of help and encouragement as needed.

4. Some children will finish a craft project sooner than others. It might be helpful to have a box of extra supplies handy, such as blank paper, crayons, markers, chalk, and a bag of homemade playdough. (Don't be surprised if some like this unstructured material better than the planned project!)

Materials Needed for Crafts

Just a few words about materials and tools may be helpful in planning craft projects. It is unnecessary to purchase many of the items suggested here. The average home has dozens of materials to work with if you keep your eyes open for possible uses of things and if you can find a place to keep your "junk." Be on the lookout for boxes, bags, containers, and so on. Only occasionally will you need to dip into your budget to buy an occasional item such as a bottle of glue or a box of paints.

It is not necessary to have *everything* suggested here. One advantage of cooperative teaching is that it allows you to ask another mother in your group if she has something you may need. For example, if a mother is planning to do the "Bald-Bert" planting project, she might ask the other mothers if anyone has some grass seed to help her out. After all, whatever you contribute to one mother or one preschool project, you give for the benefit of the whole group—a nice bonus in cooperative teaching.

Household Junk Materials

- Cardboard boxes (all shapes and sizes): large appliance boxes, moving boxes, detergent boxes, shoeboxes, shirt boxes.

- Bags: paper and plastic.

- Wood: scraps and pieces.

- Cardboard sheets: from new clothing packages or cleaning packages.

- Used containers: oatmeal boxes, shortening cans with lids, frozen juice cans, liquid detergent bottles, soup cans (check for rough edges).

- Sewing materials: felt, fabric scraps (all kinds), buttons, beads, yarn, lace trims.

- Paper: white drawing paper, colored construction paper, tracing paper, typewriter paper, newsprint (ends of rolls).

- Molding materials: clay, homemade playdough, baker's clay (see recipes in Chapter 23).

- Food materials: pastas, elbow macaroni, seeds, popcorn, grains, rice.

- Natural materials: stones, rocks, leaves, grass, plants, insects, sand, water.

- Special materials: pipe cleaners, stickers, tissue paper, cork, styrofoam.

- Miscellaneous things to save: old wallpaper books, styrofoam packing chips.

Tools*

- Glues and adhesives: liquid white glue, liquid brown glue, paper paste, clear cellophane tape, masking tape.

- Colorings: poster paints, watercolor paints, fingerpaints, crayons, watercolor felt-tipped markers, permanent felt-tipped markers, white and colored chalk.

- Brushes and pencils: watercolor brushes, paintbrushes.

- Other tools: ruler/yardstick, stapler, paper hole punch, scissors.

---

*You may need to purchase some of these.

Shortcuts to Successful Craft Projects

1. Keep the project **very simple,** so simple that the child is not easily frustrated. He should move easily along as it is being shown and explained. At the conclusion, he should feel pleased and proud of his work.

2. **Allow enough time;** don't rush. If the project takes an adult ten minutes to complete, it will probably take the children double or triple that time.

Allow the child to use his imagination in completing a project so each one's work is unique.

3. **Be flexible** on the spot. If it seems as though the planned project is too difficult, try to improvise on the spot to make it easier—make some quick changes, or even toss it out and do something else in its place. Using quick thinking, you may be able to come up with something different and yet fun and effective. Example: Just before Thanksgiving one preschool group was folding paper in a way to form Pilgrim hats, but the folding was too difficult for the four-year-olds. Therefore, the quick-thinking mother simply asked the children to color them instead and she did the folding for them when they finished.

4. The **process** is more important than the end product. The actual experience of doing is the priority. Remember, we're not trying to achieve perfection.

5. **Keep the project time very short** in order to hold their attention and motivation. The maximum for most three-year-olds is about 15-20 minutes. The maximum for most four-year-olds is about 20-30 minutes. (The interest and enthusiasm of the children will determine how much time to spend on a project.)

6. A finished **sample** of the project will help the children get a visual idea of what they are going to be doing. Children are highly visual learners, so a sample, along with clear verbal instruction, should make it easier for them.

7. **Allow room for their own imagination** and creativity when possible. A young child will often see things in different colors, positions, etc., than the sample. Let the children express themselves at their own levels of development whenever appropriate. Give them choices of color, sizes, placement, subject, etc., if it is possible.

8. Children will learn the skills most easily through imitation. A sample is just a tool. More important is that the mother demonstrate with them or just before they start. **But be sure to show and tell one small step at a time.** Example: (a) First, pick up your pencil; (b) Next, find a cardboard circle shape; (c) Place your circle on your piece of red paper; (d) Now hold the shape down with one hand and trace around it with your pencil.

9. The best encouragement we can give is **lots of praise**. Be sure to compliment "trying" as well as achieving. Pats on the back work well, too. Children thrive on this well-deserved attention and usually respond positively. They will keep going with a good attitude even if some part is a little too hard for them. And they will finish feeling very proud of themselves and their projects.

The parent should prepare a sample of the project in advance to be sure she can explain it step-by-step.

Suggestions for Craft Projects

Crafts can be so easily applied to whatever other things are happening in your preschool. They can be adapted to themes, holidays, field trips, or any other special events going on in the group.

The projects are listed by month from September to May according to the seasons and holidays usually celebrated in the US. They can be adapted or modified to suit whatever seasons or holidays are appropriate where you live.

September

AUTUMN TREE

What you need:

Construction paper; white 8-½"x11", brown, ½" x 6" strips
Tempera paint (or water paint); red, yellow, orange
Sponges, cut in small 1" x 2" pieces
Water (for clean-up)

What you do:

1. Use a piece of white construction paper for background.
2. Put a small puddle of paint, one color per bowl. Have 2-3 sponge pieces with each paint bowl.
3. Glue on brown strips for tree trunk.
4. Moisten sponges, squeeze out excess water. Dip ends into paint and dab on white paper to resemble autumn leaves. Can overlap colors for more realistic look.

DRIED FLOWER ARRANGEMENT

What you need:

Natural dried flowers, twigs with berries, leaves, weeds, etc.
Container such as a sea shell, vase, clay pot, hollowed out piece of clay, playdough or oasis (a light-weight, foam plastic for flower arranging)
Ribbon (optional)

What you do:

1. Go on a nature walk to collect many dried flowers, weeds, etc.
2. Choose a container. Put a lump of clay, playdough, or oasis at bottom.
3. Arrange dried pieces. Add a ribbon, if desired.

BOOKMARKS

What you need:

Wildflowers
Small flat seeds
Leaves
Clear contact paper or
    wax paper
Scissors
Iron

What you do:

1. Cut 2 strips of contact paper the size of a bookmark, about 2-½″ wide and 8″ long.
2. Peel off the backing on the contact paper.
3. Arrange flowers, leaves, and seeds on sticky side of one piece of contact paper.
4. Place the other piece of contact on top, matching edges. Press together. Trim, if needed.
5. If you are using wax paper, place it between sheets of newspaper and iron with a hot iron just until the wax is melted and paper is stuck together (a few seconds).*

*Adult should help with this step.

PINE-NEEDLE PILLOW

What you need:

Large needles (pre-
    threaded with yarn or
    heavy thread)
Bags (prestitched)
Pine needles (collect on
    nature walk)

What you do:

1. Ahead: sew a small bag out of scrap fabric (5″x5″), leave open on one side.
2. Fill with pine needles.
3. Hand stitch the open side. (Mother helps with stitching.)

October

HALLOWEEN SCENE

What you need:

Construction paper:
    black, 11″x14″
Construction paper: yel-
    low scraps
Colored gummed stars
Polyester fiberfill (pil-
    low or blanket
    stuffing)
Paste
Black markers

What you do:

1. Use black construction paper for background.
2. Paste small wad of fiberfill on paper, 3″-4″ size, to resemble a ghost. Draw on two black eyes.
3. Lick and stick on about 10-12 stars.
4. Use yellow construction paper, cut out a circle, 1″-2″ diameter, for moon. Paste on.
5. Use another scrap for a balloon with the word "Boooooo"; let children print letters if they are capable.

Allow plenty of time for children to complete a project, then help them clean up after themselves.

HALLOWEEN WITCH

What you need:

Construction paper
Cardboard shapes
Scissors
Glue or paste
Crayons

What you do:

1. Use construction paper for the following parts of the witch. Use cardboard forms to trace, then cut.
    head: yellow circle
    hat: black triangle
    dress: black, large triangle
    2 arms: black rectangles
    2 legs; orange rectangles
    broom: green rectangle and triangle.
2. Position pieces.
3. Glue in place.
4. Draw face with crayons.
    NOTE: Younger children may not be able to trace and cut so many pieces. Adult may want to precut the pieces and let children position them and glue.

BLACK CAT PUPPET OR MASK

What you need:

10″ paper plate
Construction paper, black
2 pipe cleaners, 12″
Crayons, black and red
Scissors
Popsicle stick
Masking tape

What you do:

1. Cut 2 circles out of paper plate for eyes.
2. Color back of plate completely black.
3. Color black nose, red tongue.
4. Out of black construction paper, cut 2 small (2″) triangles for ears.
5. Add 2 pipe cleaners for whiskers by poking from back through plate to the front, one on each side of the nose.
6. Tape ears on back. Tape popsicle stick on back for handle.
7. Note: Black cat can be used as a puppet or a mask. Practice "Meows"!

PAPER OWL

What you need:

Construction paper:
    brown—11″ x 14″
    yellow and orange
        scraps
Pencil
Crayon
Scissors
Paste

What you do:

1. Out of brown construction paper, trace and cut out owl.
2. Out of yellow and orange scraps, cut out eyes (two yellow circles slightly smaller than two orange circles). Paste on.
3. Cut out orange triangle for beak. Paste on.
4. Use black crayon to draw on many "V's" to resemble feathers on owl's chest and wings.

FLYING BATS

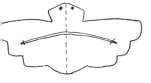

What you need:

Black construction paper
Rubber band
String
White chalk
Scissors
Cardboard form

What you do:

1. Use cardboard sheet to make a bat to trace.
2. Use black construction paper. Trace bat using white chalk. Cut out. Fold down center of bat.
3. Attach a rubber band piece from wing to wing. Staple the rubber band to the wings. (The rubber band should be 1″-2″ shorter than wing area. This will raise up the wings.)
4. Attach a string to center of rubber band to suspend from ceiling or window.

PUMPKIN MAN

What you need:

Construction paper:
  18"x24", orange,
  black, green
Crayons
Scissors
Paste

What you do:

1. Out of orange construction paper, cut large oval with stem to resemble pumpkin.

2. Out of black construction paper, cut out eyes, nose, and mouth for pumpkin. (These pieces may be pre-cut and ready to paste on.) Paste in place.

3. Out of green construction paper, cut four long 24"x1-½" rectangles for arms and legs. Accordian-fold these. Trace child's hands and feet and cut out. Paste paper hands and feet on green arms and legs. Paste onto pumpkin on back side.

November

WALL HANGINGS FROM LEAF RUBBINGS

What you need:

Leaves—various sizes and
  kinds
Fabric—12"x18" (old
  sheet or white dish
  towels work well)
Crayons
Dowel rod or long stick
  or old ruler
String
Tape—double-stick or
  cellophane
Old newspaper

What you do:

1. Collect many leaves of various sizes and shapes.

2. On a table arrange the leaves, vein-side up. Secure to table with a piece of double-stick tape. This will prevent the leaves from slipping.

3. Carefully lay fabric on top of the leaves. Tape corners of fabric piece in place.

4. Rub the long, flat side of a crayon over the fabric to get a good impression of the leaves underneath. Use different colors.

5. Place the fabric between 2 pieces of newspaper and iron with hot iron (to set the wax onto the fabric.)*

6. Attach a dowel rod or long stick and string to hang.

*Adult should assist with this step.

INDIAN HEADBAND

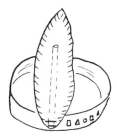

What you need:

Construction paper, various colors
Drinking straw
Pencil
Crayons
Scissors
Stapler
Cardboard stencil of large feather

What you do:

1. Take a piece of construction paper. With a pencil trace the feather shape. Cut out the feather.
2. Use scissors to cut slits on the edges of the feather.
3. Cut a strip of paper, about 1-½ " wide and 24" long, to be used as a headband.
4. Optional: Decorate the band with crayons. Children may copy a pattern or a series such as a sequence of shapes or other design. Let them finish the sequence on the length of the band.
5. Staple the band together. Measure it to fit the child's head. Staple the feather—and the drinking straw for support—to the inside of the band.

PINECONE TURKEY

What you need:

Pinecone, large and round
Construction paper, brightly colored scraps
Scissors
Pipe cleaners
Pencil

What you do:

1. Lay a round pinecone on its side.
2. Cut several strips of paper, different colors, about ½ " wide and 3" to 4" long.
3. Roll the strips of paper onto pencil to make them curl on one end.
4. Poke the strips between the petals of the pinecone, toward the more open end and with the curls going back. These are the turkey's feathers.
5. Take a pipe cleaner, about 6" long, and bend it into a neck and head.
6. Take a small piece of construction paper. Cut an oval to be used for the wattle of the turkey.
7. Push the pipe cleaner through the wattle and push it up to the top of the neck. Now poke the pipe cleaner into the tight end of the pinecone.

Suggestion: Turkeys make nice centerpieces.

TURKEY HANDS

What you need:

A child's hand
Construction paper
Pencil or marker
Crayons

What you do:

1. If a child is right-handed, place his left hand on the paper. Let him trace his own hand with a pencil or marker. Be sure his fingers are spread apart. (Reverse the directions for a lefty.)
2. With crayons, draw on legs, eyes, beak, wattle, etc. Add color to the four fingers that represent the tail feathers.

THANKSGIVING PLACEMATS

What you need:

Wallpaper—sheets from a sample book or pieces cut off ends of old rolls,
OR use construction paper
Old catalogs, newspapers, and magazines
Scissors
Glue—mucilage type
(Clear contact paper)

What you do:

1. Cut wallpaper to a size about 12"x16" for the background.
2. Look at pictures in old magazines, newspapers (advertisements), or catalogs. Find pictures of things to be thankful for.
3. Glue the pictures with mucilage onto the background.
4. Optional: Cover the entire front with clear contact paper. This will make it washable.

THANKFUL TURKEY

back

What you need:

Styrofoam drinking cup
Construction paper
Crayons
Glue—mucilage type
Scissors
Cardboard stencils of tail feather and turkey body and head

What you do:

1. Using different colors of construction paper, trace with a pencil 4 or 5 feathers. Cut them out.
2. Trace a turkey front and head. Use black crayon to draw eyes and a red crayon to draw a wattle. Cut out the turkey front and head.
3. Adult can write the words on the tail feathers. Write names of things that each child is thankful for.
4. Glue tail feathers onto one side of cup and the turkey front and head on the other side. Suggestion: Fill the cup with a nutritious snack such as popcorn or a nut mix.

TOTEM POLE

What you need:

Cardboard cylinder (from paper towel or foil)
Construction paper
Crayons
Glue
Cardboard stencils of basic shapes.

What you do:

1. Optional: Cover cardboard cylinder with a piece of construction paper. Glue the paper in place.
2. Use cardboard stencils to trace 5 shapes. Cut out the shapes.
3. Use crayons to draw different faces on the shapes.
4. Arrange the shapes on the totem pole. Glue them in place.
   Suggestion: Talk about the feelings that the various faces show.

December

SANTA'S BEARD

What you need:

Construction paper—large sheet for background
Construction paper— scraps of red, white, black, and beige
Glue—mucilage type
Crayons
Cotton balls
Cardboard stencils for face parts

What you do:

1. Lay out construction paper bacground—Dark blue works well.
2. Cut out the following shapes from construction paper scraps. Children may be able to trace these from the cardboard forms you provide for them, OR you may want to have these parts already cut out for them.
   large oval (face): light brown or beige
   2 small ovals (eyes): white
   2 smaller circles (eye centers): black
   small half circle (mouth): red
   triangle (hat): red
3. Using mucilage, glue on all the face features and the hat.
4. Glue cotton balls: 1 for hat pompon, 1 stretched for each eyebrow, 2 stretched for a mustache, many for a beard.
   Suggestion: If you do this early in the month of December, children can keep the cotton balls (up to 25) in a little bag. Each day before Christmas, they can glue on one more cotton ball until their bag is empty and Christmas day arrives.

HOLIDAY WREATH

What you need:

Paper plate, 9″
Crepe paper or construc-
    tion paper scraps,
    green
Red cinnamon candies
Scissors
Glue
Yarn, small piece

What you do:

1. Cut out the center of the paper
   plate leaving the rim, about 2″
   wide, intact.
2. Take the green crepe paper and cut
   or tear small scraps, 1″-2″ size.
3. Glue the paper pieces to the rim of
   paper plate. Glue on some red cinnamon candies to look like holly
   berries.
4. Attach a piece of yarn through a
   hole in the rim to be able to hang
   the wreath.

PINECONE ANGELS

What you need:

Medium-sized pinecones
Acorns with caps
Milkweed pods
Glue and brushes
Scissors
Styrofoam ball for head
Cardboard or paper for
    wings
Glitter

What you do:

1. Stand pinecone on flat end.
2. Glue acorn on top of pinecone to
   use as head. OR use a tiny
   styrofoam ball and glue on the top.
3. Split open the milkweed pods.
   Throw away the seeds. Glue the
   two pieces on the back of pinecone
   for wings.
4. Let dry.
5. Optional: Brush glue on the wings,
   the top of the head, and the pinecone petals. Sprinkle glitter on the
   glue over a large bowl (for easier
   clean-up.)

STAR OF DAVID

What you need:

Construction paper,
    9″x12″, blue
Construction paper,
    9″x12″, white
Scissors
Pencil
Glue—mucilage type
Cardboard triangle

What you do:

1. Use a large cardboard triangle to
   trace on each sheet of construction
   paper, blue and white.
2. Cut out the triangles.
3. Glue one triangle on top of the
   other to form a six-pointed Hebrew
   star.
4. Attach a string through the top
   point for hanging.

CHRISTMAS BELLS

What you need:

Styrofoam drinking cups
Pipe cleaner
Small round bell
Glue
Scissors
Markers
Stickers
Glitter
Gold braid or trim
Ribbon

What you do:

1. Use a pencil point to poke a hole in the bottom of a styrofoam drinking cup.
2. Push a round bell onto a pipe cleaner. Bend the end to hold the bell on securely.
3. Push the other end of the pipe cleaner through the hole in the cup. When the bell is about halfway into the cup, bend the top of the pipe cleaner to make a hanger on the top.
4. Decorate the outside of the bell, with any of the following:
   Christmas stickers
   Dribble glue around, sprinkle with glitter. Add a band of gold braid or trim.
   Use markers to draw designs.
   Add ribbon around edges.

CHRISTMAS SHAPES MOBILE

What you need:

Cookie cutters in
   Christmas shapes
Construction paper
String or yarn
Plastic lid from coffee can
Paper hole punch
Pencils or markers
Hammer and large nail

What you do:

1. Trace 5 cookie patterns onto construction paper of different colors.
2. Cut out the shapes. Or have these shapes already cut out for the children to use.
3. Punch a hole in the top of each shape.
4. Cut various lengths of string or yarn, about 12″ to about 20″ long.
5. Use a hammer and large nail to punch 5 holes around the outer edge of the plastic lid and one hole in the middle.
6. Tie the yarn pieces through the holes in the Christmas shapes. Then tie the other end through the holes in the lid.
7. Tie an extra piece of yarn in the center of the lid for a hanger.

PAPER CANDLES

What you need:

Construction paper—
  yellow, orange, and
  black
Scissors
Pencil
Glue—mucilage style

What you do:

1. Cut a circle for a base out of black construction paper.
2. Cut a rectangle for a candle out of yellow construction paper.
3. Cut an oval for a flame out of orange construction paper.
4. Use mucilage to glue the 3 parts of the candle to a background piece of paper.
   Suggestion: Fold the background paper in half before positioning and gluing. This can be a Christmas card. Let the children think up a message; print it inside for them.

GIFT CONTAINERS

What you need:

Container—any of the
  following:
  old tins
  coffee cans
  oatmeal boxes
  ice cream tubs
  boxes with covers
Things to use for
  decorating:
  old Christmas cards
  stickers or labels
  foil
  colored cellophane
  wrapping paper and
    ribbon
  markers
  paint

What you do:

1. Select a container.
2. Choose a covering. Measure and cut it to fit. Glue in place. OR spray paint the outside.
3. Decorate the entire container using any of the suggested items. Christmas card pictures, stickers, and ribbon are easy for young ones to handle.
4. Be sure to decorate the lids, too.

January

WINTER MOBILE

What you need:

Clothes hanger, thin wire
Yarn
Construction paper
Old catalogs or magazines
Glue—mucilage type
Scissors

What you do:

1. Look in old magazines or catalogs for pictures of winter things:

coats	mittens
hats & scarves	skis
sleds	ice skates
snow scene	

2. Cut out the pictures.
3. Glue them to the construction paper with mucilage.
4. Cut around the pictures on the paper.
5. Punch a hole in the top of each picture.
6. Cut various lengths of yarn. Tie one end of the yarn around the hanger, the other end through the hole in the picture.

    Suggestion: Talk about the signs of winter and the changes in their lives due to the season.

PAPER BAG PENGUIN

What you need:

White lunch bag
Sheet of black construction paper
Small pieces of orange and white construction paper
Old newspaper
Scissors
Glue
Black marker

What you do:

1. Fill paper bag about two-thirds full with loosely crumpled newspaper. Close the top and fold over once.
2. Trace and cut out the penguin's back, head, and wings from the black construction paper. (You may want to have these already cut out for younger children.) See diagram.
3. Coat the body area with glue. Attach this to the back of the paper bag, lifting the beak over the fold.
4. Cut out two white circles for eyes. Fill in pupils with black marker. Glue onto the black head.
5. Cut two feet out of the orange construction paper (each strip is about 1-½ " x 3"). Glue the feet to the bottom of the bag.

LIFE-SIZED SNOWMAN

What you need:

Very large pieces of heavy
white paper such as
bulletin board paper
or table covering
paper
Construction paper scraps
Cellophane tape
Markers
Scissors
3 large circles to trace—
such as a garbage can
lid, a saucer sled, a
hoola hoop, or a large
pizza pan

What you do:

1. Using large white paper, trace 3
   different sized circles.
2. Cut out the circles.
3. Fasten circles together with tape (on
   the back) to look like a snowman.
4. Use markers to color in face
   features.
5. Use construction paper scraps to
   draw and cut out hat, scarf, and any
   other parts of snowman.
6. Hang it on a door.
   Suggestion: This works well as a
   group project with each one taking
   a certain job to complete the project. Also, children can make up
   their own "snowman" song to sing
   to him.

FINGERPAINT CRITTERS

What you need:

Ink pad, any color
Construction paper or
plain drawing paper
Felt-tipped, fine-line
markers
Tub of warm water and
soap
Old towels

What you do:

1. Press finger tip onto ink pad. Then
   press finger straight down on the
   background paper.
2. Print any design of plants, animals,
   or any other critters. HINT: Do not
   try to paint or draw the ink—only
   print it.
3. Wash and dry hands.
4. Optional: Use fine-tipped markers to
   add little details like tails, eyes,
   whiskers, etc.

MACARONI SNOWFLAKES

What you need:

Waxed paper
White glue
Macaroni noodles, all
    shapes and sizes
White yarn or clear fish-
    ing line

What you do:

1. Give each child a large sheet of
   waxed paper to use as a working
   surface.
2. Pour a small amount of white glue
   on the waxed paper and spread
   around.
3. Have small bowls of different noodles on the table. Dip the edges of
   macaroni into the glue. Stick them
   together to form a design.
4. Let dry. Carefully peel off the waxed
   paper backing.
5. Cut out a piece of yarn or fishing
   line about 8″ long. Poke it through
   one of the edge noodles and tie
   ends. Now the snowflakes can be
   hung up in a window.

RED BIRDS

What you need:

2 styrofoam balls, one
    larger than the other
Tempera paint and
    brushes
Heavy thread or fishing
    line
Toothpicks
Cloves (for eyes)
Glue

What you do:

1. Using glue (a hot glue gun works
   well), put together the two
   styrofoam balls. (You will probably
   want to do this ahead of time.)
2. Use thinned tempera paint and a
   brush to paint the balls a bright
   color. Let dry for a little while.
3. Use a needle and thread, or fishing
   line, to poke through the head —the
   smaller ball—to make a hanger.
4. Take toothpicks to form tail feathers.
   Use broken toothpicks for wings
   and two for a beak.
5. Poke a clove into the sides of the
   head for eyes.

A parent's interest and encouragement let children know their efforts are worthwhile.

February

VALENTINE CARDS

What you need:

Construction paper, different colors
Heart-shaped paper doilies
Lace, ribbon, or rick-rack scraps
Crayons or markers
Glue
Scissors

What you do:

1. Fold a piece of construction paper in fourths or halves for a card.
2. Show children how to cut out hearts if they are able to. Or have a supply of hearts—different sizes and colors—already cut out for their use.
3. Give the children the folded paper hearts, the doily hearts, the lace, etc., to create their own Valentines. They will also need the scissors, glue, and crayons or markers to use.
4. Inside their cards, print a message for them in their words. Let them sign their names if they are able, or sign for them.
   Suggestion: Let the children mail their cards to someone special, perhaps daddy or a brother or sister. They will enjoy waiting for it to arrive.

NEWSPAPER HATS

What you need:

Sheets of old newspaper
Construction paper
    scraps, all colors
Scissors
Glue
Cardboard forms of vari-
    ous sizes of hearts

What you do:

1. Use cardboard forms—all sizes of hearts—to trace onto construction paper. Cut these out. (These may have to be pre-cut for younger children.)
2. Fold a large sheet of newspaper (2 or 3 sheets together for extra firmness) into a boat shape.
   a. Keep the newspaper folded in half. Fold outside top corners down and to the center, edges together to form a center point.
   b. Fold up the bottom edge, 2 folds, and tape in place. Do this on each side.
3. Glue lots of hearts all over the sides.
4. Wear as a hat.
   Suggestion: This project can be adapted to many holidays: St. Patrick's Day—shamrocks, May Day—flowers, Easter—eggs or flowers, Halloween—pumpkins or ghosts.

SEED MOSAIC HEARTS

What you need:

Heavy cardboard, or use
    a stiff box with shal-
    low sides
Several kinds of seeds
    such as poppy seeds,
    sesame seeds, oats,
    peppercorns, celery
    seed, dill, mustard
    seed, etc.
White glue
Cardboard form of a
    heart shape

What you do:

1. Draw or trace the shape onto the cardboard or the inside of the box.
2. Have the seeds each in a small shallow bowl or pie tin, with a spoon in each.
3. Put a drop of glue on one section of the heart and smear it around. Hold the cardboard over the bowl and spoon some of the seeds onto the glue. Shake off the extra seeds.
4. Put a drop of glue and smear it on another section. Sprinkle on more seeds. Repeat this process until the shape is completely filled in.
5. Let it dry.

LACING CARDS

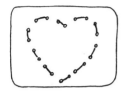

What you need:

Styrofoam meat tray
Yarn (2-3 ft. length)
Cellophane tape
Pencil

What you do:

1. Draw an outline of a simple picture. (Trace a shape if needed.) Use a heart shape for Valentine's Day, or other shapes at different times of the year.
2. Punch holes on the outline, about ½ " to ¾ " apart, using the point of a pencil.
3. Prepare the yarn by knotting one end. Wrap a short piece of cellophane tape tightly around the other end.
4. Starting from the back side, pull the yarn through. Lace the yarn in and out around the shape. Tie the loose end in the back.

HEART-SHAPED PUZZLES

What you need:

Lightweight cardboard or posterboard
Crayons
Scissors
Large envelope

What you do:

1. Cut the cardboard to about 8" x 11".
2. Trace a heart shape or draw a heart.
3. Use crayons to color the heart in any manner.
4. Use scissors to cut the heart in half. Then cut each half in two or three more pieces.
5. Practice putting the broken heart back together.
6. Keep the pieces of the heart in a large envelope with the child's name on it.

Suggestions:

1. A picture from an old magazine may be glued on the cardboard first. Then outline the heart over the picture.
2. OR, older children may print a simple message in the heart. Example: "I Love Daddy."

March

MARSHMALLOW BUNNIES

What you need:

2 large marshmallows
1 small marshmallow
Powdered sugar frosting,
　　thick and pink
Scissors
Table knife
Toothpicks
Construction paper, pink
　　scraps

What you do:

1. Mix powdered sugar frosting to be used as "glue." (Mix confectioners sugar with a dribble of water; add a drop or two of red food coloring; make it thick.)
2. Use a table knife to spread "glue" between two large marshmallows— one is the body and the other is the head. "Glue" a small marshmallow at the bottom edge for a tail.
3. Cut out 2 long ears (about 1″) from pink construction paper. Fold slightly, lengthwise, through the center. Use frosting to "glue" the ears on the head.
4. Use a toothpick dipped into the "glue" to dot on two eyes, an inverted "V" for a nose, a mouth, and whiskers.
5. Let dry.
   Suggestion: Use as a table decoration or may be eaten—except for ears.

PAINTED EGGS

What you need:

Hard-boiled eggs (do not
　　boil in aluminum pan)
Paint—acrylic is best, but
　　tempera or watercolor
　　paint will do fine
Clay or playdough
Paintbrushes
Paper towel

What you do:

1. Prepare paint ahead. Make a miniature pallet for each child by putting the paint on a plastic lid such as the lid from a margarine tub.
2. Give each child a cup of dipping water, a paint pallet, a brush or two, and some sheets of paper towel.
3. Have available some painting utensils such as toothpicks, popsicle sticks, cotton-tipped swabs, tiny sponges, and a variety of brushes.
4. Put the egg in a small wad of clay or playdough so it won't roll away.
5. Let the children create designs, faces, etc. Let the eggs dry.
   Suggestion: Have several extra eggs to use as some will crack.

BUNNY PUPPET

What you need:

9″ paper plate
Construction paper
   scraps, white and
   pink
Popsicle stick
Scissors
Glue
Pencil
Crayons
Cardboard stencil of rab-
   bit ear

What you do:

1. Use white construction paper to
   trace and cut out two bunny ears.
   Use pink paper to trace and cut out
   two smaller ear shapes (for the inside of the bunny ear).
2. Glue the pink inside ears to the
   white outside ears.
3. Cut out pink nose; glue in place on
   plate.
4. Use a black crayon to draw a mouth
   and whiskers under the nose.
5. Cut out holes for eyes.
6. Glue the ears on the top, pink side
   forward. Glue a popsicle stick on
   the back of the bottom edge to be
   used as a handle for the puppet.
   Suggestion: Put a blanket over the
   edge of the table for a stage. Let
   kids use bunny puppets to put on
   an impromptu play, such as "The
   Bunny Who Slept through Easter"

SHAMROCK STENCILS

What you need:

White drawing paper
Sponges, small pieces
Tempera paint, thinned,
   green
Cardboard "shamrock"
   stencils

What you do:

1. Position the stencil(s) on the white
   drawing paper.
2. Dip the sponge into a small dish of
   thinned tempera paint. Very lightly
   dab or dot the sponge over the open
   area of the stencil.
3. Cover the entire stencil area, even
   overlapping the cardboard. But do
   not brush with the sponges. Dab
   paint on and off so it stays light.
4. Carefully lift the stencil off. Let it dry.

Suggestions:

1. Try an acrylic paint on a dish towel
   to give away as a gift, perhaps to a
   grandmother.
2. Other ideas for stencils: use geometric designs or design the cover of a
   card.

RAINBOWS

What you need:

Construction paper
Colored chalk
Water

What you do:

1. Wet a sheet of construction paper by briefly holding it under running water. Shake off the excess water.
2. Use colored chalk to draw half circles, one above the other, using many colors.
3. Blend the colors by smearing them together with your fingertips.
4. Let dry.

Suggestions:

1. Have lots of extra paper as children will want to experiment with many other designs.
2. You may be able to introduce the color spectrum while they are concentrating. Compare the rainbow to the color spectrum of light through a prism or the light pattern of an oil puddle.
3. You may be able to suggest how the colors similar to each other are near each other in the rainbow.

KITES WITH TAILS

What you need:

Wallpaper books
Craft ribbon, 1″-2″ wide
Scissors
Glue—white liquid
3' ruler

What you do:

1. Look through the wallpaper books. Choose two pages. Tear them out, then cut out a diamond. Use a ruler to draw the four diagonal lines.
2. Cut the four triangle scraps in half through the centers. These pairs of small triangles will be the bows on the tail.
3. Cut a long 5' length of craft ribbon.
4. Glue the two large diamond shapes together. Glue the end of the tail piece in between the two halves.
5. Glue the triangle scraps of wallpaper to the tail to make bows.
6. Let them dry. Hang or fly them. Suggestion: Ask the children ... if they could sit on their kite, what would they see? Where would they go?

LION-LAMB PUPPET

What you need:

2 paper plates, 6"
Construction paper, white
Felt—black, light brown
    or beige
Buttons, black
Popsicle stick
Cotton balls
Stapler
Scissors
Glue
Tape

What you do:

Lamb:

1. Trace 4" ears using cardboard forms on white construction paper. Cut out. Fold lengthwise through the middle. Staple the ears onto one paper plate, about 3" apart.
2. Glue cotton balls all over this same plate.
3. Out of black felt, cut 2 small eyes and 1 nose. Glue onto cotton balls.

Lion:

1. Use light brown or beige felt. Cut out 8" circle; cut out 4" circle in the center. Now cut lots of triangles around the outer edge to resemble lion's shaggy mane. Cut out felt ears in the shape of a teardrop.
2. Glue the mane onto the other 6" paper plate. Glue on black felt eyes, a black button nose, and felt whiskers.
3. Add the popsicle stick taped in place to the back side of one plate. Stape the two plates together with lion and lamb on front and back.

SHOELACE NECKLACES

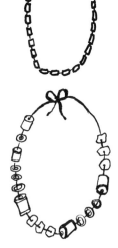

What you need:

Long shoelaces or yarn
Stringing things such as:
Cereal with holes
Noodles (macaroni,
    mostaciolli, rigatoni)
Marshmallows
Styrofoam packing chips
Empty spools
Drinking straws, cut in
    ½"–1" pieces
Clay shapes, dried

What you do:

1. Use a length of yarn 24" or longer. Make a poking tip by wrapping a short piece of cellophane tape around the end of the yarn.
2. Slip on the first item to be strung and tie the yarn around it. Knot it. Now everything else will stay on the string.
3. String the things.
4. Tie the ends together.
5. Wear as necklace or belt or headband.

April   **BABY ANIMAL COLLAGE**

What you need:

Old magazines or catalogs
Large sheet of construc-
tion paper
Scissors
Mucilage

What you do:

1. Look through old magazines and
   catalogs to find pictures of baby
   animals. (You may have to hunt
   down the right type of magazines
   ahead of time.)
2. Cut out the pictures, free form.
3. Use the sheet of construction paper
   as a background. Use mucilage to
   glue the backs of the pictures onto
   the paper. Arrange them in any way.

Suggestion:

1. Talk about the names of the mother
   animal and the baby animal. Example: cow/calf, sow/piglet, mare/colt,
   etc.
2. Talk about the sounds that each animal makes and how it is different
   than any other animal sound.

BALLOON EGGS

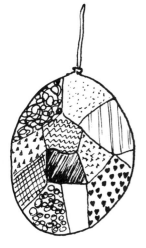

What you need:

Balloon, any size, round
or oval
Fabric scraps
Wheat paste (wallpaper
paste)
Scissors

What you do:

1. Blow up balloon; tie off opening.
2. Cut fabric into small pieces.
3. Dip the fabric pieces into the wheat
   paste and apply them to the
   balloon.
4. After the balloon has been covered,
   set it on a piece of waxed paper to
   dry thoroughly.
Optional:
5. After it has dried, cut an opening
   into the side of the balloon. Pop
   balloon and take it out.
6. Children may put straw and jelly
   beans or other small treats inside.
   Or they may decorate the inside
   with a yarn chick or bunny.

PUSSYWILLOW BOUQUET

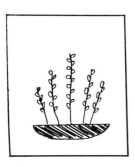

What you need:

Construction paper, 8-½ "
    x 11", dark back-
    ground color
Construction paper,
    scraps
Tempera paint, mixed,
    white
Scissors
Glue
Crayons

What you do:

1. Use construction paper scraps to
   draw and cut out a bowl shape.
2. Glue the bowl to the bottom of the
   background paper.
3. Use a crayon to draw several stems
   coming out of the bowl.
4. Use white liquid tempera paint;
   pour a small portion into a shallow
   bowl or lid. Dip fingertip into the
   paint and then press fingertip onto
   the paper to make pussywillows on
   the branches.
5. Optional: Glue real pussywillows to
   the paper.

SPRINGTIME BOUQUET

What you need:

Styrofoam egg cartons,
    various colors
Construction paper,
    scraps
Paper cupcake liners
Pipe cleaners
Clay or playdough
Pencil
Crayons
Scissors
Small jar or bowl such as
    a margarine tub

What you do:

1. Using a simple shape such as a tulip,
   made out of a cardboard form, trace
   onto bright color of construction
   paper. Cut out.
2. Cut out a single section of an egg
   carton. Cut out points around the
   edges to resemble a flower.
3. Use a cupcake liner. Take a crayon
   to draw a simple face on the inside
   center of the paper.
4. For stems: take 5", 6", or 7" lengths
   of pipe cleaners and puncture the
   center of each flower with the tip
   of each pipe cleaner. Bend over
   about ¼ " of the pipe cleaner to
   hold it in place.
5. Out of green construction paper,
   cut out long leaves.
6. Arrange the bouquet by poking the
   flower stems and the leaves into a
   small ball of playdough or clay to
   hold them in place.
7. Set the arrangement in a small jar or
   bowl such as a margarine tub.

May **TISSUE PAPER BUTTERFLIES**

What you need:

Large sheet of tissue
    (wrapping) paper
Scissors
Pipe cleaners
Clothespin, straight type
Black felt-tipped marker
White glue

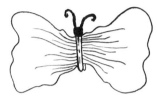

What you do:

1. Lay out a large sheet of tissue paper and fold in half.
2. Draw a large 3″ shape on the folded edge.
3. Cut on the line, through both pieces. Open up the paper.
4. Spread a thin line of white glue inside the legs of the straight clothespin.
5. Squeeze the tissue paper together at the center and slip it into the legs of the clothespin.
6. Wrap a pipe cleaner around the neck of the clothespin and shape it into two antennae.
7. Use the black marker to dot eyes on the head of the clothespin.
Suggestion: If you want to hang the finished butterfly, add a length of string around the neck.

ROCK CREATURES

What you need:

Stones, different shapes
    and sizes
Buttons
Cotton balls
White glue
Felt-tipped markers

What you do:

1. Arrange stones into creatures. Larger stone may be used for a body, smaller ones for head, eyes, arms, legs, etc.
2. Join stones together with bits of cotton soaked in liquid white glue.
3. Allow each part to dry before adding a new part.
4. Small details may be drawn on with black markers.

Suggestions:

1. Use a large rock. Design and color a "monster" using many colors of markers.
2. To prevent the rock from scratching the furniture, glue a piece of felt to the bottom side.

SPONGE-PAINTED FLOWERS

What you need:

Construction paper for background
Construction paper, green scraps
Scissors
Tempera paint, mixed, 2 or more colors
Pieces of sponge, different shapes
Glue

What you do:

1. Use green scraps to cut strips into stems and leaves of various heights.
2. Glue stems on the background paper.
3. Put the mixed paints into flat dishes or lids. Put 3 or 4 sponge pieces with each color of paint.
4. Dip the sponges into the tempera paint and then sponge onto the paper, positioning in the stems. (Do not "paint" the sponges; dab up and down.)
5. The children might want to sponge paint on outlines of butterflies, birds, etc.

LADYBUG ARM PUPPETS

What you need:

Construction paper, red and black
Scissors
Mucilage
Stapler

What you do:

1. Cut a large oval and a smaller oval out of red construction paper. This will be the body and head of the ladybug. Position the smaller oval sideways on the end of the larger oval and glue in place with mucilage.
2. Cut out black circles for the two eyes and the ladybug's spots. Glue on.
3. Cut a strip of red construction paper, approximately 8" long x 1" wide. This will be the arm band.
4. Staple the arm band onto the body.

DOILY FLOWERS

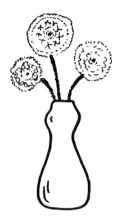

What you need:

Several paper doilies
Fine wire
A small vase such as an empty small dish soap bottle with the labels removed
White glue
Scissors

What you do:

1. Cut small flowers from paper doilies.
2. Cut wire to various lengths to stand above the opening of the vase.
3. Glue the doilies onto the tips of the wires. A small bend of the wire will help to hold it in place.
4. Arrange the flowers in the vase.

Ask the children what they would see or where they would go if they were inside a big bubble carried away by the wind.

HOMEMADE SOAP BUBBLES

What you need:

1 C. liquid dish detergent
2-½ C. water
2 T. sugar (or glycerine)
Thin wire (for hoops)

What you do:

1. Make a bubble hoop. Use thin wire to make a loop 1″ in diameter with a wire handle. Use a pie pan for the bubble tray.
2. Mix together the liquid detergent, water, and sugar.
3. Play with the bubble mixture.

ROCK PAPERWEIGHTS

What you need:

Large rock (but small enough for a child to handle)
Markers

What you do:

1. Wash the rock. Dry with old rag.
2. Use markers to make designs or faces, or animals, etc.
3. Glue a small piece of felt to the bottom (to prevent scratching of furniture).

DOUGH FLOWERS

What you need:

A batch of dough (See
   recipe below)
A baking sheet
Acrylic paints (optional)
Piece of wood, painted,
   stained, or covered
   with felt
Glue
Gummed picture hanger

What you do:

1. Use a hunk of dough to shape various parts of a flower: stem, leaves, petals, etc.
2. Assemble the flowers on a baking sheet.
3. Bake at 350° for 1 hour.
4. Flowers may be left natural or painted with acrylic paints. Let dry.
5. The flowers may be glued in place on the prepared piece of wood.
6. Attach a gummed picture hanger to the back for hanging.
   Suggestion: This might make a nice Mother's Day gift from the children.

DOUGH RECIPE

What you need:

4 c. flour
1-½ c. water
1 c. salt
Food coloring (optional)

What you do:

1. Mix together with your hands. If dough is too sticky, add more flour. Knead 4-6 minutes.
2. Dough can be used immediately or stored in plastic wrap.
3. To use: Shape desired figures, place on aluminum-covered baking sheet. Bake 350° for 1 hour until golden. (Thick items 250° for 3 hours.)

Anytime

PINECONE CREATURES

What you need:

Pinecones, milkweed
   pods, acorns, or other
   shells or pods
Clay
Cotton balls
Pipe cleaners
Construction paper,
   scraps
White liquid glue

What you do:

1. Start with a base of clay or a chunk of styrofoam to keep your sculpture from falling.
2. Work from the bottom up, using pinecones, seeds, and pods.
3. Fasten with glue-soaked bits of cotton.
4. Use construction paper scraps to cut out and make additional features such as eyes, ears, whiskers, etc.
5. Use pipe cleaners to form legs, tails, ears, etc. Twist them, then push or glue them in place.

PEEK-A-BOO PUPPET

What you need:

Plastic drinking straw
Small plastic or styrofoam
 cup
Styrofoam ball, about 1″
 diameter
Yarn, 5-6′ length
Construction paper,
 scraps of black,
 brown, pink
Straight pins
Glue
Paper punch
Scissors

What you do:

1. Head of puppet: Use a paper punch to make 2 circles for eyes and 1 nose out of construction paper scraps. Position the 3 small circles in place with 3 straight pins into the styrofoam ball.
2. Hair: Cut 10-12 lengths of yarn for puppet's hair; cut 6″ lengths for a girl's pigtails; cut shorter pieces for a boy. Glue hair on top of styrofoam ball.
3. Poke drinking straw up through the bottom of the plastic cup.
4. Poke the straw into bottom of puppet's head. (Use a dot of glue, if needed, on the end of the straw to hold it in the ball.)
5. Doll can play "peek-a-boo" by moving in and out of the cup (pull up and down on the straw.)
 Option: Use a tiny yarn and pompon chick as a puppet.

WEATHER CHART

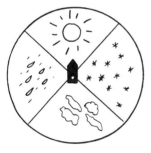

What you need:

Paper plate
Construction paper
Crayons
Glue
Pencil
Paper fastener (brass brad)

What you do:

1. Take a paper plate. Draw criss-cross lines through the center to divide it into 4 sections.
2. Use construction paper to cut out a 2″ paper arrow.
3. Use a pencil point to puncture a hole in the flat end of the arrow and another hole in the center of the paper plate.
4. Use crayons to draw a weather symbol in each quarter section: sun, raindrops, snowflakes, clouds. (Use weather symbols appropriate to your climate.)
 Suggestion: Child can turn the arrow each day to indicate the weather. This project may be used with a science activity about weather.

STOPLIGHT

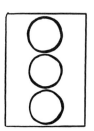

What you need:

Construction paper,
9"x12", for
background
Construction paper,
scraps of red, yellow,
and green
Scissors
Pencil
Mucilage

What you do:

1. Cut out 3" diameter circle of cardboard for tracing. Trace a circle on yellow, red, and green construction paper. Cut these out.

2. Cut out a rectangular background approximately 12"x6".

3. Glue the three circles on the background paper in the order of a stoplight.

Suggestions:

1. This is a good project to tie in with safety when crossing streets.

2. Talk about colors red, green, and yellow. Talk about "circles."

3. A safety saying goes like this: "Red light means stop. Green light means go. Yellow light means wait until you know."

VEGETABLE PRINTING

What you need:

Paper
Poster paint
Paintbrushes
Vegetables (potatoes work
well)
Paring knife
Cookie cutters—(suggested shapes: heart,
pumpkin, ghost,
candy cane, star,
flower, leaf)

What you do:

1. Choose a shape. Press the cookie cutter into the smooth side of a vegetable that has been cut in half.

2. An adult should cut away the edges, leaving the shape raised. (This is called relief.)

3. Brush paint on the surface of the shape.

4. Then stamp the shape onto the paper, randomly or in a pattern. Small pieces of folded paper may be printed for cards. Tissue paper or table-covering paper may be used to make wrapping paper.

FOOTPRINTS

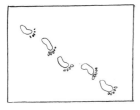

What you need:

Construction paper or
   white drawing paper
Tempera paint, any color

What you do:

1. Spread tempera paint in a wide, shallow dish or plate. Make a fist and dip the side of your hand into the paint.
2. Press your hand on the paper. (It looks very much like a footprint minus the toes.)
3. Dip five fingertips into the paint, then press them on the paper just slightly above the "foot" print.
4. Make a design or make them walk in a line. You will have to use both left and right hands to make both feet.
   Suggestion: This project may be tied into learning about animal footprints.

COUNTING CHART

What you need:

Posterboard or very stiff
   cardboard, approxi-
   mately 12"x15"
Crayons or markers
Miscellaneous small
   objects
White glue

What you do:

1. Ahead of time, draw 10 lines across the posterboard.
2. On the left side—going down— print the numbers 1 through 10, one per line. Or make dotted numbers that the children may trace over.
3. Put a handful of each of ten different objects in separate bowls. The children count out the objects, matching the amount to the printed number. Glue the objects in a row.

Suggestion:

If 10 is too many for your group of children, do only 1 or 2 numbers at each session. This can be a continuing project.

Puppets Make Learning Fun

Puppets are ideal learning toys for preschoolers. When a young child puts a puppet on his hand, on his finger, or over his face (head), his imagination takes over. He can very easily become that character for a few moments. He lets go of himself to take on the voice and mannerisms of his puppet. What an adventure into fantasy!

Your little one—with a few simple suggestions—will talk for his character. Language skills are practiced. Communication takes place. Sometimes a particularly shy little person will surprisingly open up while hiding behind a homemade theater. He can tell simple stories through his puppet. He has a chance to verbalize real concerns, fears, and worries when in character. He can act out dad, mom, brothers, sisters, and any other significant people in his life. You may need to suggest an idea or situation to play out, but a young child usually takes over very easily. For example, you might say: "Pretend you are going on a picnic in the woods, but it begins to rain just as you take your first bite of sandwich." The puppeteers will take it from there.

In the process of making their own puppets, children give life to a puppet. Each one is very individual. The puppet sometimes will take on characteristics unique to its maker.

A few extra benefits come with the process of making a puppet. For example, small muscle skills are used in drawing, coloring, cutting, gluing, arranging, and designing. Also verbal and visual directions must be followed. Each puppet will have its own personality. The child who made it will develop the personality of his puppet as he is given a chance to "talk" and to "perform."

SOCK PUPPETS

What you need:

Sock—old, clean, white
Construction paper—pink or red
Felt scraps—red
Yarn
Buttons
Needle and thread
Glue
Scissors
Markers

What you do:

1. Use pink construction paper and cut out oval. Glue it to the end of the sock. This is the mouth.
2. Sew on two dark-colored buttons for eyes.
3. Cut out a tongue-shaped piece of red felt. Glue it to the back of the mouth.
4. Cut yarn into short or long pieces. Glue it to the top and back of the head.
   Note: You can use construction paper strips, curled around a pencil, for hair. You can color with a red marker for the mouth.

PAPER BAG PUPPETS

What you need:

Paper lunch bags
Construction paper—various colors
Miscellaneous decorations: yarn, buttons, stickers, fabric, felt
Crayons/markers/paint
Scissors
Glue

What you do:

Bunny

1. For ears, cut 2 long, narrow ovals out of white construction paper. Cut 2 more ovals—a little smaller—out of pink construction paper. Glue pink onto white. Glue the ears on the top back edge of the folded bag.

2. For whiskers, cut long, thin strips out of black construction paper. Glue onto the bottom of the bag.

3. For eyes and nose, use black marker or crayon.

4. For teeth, cut 2 rectangles out of white construction paper and glue under edge of flap.
   Note: Put your hand in, fingers up over fold, and make him talk.

Owl

1. For ears, cut 2 small triangles out of brown construction paper. Glue on top edge.

2. For eyes, draw with markers or crayons.

3. For beak, cut a diamond-shape out of yellow construction paper. Fold it in half to form a triangle shape. Glue to folded edge of the triangle under the edge of the flap.

4. For feathers, tear pieces of brown construction paper. Glue on paper bag.
   Note: Now practice "hooting"!

Cat

1. For ears, cut 2 triangles out of construction paper. Shade insides with pink crayon. Glue to top back edge of folded bag.

2. For eyes, draw with markers or crayons.

3. For nose, glue on a small flat button or a tiny pompon.

4. For whiskers, draw on with black crayon or markers.

5. For tongue, cut a pink tongue out of construction paper. Glue it to paper bag under the flap.

Elf

1. For the hat, cut a triangle shape. Glue it to the top folded edge. Glue pompon onto the point of the hat.

2. For face, draw on eyes, mouth, cheeks, lips, etc., with markers or crayons.

3. For buttons, glue on 3 more pompons or 3 stickers to front of center.

4. For arms and hands, cut rectangular shaped arms out of green felt, and white oval-shaped mittens. Glue the mittens to the arms; glue the arms to the puppet.

5. Small round bells (optional) can be taped or pinned in place on each side of the bag.

Stuffed Head

1. Take a lunch bag. Use a sheet of newspaper, wadded into a ball, to stuff inside bag for a head.

2. Use crayons to draw on a simple face.

3. Use a length of yarn, tied around bag right below face!

4. For hair, cut strips of construction paper, curled on a pencil. Glue these in place on the head.
   Suggestion: Give your puppet a rhyming name. (Match the rhyme to the child's name.) Example: Scarry Kari or Merry Larry or Bim Tim.

FINGER PUPPETS

What you need:

Paper—white or other colors
Scissors
Black marker
Tape

What you do:

1. Cut a strip of paper about 1″ high by 1-¼″ long (to fit a child's finger).
2. Take a black marker to draw a face and features of a person or animal.
3. Slip the paper around the child's finger and tape it to fit.

Suggestions:

1. Each person may wish to make 2 or more of these simple finger puppets.
2. Make a theater from a shoe box (a hole cut from its side) for these little puppets.

FINGERLINGS
(A fingerling is a tiny puppet with only a finger, a face, and a hat.)

What you need:

Felt-tipped, colored, washable markers
Construction paper—various colors, scraps
Circular objects such as coins, cans, lids (for tracing)
Scissors
Glue or mucilage
Tape
Pencil

What you do:

1. Draw a face on your finger, using colored markers.

2. Put a hat on your finger tip. Here are some different hats to make:

Circle with brim hat:

1. Trace a circular object pop can. Cut out the circle. Cut out a center circle.

2. Cut another smaller circle, slit to the center, and form a cone. Slip the cone inside the open circle. Tape in place.

Indian headband:

1. Cut a slip of paper about 1-½ " long by 1" high.

2. Cut points (for feathers) on top edge.

3. Use markers to decorate feathers.

4. Wrap the Indian headband around your finger and tape in place.

Beret

1. Trace a circular shape out of construction paper. Cut out.

2. Glue on a pompon in the center.

3. Make a tape ring to hold it on the tip of your finger.

From *Plenty of Puppets to Make,* reprinted with permission.

EGG CARTON PUPPETS

What you need:

Cardboard egg carton
Construction paper—
    several colors, scraps
Loose leaf reinforcements
    (gummed circles)
Scissors
Tape
Black marker
Pencil
Glue or mucilage

What you do:

1. From the egg carton, cut out the tall crowns (six) that separate the eggs. This will be the head of the puppet. You will put it on your middle finger. Your other fingers are the legs.
2. Use the loose-leaf reinforcements for eyes; or draw eyes with marker.
3. Use the construction paper scraps to cut ears, horns, or other features of an animal. (See illustrations)
Note: If the head is too large and slips off your finger, tape it on the underneath side to your finger.

From *Plenty of Puppets to Make,* reprinted with permission.

TENNIS BALL PUPPETS

What you need:

Tennis ball (old)
Felt-tipped colored markers
Yarn
Scissors
Glue
Fabric or felt
Cardboard tube, about 4-5″ long, such as paper towel roll

What you do:

1. Take an old, worn-out tennis ball. Cut a hole in it just large enough to put in a cardboard tube snugly.
2. Use markers to draw features of a face.
3. Cut lengths of yarn. Glue onto top, back, and sides for hair.
4. Make clothes out of fabric
   Option A: Cut a criss-cross slit in a large circular piece of fabric. Slip over end of tube. Cut 2 slits for fingers to stick through.
   Option B: Sew a simple shirt out of felt, leaving a neck hole to slip over the tube.
5. Put puppet pieces together. Put the clothes over the tube, then put the head onto the tube through the cut hole. Note: Slip your hand under the clothes, putting your first two fingers in the tube, thumb and little finger in the arm holes.

From *Learning Through Play,* reprinted with permission.

STICK PUPPETS

What you need:

Popsicle stick, tongue depressor, or paint stick (used for stirring)
Paper plate
Crayons/markers/paints
Miscellaneous decorations: construction paper scraps, pipe cleaners, yarn, fabric scraps, felt, buttons, corks, sequins, stickers, ribbon, styrofoam balls, balloons
Glue and tape
Scissors

What you do:

Happy/Sad Face:

1. Take 2 paper plates.

2. Use a crayon to draw a simple face on each plate. Make one mouth "happy" and the other mouth "sad."

3. Put dots of glue on the back of each plate. Place the end of the paint stick inside the plates, about half-way up, and press together.
   Suggestion: Play a "happy-sad" game with the children. Q.1.—If you were invited to a friend's birthday party, how would you feel? Q.2—If your big brother is angry at you and wants to punch you, how would you feel? Q.3.—Tell some times when you feel happy.

Clown Face:

1. Take a paper plate. Use a pencil point to puncture a small hole in the center.

2. Use crayons/markers to design and color a clown face.

3. Cut pieces of yarn or felt for hair. Glue in place.

4. Poke a balloon into the hole so that the blowing end is in the back. Now blow up the balloon—just a little bit. Tie a knot in the balloon's stem. This is the clown's nose.

5. Glue or tape the paint stick to the back for a handle.
   Suggestion: This puppet can be used as a mask if you cut slits for eyes.

Shaggy Dog:

1. Take a paper plate and cut two slits, one on each side, where ears should be. Cut out 2 floppy ears from construction paper, felt, or fabric scraps. Push the ears through the slits and tape them to the back of the plate.

2. Draw eyes with crayons. Shade around one with a dark color, if desired.

3. Use a large button, glued or taped in place, for a nose.

4. Cut out strips of yarn—various lengths—for shaggy hair. Glue to plate all around edge.

5. Tape a paint stick to the back for a handle.

Girl with braids:

1. Take a paper plate.

2. Make braids of heavy yarn. Use short pieces of yarn for bangs. Glue the yarn in place.

3. Glue on paper stars for eyes.

4. Paint on rosy cheeks and mouth.

5. Glue or tape a paint stick to back of plate for a handle.

Duck:

1. Take a paper plate.

2. Draw on oval eyes and add pupils.

3. Cut out 2 eyebrows from black paper. Glue on.

4. Cut out 3 small triangles. Curl them on a pencil. Glue them to the top of duck's head.

5. To make a bill, cut out 2 circles 6″ in diameter. Make one pink and one yellow. Glue the two circles together and fold in half—yellow outside.

6. Cut a triangle out of orange paper for a tongue. Glue it inside the pink mouth.

7. Glue the beak to the face. Draw 2 black dots on top of the beak.

From *Learning Through Play,* reprinted with permission.

PUPPET THEATERS

Table Top:

Use a table covered with a long tablecloth. Children sit or kneel behind it with puppets above their heads. The table is very helpful for props.

Cardboard Box (on table):

Place a cardboard box on its side. The entire back should be open for puppeteers. The bottom of the box will be stage front. You may cut 2 doors, folded back on sides ... or you may cut an opening and cover it with a towel or cloth.

Shoe Box (placed on a table edge):

Cut a rectangular opening on the bottom of the shoe box. The entire back must be open. This theater is very good for finger puppets and fingerlings.

Appliance Box:

(A freezer or refrigerator box works well. Just ask a local appliance dealer to save a box for you.)

1. Stand up the box. Cut out a rectangular opening at the top of one side for a stage front.

2. Cut out a door (three sides) and fold it (to be opened and closed) in the back. Two to four preschool-aged children can usually fit inside a box of this size.

3. For a curtain, attach a dowel rod to the cardboard above the opening. Use craft wire—poked through box front and back out and around the dowel. Sew a rod pocket in a set of old bath towels or sew your own curtains. Use 2 to 2-½ times the measured width of the opening for curtains.
For example: if opening is 20″ wide, then make each curtain 20″ wide (total 40″). Make the length as long as the measured length plus 4″ (2″ for rod pocket, 2″ to hang below opening).

SIMPLE MARIONETTE

What you need:

Soda pop can (for tracing)
A quarter (for tracing)
Two large rubber bands
Thread or string
Tape
Pencil
Black crayon
Construction paper—red, black, and white

What you do:

1. Draw around a soda pop can to make one circle on white paper, one circle on red paper, and two circles on black paper.

2. Draw around a quarter to make four circles on white paper.

3. Cut out all the circles.

4. Draw a face—eyes, nose, and mouth—on the large white circle with a black crayon.

5. Cut each rubber band in half.

6. Tape one piece of rubber band to each of the four small white circles—for arms and legs.

7. Tape the two large black circles to the back and top of head— for ears.

8. Tape the large red circle to the back and bottom edge of the large white circle—for a body.

9. Tape the four rubber bands—arms and legs—to the back of the body.

10. Tape a piece of thread (or string) to the back of the head.
    Note: To make your puppet "dance," just move the thread up and down. You can make his arms and legs move.

From *The Mickey Mouse Make-It Book,* reprinted with permission.

Creativity: Art

Dribbles and Dabbles

My daughter is bright and inquisitive, which I knew, but I also realized she very much needs to be her own person and do things her way.

Carolyn Fischer, mother of Darcy, Heidi, and Brad

Creativity is a lot like walking, it comes naturally to a child. It cannot be pushed or forced; it just happens. It comes from within the individual. What you can do to foster creativity is to provide an environment in which artistic creativity can develop.

Artistic creativity in a child is his beginning experience in learning to plan and to organize. A child will express himself—his ideas and feelings—in the media of art when he has the opportunity to do so. What he creates will illustrate his growing ability to plan and to organize. Therefore, your goal is not to have your children produce a specific product, but to give them an opportunity to exercise their growing minds through expression in art.

Parents can help their young children with art by first remembering the differences between art projects and craft projects. Bev Bos in *Don't Move the Muffin Tins* sums it up this way. "I make my own distinction between 'art' and 'craft' by asking how much participation by an adult is needed once I have presented materials. When the activity is truly art and genuinely creative, all I have to do is to put a name on the paper or perhaps stand by to add to the supplies."

After the children's needs are considered, the materials can be presented so children can grow in creativity. Bev Bos provides some insight, "When we think of art for children, we too often think of media and product first and then the child. We need to be sensitive to the child first—sensitive to growth and development, aware of the child's needs. Then we can appropriately think about media. Children do not need to be coerced into doing art. If program materials are presented in the right way, the child will use them to grow and develop."

Stages of Creativity

The stages of creativity in children are universal; that is, they are the same in children all over the world, and they are sequential, meaning that one stage follows another. Let's take a brief look at the stages of creativity.

The scribble stage

Children of about two to four years old are generally in this stage of creativity. The scribbling stage can be identified by several phases, sometimes overlapping each other. The first phase, called the "disordered scribble" may be seen roughly at about eighteen months to early two years old. A child in this phase uses whole arm movements to scribble. He has no idea what he is doing. His first attempts at creative expression will be lines that are random and uncontrolled.

The second phase is called the "controlled scribble." About six months after the disordered scribble begins, the child has better coordination and control. He starts to make a connection in his mind with what he is doing. You may observe longitudinal scribbling in which the lines mostly go up and down or back and forth.

A little later in creative development, circular scribbling takes place. By the time a child is about three years old, he will be able to draw a circle.

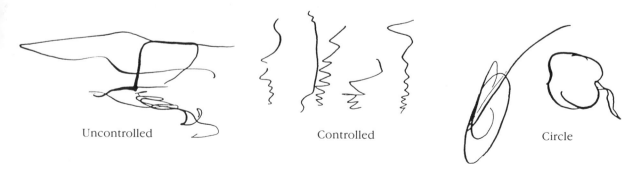

Uncontrolled   Controlled   Circle

Art begins with feelings on the inside of the artist. Whatever it is that makes us want to express ourselves is something that is taking place within ourselves.

Fred Rogers

A little later, the "named scribbling" phase will appear. In this phase the child may name something only after it is drawn. He has no idea in his mind of what he is going to draw. For example, after drawing a lumpy sort of circle, Sarah brightened up and exclaimed her picture to be a "hippopotamus." She named her art only after it looked like something to her. With a little more development in this phase, a child may first think of what he wants to draw, yet he really isn't able to draw it very well. That is, to us the drawing doesn't look like the real thing although to him it looks like what he says it is.

The preschematic stage

The next stage of creativity is the "preschematic stage" which generally occurs between the ages of four to seven years. A characteristic of this stage is that children's drawings contain certain symbols. These are typical symbols seen in this stage.

Another characteristic of this stage is that the child first draws an outline of what he imagines and then he fills in the spaces of his drawing.

The schematic stage

The "schematic stage," prevalent in the seven- to nine-year-old, can also be seen in some five- to six-year-olds. In this stage, the child will draw human figures placed on a baseline like grass, floors, etc. In their drawings, things that are larger and brighter are more significant or important to them. However, adults need to be careful in analyzing children's artwork.

Named   Preschematic   Schematic

247

Stages in Molding

Along with the stages of scribbling, stages in molding are experienced universally by children. The first phase is the "kneading period." In this phase the child investigates the molding material such as playdough or clay. He plays with it—pinches it, hits it, punches it—just for fun. The next phase of molding is the "integrative stage" during which the child does a lot of rolling into cylinders and balls. The next stage is the "representation stage." At this time he attempts to make things as they really appear.

Nourishing Creativity

With this brief discussion of the stages of creativity in the young child, you can understand that it is developmental; creativity just happens in the child without force or push. So you may ask, "How do I encourage creativity?"

Physical environment

By creating a stimulating environment, parents can help release artistic creativity from within their children. Here are some tips on preparing the physical environment for art projects:

1. Use good materials and tools—things that are safe and sturdy.
2. Materials need to be readily accessible.
3. Try the project ahead of time. Make a sample—mainly to help you plan and to check out your materials, the set-up, and the approximate length of time you will need. Many problems can be avoided when the leader is ready.
4. Have children use paint shirts or old t-shirts as cover-ups if they do so willingly. Creativity is often messy.
5. For a very young child, you will want to offer only one or two materials at a time—so that they are not overwhelmed with too much and so that they can spend a lot of time experimenting with each type of media.
6. You can occasionally offer special projects that need supervision or instruction such as fingerpainting.
7. Be ready. Before beginning a project parents need to have the work space and materials ready. This will help you to focus on the children and their needs without having to run around and find materials.

Experiential environment

To stimulate creativity in your children, you can set up an experience in which all their senses participate. The best way to do this is to take a field trip. Take the children where they can experience by seeing, hearing, smelling, tasting, and touching. One group of children went to a forest preserve and spent quite some time with the ranger near a pond. Birds singing, frogs jumping, turtles sunning on a log, ladybugs crawling up young spring shoots were all part of this scene. The boys and girls tasted and smelled onion tops, dill, and asparagus. Just being there gave them vivid and lasting impressions which they expressed a few days later with crayons on large sheets of blank paper.

A secondary way to give the children an experiential environment is to bring the world to them. Bring in things from places they haven't been or cannot go: sea shells, tumbleweed, cotton plants, whole coconuts, or sombreros. Or you can invite someone to speak to the children about a special trip or experience. The parents of your preschool children have probably had interesting experiences they could share with the group.

hildren need only to please themselves.... Once you've presented the materials, forget how you intended them to be used. Sometimes it's difficult. You may have one end product in mind, but the child may have another idea. If that's the case, hands off! It's easier to observe this principle in art activity than in crafts because there is no right or wrong in art.

Bev Bos

Spiritual environment

As parents, you can provide the nurturing spiritual environment needed to foster the creative process in your children. You simply need to remember that the most important aspect of creative expression is **the process, not the product.** Some guidelines to support a positive spiritual framework are listed here.

1. Be uncritical. Also, protect the child from others' criticism.

2. Show the attitude that "every person's art is special and important and good."

3. Use gentle guidance in giving instructions on the use of materials. Take things calmly and slowly. They will be likely to follow your lead.

4. Help them be unafraid of mistakes and disapproval by giving lots of encouragement.

5. Let the children express their own ideas and feelings.

6. Respect the child's name on his or her art. Don't try to correct it or rewrite it or cover it up in any way. His name is important to the child.

 hildren who are encouraged in their own unique forms of artwork can come to use them as very reliable aids for understanding and coping with the stresses that accompany all their growing.

Fred Rogers

Emotional environment

You can further enhance the environment for creative expression by your attitude toward the children and their artistic work. The degree of your enthusiasm and support can give them a red light or a green light in their development.

When one of your preschoolers shows you his artwork, it may not look like anything special to you. But to him it is the world as he sees it. It has been shown that the way you talk to him about his work will influence his ability to continue to be creative.

Ask children to tell you about their artwork rather than trying to guess what it is.

atch a child paint. *You see immense seriousness and concentration. There is freedom, too ... freedom to get lost in colors! A child can naturally concentrate within himself. He enjoys the experience for its own sake—not for what people will think or what the finished product will look like.*

Sandy Jones

How do you talk to your scribbler? Try not to figure out what he has made and guess what it is. Instead, ask if he would like to tell you about his picture. He may not, because it may not really be anything. If this is what happens, then you can comment on something specific such as "the long red lines" or the "many circles." Other things you might be able to comment on are the softness of the lines or how he must have gone "really fast to make those lines." As you do this you can point to the color or trace the shape you are mentioning. By doing this you are helping him to learn his colors and shapes as well as being aware of his feelings.

More Tips for Creative Experiences

1. Let the children experiment.

2. Avoid an art model; let them express their own ideas, not the ideas of someone else.

3. Give them plenty of time.

4. Give blank paper of all kinds.

5. Don't correct or add to a child's artwork. "Hands off" is a good rule to follow.

6. Don't ask "What is it?"; rather say, "Would you like to tell me something about your art?"

7. If displaying artwork, display everyone's and hang them at the children's eye level.

8. Always remember it is **the process, not the product** which is most important.

9. Don't feel guilty if you are more comfortable encouraging crafts at the expense of art. Rather look ahead to offering more art opportunities in the future.

10. Remember: "If it is really creative, a child of any age can do it."

Let the children experiment with different forms of creative expression, such as using chalk outdoors on a sidewalk or patio.

Art for preschool children is valuable in allowing them to release their creativity. By providing the right kind of environment you can give your children opportunities to express their ideas and feelings. You can open doors to allow them to illustrate their developing minds. Because artistic creativity cannot be hurried in children, you know that the best thing you can do for them is to give them a nourishing environment, including much praise and encouragement.

Dribbles and Dabbles

Materials to use

Paper

Cardboard
Coffee filters
Construction paper
Duplicating paper
Fingerpaint paper (butcher paper is much less expensive)
Foil
Newspaper, printed or plain
Paper bags, large and small

Paper napkins
Paper towels
Paper plates
Sandpaper, different grades
Styrofoam meat trays
Tissue paper
Wallpaper, rolls and sample books
Waxed paper
White drawing paper
Wrapping paper

Paints and brushes

Watercolors
Water with food coloring added
Tempera (dry is less expensive, but takes slightly longer to mix)
Poster paints
Liquid starch, also known as "goop" (See recipe in section on paints)
Brushes, all sizes and thicknesses, watercolor brushes up to house-painting brushes
Other things to paint with: sponges, styrofoam, pencils, popsicle sticks, cotton swabs, twigs, pastry brushes, feathers

Drawing tools

Crayons, thick and thin
Felt-tipped markers, fine and broad
Ink pens, all colors
Pencils, gray and colored
Chalk, white and colored

Clay and playdough (try a homemade recipe)

Collect all kinds of things for collages and sculptures

Fabric scraps, ribbon, lace, trims, buttons
Yarn and string
Stickers, adhesive backed and lick-ons
Beans
Seeds
Spices
Pastas
Wood scraps
Paper scraps
Plastic scraps
Styrofoam packing chips
Miscellaneous household items: cotton balls, cork tops, bottle caps, rubber bands, etc.

Ideas for art

Paper

Paper, so commonplace, can be used in a wide variety of ways to stimulate the creative process. Here are some ideas on how you can get more out of paper.

- Put paper in various places besides on the table. Try on the wall, on the floor, on lap boards, or outside on sidewalks or patio.

- Try many different kinds of paper from brown paper bags to computer cards to tissue paper and waxed paper.

- Vary the size, the shape, and the color of paper.

- Try a "negative space" paper. Use any paper with a hole cut into it. The hole may be any size, shape, or position on the paper. Give children paints, markers, or crayons to use. (Use only one or two colors to begin with.) Don't talk about the hole. Just let the children do what they want to do with their materials. You might be surprised at their art!

- Put paper on paper on paper. Give the children two or three different kinds of paper. Also give them scissors and white glue. Let them create whatever comes to their mind with these materials.

Crayons, markers, chalk

- Use crayons on different textures: waxed paper, foil, sandpaper, fabric

- Try markers on absorbent paper: tissue paper or paper towels

- Look for "Cookie crayons" in *Don't Move the Muffin Tins* by Bev Bos

- Use chalk on: white or colored paper, wet paper, sidewalks

- Draw to music: slow and lyrical, fast, marching, etc. Encourage whole arm movements.

- Trace shapes (the outside edge): such as cookie cutters, shape sorter pieces, cardboard forms, children's hands and feet, household items.

- Trace stencils (the inside edge of a template): use a plastic lid with a hole cut in the center for your templates, or use cardboard templates.

- Do rubbings: place paper on any textured surface; try floors, walls, unfinished wood, carved wood or metal, coins, leaves, etc.

Collages

A collage is a collection of similar objects glued to a background to create a design, geometric or free form, or a picture. The background may be any sturdy material like tagboard, cardboard, scrap lumber, heavy fabric, or styrofoam trays. An art collage, has no particular end product in mind. There are endless varieties. The only thing needed is the collection of objects which will be glued or pasted on the background. Here are some ideas for different collages.

- Beans: pinto, navy, white, split peas, lentils, blackeyed peas

- Seeds: poppy, dill, sesame, peppercorns, carrot, bean, melon, apple, pear, celery, maple tree, walnuts, pecans, peanuts

- Yarn: all sizes, lengths, thicknesses

- Fabric: scraps, all types, thicknesses, textures, weaves; also can add ribbons, rick-rack, lace, buttons, trims, pompons

- Spices: dill, sage, basil, oregano, pepper, salt, cinnamon, cloves, parsley, sage, thyme (Spices may be shaken out of small jars that have plastic lids with holes.)

- Household items: scraps of plastic and paper, rubber bands, string, cork, twist ties, cotton balls, beads

- Paper: scraps of all sizes, shapes, colors. Keep pieces somewhat large for handling by small hands.

    torn construction paper
    torn tissue paper
    crepe paper

- Nature: items which are allowed to be picked off the ground; this is especially good to do on a nature hike. Look for twigs, seeds, seed pods, acorns, walnuts, thistles, feathers, etc.

- Wrapping paper: designs or pictures cut from wrapping paper and then glued on

- Shapes: various sizes of the same shape such as circles

- Colors: the same color—such as red—cut from many different media

A child of any age can do an art project as it is the creative process that is important not the end product.

Printing

Printing is the process of dipping objects in paint or ink and then pressing onto paper to create a pattern, design, or free-form art. The background to print on may be paper, cardboard, wood, or fabric. Tempera paint, mixed to a medium thickness, may be used. Ink, on stamp pads, may also be used. You will probably want to keep a bucket of sudsy water handy for clean-up. Some printing ideas are listed here.

- Cookie cutters: especially good during holidays
- Shape printing: use blocks from a shape sorter toy (Fisher Price, Tupperware, or Child Guidance); dip the shape into the paint and print
- Cork tops: leave smooth or carve a design into them before printing
- Vegetable such as carrots, potatoes, and squash: cut a design or shape onto the top; dip and print
- Sponge printing: use various sizes and textures of sponges
- Finger printing: use finger tips pressed on ink pads and then pressed on paper (Use markers or ink pens to add lines to the prints to create pictures such as animals, plants, etc.)

■ Object printing: use miscellaneous household objects to dip and print; try popsicle sticks, toothpicks, rubber bands, pencils, fork, penny, etc.; unusual shapes and patterns will emerge.

Miscellaneous art ideas

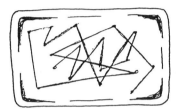

■ Stringing: use a string or yarn with a pointed tip. Wrap a small piece of cellophane tape on end or dip into clear nail polish and let dry into a point. Things to string: cardboard or paper shapes, cereal with holes, pasta, beads made from homemade clay or playdough, styrofoam packing chips.

■ Sewing cards: use yarn or string threaded through a blunt-tipped needle and a background. Here are a couple of varieties of backgrounds:

1. styrofoam meat trays: can use a pencil point to make small holes as you sew;

2. burlap stapled onto an open cardboard frame.

■ Color absorption: use a paper towel, folded several times, and drip or dot on with a brush tip tempera paint thinned with water or use food color. You can also dip the corners. Open up the towel and let dry.

■ Pipe cleaners: use all different shapes, thicknesses, lengths, and colors. Let the children sculpt anything they wish.

■ Yarn weaving: weave or sew yarn pieces through plastic mesh pieces that have no pattern. Let children create their own free flow designs or pictures.

Painting

■ Drip painting: place a piece of paper, any size or shape, on the floor and let paint drip off the paintbrush. Do not throw the paint; young children may want to also brush their drips; try black paper.

■ Fingerpainting: use a shiny surfaced paper such as butcher paper; place a small glob of paint in the center of the paper; have a bucket of warm, sudsy water and old towels handy for clean-ups. You might want to do this outside, in a garage, on a sidewalk, or a driveway or simply bring the wet papers outside to dry.

- Pudding painting: make the recipe on the box; be sure it is instant pudding. This one is great for finger-licking!

- Shaving cream painting: use an aerosol shaving cream; add a few drops of food coloring. Let children spray in the center of their own papers and choose their own color.

- Mirror painting: fold paper in half and then open up again. Tempera paint or poster paint may be dabbed with brush or spoon on one side only. Then fold paper over and gently press. Open to reveal the mirror image that was painted.

- Foot painting: use a fairly large piece of paper and paint with feet. Either sit on a chair and paint with toes, or walk on the paper. The paint may be spread thin in the bottom of a plastic dishpan so that children may walk right in the paint. Also, keep a pail of warm, sudsy water and old towels ready nearby for an easy clean-up.

- Sprinkle painting: spread a thin layer of white glue on a piece of paper. (The glue may be slightly diluted with water to spread more easily.) Then sprinkle on: rice, herbs such as parsley flakes or oregano, colored cookie sprinkles (sugar) or colored salt, or seeds such as poppy or dill. Just use one or two sprinkles. These may be sprinkled on with fingertips from small bowls or by shaking small bottles that have plastic lids with holes (such as the ones spices come in).

- Spatter painting: you will need a small piece of screen, about 4"x5", with the edges taped so they will not injure the artists. You will also need old toothbrushes and tempera paint. Dip the bristles of the toothbrush into the paint, brush on the screen with the paper placed below. Try layering different colors of spatters.

- Sponge painting: use several pieces of sponge cut into chunks or strips. Dip these into small bowls of tempera paint, each a different color. Then paint or print with the sponge onto paper. You may also use sponges that are cut into specific shapes such as circle, square, triangle, heart, star, shamrock, etc. Let the child do what he wants with the sponge painting; it is his own art.

- Straw painting: use a drinking straw dipped into liquid tempera paint, dripped onto the paper, and then blow through the straw to move the paint. Try drips in several places on the same paper to make a design.

- String painting: fold a heavy piece of paper in half and open up again. Cut a length of string about 18″-24″ long and dip it into a bowl of paint. Lay the wet string onto one side of the paper, leaving about 1″ hang off. Fold the paper over, pressing slightly. Let the child pull out the string (fast, slowly, wiggly, or straight). Open up the paper to see interesting designs. Try two strings in two different colors of paint.

Clay/playdough

Homemade clay or playdough offers a wonderful medium for true art. This is something that any aged child can do. Some suggestions when offering clay or playdough are:

1. An old oilcloth on the floor or table makes a good surface for lots of experimenting and for an easy clean-up.

2. You will not need to suggest but will probably see these as the children work with their clay or playdough: cylinders, balls, pancakes, handprints, or animal shapes.

3. Dowels, ½″ to 1″ thick, or cylinders from building toys make good rolling pins.

4. Use any kind of kitchen utensils for creating; try knives, forks, spoons, scissors, meat hammers, potato mashers, cheese slicers, toothpicks, popsicle sticks, etc.

5. For shapes and designs, give the children cookie cutters or the shape pieces from shape sorter toys.

Cylinders from building toys make good rolling pins for playdough.

COOKED PLAYDOUGH

What you need:

1 c. flour   1 c. water
½ c. salt   2 T. oil
2 t. cream of tartar   1 t. food coloring

What you do:

1. Cook over medium heat, stirring constantly, until it forms a ball.

2. Remove and knead.

3. Store in air-tight plastic containers or in plastic bags.

Cooking Up Learning by Jackie Jundt and Lucy Rumpf

COOKED CLAY

What you need:

2 c. salt   1 c. cornstarch
⅔ c. water   ½ c. cold water

What you do:

1. Mix salt and ⅔ cup water in a saucepan and stir over heat for three or four minutes.

2. Remove from heat and add cornstarch and remaining water.

3. Stir until smooth. This clay won't crumble.

Don't Move the Muffin Tins by Bev Bos

NO-COOK PLAYDOUGH

What you need:

3 c. flour   1 c. water, more if necessary
1 c. salt   A few drops of food coloring

What you do:

1. Mix all ingredients together.

2. Knead well. This recipe takes lots of kneading; let the children help.

Cooking Up Learning by Jackie Jundt and Lucy Rumpf

HOMEMADE FINGERPAINT—#1

What you need:

¼ c. cold water
1 c. powdered laundry
starch

5 c. boiling water
½ c. soap flakes
Food coloring

What you do:

1. Mix the starch and cold water in a saucepan;
2. Mix until it is a smooth paste.
3. Add the boiling water and cook until the mixture is shiny.
4. Remove from the heat and add food coloring. Let cool and pour into jars with airtight lids. This may keep a week or longer.

HOMEMADE FINGERPAINT—#2

What you need:

3 T. sugar
½ c. cornstarch
2 c. cold water

food coloring
detergent

What you do:

1. Mix the first two ingredients and then add water.
2. Cook over low heat, stirring constantly, until well-blended.
3. Divide the mixture into 4 or 5 portions and add a different food coloring to each, plus a pinch of detergent, to facilitate clean-up.

Feed Me! I'm Yours by Vicki Lansky

HOMEMADE FINGERPAINT—#3

What you need:

1 c. laundry soap
1 c. cold water
4 c. hot water

1 c. laundry soap
1 c. cornstarch
Food coloring

What you do:

1. Mix first three ingredients and cook until clear.
2. Add next three ingredients, cook until thick, stirring constantly.
3. Cool and use.

Nourishment: Foods and Cooking

Make It Munchy

My initial involvement in playgroups and later in at-home preschool has helped me spend time where my values are—with my children—rather than getting caught up in the everyday details of living.

Molly Pierce, mother of Suki, Treva, and Tosh

Eating is fun! And cooking what you eat doubles the fun! Your at-home preschool has all the ingredients needed for some very delicious learning experiences. The kitchen is the place and the foods you need are probably right there, too.

Learning and Cooking

Your preschoolers have much to gain from cooking and eating nutritious foods in addition to the obvious fact that "it tastes good." They will have the opportunity to learn many things while they have a terrific time concocting their delectable edibles.

1. They will be able to **learn about foods and which ones are good for you.** They can be introduced to the basic four food groups. Parents can emphasize choosing foods high in nutrition for snacks.

Your preschooler will have a terrific time learning by cooking and eating nutritious foods.

2. **Following directions** is a must in cooking projects. They will have to follow directions such as "stir slowly" or "it's in the lower cupboard" in order to get good results. The final product is proof of a good listener.

3. **Simple number skills** are reinforced by preparing various foods. Counting is needed while measuring and following the recipe. Count "3 eggs" or "2 cups of flour."

4. Other **basic concepts** are reinforced. Colors of foods can be highlighted during food preparation. A simple game related to this is:

   "Name 3 foods that are red."
   "Tell me 4 kinds of green vegetables."
   "Tell 3 things that come from dairy cows."
   "Name 5 kinds of red meat."

 ooking and working in the kitchen provide an excellent atmosphere for learning for your child. He will learn how to follow directions and read, work out simple math and science problems, and develop better coordination. Most of all, he will learn about good nutrition. You may be surprised what your child will eat if he makes it himself.

Whole Foods for the Whole Family

5. You can make up general categories of foods based on **color, food group, source of food,** and so on. This game is excellent for learning categories of like things.

6. **Sizes and amounts** are talked about while preparing food. For example, "The measuring cup is half full. So it is ½ cup," or "Find the large cooking pot." Ordering by size and amount will come up. "Let's measure the flour into the largest mixing bowl. Which one is the next smaller? Which one is the smallest?" or "Which spoon holds the most salt?"

7. The **sequence** of following the recipe shows them that the ingredients and steps in making something must be done in a certain order. Following the correct sequence of events will result in something good to eat.

 he kitchen is the best learning laboratory in your house! Where else can you and your child practice science, math, language, and art right from the equipment and materials provided there?

Sandy Jones

 ooking is an exciting and pleasant sensory experience for children. It also provides avenues for the development of concepts in mathematics, language, science, and social studies.

Jackie Jundt and Lucy Rumpf

8. **Vocabulary** is strengthened. The children can be exposed to many new words. Some examples are "blend, chop, grease, grind, dice, slice, stir, fold," and so on. They may also learn the names of foods which they may not have heard of before such as zucchini, parsley, almond extract, yogurt, etc.

9. The children, fascinated and curious about foods uncommon to their experience, are usually excited to taste and touch and smell the unusual. Cooking can be a very **sensory experience.** Homemade bread dough is a not-so-common product and children fully enjoy feeling it as they knead it—pushing, pulling, punching, tearing, rolling, etc.

10. Some **basic science concepts** are also naturally incorporated. With a small group of preschoolers, they can all participate in simple experiments of discovery, such as:

How does ice melt?

How does something get frozen? Make freezer pops with fruit juices; watermelon juice is especially good.

What happens when you cook a raw egg for 2 minutes? 10 minutes? in the shell? out of the shell?

Why does the apple turn to mush when it is cooked?

Where does steam come from?

11. **Small motor skills** are needed while cooking. Using utensils such as a knife, hand beater, ice-cream scoop, spatula, and measuring spoons help develop eye-hand coordination, balance, and strength of small muscles. Preparation tasks involve accurate measuring and pouring, stirring and mixing, kneading, spooning, etc. Decorating tasks require more exact fine motor movement.

t first it may take some time and patience on your part to be sure that your child can handle a given set of skills. Working with your child this way will also provide an opportunity for you to spend some special time with her.

Whole Foods for the Whole Family

e believe that a child can gain more self-esteem in a kitchen than anywhere else, for to him cooking probably is the most important job in the world.

Marguerite Kelly and Elia Parsons

12. **Getting along socially** is reinforced when all the children must coooperate on a group project. Usually cooking lends itself to one end product such as a batch of cookies or a pot of soup. Although there may be only one big thing at the end, many little steps give each child a chance to help.

Rules to Use with Preschoolers

There are some basic rules to follow while cooking with preschoolers. These rules need to be reinforced, mainly for the children's safety.

1. Always wash hands before cooking.

2. Let an adult turn on and off stove and other electrical appliances.

3. Do not try to plug or unplug anything; let a parent do it.

4. Listen to directions carefully.

5. Find all the things you need for the recipe before you start.

6. Turn the handles of pots and pans away from you to the side (but not over the burner).

7. Use potholders to avoid burns.

8. If you spill or break anything, clean it up immediately; ask for help if it is broken glass.

9. Clean up all dishes, counters, etc.

10. Put away all foods.

It is a good idea if we take that extra minute or two and explain the reasons why we have a rule. It will make much more sense and will be remembered longer, too. Young minds are capable of a great amount of understanding when things are explained.

Washing the dishes after a cooking session or snacktime is a lesson in being responsible.

Snacktime

Snacktime gives the children another enjoyable opportunity to grow. Taking a short time-out from their activities to eat a nutritious snack gives them a refreshing lift, both physically and mentally. Try to choose foods that are simple yet high in nutrition. Regardless of how busy the children may seem, they are never too busy to prepare and eat a snack.

The tasks related to eating offer more opportunities for learning. For example, setting the table with napkins, cups, and utensils, passing out napkins or food, cleaning up, wiping the table, even washing dishes are all valuable ways of learning responsibility.

Furthermore, snacktime gives our preschoolers a perfect social setting in which to listen, to respond, and to practice using table manners. They can practice appropriately saying "please," "thank you," "excuse me," and so on. They can learn the courtesies of waiting until all are seated before beginning to eat and waiting until all are finished before leaving the table. Some children may wish to say a prayer of thanks; give them the freedom to do so. This may be a first experience for the others to learn about religions of different denominations and/or faiths.

Lessons in Nutrition

Choosing nutritious foods for your snacks helps children learn about good food. They can experience the variety of the four food groups. Often children will try new foods if they see others eating and enjoying them, especially if they've helped to prepare the food.

Sitting around the table to share a snack gives the opportunity to practice table manners and social interaction.

One way to help children remember which foods are better than others is to assign a point value of one to five to each food. For example, a candy bar might get only one point, but a peach or apple might get three points. They will quickly see that the higher number stands for a better food.

Another example of learning food groups is to put an example or two of each of the four food groups in a plain paper bag. Let the children tell which food group each one belongs to:

Apple and potato	(Fruit and vegetable)
Package of meat	(Meats)
Cheese	(Dairy)
Slice of bread	(Cereal)

Take a real or pretend trip to a fast-food restaurant, letting the children order their own food. Now ask them to tell which food groups their own orders fit into. Be sure to include a discussion of a non-food item such as soda pop.

Help the children make picture scrapbooks illustrating good breakfast ideas, nutritional snack ideas, or favorite lunches.

Favorite Recipes

There are many cookbooks for children and many other recipes children can prepare from regular cookbooks. We list here a few good recipe ideas that have been tested and found to be easy, tasty, and fun. For each letter of the alphabet, there are ideas for happy cooking.

A *is for ...*

APPLESAUCE

6 apples—peeled, cored,
   and cut up
½ c. water
1 t. lemon juice
Sugar or honey, if desired

1. Mix together all ingredients.
2. Cook until tender.
3. Add a dash of cinnamon.
4. Press through a colander or food mill.

Cooking Up Learning by Jackie Jundt and Lucy Rumpf

ANTS ON A LOG

Celery stalks
Peanut butter
Raisins

1. Break celery stalks in half.
2. Spread peanut butter on celery.
3. Decorate with raisins.

Whole Foods for the Whole Family

APPLE STARS

Slice apples across the core to show seeds in a natural star formation.

AGGRESSION COOKIES

1 c. brown sugar
2 c. oatmeal
1 c. margarine
1 c. flour
1 t. baking soda

1. Put all ingredients into a large bowl and mix with your hands. (The more you mash and squeeze the better you feel and the better the cookies taste.)
2. Then form into small balls and put on an ungreased cookie sheet.
3. Butter the bottom of a glass or plastic cup.
4. Dip the glass in granulated sugar.
5. Mash each ball flat with the glass.
6. Redip the glass in sugar before each cookie.
7. Bake at 320° for 8-10 minutes.

Cooking Up Learning by Jackie Jundt and Lucy Rumpf

B *is for ...*

BANANA BOATS

1 banana
2 T. peanut butter
2 T. coconut
1 T. granola

1. Peel banana and slice in half lengthwise.
2. Spread peanut butter on each half.
3. Sprinkle with coconut and granola.
4. Share with a friend.

Whole Foods for the Whole Family

BUTTER

Whipping cream, chilled

1. Pour 1 T. whipping cream into a baby food or other small jar with tight lid.

2. Shake well until solid butter forms.

3. Spread on bread or cracker.
   Note: Shake with a partner so arms can rest. One counts to 25 while the other shakes. Take turns.

Kinder-Krunchies by Karen S. Jenkins

 **C** *is for ...*

CUT-OUT COOKIES

1. Begin by making a basic sugar cookie dough. (Use whole wheat flour and honey to make it more nutritious.)
2. Cut out with cookie cutters of basic shapes: square, rectangle, circle, triangle. Frost with peanut butter, if desired.

CHEESE CUBES

1. Use cheese such as colby, brick, mild cheddar; cut into small cubes.
2. Stab with pretzel sticks for preschool "hors d'oeuvres."

CLOWN FACES

Bread slices, cut round
Peanut butter, spread on bread
Shredded carrots—for hair
Raisins—for face
Banana pieces—for face

Apple slices—for face
Grapes—for face
Cherries—for face

Mix with imagination!

 D *is for ...*

DILLYBOBS

Dill pickles
Frankfurters
1 T. salad oil
Skewers—1 per person

Dads join in the fun!

1. Cut whole dill pickles into 1-inch chunks.
2. Cut each frankfurter crosswise into 5 equal pieces.
3. Place frankfurter piece on each skewer, than one pickle, then one frankfurter piece, and so on, until 5 frankfurter pieces and 4 pickle pieces are on each skewer. Brush kabobs with oil.
4. Cook kabobs on grill 5 minutes on each side, turning with tongs.
5. Note: Adult supervision is essential with young children.

Variations:

1. Frankabobs—use pineapple chunks, drained, in place of the dill pickles.
2. Potatobobs—use small canned potatoes, drained, in place of the dill pickles. Sprinkle with salt and paprika before cooking.

Betty Crocker's Cookbook for Boys and Girls

DELICIOUS DIP

¼ c. cottage cheese
2 T. grated cheddar cheese
¼ t. dill weed
½ t. Worcestershire sauce
¼ t. salt
Raw vegetables

1. Mix cottage cheese with cheddar cheese.
2. Add dill weed, Worcestershire sauce, and salt.
3. Mash with a fork.
4. Dip raw vegetables in and eat.

Kinder-Krunchies by Karen S. Jenkins

 *is for ...*

ELEPHANT TRUNKS

Bread, without crusts
Peanut butter, spread on bread
Raisins, banana pieces, or anything else, on top of peanut butter.
Roll up sandwich, like an elephant's trunk.

EGG BOATS

Eggs
Mayonnaise
Salt
Pepper
Onion salt
Cheese slices

1. Put eggs in boiling, salted water. Boil on medium temperature for about 20 minutes, until hard boiled. Rinse eggs in cold water until cool.
2. Peel eggs.
3. Cut eggs lengthwise into halves.
4. Take out the yolks and mash them with a fork.
5. Mix mashed yolks with mayonnaise, about 1 t. per egg. Season with salt, pepper, and onion salt. Mix.
6. Put yolk mixture back into whites of eggs.
7. Take a square of sliced cheese. Cut diagonally into 2 triangles. Use a toothpick to hold upright and push into each egg for a sail.

"EVERYBODY HELPED" SOUP

A soup bone
A beef bouillon cube
Water
Seasonings
Vegetables, potato, onion, carrot, tomato, peas, green beans, corn, broccoli

1. Have each child choose a different vegetable to bring.
2. Chop up all the vegetables.
3. Put in a slow cooker with the soup bone, bouillon cube, water, and seasonings.
4. Cook all day or parts of several days.

Cooking Up Learning by Jackie Jundt and Lucy Rumpf

F *is for ...*

FRUITSICLES

One or more juices:
Apple   Pineapple
Cherry   Orange
Pear   Strawberry

1. Use one or more flavors of juice and pour into ice cube tray or popsicle freezer containers.
2. Freeze 2 or more hours. Remove.

FONDUE

Cheeses: many different kinds such as colby, mozzarella, cheddar, American
Milk

1. Chop or grate cheeses into a saucepan (glass bowl if for microwave).
2. Dribble ¼ c. (or more) milk on top.
3. Heat and stir until cheese is melted and blended with milk.
4. Serve with crackers, chips, or apple wedges.

FANTASTIC CAROB FUDGE

½-1 c. honey
1 c. peanut butter
1 c. carob powder
1 c. chopped nuts
½-1 t. vanilla
Optional:
1 c. coconut
½ c. wheat germ

1. Put honey and peanut butter in pot. Cook over low heat. Stir with wooden spoon.
2. When this is liquid, remove pot from burner. Add carob powder, nuts, vanilla, and coconut or wheat germ; mix well.
3. Spoon and spread mixture into 8 x 8-inch pan.
4. Put in refrigerator to harden for an hour or more. If you cannot wait that long, put pan in freezer for about 30 minutes.
5. When ready, cut in bite-size pieces and enjoy.

Whole Foods for the Whole Family

 **G** *is for ...*

GOOD GRANOLA

1 c. oatmeal
⅓ c. wheat germ
¼ c. coconut
¼ c. sunflower seeds
¼ c. powdered milk
1 t. cinnamon
2 T. honey
2 T. oil
1 t. vanilla

1. Mix the oatmeal, wheat germ, coconut, sunflower seeds, powdered milk, and cinnamon.
2. Add honey, oil, and vanilla. Mix well.
3. Spread on cookie sheet.
4. Bake at 375° for 8-10 minutes. (Watch it!)
5. Cool on paper towels.

Kinder-Krunchies by Karen S. Jenkins

GELATIN SQUARES

1 T. unflavored gelatin
2 c. naturally sweetened
   fruit juice
1-2 c. sliced fruit:
   peaches, pears,
   grapes, bananas, ber-
   ries, etc.

1. Mix together ¼ c. juice and gelatin.
2. Measure another ¼ c. juice, boil it,
   then add the hot juice to the gelatin
   to dissolve.
3. Add the remaining juice, stir.
4. Add fruit slices and pour into an 8-
   or 9-inch pan.
5. Chill in refrigerator to set.
6. Cut into small squares—an easy finger food.
   Note: Cut squares into letters or
   numbers for fun and learning.

GREEN VEGGIES

Broccoli
Green beans
Green peppers
Brussels sprouts
Zucchini
Asparagus
Peas
Celery
Cucumbers

1. Let children wash and chop (using
   table knives).
2. Serve plain or with a dip
3. This is a good snack to help learn
   the color green.

 is for ...

HAWAIIAN POPS

1 can (16 oz.) peach slices
3 c. of red fruit punch
   drink
1-2 muffin pans
12 paper cupcake liners
12 wooden ice cream
   sticks

1. Line the 12 muffin cups with cupcake liners. Divide the peach
   slices and syrup among the 12 cups.
2. Freeze 1 hour or until firm enough to hold an ice cream stick upright. Poke a stick into each pop.
3. Fill each cup to the top with fruit punch drink (about ¼ cup).
4. Freeze about 2 hours or until firm. To loosen, quickly dip each
   muffin pan almost to the rim in hot water. Loosen the pops with
   a table knife.
5. To serve, peel off the baking cups. (It's a good idea to slide a
   clean baking cup over each stick to catch drips.)

Betty Crocker's Cook Book for Boys and Girls

HONEY HEARTS

⅓ c. butter
¼ c. honey
⅓ c. oats
⅓ c. dry milk
4 t. water
¾ c. flour
1 t. baking powder
¼ t. salt

1. Mix butter and honey.
2. Add oats, dry milk, and water. Mix well.
3. Add flour, baking powder, salt.
4. Roll dough ¼ ″ to ½ ″ thick.
5. Cut with heart-shaped cookie cutter.
6. Bake at 325° for 10-15 minutes
Note: You may chill dough after step 3.

Kinder-Krunchies by Karen S. Jenkins

 is for ...

ICE CREAM

Ice cubes
1/4 c. whipping cream
1/8 t. vanilla
½ T. maple syrup
A pinch of salt
A small metal juice can
A large container

1. Crush ice cubes in a plastic bag.
2. Mix whipping cream and vanilla in a small metal juice can.
3. Add maple syrup and salt.
4. Stir until dissolved.
5. Put in a larger container. Surround with crushed ice and lots of salt.
6. Stir once every 5 minutes for 30 minutes.
Note: Be careful that no salt gets into the ice cream.

Kinder-Krunchies by Karen S. Jenkins

INSTANT BANANA PUDDING

½ small banana
3 T. applesauce
1 t. plain yogurt

1. Mash the banana.
2. Add applesauce.
3. Stir in plain yogurt.
Note: Use a very ripe banana.

Kinder-Krunchies by Karen S. Jenkins

INSTANT ICE CREAM

2 c. frozen fruit (blueberries, strawberries, peaches, or bananas)
1 c. milk or cream
2-4 T. honey (optional)

1. Put fruit, milk, and honey into blender.
2. Blend on high speed until smooth. You may have to stop the blender to scrape down the sides; replace cover and blend some more.
3. Serve immediately as soft ice cream or pour into plastic cups and freeze for an hour or so.

Whole Foods for the Whole Family

 **J** *is for ...*

JUICIFUL FRUIT KABOBS

Apple
Orange
Banana
Melon
Grapes
Cheese
Wooden skewers

1. Cut fruits into large chunks.
2. Cut cheese into cubes.
3. Slide different fruits and cheese cubes onto a wooden skewer. (Try sequencing a pattern.)
4. Serve and eat.

JACK O'LANTERN COOKIES

1 graham cracker for each person
Orange frosting (or peanut butter)
8 raisins (or chocolate pieces) for each cookie

1. Spread frosting on graham crackers.
2. Arrange raisins to make a Jack O'Lantern face.

Cooking Up Learning by Jackie Jundt and Lucy Rumpf

 **K** *is for ...*

KICKERS

1 c. peanut butter
1 c. honey
1 c. powdered (dry) milk

1. Mix all ingredients well.
2. Shape into "footballs" by rolling between palms.
3. Refrigerate
4. Eat later. You'll get a "kick" out of them!
   Note: Roll Kickers in wheat germ, shredded coconut, ground nuts, or sesame seeds. Or hide a couple of carob chips inside each one.

KRAZY KITES

1 square slice of bread
Cream cheese and honey spread (or peanut butter)
Sesame seeds, sunflower seeds, poppy seeds, granola, or wheat germ
Apple slices (or orange sections)

1. Cut bread, crisscross, into 4 triangles.
2. Spread with cream cheese or peanut butter.
3. Sprinkle with one or more toppings on each triangle.
4. Arrange apple slices or orange section for a tail.

 **is for ...**

LITTLE RED HEN BREAD

1. cake of yeast
2 c. cold water
½ c. melted lard
½ c. sugar
1 t. salt
3 c. wheat flour
3 c. white flour

1. Dissolve yeast in water.
2. Add next 5 ingredients in order.
3. Grease top and put in refrigerator for 24 hours.
4. Remove and form into 12 small loaves or rolls.
5. Allow to rise until they look puffy.
6. Bake at 400° for about 12-15 minutes.

Cooking Up Learning by Jackie Jundt and Lucy Rumpf

LION FACES

Oranges
Pretzel sticks, thin
Raisins
Cheddar cheese

1. Peel an orange, then slice horizontally.
2. Make a lion face on the orange slice using: Pretzels for whiskers, raisins for eyes and nose; shredded cheddar cheese for shaggy mane.

 **is for ...**

MUNCHING COLORS

Red—apples, strawberries, cherries
Yellow—lemons, grapefruit, cheese, corn
Orange—oranges, tangerines, carrots
Blue—blueberries
Green—green grapes, avocado, lettuce
Purple—purple grapes, plums
Brown—brownies, chocolate, mushrooms, peanuts
Black—licorice
White—milk, yogurt, cream cheese, marshmallows

MOLLY'S COUNTING MUFFINS

2 c. baking mix
⅓-1 c. milk or juice
1-2 eggs
¼ c. honey
Raisins or chopped dates
Variations:
    add 1 cup blueberries
    apples, dates, etc.; cut
    liquid down to a few
    tablespoons

1. Combine all ingredients. (The batter will be lumpy.)
2. Grease muffin tins. Fill ⅔ full.
3. Bake at 375° for 20 minutes.
4. While muffins are still very warm, use raisins or date pieces to "count" the muffins.
5. Put one raisin on one, two raisins on the next one, three raisins on the next, four on the next, etc.

1. Foods come in all colors. Talk about colors as you eat.
2. Optional: Gelatins and jelly come in many colors; coconut and cream cheese can be tinted any color with food coloring.

Cooking Up Learning by Jackie Jundt and Lucy Rumpf

is for ...

NAME COOKIES

1. Use a cookie dough which can be rolled and shaped—such as sugar cookies—to form the first letter of the child's name. (He may be able to form all the letters of his name.)
2. Bake and eat.

NUTTY TIME SNACK

Nuts—walnuts, pecans, peanuts, almonds, cashews
Dried fruits—apples, pineapple tidbits, apricots, banana chips, raisins, dates
Seeds—pumpkin, poppy, sesame, sunflower
Crackers, sesame sticks, pretzel rods, etc.

1. Mix together one (or more) of each kind of nuts, dried fruits, seeds, crackers, etc.
2. Store in air-tight container in refrigerator.
3. Note: reverse this recipe, and it is a good game for sorting out "like" things. Use an egg carton as a sorting box.

  is for ...

ORANGE FLOAT

3-4 c. orange juice
Banana
Strawberries
Orange

1. Peel banana; slice into circles.
2. Wash strawberries; slice into halves.
3. Slice orange across into circles; take off peel; break orange into triangle segments.
4. Put some of each fruit into 6 glasses
5. Pour orange juice over fruit.

OLD FASHIONED LEMONADE

4 lemons
¼ - ½ c. honey or sugar
7 c. water (½ gal.)
1 c. ice cubes

1. Cut lemons in half; squeeze out juice on a juicer
2. Dissolve honey in the lemon juice; pour into 2-quart pitcher.
3. Add water and ice; stir. Note: Can add slices of lemon rind (but don't leave in overnight.)
4. Pour over ice in tall glasses. Serve.

P *is for ...*

PIZZA

1 pkg. refrigerator biscuits
1 small can tomato paste
Toppings:
cheese   mushrooms
olives   ground beef,
onions   browned
spices

1. Give each child a canned refrigerator dough biscuit. Flatten out the biscuit to be the pizza crust.
2. Spread with tomato paste.
3. Sprinkle on toppings of your choice.
4. Bake at 400° until brown.

Cooking Up Learning by Jackie Jundt and Lucy Rumpf

PEANUT BUTTER

1 c. peanuts, shelled
2 t. margarine or vegetable oil

1. Put peanuts through a food processor or meat grinder. Crush until smooth.
2. Add margarine or oil and stir.
3. Spread on crackers or celery sticks to serve.

Q *is for ...*

QUICK ENERGY SNACK

1 c. peanuts (roasted, salted)
1 c. almonds
1 c. carob chips
1 c. raisins

1. Measure and mix all ingredients.
2. Store in air-tight container.
3. Munch and enjoy!

QUESTION FOODS

Question foods to try:
Dill weed, onion, chocolate, lemon
Cinnamon, black pepper
Vinegar, fresh orange, milk
Fried egg, fresh bread
Raisin, coffee, sugar
Banana, broccoli

1. Close your eyes tight. Or use a scarf as a blindfold.
2. Choose a food to smell and/or taste.
3. Guess what the food is.
   Suggestion: Try teams. Keep point totals—one point for each correct guess. How good are your tasters?

R *is for ...*

ROASTED PUMPKIN SEEDS

Pumpkin seeds
1 c. water
2 t. salt

1. Wash pumpkin seeds.
2. Soak washed seeds in mixture of 1 c. water and 2 t. salt overnight.
3. Drain; let dry slightly.
4. Bake at 300° about 30 minutes.—Do not brown.
5. Cool and eat.

RAISIN SALAD

1-3 apples, diced
1-3 carrots, grated
1 c. pineapple, chunks or
    crushed, with juice
½-1 c. raisins
½ c. nuts or sunflower
    seeds (optional)

1. Prepare fruit and vegetables.
2. Mix all ingredients in bowl.
3. Chill in refrigerator for 2 hours.

Whole Foods for the Whole Family

DRESSING (Optional)

¼ c. mayonnaise
¼ c. yogurt
Pinch of cinnamon and/or
    nutmeg
Drip of honey, if you like

1. Combine all ingredients in small
   bowl or cup.
2. Add to salad and mix well to coat
   fruit and vegetables.

Whole Foods for the Whole Family

 is for ...

SNOW CRACKERS

24 soda crackers
2 egg whites
¼ c. sugar
¼ t. vanilla

1. Arrange crackers on a baking sheet.
2. Beat egg whites with a rotary beater
   or electric mixer just until frothy.
3. Gradually add sugar. Beat until stiff.
4. Stir in vanilla.
5. Spoon "snow" onto crackers.
6. Spread to edge of each cracker.
7. Bake at 400° for 6-8 minutes or until
   golden brown. (Do not overbake.)

Cooking Up Learning by Jackie Jundt and Lucy Rumpf

SHAMROCK SALAD

Green vegetables:
   celery
   broccoli
   green peppers
   zucchini (squash)
Vegetables (optional):
   carrots
   cauliflower

1. Wash all vegetables; drain dry.
2. Cut into thin slices or break into
   pieces (broccoli and cauliflower).
3. Toss together in a salad bowl.
4. Eat plain or dip into Fondue or Delicious Dip.

 **is for ...**

THANKSGIVING CIDER

½ gallon apple cider
2 whole cinnamon sticks
3 whole cloves

1. Pour cider in large pan.
2. Add cinnamon sticks and cloves.
3. Simmer slowly for ½ hour or more.
4. To serve, use ladle (do not put spices into cups).

TRAIL MIX

Dried fruits, such as apples, apricots, pineapple, raisins, dates, figs
Seeds, such as pumpkin seeds, sunflower seeds
Nuts, such as almonds, peanuts, pecans, walnuts, filberts, coconut

1. Put several choices of fruits, seeds, nuts into small bowls.
2. Let children choose a few handfuls, making their own combinations of 3 or more ingredients.
3. Mix together. Keep in a jar or airtight plastic bag to stay fresh.
   Note: Nutritious snack to take with on a "trail hike."

 **is for ...**

UFO'S—UNINDENTIFIED FRYING OBJECTS

1 egg
1 slice bread
1 T. butter
Salt and pepper—dash

1. With burner on medium heat, melt ½ T. butter in skillet.
2. Spread ½ T. butter on bread.
3. Cut a hole in center of bread with biscuit or cookie cutter.
4. Fry both pieces of bread, buttered sides up in skillet, until bottom is brown.
5. Turn bread over with pancake turner and break egg into the hole.
6. Add dash of salt and pepper.
7. Continue cooking slowly until egg starts to set.
8. Turn bread, just long enough to cook other side of egg.
9. Use turner to place UFO and cut out circle onto plate.

Whole Foods for the Whole Family

UNBELIEVABLE JAM

Fruit in season (strawberries, peaches, apricots, raspberries, blackberries, blueberries, or nectarines)
Honey, small amount

1. Mash or crush fruit in bowl with potato masher or use blender on medium speed.
2. Set strainer over another bowl large enough to collect juice from mashed fruit; spoon or pour fruit into strainer.
3. Put in refrigerator overnight to allow juice to drain into bowl.
4. The next day, add honey to "jam" if you like.
5. Spread on bread or crackers.
   Note: You may drink the juice.

Whole Foods for the Whole Family

 is for ...

VALENTINE CAKE

Cake ingredients
Strawberries
Whipping cream

1. Make any cake (box mix or from scratch recipe). Bake in one round and one square 8″ or 9″ inch pans.
2. Cool. Then cut round layer in half and arrange pieces to form heart shape.
3. Spread with frozen or fresh strawberries.
4. Serve with whipping cream.

VEGGIE DIP

½ c. sour cream
½ c. mayonnaise
½ t. onion flakes
½ t. dried dill weed

1. Measure and stir ingredients together.
2. Use fresh vegetables to dip: carrots, celery, cucumber, green pepper, cauliflower, broccoli, mushrooms, zucchini.
3. Makes 1 cup.

 *is for ...*

WITCHES BREW

1 gallon cranberry juice
1 gallon apple cider
12 oz. can orange juice concentrate, thawed

1. Pour the cranberry juice into a large pot.
2. Add apple cider.
3. Stir in orange juice concentrate.
4. Drink with Halloween Spirit!

Kinder-Krunchies by Karen S. Jenkins

WACKY CAROB CAKE

1 ½ c. whole wheat (pastry) flour
⅓ c. honey (or ½ c. brown sugar)
1 t. baking soda
½ t. salt
⅓ c. carob powder
1 t. vanilla
1 t. vinegar
⅓ c. oil
1 c. water
½ c. raisins (optional)
½ c. nuts, chopped (optional)

1. Preheat oven to 350°.
2. Combine dry ingredients in ungreased pan.
3. Add vanilla, vinegar, oil, honey, and water.
4. Blend well with fork, scraping sides to be sure that all the flour is mixed in.
5. Stir in raisins and nuts, if you like.
6. Pour into 8-inch square pan, greased and floured.
7. Put in oven; bake for 25-30 minutes, or until done.
8. Let cool before cutting.

Whole Foods for the Whole Family

is for ...

"X" AND "O" PRETZELS

1 cake of yeast (or 2 t. of active dry yeast)
1 ½ c. warm water
¾ t. salt
1 ½ t. sugar
4 c. flour
Egg, beaten
Salt

1. In a large bowl, soften 1 cake of yeast in 1 ½ c. warm water.
2. Add ¾ t. salt and 1 ½ t. sugar.
3. Add 4 c. flour and knead mixture into a soft dough. Do not let the dough rise.
4. Cut into small pieces immediately and roll into ropes. (Do not make the ropes too thick because they swell in baking.)
5. Shape them into "X" and "O." Lay them on a foil-covered cookie sheet dusted with flour.
6. Brush with beaten egg and sprinkle with salt.
7. Bake at 400° until golden brown. Makes 3-6 dozen.

X-TRA FRESH LIMEADE

1 small lime or ½ large lime
⅓ C. water
1 t. honey
Ice cubes

1. Cut lime.
2. Squeeze.
3. Put into glass.
4. Add water and honey.
5. Stir.
6. Add 2 ice cubes.

Kinder-Krunchies by Karen S. Jenkins

 *is for ...*

YOGURT SUNDAES

4 c. plain yogurt (or flavored)
1 t. vanilla
2 T. honey
Toppings: Choose any or all
  Bananas, sliced
  Fruit in season
  Raisins or other dried fruit
  Nuts, chopped
  Coconut, shredded
  Fruit juice concentrate

1. Mix yogurt, vanilla, and honey in bowl.
2. Chop, or cut up, or slice any fruits or nuts you choose.
3. Put scoop of yogurt in dish. Add toppings of your choice.
4. Makes 4-6 servings.

Whole Foods for the Whole Family

YUMMERS

6 t. cheese
2 T. butter
10 t. flour
10 t. crisp rice cereal

1. Grate 6 t. cheese
2. Add butter, flour, rice cereal
3. Form into little balls
4. Bake at 375° for 10 minutes. Yummy!
Note: This recipe is named after the storybook *Yummers* by James Marshall.

Kinder-Krunchies by Karen S. Jenkins

 *is for ...*

ZUCCHINI MUFFINS

½ c. zucchini
1 egg
2 T. oil
¼ c. honey
¼ t. grated lemon peel
¾ c. flour
½ t. baking powder
¼ t. salt
¼ t. cinnamon

1. Grate the zucchini. Measure ½ c.
2. Add egg, oil, honey, grated lemon peel.
3. Add flour, baking powder, salt, and cinnamon.
4. Put into muffin tin.
5. Bake at 400° for 20 minutes.
6. Eat! Zowie!
Note: A small zucchini makes ½ c. grated. Don't forget the lemon peel!

Kinder-Krunchies by Karen S. Jenkins

Music: Rhythm and Sound

Sing and Dance a Melody

I have always enjoyed playgroup experiences—we've been in three with various children now. In a co-op playgroup I think mothers learn a lot from each others' good qualities: one is artistic, one is more patient with baking with the children, another loves to sing or dance, another tells great stories and loves to read. The children profit by being exposed to the expertise of each one.

Colette Henley, mother of David, Benjamin, Peter, and Deborah

Young children are eager for music and rhythmic experiences. For most children, singing is as natural as running and jumping. Besides the obvious fact that music is fun, there are other reasons to offer music to young children. Tunes and rhythms can be learned quickly and easily through imitation; basic musical concepts such as melody, tone, pitch, volume, rhythm, and tempo can be introduced naturally through simple exposure. Also, singing—one aspect of music—builds and reinforces language skills. Musical activities that include movement benefit the children in areas of body awareness, muscular coordination, rhythmic proficiency, and auditory discrimination.

Singing is easy and fun to include in any preschool program. When the children hear a catchy melody such as "This Old Man" or "Did You Ever See a Lassie," they naturally are invited to move, to dance, to hum, and to sing.

Parents need not be concerned about their musical abilities. You will happily discover that no special talents or abilities are needed in order to offer singing or music to preschool children. At this age, they are at the very beginning of their understanding of music. And young children are extremely non-judgmental. They don't know an untrained voice from a trained one. They are too young to even know about keeping on pitch. What will affect them the most is their parents' enthusiasm. Therefore, you will do best with songs that you are most familiar with. If **you** feel confident and enthusiastic, the children will pick up on this and respond accordingly. Given the different backgrounds of all the parents, the variety of songs will be numerous.

 ong before your child ever begins to play a musical instrument or even sing, his ear will record a dictionary of sounds, categorizing noises, imitating them, and creating new ones.

Marguerite Kelly and Elia Parsons

If a mother happens to have a particular interest or training in some aspect of music, she can really take advantage of her talents and expand the music she presents to the children. She will add a special touch if she plays the piano, guitar, flute, or any other instrument. The children, of course, will really like it.

Children are most capable of learning music through imitation. A preschooler usually will not be able to explain tone, volume, melody, rhythm, or tempo. Neither can many parents. But they can learn something about these simply through following the example and instructions of their parents. For example, they can copy the "loud" and "soft" verses of "John Jacob Jingleheimer Schmidt." Or a slightly older preschooler will have fun with the rhythm when he claps to "B-I-N-G-O." Or if the parent sings a song slowly, they will copy the tempo, singing it slowly, too. And so the preschooler will learn about the basic characteristics of music very simply and naturally.

Expanding Music Activities

Music can be easily expanded beyond singing. For example, try humming, clapping, and foot-tapping to liven up an old song. Using records or cassette tapes, the children can sing along. With less concentration on words or melody, you can demonstrate actions. For example, "Do a Little Dance With Me," sung by David on the "Sesame Street" record, *Bert and Ernie Sing-Along,* is a very good song for large muscle movement. The children enjoy keeping up with the tempo as they follow the directions "Clap your hands, stomp your feet, pull your ears, turn around," and so on.

Music for preschoolers may be expanded in many other ways:

- The child can hum, whistle, or clap.

- Ask the children to feel their own (or your) vocal cords as you sing high and low notes.

- Let them have an opportunity to play a real musical instrument. (A friend, neighbor, or babysitter may play an instrument; arrange a get-together outside of regular preschool time, if necessary.)

- Attend parades, school concerts, musical plays; arrange ahead of time for a backstage tour.

- Go to a music store to see and hear a variety of instruments; talk to the manager or salesman about music.

- Visit the local library to check out records or cassettes.

- Use a cassette recorder. Tape-record the children and let them listen to themselves.

- Use a record player. The children can learn to work it. They are usually fascinated with knobs and buttons. After they learn "how to," they like the feeling of mastery over this machine.

- While working with a song, add simple body movements such as marching, swaying, hopping, or jumping. Use scarves while dancing; swoosh around for rhythm and color.

 bove all, try to be flexible; change or shorten or improvise as the spirit moves you. Add, subtract, multiply, or divide, and become part of the "folk process," an ancient and honorable tradition in which individual creativity takes what is given and shapes and alters and passes it along to the next generation to use and reshape or keep intact.

Tom Glazer

Homemade Instruments

Playing homemade instruments will reinforce the children's understanding of rhythms and tunes. Some instruments which can be made or put together easily are:

Blocks—wood blocks, with or without a hand strap

Drums—pots with metal or wooden spoons

Cymbals—metal lids from pots and pans

Triangle—metal piping formed into a triangle with metal stick

Maracas—a long-necked plastic bottle (a shampoo bottle) with some popcorn seeds (be sure to tape tightly closed).

Tambourine—decorated paper plates, stapled together with bean seeds inside.

Kazoo—comb with strip of waxed paper folded over teeth; say "toot" while blowing on it with mouth.

Guitar—cigar box with rubber bands stretched to various tensions; pluck for notes.

Xylophone—glasses or pop bottles, filled to various levels with water to achieve different notes in scale; tap with spoon for notes.

Bells—*flowerpots in graduated sizes for different notes.*

Ankle or wrist bells—*small round bells sewn on elastic bands.*

Spoon castanets—*two old spoons fastened together with rubber band.*

Drum—*empty can with a damp chamois cloth stretched over end and tied around the rim.*

Kazoo—*made from cardboard paper roll.*

Dimestore instruments—*such as plastic horns and harmonicas*

Tips for Teaching Music

Although music is generally very easy to include in a preschool program, these tips will help you select songs and teach them to your preschoolers.

1. **The songs need to be very simple** in tune and in words. The easy, simple songs are learned more quickly, therefore giving the child a more immediate sense of reward. And, of course, if he is pleased with himself, he will be more willing and eager to learn another song.

2. **Write the words** of a song that is new to you on a 3x5 notecard. You will feel more confident with it.

3. **Repetition**, in small amounts, is an effective way to learn a song. The children need to hear a verse of the song to get an idea of its tune, rhythm, and style. So, first, slowly and clearly **sing** (or play) a whole refrain or chorus for the chil-

Children learn best when parents are enthusiastic about what they are doing.

dren. Next, **say** a line or two and ask the children to repeat it. Do this through the refrain. Then do the same, having the children **sing** it with you. Finally, sing the whole song together. Do it a second time and you'll see how quickly they improve. Perhaps, later in the preschool session the children can sing it again. Just before or after snacks or just before a story or quiet game, you might want to try the new song again.

4. Encourage children to **sing softly** enough so that they can listen to each other. This will help to develop their sense of pitch and quality of tone.

5. Be sure you can **look at their faces** and sing with them.

6. Have them **sit up straight**. Good posture will help them sing better.

7. Ask them to **open their mouths wide** when singing and use their tongues to articulate the words. Your example is one of the best reminders to them to practice these skills.

8. **Balance old and familiar songs with new and different ones.** By occasionally repeating the old songs, you will help the children feel a sense of achievement. By introducing new ones, you will help them move ahead in their understanding of music.

9. **Expand the songs** when you, or they, have the interest. Include movement, dance, or instruments.

10. Have fun with music by **changing tempo and volume**. Create your own dances. Make up verses when a song lends itself to this.

Enjoy music with your preschool children and it will become one of their favorite times of day.

hildren adore humor, even zaniness, as well as fancy, fable, and fantasy, the basic "F's," I think, of their creative lives, so that I know of no better way to get educational ideas across than through these devices of enchantment. It has been pointed out so wisely that learning can be accomplished in two major ways: through fear or through love.

Tom Glazer

Music Activities

The following activities can help children become aware of the tempo or speed of music. A parent should beat on a drum (a homemade one will work fine) to indicate the tempo and the changes in tempo.

- Children can pretend to be at a picnic. They see a storm coming and start to go home. As the rain falls, they must go a little faster. When the thunder crashes and the rain comes down harder, they run even faster to get to safety.

- Children can pretend to be the horses on a merry-go-round and show the up and down movement. As the merry-go-round gets faster and faster, or slower and slower, they follow the speed of the music with their body movement.

- Children walk slowly as they pretend to walk up a steep hill. And they run easily down the other side.

- In time with the beating drum (and as it changes tempo), children can pretend to chop wood, saw a board, pull a rope, hammer a nail, slice potatoes, brush teeth, and so on.

- Children can pretend to roller skate to the tempo of the drum. The drummer can add some surprise stops and starts.

- One child stands in the center of the circle of children. He pretends to be the flame of a candle on a birthday cake. Each child, alone, takes a turn to try to blow out the flame. As the tempo becomes slower and slower, all the children blow together and blow out the flame. The flame falls to the ground as it is put out.

- One child is the leader of the group. He may choose to hop, skip, walk, run, gallop, and so forth, in tempo with the drum. The others in the group must try to follow him exactly.

- Children may clap to the rhythm of the drum. Encourage them to stick with it, trying to clap together with the group.

- The children can pretend to be backpacking with a heavy load strapped on their backs. They start out with lots of energy and speed. As they walk on, they get more tired and walk slower and slower. Finally, exhausted, they fall slowly to the ground. (The drummer will lead the movement with the tempo of the drum.)

- Use homemade rhythm instruments. Play to the rhythm of the lead drum. The drummer will vary the tempo.

- Children can wave scarves, pompons, or long ribbons to the tempo of the music.

- Try a song with a pattern. Let the children make up their own verses. Examples:

  Verse 1. Chicken soup has a friend (3 times)
  And his name is soda crackers.

  Verse 2. Peanut butter has a friend (3 times)
  And her name is strawberry jelly.

  Verse 3. Mail box has a friend (3 times)
  And his name is letters.

Certain activities can also help children become aware of dynamics, the loudness/softness or intensity of music. It does a lot to give music a certain feeling or mood.

- Children can pretend to be tornados, turning around and around to a loud and fast section.

- Children walk, run, or skip quietly to soft music. As the music gets louder, they can make larger movements.

- Children beat their own drums, marching high and beating loudly to loud music. They can tiptoe and beat quietly to soft music.

- Children can pretend to be Raggedy Ann and Raggedy Andy dolls. They can move around in a floppy way. When the music goes down softly, they collapse to the floor.

- Sing or play "Pop Goes the Weasel." Children skip or gallop in a circle quickly. When they hear the world "pop," they jump high in the air and land in a squat.

- Children pretend to be flowers. When the music gets louder, they open up (open their arms). As the music gets softer, they close up again.

These activities will help children become aware of pitch and melody. Pitch is the highness or lowness of tones; melody is the pattern of notes as they move up and down the scale.

- Children get into two groups and echo each other line-by-line. The first group sings a simple line of a song. The second group "echoes" it, trying to match it as closely as possible. Do the whole song.

Using homemade or toy instruments gives children a sense of what it's like to create music.

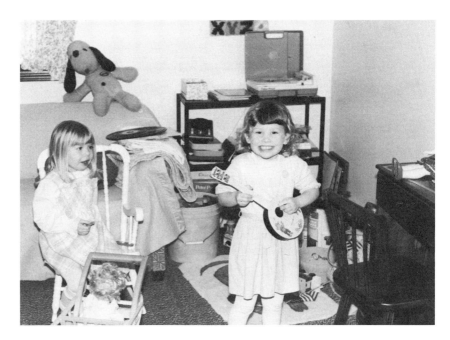

- Practice singing the melody into pretend microphones (made out of sticks, Lincoln Logs, or Tinker Toys).

- Let the children volunteer to sing "solo" lines of a song. Ella Jenkins' album entitled *Early, Early Childhood Songs* and *Burl Ives Sings Little White Duck and Other Children's Favorites* include songs that lend themselves to having the children join in at certain points.

- Parent hums the melody, then the children copy and hum the melody. Try a phrase at a time.

- Pretend to be birds flying. As the notes go higher on the scale, fly high; as the notes go lower, fly lower. When the music stops, the birds stop flying and land.

- Use "la-la-la" or "do-do-do" or some other syllable as you make up a simple melody. Let the children copy your melody. Then reverse and let a child volunteer to make up a series of notes (no words), and you and the other children copy his melody.

- Try to sing the melody in a high voice and then in a low voice.

- Sing one note. Let the children match their voices to that note. Try a few more notes—one at a time.

- Children raise arms up as notes go up, and lower arms as notes go down.

- Children walk forward as the notes go up and backward as the notes go down.

Some favorite songs of preschool children

"The Ants Go Marching"
"B-I-N-G-O"
"Did You Ever See a Lassie?"
"Do Your Ears Hang Low?"
"Down By the Station"
"The Farmer in the Dell"
"Head, Shoulders, Knees and Toes"
"Here We Go 'Round the Mulberry Bush"
"He's Got the Whole World in His Hands"
"Hokey, Pokey"
"I Love the Mountains"
"I Point to Myself"

"If You're Happy"
"I'm a Little Teapot"
"I've Been Workin' on the Railroad"
"John Jacob Jingleheimer Schmidt"
"Little Cabin in the Woods"
"London Bridge"
"Make New Friends"
"Michael, Row the Boat Ashore"
"Miss Mary Mac"
"The Muffin Man"
"Oh, Susanna"
"Old McDonald"
"Pick a Bale of Cotton"
"Polly, Put the Kettle On"
"Pop! Goes the Weasel"
"Rise and Shine"
"Row, Row, Row Your Boat"
"Sarasponda"
"She'll Be Comin' Round the Mountain"
"Skip to My Lou"
"Sing a Song of Sixpence"
"Sing Your Way Home"
"Ten Little Indians"
"Ten in a Bed
"This Old Man"
"Who Stole the Cookies from the Cookie Jar?"
"Who's That Knocking on My Window?"

Fingerplays

A poem set to music and action is called a fingerplay. Dancing fingers set to poetry or music become "finger puppets" in this form of creative expression. Words accompanied by actions bring language to life. By matching an action to words children must listen carefully and sequence their movements to the words of the song. Babies love playing "This Little Piggy" and "Pat-a-Cake" because it involves movement and song. Young preschoolers love rhymes using their whole body in action songs such as "Ring-Around-A-Rosy" and "Teddy Bear." Older preschoolers can make more refined finger movements such as those required in "Eensy Weensy Spider."

Fingerplays encourage creative movement and language. They help preschoolers use fine finger movements without being tedious or difficult. Often children who are usually quiet are fascinated with the actions

Fingerplays encourage creative movement and language while using small muscle skills.

and suddenly find themselves singing along. Fingerplays can provide a nice transition between other activities of your preschool day. During field trips or walks outside, they entertain and pass the time quickly.

Sign language is a sister to fingerplay. By communicating with their hands and bodies, children can use sign language to put thoughts into actions without words. We were amazed at how this form of expression intrigued our four-year-olds. *Sesame Street Sign Language Fun* is an excellent source for information on sign language at the preschool level. A trip to a deaf class brought the lesson to life.

Here are a few tips for presenting a new fingerplay:
1. Present it slowly, breaking down the necessary movements;
2. Tell it like a story put to action;
3. Let the children join when they feel comfortable;
4. Repetition ensures success;
5. Introduce one new fingerplay at a time, though old familiar ones can be repeated often.

A few fingerplays or action songs have been handed down through the generations such as the nursery rhymes "Pat-a-Cake" and "Teddy Bear." Some we remember from jump rope songs that were elementary school favorites. Don't be afraid to expand on a few or let the children dramatize their own poems and songs, too. A favorite book we discovered to be rich with ideas for fingerplays is *Ring-a-ring-o'roses: Stories, Games and Fingerplays for Pre-school Children*. It is available from the Flint Public Library, 1026 E. Kearsley, Flint MI 48502 USA.

Two other good books, both by Tom Glazer, are *Eye Winker, Tom*

Tinker, Chin Chopper and *Do Your Ears Hang Low?* Good fingerplays can also be found in *Wee Sing: Children's Songs and Fingerplays* by Pamela Beall and Susan Nipp.

To help you get started, some favorite fingerplays of preschoolers are listed here, titled by first line. (For complete words and finger/hand directions, go to the available sources.)

"Teddy bear, teddy bear turn around"
"The wheels on the bus go round and round"
"The eensy weensy spider climbed up the waterspout"
"There was a little turtle who lived in a box"
"There were two little blackbirds sitting on a hill"
"This is the mother so fine and good"
"Way up in the apple tree, two little apples smiled at me"
"Open, shut them, open, shut them, give a little clap"
"Five little monkeys jumpin' on the bed"
"Where is Thumbkin?"
"Johnny works with one hammer, one hammer, one hammer"
"Here are Grandma's spectacles"
"Hickory, dickory, dock"

How to have a bear hunt

Have the children sit facing you with their legs crossed. They repeat all your words and actions throughout the game. Begin by slapping your thighs alternately in a steady rhythm to simulate walking. Everything that is said, is said in this rhythm. Since the children repeat all your words and actions, only your lines are given.

(Start walking rhythm) Want to go on a bear hunt?/ Okay/ Oh, look/ I see a wheat field/ (stretch neck to look over wheat field) Can't get over it/ (Lower head to look under) Can't get under it /(swing body and head to look around) Can't get around it/ Let's go through it/ Okay/ Let's go/ (Rub hands together to make swishing sound of walking through the wheat.)

(Resume walking rhythm) Oh, look/ I see a river/ Can't get over it/ Can't get under it/ Can't get around it/ Let's swim it/ Okay/ Let's go/ (Make swimming motion with arms)

(Resume walking rhythm) Oh, look/ I see a bridge/ Can't get over it/ Can't get under it/ Can't get around it/ Let's cross it/ Okay/ Let's go/ (Beat fists or heels on floor.)

(Resume walking rhythm) Oh, look, I see a tree/ Can't get over it/ Can't get under it/ Can't get around it/ Let's climb it/ Okay/ Let's go/ (put hand over hand and rise until all come to full stand)/ Jump!/ (Jump and then all sit.)

Action songs and fingerplays with whole body movements can be a fun part of your preschool day.

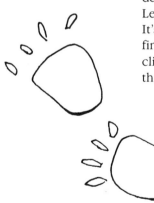

(Resume walking rhythm) Oh, Look/ (Stop rhythm, point, lower voice) I see a cave/ (suspenseful whisper) Can't get over it/ Can't get under it/ (Build excitement) Can't get around it/ Let's crawl through it/ Okay/ Let's go/ (Tiptoe with fingertips on knees) Tiptoe, tiptoe/ (Close eyes) It's dark in here/ Whoo/ Ohhh/ I feel something soft/ (Stroke knee with fingertips) and warm/ and furry/ It is a bear/ (Running rhythm, jump up, climb down tree, jump down, run, cross bridge, run, swim, run, go through wheat field, run home.)

Language: Senses and Words

See It, Say It

In our cooperative at-home preschool, I began to understand better what to expect of my child. I saw him learning and sharing creatively. I began to worry less about his academic skills and more about his attitudes. I began to understand that learning cannot be forced, that young children learn in spurts, and that happy children catch up if they are encouraged and not pressured.

Cheryl Sullivan, mother of Tara and Darren

Children learn about the world by using their senses. A baby takes in information about his surroundings through his senses. Some of a baby's first learnings are the smell of his mother, the taste of her milk, the feel of her heartbeat and the sound of her voice. He learns about himself through movement; he learns about the world through his senses. As he grows into toddlerhood and into the preschool years, he continues to use his senses to learn. When he has gathered enough information from his senses, he will begin to order and classify the experiences. The sensations children experience become meaningful when they are organized and reinforced over and over again.

Perception is the learning process midway between sensations and thought. Children understand before they can express their thoughts in words. The ability to talk to another person opens up a whole new form of learning. Yet, language has its foundation in movement and sensory awareness.

Arranging long rows of round containers in size or color sequence provides sensory information.

Sensory Awareness

The more a child is talked to, the sooner he will begin using words to order his world. He needs time to experience and time to connect the word with the idea. For example, a toddler sees water in a lake and understands it will feel wet when he touches it, just like the water from a faucet at home, because he has seen, touched, and heard the word water associated with these sensations. He listens to the sound of a wave or a splash and understands that he can experience the same sound in the bathtub or the lake or a pool. He sees and feels the "wet" quality of it. He reinforces his understanding of the word "water" through sensory processes.

Soon he is ready to learn about colors. Perhaps he first becomes aware of "redness" when a red ball is pointed out to him. Then he sees a red tractor and a red rose and hears the word "red." He sees the color and he begins to understand the meaning of the word. Now he must sort out the objects he sees that are red from all the other colors he sees. He connects the word "red" with the color even though various hues and intensities of red are seen. He is beginning to organize his perception of colors.

Later in your child's learning he refines his ability to organize sensory information even more. He will be able to sort shapes—triangles from squares—simply by touch. Having been exposed over and over to the shape and the word to identify it, his perception of "triangle" becomes internalized. His eyes and fingers provide the sensory information and his mind sorts and classifies the information. He remembers the word to express his experience and can now build further mathematical learnings from his perception of a triangle.

Sensory information is continuously being processed, refined, and labeled by a child's computer-like mind. Unlike a computer, he adds a touch of imagination and excitement to each newly learned experience.

Maria Montessori observed that the child takes a special interest in sensorial impressions of all kinds—in color, sound, shape, texture, and so forth, before the age of reasoning sets in. This is the special time to provide children with many opportunities to refine their sensory experiences. These learnings are the foundation for future readiness skills and concepts: mathematical, scientific, social, and so forth.

Guide your children's understanding of their world by providing playful practice with sensory experiences. It is important for children to begin ordering sensory experiences. The most fundamental is to simply help children properly **label** basic perceptions such as color names and shape names. Help children use words to label what they see, hear, feel, taste, and touch. Labeling basic descriptions such as hard or soft, light or dark, and so on, can be a challenging learning experience.

Matching and Sorting

Matching and sorting these sensory experiences will allow children to classify and discriminate between sensations. Sorting buttons or blocks by color, size, or shape is an example of a matching and sorting game. Sorting and matching letters, numbers, and words are more advanced discriminations your child will experience in later years. More ideas for matching and sorting will be listed at the end of this chapter.

 hether you help him or not, your preschooler will constantly be sorting out and combining and reorganizing and shifting the great mass of sensory impressions he is receiving and the perceptions he is acquiring, as he tries to understand the world around him. Often he makes mistakes. Often he draws incorrect conclusions. But usually the fault is not in his way of thinking or in his reasoning abilities. He just doesn't have enough of the right information to begin with.

Joan Beck

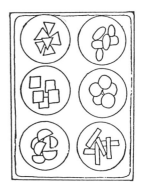

Memory

Another way to exercise sensory awareness is through memory games. Allow children to practice their touching or listening memory by using a blindfold. Ask children to sort and match fabric swatches by touch. Exercise visual memory by having children watch a movement and then try to imitate it. Try creating simple movement patterns. Challenge the children to move with you and then demonstrate whether they can remember the sequence. For example: Stand with your feet together, jump with feet apart, then jump with one foot forward and one foot back, then put both feet together again. Repeat a sequence several times, then let several children lead the group to create their own patterns.

When children exercise their memory, they become better able to remember in a specific order or sequence. Sequencing beads by shape and color and stringing them in a certain pattern is yet another example of sequencing. Remembering the sequence of letters in a word—spelling—is but another refinement of this skill.

 ncourage children to explore their surroundings and to play with objects so they can describe them and differentiate one from another. Try all the senses—sight, touch, smell, sound, and taste. Only through real experiences can children develop classification skills.

Rosalie Jensen and Deborah Spector

A special time slot can be provided for sensory awareness during your preschool day or it can be incorporated into an art, craft, math, reading readiness, or cooking activity. A variety of seeing, hearing, and touching games will help children exercise their language skills. A few materials to aid in matching and sorting include:

blocks of various sizes and colors	plastic shapes
fabrics of various textures	pictures from magazines
egg cartons for sorting	muffin tins for sorting
puzzles	playing cards
sound/music makers	various sized containers
small jars	

Games for learning to label colors, shapes, sounds, and textures

COLORS

Begin with primary colors first—red, blue, green, yellow; then secondary colors—purple, orange, pink, brown, etc.

- A Color Hunt: Walk around the house hunting for "red" objects. Try going outside, too. Look for butterflies and flowers in the garden or fields. Toys can also be used to label colors; have the children sort out all the red toys, then green, etc.

- My Book of Colors: Using pictures from magazines, let the children design each color page by pasting in their favorite red pictures. Use the primary colors for the assorted pages.

- Color Tray: Provide color squares to be paired with their match on the tray; try using two colors such as a red square with a blue circle in it to be matched, having about six color combinations.

- Rainbows: Using fingerpaints, watercolors, or chalk, let the children design a rainbow.

- "Mary Wore Her Red Dress": Sing: "Mary wore a red dress, red dress, red dress. Mary wore a red dress all day long" (add other clothing pieces: red hat, red shoes, etc.). "Who wore some pink pants, pink pants, pink pants? Who wore some pink pants all day long? Nancy wore some pink pants ... all day long."

SHAPES

Circle, square, rectangle, triangle, cross

- My Book of Shapes: Same as with colors, children need to be able to see the circle in a magazine picture of a car or bike; this activity involves some discrimination.

- Shape Mobile: Use a hanger and make shapes from construction paper to hang at varying lengths.

- Rope Shapes: Use a long rope to make a circle for the children to march on.

- Template Tracing: Cut simple shapes, about 12 inches in size, in heavy cardboard, and let the children color inside the shape; you might want to tape the paper under the template; later children can practice outlining the shape with a crayon.

- Traffic Signs: Discuss the shapes of the traffic signs or have the children construct the signs.

- Sorting Toys: Use shape sorting boxes (found in most toy departments).

- Stacking Toys: Stack boxes (squares) or cups (circles) of various dimensions; this adds the size element to labeling the shapes.

SOUNDS

- What Is It? Have children close their eyes and identify sounds:

Clap	Bounce ball	Knock on door
Open window	Snap rubberband	Crinkle paper
Whistle	Clear throat	Cut paper
Blow nose	Shuffle cards	Snap fingers
Turn page	Pour water	Jiggle money
Sneeze/cough	Sweep a broom	Close door

- "Old McDonald Had a Farm": This will help children identify animal sounds.

TEXTURES

- What Is It Made of? Let children discuss what material objects are made of. Use a piece of wood to teach hard and cotton to teach soft.

Games for learning to match, sort, or classify

- Picture Puzzles: Cut up a picture of a face—first in half, then several parts. Let the children identify it by the parts. Then try simple animal or food pictures cut into parts.

- Sorting Tray: Sort objects that go together: crayon, apple, pencil, pen, banana, dog, peach.

- Classify Objects: Sort objects or pictures by color, shape, size, age, or letters. Example: use various buttons and try sorting them by colors, size, or shape. Use an egg carton or

Sorting various items in egg cartons teaches children to match and classify.

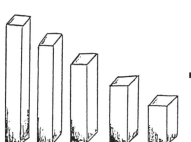

muffin tin to sort in. (This can also be done with various screws, nails, or coins.)

- Old Maid and Dominoes: These games are matching tasks.

- Color Chips: Use the paint store color samples to sort shades of colors.

- Cards: Sort a deck of cards by numbers, colors, or suits.

- Near or Far: Let the children identify sounds by how close or far away they are. Then try varying sounds by loud/soft, fast/slow, or same/different.

- Sound Bottles: Use 12 identical containers (small jars can be covered with construction paper of the same color); film containers and cigar holders work well. Fill six pairs with the same substance: beans, rice, sugar, rocks, air, noodles, etc. Let the children match the sounds. This also works well with odors; try using spices.

- Wooden rods: Make wooden rods (one-by-ones) of the same color, varying only in length. If you make the length difference consistent such as 5 inches, 10 inches, 15 inches, etc., they can make steps. The book *Teaching Montessori In the Home* by Elizabeth Hainstock explains this in detail.

- Shape Sorting: Use one shape cut from the same color construction paper but vary the size of the shape. For example, make eight circles of graduated sizes. Have the children sort the largest to the smallest. Later try having children sort polygons cut from the same color paper. Have them sort the shapes with the least number of sides to the most.

- Rhyming Words: Play a game of listening for letter sounds by having children listen for rhyming words. For example, you might say red/bed—those rhyme; then say tree/light—now those don't rhyme. Vary this a little by having the children turn so they can't see your lips; have them tell you if you are saying the same words or two different words. Try red/bed; stick/fix; puff/push; max/mask, etc. This is an excellent way to catch any hearing difficulties.

- Word Game: Discuss why two words are the same such as milk and water; a peach and an orange; then have them tell why the two words are different (milk and water are both wet, yet one is clear and the other white).

- Feely Bag: Let children identify various groups of food, toys, shapes, or letters by reaching into a bag (or box) with holes in it so they cannot see the object.

- Make a Material Scrapbook: Have categories to sort materials into such as hard, soft, smooth, rough, etc.

- Fabric Fun: Glue different textured fabrics on cards for the children to match. Silk, terry cloth, corduroy, and velvet work well.

- Rough and Smooth: Use various textured sandpapers glued to cards for children to arrange from rough to smooth. (Purchase several grades of sandpaper at the hardware store.)

 here is a big difference between expressive language and receptive language or understanding, which the child achieves much earlier.

Mary Ann Spencer Pulaski

Games for learning to use memory

- Concentration: Put four objects on a table for the children to remember, remove one object while the children close their eyes, and then ask them to identify the missing object. You might try removing more than one object when they become sharper at identifying the missing object. Also you may try to add an object instead.

- Shape or Color Concentration: As above but using only shapes and colors.

- Movement Memory: Move arms up, around, etc. Let the children watch, then try to repeat your movements.

- Follow Directions: Give simple directions for children to do, gradually add commands or make them more complex: "Open the door and clap two times"; "Open the door, touch your head, clap slowly three times," etc.

- Simon Says: Children must remember when to move by listening for the key words "Simon Says."

- Trees: Children must stand on tiptoe when you say "trees," stand straight when you say "soldier," or stoop when you say "ant."

- "Cookie Jar": Sing: (Group chants) "Who stole the cookie from the cookie jar? Tara (one child's name) stole the cookie from the cookie jar." Tara: "Who, me?" Children: "Yes, you." Tara: "Couldn't be." Children: "Then who?:" Tara: "Laura stole the cookie from the cookie jar!" Laura: "Who, me?" etc.

- Wrong Word: When saying a nursery rhyme, change a word and see if the children can catch you. Example: Jack and Jill went up the mountain to fetch a basket of water.

Games to enhance sequential memory

- Bead Patterning: String beads or noodles in a certain order. Try dying them different colors with food coloring and vinegar.

- Phone Numbers: Practice dialing their own phone numbers. If a child has trouble learning his phone number, try using a melody.

- Days of Week: Put the days of the week to a melody.

- Rap-A-Tap: Have children copy rhythms, tap on the table two times, then add a tap and vary the rhythm.

- "I Know an Old Lady Who Swallowed a Fly"

- Use pictures to tell a simple story. Cards can be purchased or made. An example might be a seed, plant, flower, and last, the fruit growing.

Forming Concepts

Once children have experimented again and again with sensory experiences and formed some basic perceptions, they will begin forming more abstract ideas. Simple observations soon become organized and lead to more complicated discoveries. Children begin to form concepts.

 e seldom appreciate the magnificent job that we have done in teaching our children the English language. We haven't been conscious of being language teachers, yet from the time our children have been babies we have repeated words to them, talked to them, and corrected their mispronunciations and faulty syntax.

Sandy Jones

A concept is similar to entering a dark room, experiencing the sensations in it, matching, sorting, and remembering until at last the light is turned on and a total "concept" of the room is formed. Nobody can turn on the light for another person; children develop at different paces—concepts will come in their own good time.

Concepts are best developed through firsthand experiences. Children need to have many chances to hear new words, to label sensations, and to practice expressing them with words.

Parents can provide children with experiences for building this kind of vocabulary by using word-guessing games. Words you can stress for three- to five-year-olds include words dealing with the concepts of opposites, quantities, space, and time. Along with learning the means to express thoughts, new concepts will be forming including ideas about animals, foods, air, machines, and people. You will provide activities and materials to enhance these discoveries. Your preschool activities will begin to help children answer some of their own questions.

In order to guide children in forming more abstract ideas, you will need to enhance their descriptive vocabulary when making observations. The following word games can be played at any time in your preschool day.

 ccording to Piaget, language appears along with the other symbolic functions such as deferred imitation and make-believe play. Like them, it has its roots in sensory-motor intelligence, in all the learning which precedes the ability to represent physical reality in mental images.

Mary Ann Spencer Pulaski

Games to encourage descriptions

- "I'm Thinking of..." Describe something and let the children try to name it. "I'm thinking of something that's big, it has two doors, it is very cold inside, and we store food in it (if necessary, say it's usually found in the kitchen)." Let the children try some, too. Try describing animals, foods, clothes, etc.

- "Who's Who?" Try describing another child in the group, giving one clue at a time. Describe clothes and facial features that the others can see first. Later you can play this game using descriptions which cannot be seen such as his family, address, pets, or any other traits that set him apart. The correct guesser gets his turn to describe a person next.

- "Where Am I?" Try describing a place such as:

  a playground   a school
  a church   a supermarket

- Ask the children to finish a sentence:

  I like to go to the ...   I am ...
  My favorite food is ...   I know how to ...
  I can ...

- The Name Game: See if the children can

  name three things that have wheels
  name four red things
  name five outdoor playthings
  name four things in the sky

Opposite words

Opposites pose more difficult concepts for preschoolers to grasp. A few simple ones can be fun.

- Try playing this tricky game:

  "You say **yes**, I say **no**!"
  "I say **up**, you say ____?"
  "I want to **go**, you want to ____?"

- By using a simple story, the children can begin supplying opposites.

  Once there was a fat lady cat who lived with a man cat who was not fat at all. He was ____. The big fat cat liked to eat a great big breakfast but the man cat did not eat a big break-fast. He ate a ____ breakfast. One day the lady cat said to the man cat, "Let's go out and buy a new hat for you." "No," said the man cat. "I don't want a new hat. I like my ____ one."

- Some common opposites three-, four-, and five-year-olds can have fun with include:

up/down	hard/soft	right/left
funny/sad	good/bad	fat/thin
clean/dirty	old/new	warm/cool
open/close	long/short	laugh/cry
off/on	small/large	high/low
right/wrong		

Quantitative and spatial words

Concepts dealing with numbers, size, quantity, weight, and distance help develop a mathematical vocabulary. Help make the children aware of these concepts by continually asking for details through questions:

  How many red flowers do you see?
  Which one is the biggest?
  Which one is the shortest?

Children will begin to orient themselves in space and time by using lan-guage. A simple following directions game can introduce some spatial vocabulary.

  "Put the book **on** the chair."
  "Now put it **under** the chair."
  "Now put it **over** the chair."
  "Now put it **next** to the chair."

Stacking blocks can teach spatial concepts such as over/under, top/bottom, left/right. (Shown here is a counter top scrap used to mark a play space area or to build with blocks on an uneven surface. These are sometimes available from lumber yards.)

Some other spatial concepts the children can work with include:

in/out	near/far	around/inside
over/under	left/right	pick up/put down
in back of/in front of	top/bottom	here/there

Time words

Learning concepts relating to time is influenced by a child's experience with events. Tara was excited about Christmas and wanted to know how long a wait she had. To tell her it was a week away was impossible for her to understand; to say it would be tomorrow was still vague to this three-year-old, but when told it was two "sleeps" away she nodded with understanding. Children live in the "here and now." Only by exposing them to routines in their daily activities do they gain a sense of time. We must constantly reinforce the language of time with concrete daily examples. For instance, Darren once declared, "I want to make playdough—right now!" Saying we would be able to make it in an hour would have been fruitless without drawing upon an experience he could more easily relate to. When he was told he could make it after lunch or before naptime he relaxed.

Four-year-olds can become involved with planning future events or discussing past events. These plans enrich their understanding of time and provide an opportunity to use the language of time:

yesterday/today/tomorrow
names of the months/
  a month before

never/always/sometimes
days of the week/a week ago
special days/holidays/birthdays
calendars
clocks
seasons

Try making a clock book by either finding pictures or drawing pictures that represent certain events during the day. Eating breakfast, getting out of bed, playing, or sleeping. This gives the children a sense of order.

Ordering and sequencing life is a big chore. Concepts continue to develop all through life. They must be reinforced through many varied experiences; they are not memorized.

Learning bits and pieces of various concepts will enable children to begin to use logical thinking and reasoning. A young child's reasoning is not yet refined at the preschool age. By providing a variety of questions and experiences you provide a good foundation for logical and creative thinking. A young child's reasoning is not yet refined at the preschool age.

oncepts cannot be fully understood by looking at pictures or by memorizing the words. They have to be experienced. Concepts are not learned overnight: they must be met in a variety of settings over a long period of time.

Elizabeth Gregg and Judith Knotts

Communication: Listening and Story-telling

Once upon a Time

My son was well prepared to start school. He'd been part of a group where he learned sharing, listening, taking turns, a little structure, and a few school readiness skills.

Colleen Weiland, mother of Mike, Eric, Amy, and Matthew

Learning to use language to express themselves is a form of communication that children are learning at around two, three, and four years old. Soon they become quite talkative and able to express their feelings, thoughts, dreams, and desires. As parents working with young children you will want to encourage good communication between yourselves and the children. You will also encourage good communication among the children when they speak to one another.

Responsible communication includes good listening habits and the ability to talk clearly so others can understand what you are saying. Children can use their communicating ability in a creative way, too. Listening to stories that are read aloud encourages a desire to read; making up stories requires sequencing of events and using words to describe ideas. Children need to have opportunities to listen and to share ideas in order to develop and exercise their language abilities.

Encouraging Good Listening

Listening and speaking go hand in hand. If children have the opportunity to be listened to by concerned adults, their level of achievement will be higher because they become actively involved in learning. Children begin to listen because they have a desire to understand what is being said. Parents can excite a child's curiosity about what is being said in a number of ways.

In order to help a child use effective listening you need to set a good example. Provide an accepting atmosphere with the children. Parents should be cautious about ordering or commanding, lecturing, warning, or blaming children. Concentrate on details; describe rather than analyze. For example, saying "I see paper on the floor" is easier to respond to than "Pick up that paper; you sure are sloppy today!" You will have lots of opportunities to give directions and to guide, but do it in a gentle, understanding manner.

If the occasion arises that the children seem to be losing interest, not listening, or interrupting, then stop. You are losing them. Are they bored? Frustrated? Could they just be over-excited, bubbling over with curiosity? Don't force an activity that stifles a child's desire to listen and learn. You need to take a quick break, to alter the project, or drop it entirely if the children are losing interest. By the same token, if a project or activity is over stimulating them, try to get them to pay attention with gentle guidance and loving limits. Establish some quick rules to maintain control and yet continue their enthusiasm. Ask the children for suggestions when you are establishing rules.

Children will listen best if they know they will be listened to. Try

Children can take turns retelling a familiar story in their own words to show that they have listened carefully and understand it.

to understand what a child is feeling and what he means by interpreting his words. Try repeating what a child has said back to him in your own words. By doing this, you accept his feelings and encourage him to express himself. It helps you to listen more carefully. For example, during a craft project involving coloring and cutting, Timmy said, "This is silly." The parent-leader keyed in on his feelings and tried to get to the reason for them. Was he bored, frustrated, or just being uncooperative? She commented, "This project doesn't please you; you think it's silly." Tim responded, "Coloring is stupid." Parent continued: "It makes you angry; you are upset about coloring?" Tim: "It's hard and I'm always the last one done and mine is ugly." Parent: "Maybe we could change this project so it could be more fun. Let's talk about it." Tim was not just being uncooperative; he was frustrated. By involving him in the decision-making, the parent helped him begin to feel worthy and less defeated.

Through this interchange, the parent began to understand Timmy's problem. She acknowledged his feelings of frustration. She helped him to deal with his feelings without being critical or demanding. Timmy was able to accept his feelings because he was actively participating in altering the project so he could handle it.

Thomas Gordan's book *Parent Effectiveness Training* has some excellent examples of this reflective listening technique. *How To Talk So Kids Will Listen and Listen So Kids Will Talk* by Adele Faber and Elaine Mazlish is another excellent book on listening and communicating with children. (Both are listed in the Appendix.)

By allowing yourself to "get inside" the child, and accepting his feelings, you let him know you care about him. Children can become responsible and independent in an accepting atmosphere.

When you work to establish a warm accepting attitude about listening for the children, they will learn to use this just as effectively as they learn to listen.

Some key phrases to get children to express themselves include:

tell me about it ...
tell me more ...
let's discuss it ...
sounds like you want me to know ...

Children also need to be encouraged to listen to one another. If good listening habits are established by the parent and encouraged among the children, the children will listen responsibly when directions are being given. It is more profitable to wait for the group's attention in order to give directions rather than repeat yourself several times later. Use a sign—such as a finger to your lips—and get eye contact with your listeners, then make your point. Don't ramble or you will lose their interest quickly.

Another way to have children practice effective listening is to have them listen to the weather report and then tell what they heard. Or create a mock grocery store. One child pretends to be the grocery clerk and each child must remember a grocery list to buy.

Children soon learn to understand that what others have to say is important. Though they still have difficulty remaining patient while others speak, treat interruptions with respect. Explain that you will listen to him or her when you are through listening to the first person. Then as soon as possible, give attention to the waiting person.

Encouraging Responsible Communication

Children need to be able to express themselves so others can understand them. By encouraging them to learn their address, age, or phone number, you begin to help children be responsible for themselves as they experience more of the outside world.

One way to get serious about communicating effectively is by allowing children to practice proper telephone procedures. Teach children to respect the phone. Create a drama in which a child becomes responsible for calling the operator to get help for his mother who has just fallen down the stairs. The children usually respond when given the seriousness of the situation. Another telephone tip to teach children is not to talk to anyone if an adult is not available. Without frightening children about strangers, teach them that they do not have to give out unnecessary information unless an adult nearby says it's okay. Teach them to say, "My mother is busy now but you can call back later."

Children can be given the opportunity to tell about birthdays, Christmas, Halloween, or vacations. Encourage them to talk about the details. Allow comments and questions from the other children as long as nobody insults another person. Sharing time is more than showing off. It can be a time for children to think about the past, to sequence events, and plan for the future. Whenever possible, encourage children to participate in planning activities, discussing field trips, and talking about feelings. In this way you establish a healthy respect for each other. Communication comes more easily.

 our-and-a-half-year-olds are great discussers.
Reading a book about fires might lead to a long
discussion about the pros and cons of fires.

Frances Ilg and Louise Bates Ames

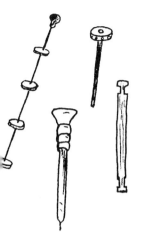

Creative Expression

By encouraging creative expression through stories, music, poetry, or drama you allow children to experience the enjoyable aspects of language. Preschoolers have a special, fresh way of looking at the world and expressing their feelings. How can parents encourage and capture some of this creativity? Even though preschoolers can't yet write, they just need a chance to experience poetry, stories, and drama, along with a little help from you, to bring out their creativity.

There are several things that seem to automatically get little ones talking. You can use toy telephones, a tape recorder, or a microphone. It can be anything from a Lincoln Log covered with aluminum foil to a real microphone. A plain box with one side cut out can become a television set and a bent coat hanger can become rabbit ear antennas. Tuning knobs made from buttons finish the look. Puppets and puppet theaters are also great gimmicks to encourage language usage.

Reading Aloud

By reading stories aloud, you encourage an enthusiasm for reading that will enhance a child's desire to learn to read. Stories have been used for years to teach as well as to entertain. There is an art to telling or reading stories to young children that will make the story come alive and aid in the understanding of it. In the *Read Aloud Handbook,* Jim Trelease makes a few suggestions: "Remember that reading aloud comes naturally to very few people. To do it successfully and with ease you

Add some excitement to stories you read aloud by changing your voice with the various characters, slowing down to add some suspense, and speeding up to match the actions being described.

must practice." Read slowly; many a story loses its impact because it is read too fast. Let your imagination and acting ability flow freely and use plenty of expression.

Put new life into retelling familiar stories with the magic ingredient of questions. But don't turn it into a quiz! By asking questions you involve your listeners; open-ended questions with no right or wrong answer get thinking started. You can ask questions before you begin reading.

Talk about the main character if pertinent and warn your listeners about the predicament he gets into. For instance, before reading *Peter and the Wolf,* ask the children what they would do if a wolf came around their house. "Do you know what it means to be brave? Let's listen to this story and see if Peter was very brave." This is also a great opportunity to help children master new words. Introduce new words while reading the book, too, as long as you don't detract from the story's impact.

 eluctant readers or unusually active children frequently find it difficult to just sit and listen. Paper, crayons, and pencils allow them to keep their hands busy while listening.

Jim Trelease

Another good way to help children get involved more fully is to ask how the characters feel at certain points in the story. When the story is finished, you can get children to compare how the characters felt to how the children have felt in similar situations. Lots of descriptive feeling words can be encouraged such as: lonely, tired, warm, angry, hurt, embarrassed, and so on.

Children love lots of repetition in a story; let them join in whenever possible. Retelling familiar stories encourages children to read along with you. The more drama you can incorporate into your story, the better. Let each billy goat in *The Three Billy Goats Gruff* speak with a deeper voice. Whisper during suspenseful parts and speed up during the chase. "You can't catch me; I ran away from a little old lady, a little old man, the cow, and I can run away from you, too. Run, run, run, as fast as you can; you can't catch me, I'm the gingerbread man!" Use actions when telling a story to captivate your audience. While reading *The Little Engine That Could,* dramatize the engine with arm movements and adjust the reading pace with "I think I can, I think I can, I think I can."

*O*ne excellent means of building the confidence, imagination, and vocabulary of pre-readers is through the use of "wordless" books—picture books consisting of simple plots but no words. The pictures tell the story.

Jim Trelease

Picture books

Picture books provide a basic story that needs interpretation; the children bring it to life. Children can be given the opportunity to interpret picture books in their own words. They note details in the pictures in order to accurately describe the actions and the feelings of the characters.

In the picture book, *One Frog Too Many,* children are given the opportunity to interpret feelings, to discuss motives, and to predict the story outcome. They get a chance to solve the character's problem and think about his alternatives. Each child will "read" the story a little differently—some will add more details, some will develop characters, and some will add their own action-packed details. One exciting way to have children read a picture book is to tape-record them while they read. Each child will read in his own style, bringing the story to life.

Reading is understanding words. Picture books provide the opportunity for children to play with words, even as pre-readers. Older children will also enjoy "reading" an occasional picture book.

When picking out stories for the children, ask your local librarian to refer you to highly motivating stories for preschoolers. Another excellent resource is *The Read Aloud Handbook* by Jim Trelease. This book

A visit to the library lets children pick out the books they want.

lists favorite stories for children and also discusses the question: Why read aloud? Some favorite playgroup read-alouds include:

> *Bedtime for Frances* by Russell Hoban
> *Blueberries for Sal* by Robert McCloskey
> *Corduroy* by Don Freeman
> *Frog and Toad Are Friends* by Arnold Lobel
> *Ira Sleeps Over* by Bernard Weber
> *The Little Engine That Could* by Watty Piper
> *Little Toot* by Hardie Gramatky
> *Madeline* by Ludwig Bemelmans
> *Mike Mulligan and His Steam Shovel* by Virginia Lee Burton
> *The Story of Ferdinand* by Munro Leaf
> *Where the Wild Things Are* by Maurice Sendek
> *Chicken Soup with Rice* by Maurice Sendek
> *Noisy Nora* by Rosemary Wells
> *Can I Keep Him?* by Steven Kellog
> *Caps for Sale* by Esphyr Slobodkina
> *The Story about Ping* by Marjorie Flack & Kurt Weise
> *Swimmy* by Leo Lionni
> *The Do-Something Day* by Joe Lasker

Drama

One way to help children listen more carefully to a story is to tell them they will get to act out the story when it's finished. Then, after you finish reading it once, you go back and narrate the story, pausing when it is a certain character's turn to speak. The children bring the story to life. It doesn't matter if the children remember the lines exactly for by narrating you have control of the story. By acting out the story the children demonstrate that they understand the meaning of the story. A modification of this technique might be to tape-record the narration allowing pauses for the children to say their parts. This worked especially well with one group of four-year-olds using the old favorite *Goldilocks and the Three Bears*. The children invited their parents and put on a "play." They each had a part. The story was narrated on a tape and the children provided the action. For the broken chair, a child knelt down on all fours in a chair position and, when Goldilocks sat on him, they both crashed to the floor creating a little comic relief.

Puppet shows can also use this technique. Another group really enjoyed presenting *Peter and the Wolf* with stick puppets. First the parent read the book aloud. Then she made the stick puppets to retell the

Children can add their own dialogue and actions as you narrate a favorite story.

story aloud to the children. Next they listened to the instrumental version of the story on a record while the children pretended they were the characters in the story. Through this repetition of the same story in several different ways, the children experienced it more fully. A culminating activity to this dramatization might be to go and see a live performance or a movie of the story.

After you have read a story, there are several ways to elicit discussion about it. Try changing the story: "What if in *The Cat in the Hat* the cat didn't come back to help clean up?" "What if Peter Rabbit hadn't lost his jacket; would his mother know what happened?" Then try letting the children tell how they would feel trapped in the farmer's field. Did they ever have an experience like Peter in real life?

Let the children retell the story in their own words. Have them sit around in a circle and take turns adding the next part of the story. This involves sequencing the events and a great deal of memory.

Another idea is to let the children come up with their own group story round-robin style. Here are some tips for group story-telling:

1. Just let the children add lines spontaneously as they think of them.

2. Establish a round-robin sequence in order to ensure that all the children get a chance to participate.

3. Or let just one child at a time tell the whole story and then the next child tells his story.

4. Use picture books without words for the children to "read."

Story-telling

Children can be expressive if given a topic to make up a story about. To involve children, the stories suggested should be very simple and free flowing. Parents might need to remind themselves that when a child's mind is allowed to flow freely, the story may not have a purpose or theme or even be very logical. And they probably will not have a conclusion to their story. But the important thing is that their thoughts are their own. You can learn more about what makes them happy or sad or what things frighten them. Story-telling helps children develop creative thinking that will help them in later life.

Here are a few topics that will encourage children to tell a story:

Ghosts	Leprechauns
Animals	Children's playthings
Olden days	Made-up characters
Dinosaurs	Outer space

Some sample story suggestions to get the children started might be:

- Once when I went out for trick-or-treat I went with my friend Amy. She was dressed up like Cinderella and I was Oscar the Grouch. Then we met a ghost named Bumpy.

- When I was shoveling the snow, I moved a big pile of snow which covered a strange deep hole with a very soft blue light in it. I wondered what could be in there so I carefully and quietly stepped in. I found ...

- Tommy and Timmy were cleaning up their toys one night before going to bed. Just as they picked up the last of their blocks and flipped the light switch off, they both heard a funny little voice say, "Boys, you forgot to give me a hug and a kiss good night." They stared into the dark playroom and wondered if the voice belonged to their favorite space alien, ET. So Tommy and Timmy crept back in and ...

If the children do come up with an interesting story, let them try drawing simple pictures about their story to illustrate a group book. And don't forget that parents have a wonderful ability to make up stories, too. Let your feelings run free and let the story flow; you may surprise yourself with your creativity.

Personal books may be possible with older children. Try letting them finish starter sentences such as:

I feel happy when ...	If I could ...
I feel sad when ...	I love ...
I just learned ...	

Then write down each child's response. Some children will need more help at this activity than others. Staple each child's book together and let him illustrate the book with drawings, magazine pictures, or photos.

Poetry for Preschoolers

Poetry for preschoolers? By all means! Preschoolers are fascinated with words and language; it's like a new toy that they must fully experience. At the ripe age of two, three, and four years old, children know no limits to imagination. Sentence structure is not restricted by the formal rules of our language as it may be by age ten.

Nursery rhymes are some of a child's first experiences with poetry. Children enjoy the rhythm of poetry and the images they can conjure up with words. A cow jumped over the moon? How silly!

Rhyming words are insignificant to these budding poets though they do sense when a poem works. Tara responded enthusiastically when she was reminded to:

> *Get dressed*
> *Brush your hair*
> *Brush your teeth*
> *But don't forget your underwear!*

Encourage children to express their thoughts in a rhythmical manner and let the words flow. Shel Silverstein has some poetry that is appropriate for preschoolers in *Where the Sidewalk Ends*. His work is real and quite funny.

When trying to create poetry with preschoolers, provide them with an idea. A suggestion to start the words flowing is all that is necessary.

> *Rain, rain, rain*
> *Look at the rain*
> *A big sprinkler in the sky!*

This poem came about during a rainstorm with the suggestion: Tell me about rain. Does it remind you of anything? Just using everyday events can trigger poetic expression. A few sample poems about rainbows and thunder, made up by you, can help set the mood.

Four-year-olds love rhyming names. Tara's imaginary friends included Tara, Mara, Sara, and Bara. She was experimenting with rhyming by changing the beginning sounds. This is the foundation of phonics, learning to listen for sounds. However, poetry should not be restricted to rhyme.

Before snacktime, one playgroup provided a time to give thanks. This produced some very inspiring prayer poetry. Children took turns going around the table telling what each was thankful for.

Thank you for the rain that makes the flowers grow
Thank you for the food
Thank you for my mom and dad
Thank you for the world

This quiet time was an inspiration to all. Our little ones have such a fresh way to look at life!

In *Mothering* magazine (Summer 1982), Connie Biewald writes about poetry with preschoolers. She suggests that preschool is an ideal place to encourage the composition and appreciation of poetry. She advises giving a child a poetry idea in order to help start thoughts flowing. She provides some very good examples.

- Start every line with:

  I wish ...
  I used to ... but now ...
  If I could be ... I would
  I'm sad when ...

- In every line say something about:

  bugs   grown-ups
  hamsters   kids

- Make up a poem or story that:

  begins with the sound your name begins with
  ends with the sound your name ends with
  begins with the sound your name ends with

- Invent a magic spell!

- Describe what you see:

  in a particular painting
  in a particular photograph
  in a particular sculpture

- With my magic

  glasses, I can ...
  muscles, I can ...
  wings, I can ...

Colors and numbers are often repeated in young children's poetry. A simple poem by Sarah demonstrates a two-year-old's infatuation with colors and numbers:

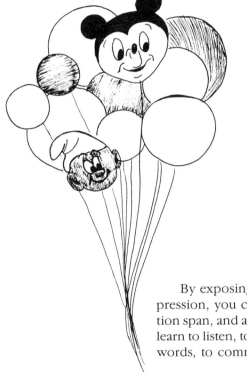

I like balloons
I like red balloons
I like green balloons
I like purple balloons
I like yellow balloons
I like two green balloons
I like two red balloons
I like Mickey Mouse balloons
I like Smurf balloons
I like to go in the sky with balloons

By exposing children to read-aloud stories and also to creative expression, you create a foundation for creative thinking, a good attention span, and a good feeling about making words work. You help them learn to listen, to organize their thoughts, to express themselves, in other words, to communicate.

Discovery: Letters, Sounds, and Reading

Breaking the Secret Code

My daughter has an excellent early foundation for learning to read. In fact, she can already read some words because of this experience.

Becky Henderson, mother of Maren, Dustin, Kirsten

Around four years of age, children can be very curious about letters and sounds and the process of reading. They are eager to learn a new skill, to break the secret code in the books they listen to and look at. Learning to interpret all those squiggly lines will open up a whole new world for them to explore. Like finding a secret code that is waiting to be deciphered, the task of learning to read challenges their eager minds.

Young children are in the process of labeling and sorting the events and materials in their lives. They spend an enormous amount of energy mastering their language. By four years old, a child's command of speech will often trigger an interest in printed words and reading. Only when children can speak with reasonable surety can they begin to break the reading code.

Generally, nursery schools and preschools provide encouragement in the areas of social, mental, and movement development. They provide experiences through exposure to new materials in order to help children meet the demands of the more disciplined routines they will encounter in elementary school. A small group such as an at-home preschool can and should provide good language development. However, due to the wide variation in abilities of preschoolers, the question of introducing reading in a group is often debated.

To Read or Not to Read?

The issue of when to introduce the letter names and sounds or writing the alphabet can be an emotionally charged subject. Individual attitudes from parent to parent will differ. In addition, the requirements of various school districts will differ; some require mastery of the alphabet upon entrance to kindergarten while others expect little or no exposure to the alphabet. Because of these differences, parents must carefully evaluate the needs of their children. The decision to introduce reading skills should be based on what is best for your children—not the expectations of others.

You can become as confused by the wide variation of requirements for entering kindergarten as by the differing opinions offered by the experts. In *The Magical Child,* Joseph Pearce expresses his concern over the separation of the child's sense of self from his actions, thoughts, and experiences. The written word is made of letters arranged to stand for symbols which stand for words which then stand for things or events. Pearce refers to the power of self, logical thinking, and imagination that must be established before moving on to more symbolic thinking. He contends that early reading will negate imaginative and creative thinking.

Piaget, a noted psychologist, is concerned that children need to be given opportunities to think and to work out problems through trial and error before they can learn the alphabet or reading. Piaget describes concrete operations as a stage children reach by about seven years old; it is at this stage that a child can begin to think logically about things he has experienced and manipulate them symbolically, as when learning to read.

Maria Montessori believed that the young child should become familiar with letters by using several senses. She recommended that children use sandpaper letters so they could feel the letter shape. Montessori also used a "movable" alphabet in which children could match individual letters to the same letters on word cards.

Montessori encouraged having children learn about letters by forming the letters in a tray of cornmeal or sand in order to get a better "feel" for the shape. Montessori observed that children from three and a half to four and a half enjoyed working with the letters from a sensory level—seeing and feeling the shapes and hearing the sounds each letter makes. In Montessori's schools "the children were not taught the names of the letters, but only the sounds they represent. Further, they were encouraged to trace the forms of sandpaper letters with their 'writing fingers,' i.e., the first and second fingers of the right hand*" (*Maria Montessori: Her Life and Work* by E. M. Standing).

---

*Today it is generally recognized that the left hand is just as good as the right for a left-handed person.

Montessori also observed that children become interested in writing letters before they have the desire to learn to read. They enjoy manipulating letters, forming the letters, and learning letter sounds before becoming interested in reading words or sentences. *Teaching Montessori in the Home—The Preschool Years* by Elizabeth G. Hainstock has some illustrations that show how to implement more of Montessori's ideas.

Donald Emery, a noted educator and author of *Teach Your Preschooler to Read,* believes that by age four, children have all the necessary experience for learning to read successfully—with the following comments. He feels that basic reading should and can be taught to four-year-olds by their parents, at home. For the most successful results, the learning situation should **not** be in a group. Parents are the most sensitive to the natural interest, readiness, and enthusiasm their child has toward reading. Parent-child time is flexible and praise can be more effective at home. Futhermore, parents can provide the one-to-one relationship needed to learn this skill at an early age.

Reading is an issue that must be discussed among the parents of your at-home preschool group. As parents you must decide whether or not to introduce letters, sounds, and/or writing with your children. You must decide if you wish to introduce reading in the group, at home on an individual basis, or not at all. We would suggest that if reading—that is, the introduction of words, letters, sounds, or writing—is done with the group, only short segments of time should be scheduled for these activities.

Fundamentals for Reading

There are many schools of thought on how reading should be introduced; yet most experts agree there are several fundamental skills needed to ensure success in reading. Whether or not you opt to become involved with the process of reading with your group, you should try to include these fundamental skills in your preschool day.

Language experience

Provide lots of language experience, the learning of words and meanings. To read, a child must relate to what he knows if there is to be any real understanding of the printed word. By providing experience with talking and building vocabulary, you help children express their ideas and articulate their words properly. If a stranger cannot easily understand what a child says, then he is probably not ready to work on sounds or letters.

The next time you read *Goldilocks and the Three Bears* ask the children what porridge is. The answer may range from oatmeal to soup.

Take this opportunity to help the children master a new word. "What was Miss Muffet eating—curds and whey? Did you ever eat curds and whey?" Here's an opportunity to discover where milk comes from and a whole lot of interesting facts about other dairy products. (See Chapter 20 for more ideas on reading aloud and encouraging new words.)

Listening experiences

Provide a variety of listening experiences. When the children are following directions and listening to what others have to say, they must learn to understand another's meaning. This is similar to—and a prerequisite for—reading. Through speech you can help your listeners understand your meaning by emphasizing certain words or phrases. For example, when you give a simple direction such as "Put the book over there," you have several choices in helping your listener understand you. You can emphasize certain words with gestures: "Put the book over there" (pointing). You can add words: "Put the book over there on the table next to my notebook." You can verbally check for understanding. Reading does not allow for this extra information.

Likenesses and differences

Help children become aware of likenesses and differences. Reading requires fine discriminations. Children must be able to distinguish between "u" and "n," "b" and "d," "s" and "z." They must become aware of sound differences such as "m" and "n," "f" and "z," and between "s" and "z." They must be aware of directional orientations as in "on" and "no," "saw" and "was." For writing they must learn the concepts of top, bottom, up, down, under, across, and have an understanding of the left to right movement used in reading. You can help develop these discriminations in many ways by helping children become aware of likenesses and differences in everyday events, by letting children sort the silverware in the tray, by letting them pick out clothes with matching colors, by choosing puzzle pieces for the proper spaces, and so on. (See Chapters 19 and 22 on Language and Math for more ideas.) Many of your preschool daily activities involve practice with skills needed for these discriminations.

Reading aloud

Develop a love for books by reading stories and poems galore. Children who enjoy listening to stories bring a strong motivation to the task of learning to read. By providing books for them to look at independently and magazines for them to "read," you can motivate children to become interested in reading. (See Chapter 20.)

Talk about the stories you read with the children. In *Goldilocks and the Three Bears,* you might want to discuss whether the biggest was the best or ask what it was that Goldilocks should not have done. Why can't you enter a strange house when no one is home? How did Goldilocks feel?

 elevision is the direct opposite of reading. In breaking its program into eight-minute commercial segments (shorter for shows like "Sesame Street"), it requires and fosters a short attention span. Reading, on the other hand, requires and encourages longer attention spans in children.

Jim Trelease

 eadiness means ... (1) a sense of self-worth, (2) a sense of trust, (3) curiosity, (4) the capacity to look and listen carefully, (5) the capacity to play, and (6) times of solitude.

Fred Rogers

Planning and thinking experiences

Increase children's attention span by reading exciting stories to them. Ask questions, act out stories, predict outcomes, and try changing story endings. Encourage children to be detectives, listening for details, interpreting "picture" books, and talking about how a problem can be solved before you read the ending. Concentration games that exercise memory and sequencing pictures and events in the proper order provide the foundation for reading skills.

Introducing Reading Skills

How can you introduce reading if you decide you want to do so? The following ideas for introducing letter names, letter sounds, letter shapes, and words can be used in a group. Each group of preschoolers differs a little and some may be eager for reading while others don't care at all. Let the children tell you if this is a good activity to continue by their level of interest. If they "burn out," you will know it. Devote only small segments of time to these activities.

Alphabet books

One at-home preschool excited the children's interest in letter names by purchasing commercial alphabet books that used stickers. The parents were able to pull out the letter or letters they wanted to introduce as they saw necessary. The children had to match the correct sticker to the letter page and then paint or color the pages. They were also able to purchase several alphabet letter card games which they played in the group. This fun little activity lasted about five minutes at each preschool session and it was greatly enjoyed.

Command cards

In the book *Teaching Montessori in the Home—The Preschool Years,* "command cards" are described. These cards are a way to introduce the written word to children by associating an action with a word. They are written on large cards in large letters so the group can see them and perform the action from a slight distance away. Action words you may choose to use include: "clap," "jump," "stand," "hop," and, of course, "stop." When making your command cards, be sure to use the proper manuscript printing, with lower case letters rather than capitals.

Introduce only one action word and the word "stop" during the beginning lesson. As the children's interest and curiosity permits, gradually add more commands in later lessons—one word at a time. As a

Providing books and magazines for children to enjoy on their own helps them develop an interest in reading.

Command cards introduce the written word by teaching the children to associate an action with a word.

group, this works nicely because the children who can read the words do the action and the others follow quickly; thus word and action become reinforced. Children really like this activity because it involves movement and learning new words in an enjoyable way.

es, you have to teach reading and math skills. They are necessary. But don't make the mistake of thinking they are the purpose of teaching or even the heart of the curriculum. Reading skills are facts; they have no life unto themselves. They cannot be loved, they cannot motivate.

Jim Trelease

Introducing letters by letter names

If you choose to introduce letter names rather than letter sounds, this very traditional method might be of interest to you. There is much controversy between the experts as to which method is easier for children to learn—either letter names only, letter sounds only, or combining both. Some children will be ready to combine the letter names with the sounds of the letters while other children will become frustrated and confused. Don't let all this controversy bother you. The children will let you know how much "reading" they can handle by their interest and attitude. Your job as a parent is to be sensitive to what the children are telling you by their actions.

Paul McKee, a noted author in the field of elementary reading, suggests this method of introducing letter names to a group. Introduce the letters in four separate groups so that no one group has letter forms that are easily confused. Use index cards for each letter. Make a duplicate set of capital letter cards for each group of letters. Have a second set for the lower case letters. Begin with the capital letters.

Letter Groups

1. M, U, D, F, I, G

2. W, E, S, T, B, X

3. P, A, N, C, K, J, Z

4. H, O, V, R, L, Y, Q

Go through each set of exercises for Group one letters before introducing Group two. Repeat each activity for each group of letters.

1. Give a letter card (with capital letters) to each child. Make sure they are holding the cards right-side-up. You keep a duplicate set of cards. Show the letter "M" from your set saying, "This is the letter 'M'; if you think you have the letter 'M,' place it under mine as you say the letter name." Now hold up "D," place it on the table to the right of "M" because you read from left to right. Ask: "Who has the letter 'D'?" and have him lay it down below your letter "D," ask if he can "read" both letter names on the table. Continue this exercise until all the letters in Group one are on the table. Let the children "read" all the letter names. You may choose to repeat the activity mixing up the letters if the children have not lost interest. The first time this activity is introduced to them, the children will be more interested; as it is repeated, they often get bored quickly.

2. Next time you use the letters, pass out all the capital letters from Group one again. This time—**without** showing the letter, say, "I am looking for capital 'M'; if you have it, put it on the table." Next call for the letter "D," having them set it to the right of the letter "M" and so on until all the Group one letters are out. You can repeat this activity calling for the letters in a different order.

Letter cards can help introduce letter names through simple exercises.

3. Now place the capital letters from Group one in a row. Ask: "Who can name these letters?" (Have children read from left to right.) They should say "capital M," "capital D," and so on.

4. Hold up the letter card for lower case "m," and say: "This is the letter 'm' too." Repeat each lower case letter in Group one. Pass out the lower case letter cards. Say: "Who has the lower case 'm'?" and have the child place it under the capital "M."

5. Mix all the capital and lower case letters. Have the children match the pairs of letters.

There is no need to continue these exercises until each child masters all the letter names; this is simply a way to introduce letter names. Some children will be ready to learn them; others won't be ready yet. You can repeat these exercises with the other groups of letters if the children are still interested.

Experience stories

Using "experience" stories has been a method of introducing reading for many years. Have the children tell about a field trip, a nature walk, or a vacation. Then, in their own words, print the story on large paper for them to see. Remember to use the correct printing forms so the children are exposed to the method of writing they will eventually use. Keep the sentences simple. Be sure to use capital and lower-case letters. The children may want to illustrate the story.

Introducing letter sounds

Another method of introducing letters to four-year-olds is to introduce beginning sounds. This method is the opposite of introducing letter names; you will want to choose only one method, otherwise it will be confusing to the children.

To introduce letter sounds, you will introduce the letters in small groups. The groups of three to four letters are divided in such a way that the letter sounds are easily distinguished. Besides learning the letter sound, the children will start to understand what "beginning" sound means. They must learn which sound to listen to in a word. Before exploring this activity with your group, be sure they understand the meaning of first, middle, and last. Use sequence cards to talk about first and last. Make three sounds: a clap, a bell, and a knock, for instance; see if they can tell you which sound came first and last.

The following letter groups work well when introducing letter sounds:

1. s, t, r	5. w, g, j (g as in goat)
2. m, f, b	6. d, z, v
3. c, p, n (c as in car)	7. k, x, q, y
4. d, h, l	

Introduce letter sounds in these groups. The Montessori method suggests introducing letter sounds as in the above groupings using a "three period lesson." Using sandpaper letters on 3x5 cards (these can be purchased or made with sand or yarn), introduce the first group of letters as follows. (For some children all three questions can be introduced in one sitting while other children will remain interested for only one of the lessons.)

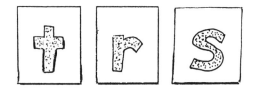

HEAR THE SOUND

1. Using your index and tall fingers (these are the fingers a child will later use to grasp a pencil), trace the letter "s" saying "ssss." Have the child(ren) trace the letter "s" saying "ssss." Repeat with all three of the Group one letters.

FIND THE SOUND

2. Now ask: "Show me 's'." The child(ren) show(s) knowledge of the letter by tracing the letter and making the proper sound. Then: "Show me 'r'," and so on.

TELL THE SOUND

3. Next simply point to one of the three letters asking: "What does this say?" Do this with each letter in Group one, mixing them up after each use.

Once the first group of letters is introduced with the "three period lesson," reinforce the sounds. Have children match small objects such as miniature dollhouse items or magazine pictures that begin with "s," "t," or "r" only. Divide a white paper in thirds. Put "s," "t," or "r" at the top of each section. Have children sort through pictures from catalogs that begin with "s," "t," or "r." Provide only objects and pictures that begin with these three letters.

After the children have completed these activities with Group one letters, introduce Group two and so on.

After each letter group is introduced, try:

- hopping from the letters as you name them (use heavy paper to print each letter for hopping on)

- tracing the letters in sand, rice, or mud

- tracing the letters in the air

- making them with their bodies

- locating them in newsprint headlines

- fingerpainting the letters

- shaping them with clay

- tracing letters with chalk on the sidewalk to walk on

- make the letters on the floor with tape to walk on

- trace them on large newsprint

Word cards

Another method of capturing a young child's curiosity about reading is to use index cards to print words your child has already asked you to spell. This is an at-home activity however, and probably should not

The children make the letter "E" with their bodies to reinforce their understanding of its shape.

be a group activity. When a preschooler wants to have a word spelled for him, put it on a card so he may save a collection of his new words. He may want to draw a picture on the word card to help him remember the word meaning. This is an activity that utilizes the "teachable moment" idea. You must be available for the spark of excitement that will motivate a child to learn purely because he wants to. This moment may come on any day at any time. It would defeat the purpose to schedule this reading activity in a group. Learning to read words is natural and easy when a child shows the desire, in other words, when he's ready.

The decision to introduce reading concepts and reading readiness activities is entirely up to your group. Choose from the suggested methods or create your own. Remember, children learn when curiosity leads them. If the children seem eager to work with reading and/or letters, follow their interest. If you decide to use a method of introducing letters, don't feel obligated to continue through all the letters if the children become bored or frustrated. Reading is a joy; children will read when they are ready.

22

Investigation: Numbers, Shapes, and Measures

As Simple as 1, 2, 3

My involvement in my child's playgroup helped me feel more aware of my child's strong points and weaknesses, what he is capable of, and his interests.

Judy Mast, mother of Nicholas

How do you teach a preschooler about math? Measuring and solving problems dealing with space, time, and quantity—that's what math is all about. This involves more than learning to count, add, or multiply; it involves observation. Your job as parents is to help your children discover mathematics through observation. Math concepts will come through this observation and direct experience, along with the language they need to describe these new discoveries.

All around you there are opportunities for solving mathematical problems. Becoming aware of the many ways to introduce mathematics to children will aid you in helping them grow confident with these concepts. At home you use math when you cook as you measure and count teaspoons or shape the cookies. When you set the table you must sort out a set of silverware for each person at the table. Sorting laundry— darks and lights—helps in learning to classify. You measure bigness when stacking cans on the shelf or when making a block tower.

Children will begin to acquire a language of mathematics as you help them to describe their observations. With a parent's interest and awareness of opportunities to introduce math concepts and vocabulary, abundant ways to develop an understanding of math will be found.

Quantity Questions

You begin teaching math simply by asking questions that encourage children to describe their observations. How many flowers do you see? Which one is bigger? How many circle shapes are in this picture? Even before doing comparisons and counting, you will want to have children use directional words whenever possible so they will be able to describe spatial relationships. Some words to stress during other parts of your day include:

up	above	straight
down	below	sharp
outside	to the side	corner
inside	open	flat
top	round	closed
bottom	smooth	bumpy

You can also introduce some geometric or shape words:

circle	rectangle
square	triangle
oval	diamond

Introduce a measuring vocabulary also to help describe quantities:

big/little	hot/cold	wide/narrow
high/low	warm/cool	dark/light
heavy/light	loud/soft	long/short/tall
fat/thin	hard/soft	

Use questions to stress comparison concepts:

Which is bigger?	Which are the same?
Which is similar?	Which is the biggest?
Which has more?	Which is smallest?
Which is less?	

A set of cuisenaire or number rods in graduated sizes can encourage the use of mathematical language. They are available at teacher supply stores if you are interested in purchasing them.

Number words include more than learning the numeral names. Use problem-solving questions that stress mathematical vocabulary:

Is it more or less? Most? Least?	How much does it weigh?
Is it fewer? greater?	What is the temperature?
Is it none? all?	What number do you see?

More math concepts deal with the measurement of time, a difficult concept for preschoolers to grasp. Introduce them to the following words but do not expect total comprehension.

calendars	names of the months of the year
clocks	names of the days of the week
today, tomorrow, yesterday	

Counting

At three years old, most children are aware of numbers. Along with encouraging rote memory counting, you can encourage mathematical concepts of different sizes, shapes, and quantities. Children will learn what numbers mean when they hear you use them to describe quantities; as they experience more of life and become more mature, the number words take on more meaning.

Here is one example of a developing counting concept still lacking adequate number language. At two and a half years old, Darren observed his five-year-old sister discover the reason a subdivision was called "Four Hills." She counted the four foothills looming on the horizon. Darren followed by pointing to and counting each foothill: "one, two, one, two." He had comprehended the concept of making a one-to-one match when counting, but he lacked the needed number words to describe his dis-

Learning math concepts involves an understanding that goes beyond just counting to ten.

covery. Another two-and-a-half-year-old, Sarah, is able to count well past twenty sequentially, yet she is unable to count objects to match the number name to the proper object. Sarah has a good mathematical vocabulary, but the counting concept of a one-to-one match is still developing. Concepts and language must go hand-in-hand so children can describe their observations. Counting out loud and naming numbers is the first step in understanding numbers.

One-to-One Matching

One-to-one matching is another step in learning about numbers. Provide opportunities for children to place one object at a time in a container. Provide the same number of objects as containers at first. Muffin tins and egg cartons work well for this activity. Fill containers with bottle caps, lima beans or buttons. Ask the children if the sets have the same number of objects. The children learn that each "set" has one object; they learn the relationship between two sets.

Another way of helping children learn one-to-one matching is to line up a row of objects and then let the children match each of the objects with one of their own. Discuss whether the two rows are "equal" or if one has "less" and the other "more." At this time you do not have to stress counting.

 he concept of numbers develops as children are exposed to varied situations in which quantity is an important factor. Parents invest a great deal of energy teaching children to count.

Rosalie Jensen and Deborah Spector

 ne of the important goals in both mathematics and movement education is to lead children into problem-solving experiences.

Rosalie Jensen and Deborah Spector

When children have mastered putting one object in a container, see if they can put two objects in each set, then three, and so on. When the concept "equal sets" is mastered, let them put objects in sets by increasing the number each time by one. The first set will have one object, the second set has two objects, the third set has three, etc.

When children begin to associate written numbers with the proper quantities, the same kind of one-to-one games can be played. By using pennies and index cards, you can encourage number recognition. Using a hole-punch, punch one hole in the first card, print the number "1" on the card. Punch two holes in the second card and print the number "2" on that card, and so on to "10." Have children place the proper number of pennies over the holes to show the correct quantity for each number. If you give them the exact number of pennies needed, the game is self-correcting. It simply helps children associate numbers with quantities. You may use baby food jars; have each jar labeled with numbers 1-5. Have children place the correct number of checkers in each container. Be sure to provide the exact number of objects to complete the activity correctly.

Some of the many ways to expose children to math concepts include the following activities. More ideas can be found in Claudia Zaslavsky's book *Preparing Young Children for Math: A Book of Games,* Sandy Jones's book *Learning for Little Kids,* and *Teaching Mathematics to Young Children* by Rosalie Jensen and Deborah Spector.

Math Games for Younger Children

SHAPES AND SPACE GAMES

- Up then down: Play "Ring around the Rosie" or sing to the tune of "Here We Go 'round the Mulberry Bush" "Around we go on the merry-go-round, up and down, up and down, up and down we go."

- Roll a can: Have the children feel the flat side of the can and then the round side; stress the words "round" and "flat." Ask them if they can roll the can. Then stand it up and challenge them to roll it. Try this with several different cans, wheels, cylindrical blocks, spools, or cups.

- The shape of things: Place a box, a ball, and a can in a bag. Ask them to feel for the round ball and pull it out, then the rectangular box, or the round and flat can. Have the children put their hands behind their backs and place an object in each child's hands. Ask him or her to describe the shape in their own words.

- Too big—too little: Use several containers such as pans, pots, balls, boxes, etc. "Here is a ball and here is a pan; will the ball fit in the pan? Tell me why or why not." You may use stacking toys for this activity also.

- What's big? One large item and one small. "Sara wants a big doll and I want a little one. Tell me which one to give to Sara.... Yes, that's the 'biggest' doll; it is bigger than this one."

- What's longer? Use two paper straws or two pencils of equal length. Ask which object is longer or if they are both equal. You may need to show how to line them up at one end in order to judge. Try breaking the straw to see if they can tell which is longer and why. Use a bag for the children to "feel" which object is longer without looking. Let them check by comparing the two.

MEASURING GAMES

- Measure me: To see who is taller, have two children stand back-to-back while the other children compare to see who is taller. Compare yourself to one child. Use a doll to discuss the word "short" in the same way. Using blocks, have the children build short towers, a tall tower, or a tower equal to yours. Discuss how you can tell which is taller.

- We're growing: Keep a growth chart and weight chart for each child. Recheck several months later.

- Which is higher? Have the children compare various objects' heights such as a chair and a refrigerator. Which is taller? Ask what is taller than the kitchen table? How can they tell? What else can you do to prove which is higher? Try to find what is lower than the bathroom sink by asking the same questions.

- What is wide? Have a wide bowl and a tall narrow container. Have the children decide which is taller and which is shorter. Show them that the bowl is "wide" by running your finger along the rim and explain that a narrow object can fit inside a wide object.

- Detective: When the children have discussed longer, shorter, taller, higher, lower, wider, and narrower, let them try to find objects to compare such as:

  (holding a hammer) ask them to find an object that is shorter or longer

  (holding a candle) ask them to find an object that is taller, etc. (Later, try using heavy/light.)

- Pouring fun: Use containers of various sizes; let them decide which holds the most. Try beginning with beans, then use rice, cereal, sand and, when they are ready, move to water, syrup, or honey (quite difficult).

- Tricky weights: Help the children learn that bigness doesn't necessarily mean heaviest by comparing:

  a dictionary and a box of cereal
  an apple and a sponge
  a cup of rice and a cup of popped popcorn

- Big, bigger, biggest: Read *Goldilocks and the Three Bears* discussing big, bigger, biggest, smaller than, and tallest. Measure children for tall, taller, tallest.

COUNTING GAMES

- How many things: Use apples, one on one plate and two on another. Ask how many apples on each plate. Which plate has more? Are they equal? Try two apples and two apples and three apples and two apples on each plate, asking the questions above.

- One-to-one matching: At snacktime set out three plates; hand a child three spoons without saying the number and ask if he has enough spoons for each plate; how does he know? Add some plates and repeat your questions. Add cups, napkins, or forks. Let the children set the table for the proper number who will be eating.

- One went away: Have six small cars and two trays. Put three cars on each tray. Ask how many cars are in the garage? Drive one car away and ask how many? Which garage has more cars? Which has fewer? This garage has fewer cars because two is less than three. Play this game many times, stressing words like more than, less than, fewer than. The children will need many experiences with this concept.

- Bean counters: Provide five small containers (jars, cups, etc.); carefully place one lima bean in the first container, count two beans for the second, and so on until container five contains five beans. Let the children duplicate your demonstration. Try labeling the containers with the printed numbers 1-5.

 he key to teaching a preschooler about math is to set the stage for him to make his own discoveries and to present ideas in the form of games which you both enjoy. You gain almost nothing by trying to stuff his head with number facts learned by rote.

Joan Beck

Experimenting with Science

A Garden in a Shoe

I was surprised to see how eager to learn she is—like a sponge soaking up new experiences!

Carolyn Fischer, mother of Brad, Heidi, and Darcy

Why are there lines in this leaf? How does light get in the light bulb? What is thunder? How does the worm crawl? These are typical questions springing from the mind of a three- to five-year-old. His curious mind is constantly searching, wondering, asking. Add a little kindling to the flame of curiosity and you will see his mind burning for more information. Three-year-old Laura and Rachel, four and a half, who had discovered dozens of caterpillars on the marigolds in the backyard, were excited to catch these crawling, furry insects. Bubbling over with enthusiasm, they asked, "Can we have a jar?" "What do they eat?" and "Let's get the magnifying glass to see them." These furry creatures of the insect world became good friends of the two preschoolers. This is just one of the many adventures their curiosity took them on.

One of the best things about nurturing curiosity about science is that the whole world is a museum, filled with hundreds of doors that have never been opened to your little ones, but are waiting to be stepped through into the vast dimensions of knowledge. You can help open some of these doors. It's easy and it's fun! It's free for the taking. And preschoolers are great takers! Tiny red and black ladybugs crawl end-

child's world is fresh and new and beautiful, full
of wonder and excitement.... If a child is to keep alive
his inborn sense of wonder.... he needs the
companionship of at least one adult who can share it,
rediscovering with him the joy, excitement, and mystery
of the world we live in. Parents often have a sense of
inadequacy when confronted on the one hand with the
eager, sensitive mind of a child and on the other with a
world of complex physical nature, inhabited by a life so
various and unfamiliar that it seems hopeless to reduce
it to order and knowledge. In a mood of self-defeat,
they exclaim, "How can I possibly teach my child about
nature—why, I don't even know one bird from another!"

I sincerely believe that for the child, and for the
parent seeking to guide him, it is not half so important
to know as to feel. If facts are the seeds that later
produce knowledge and wisdom, then the emotions and
the impressions of the sense are the fertile soil in which
the seeds must grow. The years of early childhood are
the time to prepare the soil.

Rachel Carson

The Sense of Wonder by Rachel Carson. Harper & Row, New York, 1956.
Reprinted with permission.

lessly hand over hand. Bluejay feathers are carefully inspected and then
worn decoratively in their hair. A gurgling, shallow brook is the source
of exploration, over and under rocks, from one bank to the other.

In and around your preschool-at-home, you can offer an environment in which your children can be encouraged to work, to move, and
to develop freely. You can give them opportunities to touch, to smell,
to taste, to hear, and to see. Because a preschooler is very hand-oriented,
he learns through touch, movement, and manipulation. As he interacts
with his environment, he absorbs from the things around him.

The environment should be presented so that it will reveal the child's
growing mind, not mold it. He needs freedom to explore. The environment should allow the child to be in direct contact with objects in the
world about him. It should invite him to use his five senses. Your child
is sensitive to the many different impressions that build in him step-by-

step. He needs plenty of time to work through the discovery process. He needs a minimum of interference as his thoughts unfold. (Perhaps a simple, non-directed question or suggestion may be enough to stimulate your child's natural curiosity.) And, it is important that he has the opportunity to tell someone about his discoveries.

Through his own discovery process, he will gain a sense of understanding of who he is. He will gain knowledge about the world. And he will develop a sense of his relationship to the world. As he learns, he acquires respect for and mastery over his world without diminishing the excitement, awe, and mystery that accompany investigation and discovery.

What a Child Can Learn through Science

What can a child learn through his observations, experiments, and discussions about science?

1. **Cause and effect relationships.** Example: by playing in water, he will find that the water level will go up if he puts a brick into a tub of water.

2. **Sorting.** Example: a sack full of leaves collected on a nature hike can be sorted into different categories such as shape, size, or color.

3. **Classifying.** Example: after a visit to a farm, he can tell the piglets from their mothers, the ducklings from the ducks, and the calves from the cows.

4. **Sequence of events.** Example: after planting bean seeds and observing the various stages of growth, your young child will be able to tell you the order of natural events from seed, to sprout, to leaves, to blossom, to fruit.

5. **Labeling.** Your child can correctly identify by name many new things and events. By labeling, he is practicing language skills and will be taking the first step toward abstract thinking. Example: a three-year-old will enjoy using a big word such as "static electricity" when he experiments with a balloon rubbed on his head and stuck on the wall.

Preschoolers may enter the world of science by many doors. Sometimes the introduction to a new idea may begin with his spontaneous question such as "Why are the clouds moving?" or "Do bugs sleep?" Or his quest for knowledge may be stimulated by a planned activity such as a walk, a field trip, a story, or a prepared experiment.

A Nature Hike

One type of planned activity is a nature hike. Regardless of where you live, your natural environment is waiting to be explored. These suggestions will help you prepare for your hike.

1. Check it out ahead of time. Before you bring your preschool group, walk the paths. This will give you some idea of what to call attention to when you go with the children.

2. You will need to discuss the objective(s) in going. Make a list of needed materials (if any) to bring along and organize these things ahead of time. Anxious children don't like to wait for an adult running around getting "just one more thing."

3. You may want to talk to the children about what they will see. This will help prepare them to get the most out of the experience. Discuss the trip, its purpose, and any other background information that will help.

4. Be sure that children dress appropriately. Will they need boots? old shoes? long pants? sweatshirts or jackets?

5. Before going on your hike have the children use the bathroom, and have a drink of water.

6. You might want to bring:

   a tape recorder—to capture sounds
   a magnifying lens—to get a close-up look
   measuring tape or yardstick—to measure plants, tree trunks, etc.

7. Bring paper sacks or plastic bags to put collectibles in. Have one for each child. Write each one's name on his own bag. If children can write their names, let them do it (or they can decorate their bags ahead of time).

8. For added fun, bring the words to appropriate songs, fingerplays, or poems. These can be written on 3"x 5" notecards which slip easily into bags or pockets.

9. If it is a long walk, a thermos of cold water will be appreciated and worth carrying.

10. Ready, set, go! Encourage children to use all their five senses. Ask them simple questions such as: "Stop for a moment. Listen. What do you hear?"

Finding a worm in a backyard garden can lead to discovering more about nature.

Opportunities are everywhere. Here are some ideas of what children can discover on a nature hike.

- Under or beside a rock or log:
  slugs, snails, toads, turtles, insects, worms, lizards, snakes, small animals, damp soil, mushrooms, toadstools, moss, lichens

- On a sidewalk:
  footprints, wet leaves, leaf prints, ants, grass or weeds in cracks, ice, snow, puddles of water, worms after rain

- On, in, or under a tree or a bush:
  cattails, water lilies, swans, ducks, snakes, fish, reflections, minnows, insects, leaves, seeds, algae, twigs, grass, moss, frogs, turtles, crayfish, mud, stones, rocks, dragonflies, water spiders

- At the beach:
  sand, seagulls, water, seashells, driftwood, seaweed, insects, fish, clams, crabs

- In a pile of dirt:
  insects, seeds, worms, rocks, pebbles, different colors of soil, gravel, sand, clay, leaves, bark

- In a garden or on a lawn:
  dandelion and other seeds, anthills, flowers, grasses, feathers, worms, insects, birds

Kinds of Walks

"LOOK FOR INSECTS" WALK

- Look under rocks, logs, leaves, in soil and sand
- Use a magnifying lens for close-up look
- Small jars with lids may be used to capture insects for further observation
- Questions: What does each look like? What are they doing? Where did you find it?

"FEELING" WALK

- Touch and feel things along the way
- Questions: What can you find that feels soft? hard? rough? smooth? bumpy? prickly? sharp? wet? dry?

"SMELLING" WALK

- Smell as you walk
- Taste is closely related to smell; let children taste some safe plants such as wild strawberries, dill, clover
- Questions: What can you smell that smells sweet? bitter? dusty? damp? wet? dry? rotten? fresh?

"COLLECTING" WALK

- Look for "natural" items (on the ground, growing, if you are permitted to pick)
- Look for things that will be used for a project such as a collage, mobile, sculpture, or relief sculpture

"WATCHING THE WEATHER" WALK

- Look for the signs that show weather. Talk about the sun; the temperature of the air; the wind—direction and speed; the clouds—shape, height, color, the moisture in them; behavior of the animals
- Children can act out "wind" and "sun" and "rain."

AUTUMN WALK

■ Collect leaves of different shapes, sizes, colors; leaves are good for sorting, rubbings, preserving for arrangements

■ Questions: What are the colors of leaves? their sizes? shapes? What is the name of the tree or bush where they grew? What other changes indicate the fall season? What seeds can be found? How are the animals preparing for the winter season—their fur? feathers? storing food? hiding nuts? flocking to fly to a warmer climate?

WINTER WALK

■ Walk the same path as the autumn walk

■ Questions: What changes are there? Trees and bushes? What things stayed the same? What animals are around? What footprints can be seen—squirrels, rabbits, birds? Where do the winter animals get their food and water? What happens to the water when it gets very cold?

■ Look at the cloud formations; talk about the winter weather; how do people stay warm in the winter?

SPRING WALK

■ Walk the same path as the autumn and winter walks

■ Questions: What changes are there: Trees and bushes? Plants, seeds, shoots, buds, blossoms, leaves? What animals do you see and hear? Can you find any nests? What are the clouds like?

"COLLECTING SHELLS" WALK

■ Walk along a beach; look for and collect shells of different shapes, sizes, colors

■ These can be used for sorting, making a collage, a sculpture, jewelry, etc.

"DESERT" WALK

■ Walk in the desert

■ Questions: What does the earth and sand feel like underfoot? What plants can you find in the desert? What animals live here? Where do they find food and water? Could you live here? How? What does the sky look like?

Helping Children Learn a New Idea in Science

The realms of science are vast and complex. On a basic level, however, preschoolers are very capable of appreciating many aspects of science. Sometimes they even notice things in a more pure way than through the eyes of their teachers who often want to dissect and analyze when the simplest ideas are enough to handle. There are many different ways to explore the natural and physical world around us. How do you present a new idea to your preschool-aged child? Here are some methods of learning new ideas in the area of science.

1. **Read** a story, either factual or fiction, on the subject area. Talk about some key points.

2. **Observe** using all five senses: sight, sound, smell, taste, touch.

3. **Experiment.** Try to guess what might happen and make a prediction. Or work with the material by trial and error to make discoveries.

 hose who work with young children know that three-year-olds learn best through direct experience; they retain little of what is talked about, but remember a surprising amount of what is touched, explored, and experienced.

Robert E. Rockwell, Elizabeth A. Sherwood, and Robert A. Williams

 hildren thirst to use all of their senses. By adulthood we become more refined and restrained. We simply look and listen. Such passivity is never enough for the young child. Two gateways to the mind, the eyes and the ears, cannot do the job. The young chld has to "know" things through his lips and his tongue and his fingers and his nose.

James Hymes

To learn about science, a child needs to observe and experiment.

4. **Measure.** Young children can, with some help, take some simple measurements such as heights, weights, temperatures. If they can recognize and name numerals, they will be able to do this to some extent. If children do not know the numerical symbols, they may be able to answer a few questions such as "Which one is bigger?" "How many _____ does it have?" "Is it smaller or larger than it was last week?" "Which one is light? heavy?" "Does it feel hot or cold?"

5. **Keep Records.** Parents can write down children's comments. Children can draw something they observed. Other devices which can be used are a camera to take photographs, a tape recorder to capture sounds, and a simple "check-off" chart. Let the children help as much as possible.

6. **Discuss.** Ask children "what," "where," "how," and "why" questions. Let the children think it out; restrain yourself from saying it for them.

Science Activities for the Three- to Five-Year-Old

Listed here are science activities geared to young children. Some will be experiments; some are planned as projects. An experiment is the process of discovering an answer to a question. You may begin with acquiring some knowledge about the subject. Preschoolers may listen to an explanation or a simple story about the subject. Better yet, they like to explore the material or subject "hands on" to learn more about it. You may ask a question or two that will challenge them into making a good guess (hypothesis) based on the information available. Then do all the necessary steps to learn if your prediction is correct or incorrect. For example, when children bring an ice cube into the sun on a hot day, they can learn to "predict" that the ice will melt. Their observations, discussions, and measurements become part of the experimentation process.

A project in science is similar to a craft project because you have an end product in mind before you begin. A project is another way to learn about science because it encourages manipulation of the materials of science. A child can learn about the subject by making something out of it. For example, children learn about leaves by collecting them, sorting them, or doing leaf rubbings. Another way to learn about plants is to plant a garden of herbs in the sections of an egg carton.

WORM HOUSE

What you need:

Orange juice can, soil, large glass jar, oatmeal, soil, worms

What you do:

1. Fill an orange juice can with soil; place the can in the bottom of large glass jar;

2. Fill the rest of the jar with sand or soil;

3. Put in the worms;

4. Sprinkle oatmeal on the soil for the worms to eat;

5. Moisten the soil by poking wet cotton into the sand/soil every few days. Note: The can in the center forces the worms to the outside of the jar where they can be more easily observed.

Questions to ask:

1. Where do the worms travel to?

2. What do they eat? How much?

3. Do they communicate with each other?

4. What would happen if too much water was put in? If no water was put in?

TAKE ALONG A TELESCOPE

What you need:

A cardboard tube, such as from paper towels, foil, or plastic wrap—one for each child.

What you do:

1. Each child should have his own telescope. Print his name on it. Go for a walk. Caution: Do not look through the telescope while you are moving. Stop and stand or sit down to prevent an accident.

2. Point the telescopes at something far away, for example, a bird at the top of a tree. Ask everyone to try to find the same thing. Describe it in detail.

3. Find something up close. Ask everyone to focus on this thing. Describe it in detail.

4. Let each child have a turn at being the "spotter," having the others try to find the thing he describes. Take turns.

Questions to ask:

1. Why do you seem to notice more things using a telescope? Why can you see more details about each thing?

2. How does blocking out the surrounding view help your observations?

3. What do you think it might feel like if you were there? Pretend you are the red-winged blackbird on the top of the tree. What can you see from there? What does the ground look like?

OBSERVING ANTS

Preparation:

Read and talk about ants. Take a nature hike. Collect ants in a large clear jar (such as a peanut butter jar or a mayonnaise jar).

What you do:

1. Give the ants a small handful of dry sand and/or soil. Wait. What do they do with it?

2. Give the ants some crumbs of bread. Wait. What do they do with it? Do they eat it? Carry it? Help each other? Talk to each other?

3. Write down or record the observations of the children. The children might also want to draw or paint what they observed.

A picnic lunch adds some fun to the learning experiences of a nature walk.

LEAF RUBBINGS

Preparation:

Take a nature walk to a wooded area, park, or backyard. Collect leaves of all sizes, shapes, and colors. The leaves that are less brittle will work better for the project.

What you need:

Leaves, typing paper (or other thin but strong paper), crayons or chalk, tape.

What you do:

1. Lay a leaf on the table.

2. Place a sheet of paper over the leaf and tape the paper in place on all four corners.

3. Use the side of a crayon or a piece of chalk to rub over the leaf. Rub firmly to get a strong print showing veins, stem, and outline.

4. Variations: Overlap several leaves. Blend several colors.

Questions to ask:

1. What colors are the leaves? Sort the leaves into piles by similar colors.

2. What are the shapes? Sort the leaves by shapes.

3. What are the sizes? Sort the leaves by two or three sizes.

A SIT-UPON

A sit-upon is a small, flat seat usually made to be waterproof. It can be made out of many different materials in different ways. It is valuable on hikes, especially when the ground is damp or wet. It helps to rest tired legs and a sit-upon helps to keep bottoms dry!

What you need:

Stacks of newspaper, about 1″ thick per child; a piece of plastic such as light colored plastic bags or clear contact paper (probably more expensive); heavy tape; permanent markers

What you do:

1. Wrap the newspaper, 1″ thick, in the plastic OR cover the newspaper with contact paper;

2. Use tape to secure loose ends;

3. Use permanent markers to decorate the sit-upons. Names may be written on them;

4. Take them with you when you go on your nature walks.

"FEELY BOX"

Preparation:

On a nature walk, collect many different objects such as twigs, leaves, flowers, shells, stones, driftwood, feathers.

What you need:

Cardboard box, objects from nature walk

What you do:

1. Cut a hole just big enough for a child to reach his hand in the box;

2. Put a nature collection of bark, leaves, acorns, pinecones, and so on, inside the box;

3. Children can reach inside the box to feel an object and guess what it is.

 hat better gift can we as parents and teachers give this precarious earth than a generation of children who have learned to know and love the natural world?

Robert E. Rockwell, Elizabeth A. Sherwood, and Robert A. Williams

NEST BUILDERS

Preparation:

Read and talk about birds and their homes, their nests. Look at pictures or photographs of real birds' nests. Identify some of the ones found in your area.

What you do:

Go on a nature hike. Bring a sack to carry a bird's nest in. OR, on location, let the children hold the nest and slowly take it apart.

Questions to ask:

1. What kind of bird built the nest?

2. Where did he build it?

3. Why did he choose that spot?

4. What did the bird use to build his nest? (Twigs, mud, string, leaves, paper, feathers, hair, yarn, cloth, etc.)

BUILD A NEST

What you need:

Clay or homemade playdough; twigs, sticks, paper, feathers, leaves, yarn, etc.

What you do:

1. Using the clay or playdough as a base, shape a bird's nest. Let each child make his own.

2. Add twigs, feathers, string, yarn, etc. The children may learn that nest building is a hard job, even more so for birds who have no fingers.

BIRD FEEDERS

Preparation:

Read a story and discuss birds and their need for food in the winter. Discuss what birds eat.

What you need:

Container (see samples below), bird seed, nuts or bread crumbs, heavy string or cord.

What you do:

1. **Grapefruit shells.** Clean out the shells by eating the grapefruit. Punch 3 holes near the top for heavy string to tie into a tripod.

Tie the 3 strings into one string for hanging. Fill with food for birds. Hang up in a visible location.

2. **Milk cartons (plastic).**Cut a small 2″ hole in side of container near center. Punch a hole in all four sides near the top of the container. Thread the string through, in both directions, and tie above. Put seed in the bottom. Hang up in a place where children can see the birds.

3. **Pinecones.** Tie a heavy string around the top, long enough for hanging. Spread peanut butter on the sides of the pinecone. Roll it in birdseed. Hang it up in a tree.

SPIDERS

What you need:

A live spider that spins webs (check gardens, cellars, and window wells); a clear plastic box or a clear gallon jar; a bottle cap; a small tree branch; sand; a broom straw; a live fly and a dead fly.

What you do:

1. Cover the bottom of the container with about one inch of dry sand.

2. Set a bottle cap in the bottom and add a small amount of water to it.

3. Place the small tree branch in the jar.

4. Put in the spider. This may be done by letting it lower itself on its own dropline of silk.

5. Watch. Observe how the spider spins its web.

Questions to ask:

1. What type of web did the spider make? What does it look like? What is it attached to?

2. Add a live fly. What does the spider do? Does she eat it all? Does she save some of it? Add a dead fly. What does the spider do?

3. Touch the web in a few places with a broom straw. Make a small hole in the web. What does the spider do? Does she try to repair it?

SPROUTING CORN

What you need:

Ear of corn, pan, water

What you do:

1. Place an ear of corn on its side in a pan of water.

2. Wait a few days. Watch it sprout.

3. Draw a picture before and after it sprouts.

Questions to ask:

1. What is needed to help the corn sprout?

2. How many days did it take to sprout?

3. What does the sprouted corn look like? Color? How big? Why does it have more than one shoot?

4. Is more water needed to keep it growing?

INDOOR GARDEN

What you need:

Container, plants or seeds, soil, water, pebbles

What you do:

1. Prepare the container for the plant by putting a thin layer of pebbles at the bottom.

2. Add the growing medium: soil or water without pebbles.

3. Put in the plant and firm up the soil around it. Or follow directions for planting seeds.

4. Water lightly.

Suggestions:

Container	Medium	Plant/Seed
old shoe	soil	carrot top
egg shell	soil	grass seed
sponge	water	mustard seed
jar	water	water cress, avocado
pot	soil	flower seeds
mug	soil	onion or popcorn
egg carton	soil	different seeds in each hollow: celery seed, poppy seed, mustard seed, sweet basil, marjoram, chives

Other possibilities: coleus, marigolds, impatiens, pineapple top, sweet potato

FORCING BRANCHES TO BLOOM

What you need:

Branches from bushes or trees cut off early in spring; can, water

What you do:

1. Bring branches indoors where it is warm.

2. Put one branch in a can with water.

3. Put one branch in a can without water.

4. Observe daily over the next few weeks.

5. Write down what you see once or twice a week on a calendar.

6. Draw a picture of what you see—size, shape, and color of buds, blooms, and leaves.

7. Use a ruler to measure the size of the leaves.

8. Take a photograph once a week of your observations.

Questions to ask:

1. What happens each day? each week?

2. When do buds appear?

3. What do the first leaves look like?

4. Look at the branches on the same tree or bush outdoors. What is happening to them? Compare the indoor branches to the outdoor branches. Why is there a difference?

5. What is the difference in growth of the branches in water compared to those without water? Why?

 hildren can watch how things grow, can come to understand the plant's needs for nutrients in the soil, for water and sunshine. There is a quiet joy that comes from nurturing a living thing and with gardening the pleasures are the fragrances, the moist coolness of the soil, and the excitement of watching change.

Sandy Jones

BUTTERFLIES AND CATERPILLARS

Preparation:

Plan to take a nature hike when you know the caterpillars are in season. You might collect a few the day before in the event that your group doesn't find any.

What you need:

A clear glass container including a lid with small air holes; cotton balls; twigs

What you do:

1. After finding a caterpillar, place it gently into the container.

2. Add some leaves of the plant you found it on.

3. Moisten a cotton ball and put it in. Also put in a few small twigs.

4. Add fresh leaves and water each day.

5. Watch.

Questions to ask:

1. What does the caterpillar eat?

2. What does it need to make a cocoon or chrysalis? How does it use its own hair for this?

3. Does the color or pattern or thickness of the fur tell us anything about nature?

4. How long will it take to complete its "metamorphosis"? (You may need to look up this one in a reference book).

PETS

Preparation:

In a small group of preschool children, one child may wish to share his/her pet with the group. Read a story about the animal and talk about it. (It may be easier to have the group meet at the home of the pet rather than transporting it.)

What you do:

1. When the pet comes to the group, remind the children to be quiet and calm so they do not frighten the animal.

2. Let the pet owner (and parent) do the handling at first. If the pet and children are calm, they may be able to pet or hold the animal.

Close observation of a turtle provides an opportunity to learn about caring for animals.

Questions to ask:

1. How old is the animal? Is it male or female?

2. How much did it weigh when it was born? How much does it weigh now? How big will it get when it is full grown?

3. What does it eat? Who feeds it?

4. How does it get exercise?

5. Where does it live? Does it have a bed or cage? How do you clean the pet or its cage?

6. Do pets need love and affection to grow well?

Suggestions:

Hamster, gerbil, guinea pig, box turtle, toads, fish, guppies, lizard, dog, cat, rabbit, ants

COLLECT AND MEASURE RAIN

What you need:

Rain clothes, a clear jar, a ruler

What you do:

1. Put a clear jar out in the rain, unobstructed by buildings or drafts. Write down what time you put it out.

2. Bring the jar in after the shower ends or at the end of a designated time such as an hour or two.

3. Measure the rain with a ruler. This is a good time to use beginning numbers.

POTATO HEADS

Preparation:

Read a simple story on plants and how they grow. Discuss plant growth. Include words: seed, root, stem, light, water, soil (the plant's food)

What you need:

Large, old potatoes; potting soil; grass seed; cloves; water

What you do:

1. Scoop a hollow in the top of a big potato. Slice off the bottom so that it will stand upright.

2. Stick cloves into the potato for eyes, nose, and mouth.

3. Fill the hollow with potting soil.

4. Sprinkle grass seed onto the soil.

5. Water the seeds and soil ... lightly.

6. Watch. The grass seed will sprout in a few days. Keep it lightly watered. You may need to give the potato head a haircut!

Questions to ask:

1. Pull out one blade of grass. Where is the stem? the root? the seed?

2. What is needed for the grass seed to grow? Where does it get its food?

WATER IN A POTATO

Preparation:

Talk about the fact that water is needed for life. Water is in everything living, both plants and animals. Give some examples.

What you need:

Potato, spoon, salt

What you do:

1. Scoop a hole in a raw potato using the spoon.

2. Sprinkle about a teaspoon of salt into the hole. Leave it overnight.

3. Check the potato. What do you observe?

Questions to ask:

1. What happened to the potato? What does it look like?

2. What does the hole look like? Why?

3. Where did the water come from? (The water came from the potato absorbed by the salt.) To show absorption, dissolve a teaspoon of salt in a glass of water.

he sense of initiative, curiosity, and exploration is encouraged when parents take time to answer children's questions, when they provide opportunities to explore and discover.

David Elkind

OUTDOOR GARDENS

What you need:

Garden tools, fertile soil, fertilizer, seeds, camera (optional), ruler, paper, and crayons

What you do:

1. Dig up the soil. Sprinkle on the fertilizer and rake in.

2. Stretch a string on two sticks. Furrow a row with a hoe.

3. Drop in the seeds, following the package directions for depth and spacing.

4. Cover the seeds with soil. Tamp down lightly.

5. Water the seeds. Let them grow.

6. If you have the availability of a camera, let the children take pictures of each step in planting. Take pictures of plants in all stages of growth. OR draw pictures of plants at various stages of growth.

7. Measure the height of plants and the width of leaves with a ruler. An adult can write these down to keep records.

Suggestions for planting:

Beans, sunflowers, radishes, marigolds, cucumbers

LITTLE TERRARIUM

Preparation:

Take a walk in the woods to gather the following: mosses, lichen, tiny low-growing plants, pebbles, acorns, twigs, etc. Put these in a pail—one per child.

What you need:

Baby food jar or pint jar with lid; trowel or old spoon; pails—one per child; charcoal (can use pieces from fireplace or grill); extra soil and pebbles

What you do:

1. At the bottom of the jar, layer pebbles, charcoal, soil.

2. Arrange the woodland treasures.

3. Water just a little and put the cover on. (Add a few drops of water as needed to keep moist ... not muddy.)

4. Watch it grow.

Suggestion:

You may want to buy sterilized potting soil as regular or woodland soil is often too soggy.

MINIATURE WOODLAND SCENE

What you need:

Moss, fungi, lichens, pebbles, sand, dried plants or parts of plants, such as acorns, seed pods, galls, leaves, nuts, etc., a small glass jar or small cardboard box lid or a slab of wood cut from a small log, white glue, pails

What you do:

1. Bring pails on a nature hike and collect natural living and non-living things.

2. Use a container, lid, or wood slab as a background for your woodland scene.

3. Plan the landscape by arranging your treasures.

4. Put glue on the surface area, then sprinkle heavily with sand. Shake off the extra sand.

5. Next glue the moss in place.

6. Glue on the other articles as you planned. Let it dry for a few days away from direct sun. Adding a sprinkle of water will keep the living things growing.

Questions to ask:

1. Where did these little items of nature come from?

2. What does the moss need to grow? What does it not need?

3. Talk about the sizes of the things used.

DANDELIONS

What you need:

Lots of dandelions at all stages of growth—young, mature, dried, and seeding; magnifying lens; bowl; water; black construction paper; glue; sponge

What you do:

1. Use a magnifying lens to look at dandelion blossoms. Where are the roots? the stem? the seeds?

2. Put water in a bowl. Split some dandelion stems into three or more strips. Put these in the water and watch them curl up. Why does this happen?

3. Spread paste on black construction paper. Take a seeding dandelion and blow the seeds into the paper to see a design or pattern. What does the wind do with the seeds?

4. Try germinating the dandelion seeds by putting them on a moistened sponge or blotter. Keep it wet for a few days. What ingredients were needed to sprout the seeds?

5. For fun, make necklaces from stems by pushing the end of one into the end of the next stem, and so on. Or try weaving and tying stems together.

Suggestion:

Wear old clothes when playing with dandelions because the juice from the stems permanently stains clothing.

FOLD A FAN

Preparation:

Talk about the fact that we cannot see air. Air currents are all around us. We can feel moving air.

What you need:

A big piece of paper

What you do:

1. Fold a big piece of paper in an accordian fold. Fold it back and forth and back and forth again and again.

2. Hold the folded paper by one end. Open out the other end.

3. Wave in front of your face.

Questions to ask:

1. Do you feel something? Can you hear it?

2. What do you feel? Where did it come from?

BALLOONS

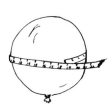

What you need:

Balloons—large ones that blow up easily (you may have to blow them up ahead of time to make the rubber more flexible and easier to blow up by a child), measuring tape (fabric type)

What you do:

1. Give a balloon to each child. Let them practice blowing it up a few times.

2. Start with empty balloons. Take a deep breath and blow one breath into the balloon. Tie off the end.

3. Measure around the balloons.

4. Compare the sizes of balloons.

Questions to ask:

1. What is inside the balloon that made it get larger?

2. Where did the air come from?

3. Who had the biggest amount of air in his/her lungs?

PARACHUTE

Preparation:

Talk about the fact that all things on earth fall down. The same things will fall down at different rates of speed if they are different shapes. This is due to air resistance. A larger surface area resists more.

What you need:

A plastic bag or a 16″ square of fabric, string, a stick, stone, or a block of wood, tape

What you do:

1. Cut a 12″ circle out of the plastic bag (or use the 16″ square of fabric).

2. Cut four 12″ lengths of string.

3. Tape the string pieces to the plastic or fabric chute. Tape the other ends of the string to a stick or stone or wood block for a weight.

4. Toss up the parachute. Watch it come down.

Questions to ask:

1. Why does it come down?

2. Does it come down slowly? Why?

3. Tie the chute closed. Toss it again. Does it seem to come down faster or slower that when it was opened. Why?

WALK IN THE RAIN

What you need:

A gentle warm rain, raincoats, hats, boots, etc.

What you do:

1. Dress up in rain clothes.

2. Walk in the rain.

3. Use all your senses to experience rain.

Questions to ask:

1. What does it feel like on your face?

2. What does it taste like as it falls on your tongue?

3. What does rain smell like? look like? sound like?

4. Where does rain go after it hits the ground?

5. When is rain helpful? When is it harmful?

MAKE A RAINBOW

What you need:

Old playclothes, a warm sunny day, a garden hose and water, glass prism

What you do:

1. Wear old playclothes or swimsuits.

2. Turn on the garden hose. Let the children enjoy playing in the water.

3. Adjust the nozzle to a fine spray. Arch the water high into the air.

4. Observe the rainbow that is made as the sun's rays strike the water droplets. The water droplets act like prisms to form a rainbow.

Questions to ask:

1. What two things are needed to form a rainbow?

2. What colors do you see in the rainbow?

3. Why is the rainbow the shape it is?

4. Read a story about a rainbow. How does a rainbow make you feel?

5. Use a glass prism to make another rainbow on a surface. Talk about how the light is bent and, therefore, broken into the band of colors as the light passes through the glass. Or just enjoy the mystery of the color spectrum.

WATER PAINT THE SIDEWALK

What you need:

A pail or bucket, sandbox pails, an empty plastic milk jug with handle on and top cut down or empty ice cream bucket, brushes (old paintbrushes or rolls of newspapers will serve as brushes)

What you do:

1. Fill buckets with water—one per child.

2. Take brushes and water, paint pictures, designs, etc., on sidewalks.

Suggestion:

This is done best on a very warm sunny day. The water pictures will evaporate quickly, erasing themselves, so more pictures can be painted.

MEASURE THE SNOW

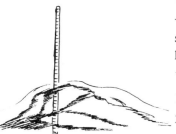

What you need:

Yardsticks—one for each child. (Check lumber yards or hardware stores for free yardsticks.) Permanent marker, sheet of paper and a pencil.

What you do:

1. Print each child's name on one end of his/her yardstick.

2. In winter before a predicted snowfall, go outdoors and let each child choose a spot for his yardstick. Suggest places in the open, next to a building, under a tree, etc. An adult can hammer the yardstick into the ground an inch or two with the name end up.

3. After the snowfall, let each child make a dot on his yardstick showing how deep the snow was in that spot. Talk about the numbers on the ruler or yardstick.

4. A parent can write down on the record sheet how deep the snow was in that spot. Write the date also.

5. Record the inches after each significant change in weather, such as a snowstorm or a thaw.

Questions to ask:

1. Why is the snow deeper in some spots than others?

2. What happens to the depth of snow after a snowfall? after the temperature gets above freezing?

3. Talk about measuring things and about what tools are used for measuring.

SPRAY PAINT A FRESH SNOWFALL

What you need:

A fresh snowfall; old spray bottles that have spray nozzles or squirt tops like those from dusting sprayers, cleaners, or dish detergents; water; food colors (optional)

What you do:

1. Fill spray or squirt bottles with water.

2. Add a couple of drops of food coloring (optional).

3. Dress warmly. Go outside. Spray paint pictures in the snow.

PLAY WITH WATER

What you need:

Choose a few or many of the following: bowls, pitchers, pump bottles, squeeze bottles, plastic tubing, plastic sandwich bags, measuring cups, spoons, shower hose, meat baster, funnel, ladle, sieve or colander, corks, sponges, pingpong ball, rubber ball, beach ball, washers, nails, salt, sugar, paper boats

What you do:

1. Pour, measure, sieve, pump, squeeze, ladle, spoon, spray, dump.

2. Float objects.

3. Sink objects.

4. Dissolve salt and sugar.

Questions to ask:

1. What objects float? Why?

2. What objects sink? Why?

3. Would you float or sink? Why? How much water would be needed for you to float?

4. What substances dissolve in water?

5. Why is water able to go down the tiny holes of the drain?

PLAY WITH MUD

What you need:

Heavy-duty plastic or wooden spoons, bowls or other containers, old muffin tins, pots and pans with handles, sticks, grocery bags, newspaper, water in a bucket and old towels for clean-up

What you do:

1. Spoon, pour, mold, mix, stir, pat.

2. Use sticks to represent a birthday cake with candles.

3. Use grocery bags or old newspaper sheets for fingerpainting with the mud.

4. Draw pictures in the mud using sticks and fingers.

5. Mold it and let it dry in the sun.

PLAY WITH SAND

What you need:

Dump trucks, funnels, sifter, sieve, colander, scoop, shovel and pail, molds, scoops made from the bottom of empty milk jugs, spoons, ice cream sticks, watering can, wooden or plastic dolls and animals

What you do:

1. Shovel, spoon, scoop, stir, pat, mold, dump, sift, push, pile.

2. Make roads, buildings, farms, etc. Let the children direct the play.

3. Use sticks to draw letters or numbers if the children show an interest in this. Sticks are also good for fences and candles on a sand cake.

PLAY WITH STONES AND ROCKS

What you need:

Stones and rocks of all shapes, sizes, colors; hammers; markers or paint; bowl of water

What you do:

1. Crack open with hammers. Look inside the cracked rock. Can you find any fossils?

2. Make paperweights. (See Chapter 15.)

3. Design rock creatures. (See Chapter 15.) Use paints and markers.

5. Make a rock garden outdoors.

Planting seeds and watching them grow can teach young children about the sequence of natural events.

PLAY WITH SHELLS

What you need:

Shells of all sizes, shapes, colors; small jar; hand drill; fishing line; egg carton

What you do:

1. Identify the shells. Talk about the animal that lived in each.

2. Collect shells. Put them in a brandy snifter or a small jar which can be used as a paperweight.

3. Use a hand drill to make a small hole in some of the shells. Use a string or fishing line cut into various lengths. Attach shells, suspending them from a dowel or piece of driftwood to make a wind chime.

4. Play a sorting game. Use the sections of the egg carton to sort by either size or color or type, etc.

5. Use shells to practice counting.

6. Make up a story about the animal that lived in the shell.

7. Use a larger shell as a container for a living plant.

MEASURING WATER IN SNOW

What you need:

Two unbreakable containers (large jars or old coffee cans) of equal size, a measuring cup, a ruler, a permanent marker

What you do:

1. Place two containers outside in a spot not protected by trees, buildings, etc., so that the snow can fall freely into it.

2. After a snowfall bring the containers inside.
(a) Measure the snow in the first container with a ruler. Mark how many inches it is with a marker.
(b) Measure the snow in the second container by spooning it gently into a measuring cup. How much is it?

3. Let it stand inside the warm house. Observe. Ask questions about what will happen.

4. After the snow has melted, measure the water in each container.
(a) Use a ruler to measure the depth of water in the first container.

(b) Pour into the measuring cup and record the amount on your record sheet.

Questions to ask:

1. What do you think will happen to the snow? Make some guesses.

2. As the snow begins to melt, ask what is happening? Accept all comments. There is no right or wrong answer.

3. Why is the snow melting?

4. What do you think will happen if you put the water back outside? Try this and see.

5. You may want to talk about temperature indoors and out. What clothes do you wear? How do your hands feel?

EXPLORING SOUND

Preparation:

Talk about sound. Sound energy does not travel in a straight line. Sound vibrations can be both seen and heard. Sound waves must travel through a medium such as air or water. Some things block sound such as fabric, cotton, or feathers.

What you need:

Various materials which demonstrate sound and/or vibrations.

What you do:

1. **Explaining vibrations.** Toss a pebble into a pond. "The shaky rings of water radiate from the splash like sound waves, engulfing twigs and rocks but getting less and less distinct the farther they travel. The bigger the stone, the bigger the splash and the more distinct the vibrating waves. A shout is like a big stone; a whisper is like a pebble" *The Mother's Almanac.* Can we see sound? Can we hear sound? Does sound travel in a straight line? Where does sound come from?

2. **Doorbells.** Have one child ring the bell while the others listen indoors. What do they hear? How does the sound get from the door to the bell and then to your ears? What other things make sounds?

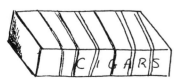

3. **Sound from a homemade instrument.** Use a stiff cardboard box. Put several large rubberbands around it and across an open side.

Stretch them differently. Then strum them with your fingers. What do you see? What do you hear? Where does the sound start and end?

4. **Different sound conductors.** Put your ear on various materials such as a wood table, a metal cabinet, a glass windowpane, even a large bowl of water. Tap with a coin or drop a coin on the surface. Which one sounds the loudest?

5. **Homemade walkie-talkie.** Poke a small hole in the center of the bottom of a paper or styrofoam cup. Poke thread through to the inside of the cup and tie a double knot at the end. Repeat this with the second cup. Use a length of string up to 50 feet. Pull it taut. Let one child listen while the other speaks softly from the other end. Reverse. Do the voices sound louder than a whisper? How does the voice travel? What is the sound conductor?

EXPLORING LIGHT

Preparation:

Talk about light. It travels in a straight line. A line of light is able to bend as it passes around corners and as it bounces off a surface such as a mirror. Light is able to pass through some substances such as glass or water. Light can break apart like a fan into colors. Bright light shows off full colors.

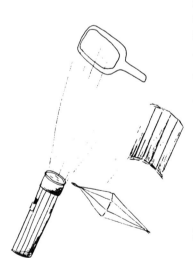

What you need:

Various things to explore light. See each activity.

What you do:

1. **Flashlights.** Use a flashlight in a dark or dim room to show that light travels in a straight line. Does the light bounce off walls? Light-colored walls? Dark-colored walls or furniture? Go to a closet with the flashlight. Leave the door open a crack while shining the light into a dark corner. Does some of the light bend around the corner or bounce off the walls and escape through the door?

2. **Mirrors.** Play with mirrors and a flashlight or other light. Does the mirror block the light when it is held close? Does it make it seem even brighter (magnifying it)? Hold the flashlight still, but move the mirror around. Can the light be made to move wherever you want it to by reflecting it off the mirror?

3. **Use a glass prism or a water hose to make a rainbow.** The light is bent and therefore broken or splintered into the band of

colors as the light passes through the glass. The water droplets act just like millions of little prisms as the sun shines through them. Does white light have all the colors in it? Talk about the colors. What are other places where you might have seen the color spectrum?

4. **Lenses.** Lenses come in six basic shapes and every one of them bends light. Lenses help the eye see better. One side of a lens must be curved. Use a spoon—either side—as a lens. Its curve will make the image upside down (on the concave side) or broad and slightly enlarged (on the convex side).

5. **Magnifying lens.** Use a magnifying lens to explore things up close. You will see many more details with it than you can see without it. A simple magnifying lens with a handle is a great take-along on nature walks. Are the sides of the magnifying glass flat or curved?

6. **Shadows.** Shadows are made when you block light. Indoors, use a lamp without the shade or a high-intensity light on a wall. Let the children make fingerplays on the wall. Outdoors, children can play a game of shadow tag, especially in late afternoon when the shadows are longest. A five-year-old might be able to trace someone else's shadow with chalk on the sidewalk.

EXPLORING HEAT

Preparation:

Talk about heat. Heat cannot be seen or heard. Heat can be felt. Everything has a temperature, from low to high. Heat rises and cold sinks in both air and water. Different kinds of materials conduct heat well, some conduct (carry) heat not so well, and some block heat.

What you need:

Various materials that will demonstrate heat, absence of heat, conductors. See each activity.

What you do:

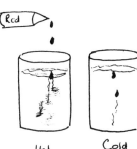

1. **Heat rises.** Fill two clear jars of the same size with water—one with hot water, one with very cold water. Put two drops of food coloring in each jar. Where did the dye go in each jar? The heated water is more active and swirls the color more evenly; the cold water is not moving as much and the dye sinks to the bottom.

2. **Heat conductors.** Give each child a coin that has been in the refrigerator or freezer. Hold it tightly in one hand. Does the penny get warmer after a few minutes? Touch the palms of your hands together. Is one hand colder than the other? Did some of the heat from your hand go into the penny? Repeat this experiment using a baked potato that is small enough to hold in one hand. This will demonstrate that heat from an object can be passed from the oven to the potato to a hand.

3. **Insulators.** Some things block out heat. Put a mitten on one hand and no mitten on the other hand. Then hold an ice cube in each hand. Does one cube melt faster than the other? Why? Try this again holding a mug of hot chocolate in each hand. Try it again holding a glass of ice water. What happens to the hot chocolate? What happens to the ice in the ice water? What does the mittened hand feel? Why?

4. **Friction produces heat.** Two slightly rough surfaces rubbed together can cause enough friction to produce heat or, perhaps, a spark. The bumps and ridges on the skin of your hands can cause friction. Rub your hands together rapidly. What do you feel? Rub together two sticks, or rub the point of one stick on cement. Touch the end of the stick. Does it feel warm to the touch? If it got hot enough, could the sticks light a fire?

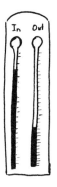

5. **Thermometers—instruments to measure heat.** Use an oral thermometer to take someone's body temperature. How warm are you? Look at an indoor/outdoor thermometer to find out the temperatures inside and out. Where is it warmer? colder? How can a thermometer be helpful?

EXPLORING MAGNETS

Preparation:

Read a story about magnets. Talk about the properties of magnets. Magnets can be used as tools. Their magnetic field is a source of power and can be different strengths depending on their size. Magnets are made from iron or steel and only attract substances made of iron or steel. A magnet has two poles: North and South. A north will repel (go against) another north, but will attract (go toward) a south.

What you need:

Various types of magnets and metallic and nonmetallic objects to show how magnets work. See each activity.

Being able to examine and test a wide variety of materials gives children a basic understanding of our world.

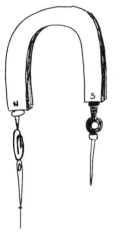

What you do:

1. **What things stick to a magnet?** Use a magnet and touch various objects: tacks, nails, paper clips, bottle cap, toothpick, rubber band, cotton ball, drinking glass, pencil, eraser, penny, nickel, dime, bobby pin, toy car, and so on. Which ones stick? Why do some stick and some do not? Sort the objects into two groups—those that are attracted and those that are not attracted.

2. **Can a magnet work through things?** Take a paper plate. Put the bar magnet below the plate and a few paper clips on top. Now move the magnet. Do the paper clips move? Do they follow the magnet? Do this again replacing the paper plate with a piece of wood, a piece of fabric, a glass pie plate, a metal cookie sheet. What happens?

3. **Can a magnet work through water?** Put a few paper clips in the bottom of a clear glass. Fill the glass with water. Use a bar magnet to go "fishing" for the paper clips. Are the clips attracted to the magnet through the water? Can the magnet lift them out of the water?

4. **Which part of the magnet is the strongest—the middle or the ends?** Spread a pile of tacks on a table. Slowly push the magnet into the pile. Where do the tacks attach? Where is the magnet's strongest pull?

5. **What happens when two of the same poles are placed together?** Use two bar magnets. Let one rest on the table. Place the second magnet's north near the first magnet's north. What happens? Place the south near the south. What happens?

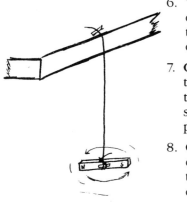

6. **Will one magnet pick up another magnet?** Use two bar magnets or one bar magnet and one horseshoe magnet. Hold one near the other, matching N with S on each end. Can one pick up the other?

7. **Can a magnet show direction?** Attach a 20″ length of string to the center of a bar magnet. Tape the other end of the string to the edge of a table. Let the magnet dangle and turn. When it stops moving, look at the ends. In which direction is the N pointing?

8. **Can you make a magnet?** Use one end of a magnet to rub a needle or a nail. Rub it 25 or more times. Always lift it and rub it in the same direction. Now test the needle. Does it attract paper clips or tacks? Is the needle a magnet now?

EXPLORING TOOLS

Preparation:

Talk about tools. Discuss the fact that tools can increase a person's strength. Some tools are simple like a spoon or bottle opener; some are complicated like a lawn mower. Each tool usually has just one purpose—that is, one use.

What you need:

Different tools and materials to demonstrate the five basic tools and how they work. See each activity.

What you do:

1. **Lever.** A lever is a tool that either lifts or pries. What are some different levers? (A shovel, a spoon, a nail clippers, scissors, or a seesaw.) Make a lever outdoors. Take a long plank—four-foot or longer. Use a concrete block as a fulcrum. Rest the lever on the fulcrum, first in the center of the plank and then at various distances from the end. Use the lever to lift something heavy such as a bag of cement or fertilizer. Is it easier to lift the weight when the fulcrum is in the middle or near the end of the plank? Why? Can you lift the weight easier by hand or by using your lever?

2. **Inclined Plane.** An inclined plane makes a load easier to carry because the slope is more gradual although it gets longer. What are some examples of inclined planes? (Ramps for moving furniture or boxes of food; ramps for wheelchairs; a sloping hill

child needs to examine all things closely and find their points of similarity and their points of difference so his knowledge can rest on firm foundations. This testing, either by experience or by observation, is the heart of science and he must do it as much as he can.

Marguerite Kelly and Elia Parsons

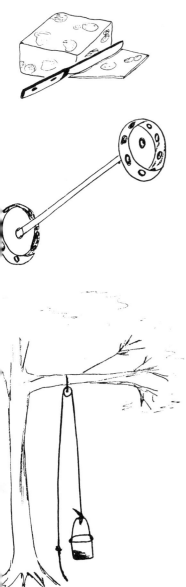

as opposed to straight up a mountain side.) Make an inclined plane. Use a table or chair to lean a ramp made from a board or stiff piece of cardboard. Use toy trucks to roll on the plane. Change the height of the plane. Do the cars and trucks go down faster on the higher or lower planes (straighter or steeper slope)? At which heights would it be easiest and hardest to climb?

3. **Wedge.** A wedge is a small inclined plane usually used to split, break, or crack open something. What are some examples of wedges? (An axe, a chisel, a hatchet, or a knife, or a triangular shaped block that holds open the door.) Use a knife to cut a block of cheese or meat. How does the wedge work to split it open?

4. **Wheel and Axle.** A wheel and axle makes work easier because the wheel rolls and because the larger the wheel's rim, the faster the wheel will go. What are some examples of wheel and axle? (The wheelbarrow, a pull cart, a wagon, roller skate, toy cars and trucks.) Make a wheel and axle out of the pieces of a toy construction set such as Tinker Toys, Legos, or others. Try different sizes of wheels. Which wheels roll farther or faster?

5. **Pulley.** A pulley is a tool that helps you lift a weight with half the effort that would be needed without it. For examples of pulleys, look around your house—a window drapes' pulley or miniblinds' pulling mechanism. A lumber yard may have machines with pulleys. Make a pulley and rope. Hook a real pulley onto the floor of a raised surface like a fort or balcony or porch. Put the rope through and tie a bucket to one end. Try to lift different loads with and without the pulley. Which way is easier?

Short Trips and Big Adventures

24

Ready, Set, Go!

Playgroup and preschool days are some of the best memories of my daughters when they were preschool-aged. The trips together with all the children and mothers punctuated a delightful and enriching experience for us both.

Anne Engelhardt, mother of Rachel, Laura, Sarah, Matthew, and Luke

Children are eager to explore their world—to experience its colors, its movement, and its sounds. Being surrounded by the many sensations our world provides is a learning experience in itself. If you have ever observed a preschooler chase a butterfly or pick a dandelion on a summer day, you will notice he is filled with wonder. He is amazed at the butterfly's darting quickness, its colors, its silent movement, its elusiveness. The delicate fuzzy white dandelion waits to be plucked and blown apart. Lighter than air, it disappears with the wind. Learning in its most natural form is taking place.

Parents can explore the world with their preschoolers. They can look at the world through their preschoolers' eyes and answer their questions. You can present new experiences for little ones to absorb and learn from. As parents in a cooperative preschool you can draw upon each other for ideas to open up doors in your curious preschoolers' minds. From a walk down the block to a big adventure in a nearby city, many learning experiences await your youngsters.

In a formal school, children will be stimulated by teachers, books, and other media found within the confines of the school building. It is a rare school that can offer excursions into the outside world whenever the teacher thinks an opportunity for learning could be enhanced. Teachers and administrators limit field trips because they are often too expensive and too time-consuming, or they lack the needed supervision, or they don't have buses. It takes an extra effort to gather a large group for outside-the-classroom learning experiences.

Yet, the children are so eager to go. They yearn for the freedom to learn from imitation and observation. These sensations and experiences are necessary for optimal learning. As cooperative preschool parents, we have the opportunity to provide these experiences for our children. In a small group, the children can explore their world in a variety of ways. All of the parents may choose to go along for the journey—each accompanying his or her own child—or the group may decide to have just one or two parents serve as the tour guides. It has been our experience that most of the parents are anxious to come along and join the fun, and this is when dad often joins in, too.

xpose your child to as much as possible; the wider his scope, the more he will learn. Take him places with you—let him meet new people, see new things, have new experiences. Children learn gradually and naturally from the people with whom they come in contact.

Elizabeth Hainstock

Opportunities for exercising curious minds seem more plentiful with a change of setting. Children stimulate each other's learning in a natural, spontaneous way. One child (or parent) starts to sing a song and the others join in. Someone creates a poem about what they see or hear while the others add their comments. Laughter is spontaneous. A parent discovers footprints in the mud and sets the stage for detectives to solve the mystery. "Why do the ladybugs have spots?" a child questions, leading his parent on a quest for the answer.

Learning can take place even traveling to and from your destination. Parents can use their imaginations and come prepared with ideas for riddles, books, or games to challenge or relax the children as needed while in transit. A field trip begins the moment you leave the doorstep—from the ride in the car to the walk across the parking lot and the waiting in line. Numerous opportunities for learning can be found along the way.

No matter what the weather, your pre-school children will enjoy a short trip or big adventure.

Short Trips

Short trips out of the house include backyard excursions, experiences in the garden, or a walk to the creek. Many times a walk to the school or playground or a hike through a field in various seasons can hold a wide variety of learning opportunities. (See Chapter 23.) Don't be afraid to follow the children's lead, and let their curiosity show you the way.

Three-year-olds will enjoy these short excursions best. Both young and older preschoolers benefit from experiencing their neighborhood. You may want to discuss safety near the home, point out dangers, and suggest precautions. You may want to use this as a lesson in independence, having the children demonstrate how to cross the street or walk home when the house is not in sight. Provide some imaginative play-time, too—some will choose the sandbox, others the play equipment, while still others may choose to create their own imaginary game to play. Even with no formal reason for an outing, learning will occur at least in social understanding.

Big Adventures

Bigger adventures—those farther from home requiring longer attention spans—can be planned for preschoolers who are four and older. A big adventure includes just about anywhere the group chooses to go. Consider the distance and time elements though; judge what your youngsters can handle. Be wary of traditional field trips to the zoo or the the big city museum that children may experience when they go to school. Sometimes these require more walking than the group is comfortable with, and provide much more input than preschoolers can handle in one day.

Some guidelines you may want to consider when planning an adventure for your group include

1. Plan your adventure ahead of time:

> The world is so full
>   of a number of things,
> I'm sure we should all
>   be as happy as Kings.
> Robert Louis Stevenson

Arrange the date with other parents.
Arrange parent-helpers and transportation (2 to 3 children per adult is a good number).
Notify the place you will be going to visit (good public relations never hurts).
Inquire about any charges or costs.
Name tags may provide some peace of mind (and may be fun to make).*

Decide on lunches or snacks to be taken along or money to buy food or trinkets.
Visit the place alone once—if possible—to check on parking, seating, and other unforeseen variables you may need to be aware of before experiencing the trip with a group of young children.

2. Prepare the children:

Use discussion time to discuss the journey.
Use playtime for acting out the roles they will be experiencing whenever applicable.
Read books to the children (use the library for help) that explain or will aid in their understanding of the excursion.
Use art or craft or music time to develop some ideas about their journey.
Establish some rules with the group; discuss do's and dont's for your journey. Let the children help. Preparation tips are listed for each individual adventure. Discuss getting lost and who they can trust.

---

* As a safety precaution, simply put the child's last name on his name tag. Unfortunately today, one must be careful of first names on name tags when children are in public. It is easier for a child to go off with a stranger when he is addressed by his first name.

After discussing "big and little," this preschool group visited a display of miniatures.

3. Plan games, songs, or snacks for travel time:

Have a jug of water and snacks if the day will be long.

Be prepared with some guessing games to play in the car, bus or train before arriving at your destination.

Be prepared with some traveling songs or fingerplays such as "The Wheels on the Bus" or "This Old Man."

Have some relaxing books or games ready for a tired journey home.

Have children use the bathroom before departing, especially if it will be a long drive.

4. Plan a follow-up activity for the children to remember their journey.

Draw a picture or free-form design of something they felt, smelled, saw, or heard while on their journey.

Let the children make up a story or poem about their experiences.

Tell a group story about the sequence of events that took place (let them illustrate the events and make their story into a book).

Tape-record them telling about their experiences while on the outing, then let them listen.

Make a craft or art project to help remember the day.

Dramatize the event using a prop box. (See Chapter 12.)

Field Trip Suggestions

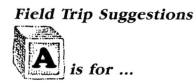 *is for ...*

ART MUSEUM

Before the trip:

Preview the works of art the children will be going to see, choose just a few halls to visit rather than trying to see too many.

Explore some art media such as: watercolors, tempera paints, clay, sculpture, noodle collages, paint rocks (see Chapter 16).

Discuss artists, why they draw, what they draw.

Tell a story about a famous artist and show some of his or her work. Talk about the media the artists use: paint, chalk, ink, etc.

During the trip:

Pick out some favorite works and discuss how you feel when you see the paintings or sculptures; have the children tell you if they like them and why.

Discuss the media in which the work is done.

After the trip:

Have children make their own artwork using different media such as clay, paint, or a texture design of noodles, beans, seeds, etc. Frame the artwork and let them take it home for display;

If possible, visit a nearby artist.

AIRPORT

Before the trip:

Talk about how people use airports for transportation. You may want to discuss making a reservation, buying the tickets, when to arrive for a flight, catching a connecting flight, where your baggage will be, and where to pick it up. There are several books on airports that can be found at the library.

You may want to study transportation as a central theme using books with pictures or easy-to-understand stories describing different kinds of transportation.

Look at the history of airplanes from Kitty Hawk, Orville and Wilbur Wright, and the various phases of flying history.

During the trip:

Find a quiet waiting area and have the children tell where they would like to go on an imaginary flight.

Look at the airplanes; talk about the flight preparations such as fueling, observing the weather, calling the tower. Observe some take-offs and landings.

If possible, meet a pilot and go out to see one particular plane.

After the trip:

Talk about their favorite part.

Have the children think about what makes the plane fly.

Talk about the size of an airplane on the ground and in the air.

AQUARIUM

Before the trip:

Before visiting an aquarium, make an underwater scene using magazine pictures of different fish. Talk about the many different kinds of fish, colors, sizes. How do fish breathe? What do they eat? Try pretending to be a fish.

A large city may have an actual aquarium; a smaller city may call for a journey to the pet store.

Before visiting a pet store, talk about fish as pets. What do they eat? What kind of care do they need?

During the trip:

Observe the many kinds of fish, colors, sizes, etc.

Observe how certain fish co-exist with other fish.

Talk about the aquarium hardware, pumps, scenery, real and unreal props.

After the trip:

Talk about how fish survive underwater.

Pretend to be a fish.

How do aquariums provide oceanlike surroundings for different types of fish?

Listen to a "Little Thinker" tape of the sea and draw the picture.

Have the children care for a goldfish. Perhaps buy it and name it. Let the goldfish travel to each house. At the end of the preschool year, draw the name of the eventual owner.

 **is for ...** BAKERY (DOUGHNUT SHOP)

Before the trip:

Visit the bakery beforehand (a phone call is sometimes enough).

Bake pretzels, nut bread, or another favorite bakery recipe with the children.

Read *Little Red Hen* aloud or *In the Night Kitchen* by Maurice Sendek.

During the trip:

Discuss rules of visiting a bakery.

Talk about the bakery goods, color, shapes, and sizes.

Compare the large bakery utensils with "at home" utensils. Why is there a difference?

Talk about the need for cleanliness.

Take some time to smell the bakery goods.

After the trip:

Have a pretend bakery; sell your pretzels or bread slices; have small juice cups for sales clerks to pour for customers.

BAND PRACTICE

Before the trip:

Contact the local high school band director for permission to see the band practice.

Dramatize a marching band

1. Make or find rhythm or wind instruments;

2. While sitting (no instruments), sing a marching song ("Mac-Namara's Band" or "The Saints Go Marching In");

3. Clap the rhythm of the song;

4. March and clap to the rhythm;

5. March and play instruments to the tune.

Provide a band instrument for the children to touch and listen to.

New words: string instruments, wind instruments, percussion instruments.

During the trip:

Enjoy the band practice.

Observe the various instruments and decide which category they belong to.

After the trip:

Do a presentation for all the parents using your musical instruments.

BUS TRIP

Before the trip:

Talk about public transportation: jets, buses, taxis, ships, trains.

Sing: "The Driver of the Bus" (and do motions, too).

Discuss street safety while waiting for the bus.

During the trip:

Allow each child to put his fare in the box (if required).

Talk about sitting safely on the bus.

Observe the emergency pull cords.

Count the passengers; add and subtract as riders come and go.

Look out the window and enjoy the ride.

After the trip:

Dramatize a bus ride by pulling children in a wagon down the block.

Listen to the "Little Thinker Tape" on *Ways to Travel*.

BOAT RIDE

Before the trip:

Schedule the time and date of the ride; discuss safety.

Talk about travel on land, in the air, and in the water.

Provide an experiment on sinking and floating various items in a tub of water.

Read *Tubby the Tug Boat*. How did Tubby feel? Where did Tubby start his journey? What kinds of water did Tubby float down—stream, river, ocean? Also read *Little Toot* by Hardie Gramatky and *The Maggie B* by Irene Haas.

During the trip:

Talk about water safety, life preservers, sitting down, etc.

Observe the means of powering the boat (motor, oars, wind, paddle wheel.)

After the trip:

Sing "Row, Row, Row Your Boat" (using actions).

Make sailboats out of wood for tub toys; paint the boats.

Make Egg Boats for a snack. (See Chapter 17.)

BALL PARK

Before the trip:

Talk to the manager; make arrangements to go on the field and meet players.

Using a felt board, describe the game and show the bases and how the umpire fits into the game.

Explain the game: strikes, pitching techniques, how each player does his job, and how the players cooperate to make a team.

During the trip:

Observe home and visiting teams, uniforms, umpire, bases.

While on the field, children can experience how vast it can feel as a hitter or outfielder.

Watch the game. It may be that the game won't hold the attention of the children the entire time. This is not unusual; leaving early doesn't dampen the excitement.

By all means, take sides and cheer—and have a hot dog!

After the trip:

Play a game or just review with felt board the names of positions.

Talk about the game itself and how it felt to be on the field.

What was your favorite part? How would you feel if: You struck out? You caught a ball? Hit a home run?

BEAUTY/BARBER SHOP

Before the trip:

Ask children what a barber/beautician does. Discuss how they are trained and what tools they use.

Have children comb each other's hair.

During the trip:

Observe tools and chairs. Perhaps children can sit in chair.

Ask barber/beautician about his or her training.

Look through books of hair styles (usually available).

Watch someone getting a hair cut.

After the trip:

Have children take turns pretending to be barbers or beauticians and clients. Use old sheet for cape. spray bottle of water for hair spray, and portable hair dryer (or just pretend). Explain why they cannot use real scissors on one another's hair.

BALLET

Before the trip:

Purchase tickets early so children will have good seats.

Listen to the music that accompanies the ballet you will see.

Allow children to listen quietly to the music while you explain what is happening; stick puppets can help you act out the story.

Discuss how the children will dress for this special occasion.

Read a book about ballet lessons.

During the trip:

Discuss ballet performances and the need for quiet.

Allow plenty of time to arrive early. Once children have found their seats, if possible, visit the orchestra.

Things to observe: lighting, costumes, music.

After the trip:

Talk about the experience, the music, and the dancers.

Practice some ballet steps: 1st position, 2nd position, 3rd position.

Listen to the music again and discuss their reactions.

If possible, have the children act out the story of the ballet or use puppets to tell the story.

 is for ...

CLEANERS

Before the trip:

Talk about the purpose that the cleaners serve.

Show the children clothing that can't be washed in a washing machine.

Let children feel fabrics and try to tell the difference between those that are washable and those that are not washable.

During the trip:

Have operator show how a garment is cleaned.

Observe machines and types of cleaners.

Also see how garments are pressed.

After the trip:

Have the children pretend to be cleaners and reenact the operator's actions.

Discuss clothing and its proper care.

A trip to the circus can give children some exciting memories.

CIRCUS

Before the trip:

Purchase tickets.

Read *Randy's Dandy Lions* by Bill Put. Ask: "Which lion tamer did you like best? Why? Why did the lions start to roar?"

During the trip:

En route: Talk about the circus—"What kind of animals can you expect to see? What are some circus acts you may see?"

New words: Ringmaster, trapeze, lion tamer.

Look at lights, nets, animals, clowns.

After the trip:

Create a backyard circus.

Balance beam (from 2 boards) for tightrope.

Give each other pony or elephant rides.

Tame the lions.

Have a box for the ringmaster to stand on to introduce each act.

Do acrobatics.

Dress up as clowns.

Sell popcorn or juice.

CAR WASH

Before the trip:

Provide a bucket and sponge to clean bikes and wagons.

Read *Harry the Dirty Dog* by Margret Graham.

During the trip:

Talk about how it feels in the car when entering and exiting the car wash.

What does it feel like inside the car wash?

Talk about how machines help us.

After the trip:

Wash the car together (arrange for children to wear appropriate clothes).

Do an art project of their impression of the car wash.

CAMPING

Before the trip:

Visit area beforehand.

Advise parents of proper clothing.

Go on an imaginary camp-out.

Plan the camp-out together: Food to bring; what to wear; where to sleep.

Put up a tent together in the backyard.

Add sleeping bags and backpacks.

Decide where to make a campfire, gather sticks and leaves (use a flashlight to represent the fire).

Sing some camp songs.

Talk about some camping rules such as protecting the environment.

During the trip:

Try walking quietly in the woods.

Collect a treasure; describe how it feels, how it smells, how it sounds.

Try to find some animal footprints, if possible. Follow them; talk about what kind of animal made them.

Collect leaves and other materials for future projects.

After the trip:

Make a collage from the leaves collected.

Read *Sleep Out* by Carol Carrick.

Do the science project, "Making a Woodland Scene." (See Chapter 23.)

CHRISTMAS CAROLING

Before the trip:

Decide where to go: senior citizen home, retirement home, hospital, handicapped school.

Choose which songs to sing; practice singing.

Make ornaments or snowflakes to decorate or give to the people they sing to.

During the trip:

Bring special handmade ornaments or artwork to give to the people or to decorate the area.

Enjoy singing.

After the trip:

Talk about how the people felt when they heard the singing.

Discuss doing things for others as important part of this season.

CHRISTMAS TREE DISPLAY

Before the trip:

Have children make ornaments and decorate tree (live one, construction paper one, or an art tree).

Read story and discuss how the decorating of the tree came to be.

Learn song "O Christmas Tree."

During the trip:

Observe decorations and sing "O Christmas Tree."

Compare the tree you visit to yours.

After the trip:

Draw the tree.

Discuss favorite ornaments.

How does the tree help us celebrate Christmas?

 *is for ...*

DIME STORE

Before the trip:

Pretend to have a store. Talk about what the store will sell.

Put price tags on some items. Use pretend money to pay for items.

Read *Corduroy* by Don Freeman.

Demonstrate the value of coins by using pennies; use
    a penny = 1 cent
    a nickel = 5 pennies
    a dime = 10 pennies or 2 nickels
    a quarter = 25 pennies or 2 dimes and a nickel

During the trip:

Allow each child to bring a small amount of money to purchase something.

Have children ask about prices; let them decide if they have enough money.

Allow children to give sales clerk their money and receive change along with their purchase.

New words: cashier, cash register, sales tax.

After the trip:

Talk about how people earn money.

Talk about saving money vs. spending it right away.

DOCTOR'S/DENTIST'S OFFICE

Before the trip:

Talk about how to stay healthy.

Try making a "health" chart for each child to complete for a week including: brush teeth, wash hands, wash face, eat a good breakfast.

Talk about how doctors help us to get well when we're sick.

Pretend a visit to the doctor (or dentist). Use a white shirt for the doctor, a gauze bandage, and any other props you may think of.

Read *Come to the Doctor, Harry* or, for the dentist, *The Bears' Toothache* by David McPhail.

During the trip:

Observe the various equipment you see and talk about its uses.

Point out the duties of the nurse, doctor (dentist), receptionist.

If possible, have the doctor or dentist say a few words to the children.

After the trip:

Discuss how it feels to go to the doctor when you are well or when you are sick.

Horseback riding can be another enjoyable outing for the children, even in winter.

DUCK POND

Before the trip:

Visit the pond area ahead of time.

Talk about animals with feathers.

Read *Chickens Aren't the Only Ones* by Ruth Heller.

Practice being various birds: chicks, ducks, blackbirds, eagles.

Find a bird's nest to examine.

Talk about eggs: color, shape, size.

During the trip:

Have a picnic.

Try bringing some bread to feed the ducks.

Enjoy watching the ducks; observe the similarities and differences in the ducks.

Find some feathers to take home.

After the trip:

Talk about migration.

Read *Make Way For Ducklings* by Robert McCloskey.

Make a bird's nest from clay, grass, or other materials.

Use feathers for an art project.

is for ...

ELEMENTARY SCHOOL

Before the trip:

Read *First Day of School* (Berenstein Bears) or *Talk About School (Lady Bird Books).*

Talk about preschool vs. elementary school.

During the trip:

If close enough, walk to school.

Have children visit classroom; if teacher is receptive perhaps the children can do an activity with students. Otherwise, observe not only the classroom but cafeteria (perhaps have lunch), gym, playground.

After the trip:

Discuss how the children feel about going to school when they are older. What did they like about the school? What was the teacher like? Plan a math or reading readiness project and explain that this will help them be prepared when it is time to go to school. (See Chapters 21 and 22.)

is for ...

FLORIST

Before the trip:

Talk about how flowers are used to decorate and to help make sick or sad people feel better, and as gifts. Using an arrangement, show the children how they are put together.

Show them artificial flowers. Perhaps have artificial flowers available to put together.

Discuss the sense of smell and sight.

During the trip:

Smell! Differentiate between smell of roses and carnations and other flowers. Observe beauty of flowers.

Watch a florist put an arrangement together.

After the trip:

Have children arrange real flowers or flowers made from construction paper. Take to nursing home.

Do craft project, "Making a Spring Bouquet." (See Chapter 15.)

Try planting flower seeds for a science project. (See Chapter 23.)

FAIR

Before the trip:

Preview the fairgrounds; pick several areas to see; limit the time.

Talk about fairs; what might be at a fair. If there are any children's exhibits or baking contests, enter something as a group.

Pick one or two exhibits to talk about with the children; plan some activities to help them better understand their purpose.

During the trip:

Talk about how to be safe in a crowd.

Have brown bag lunches, or sample food sold at booths.

Enjoy and talk about the various exhibits. Stop and experience the smells and sounds.

After the trip:

Let each child tell about which area he enjoyed and why? Talk about the smells they experienced, and the sounds they heard.

Plan a craft project related to one of the exhibits they saw.

FIRE STATION

Before the trip:

Call local fire station and arrange for tour time.

Inform the person giving the talk of the age of the children; help him/her be aware of their level of understanding.

Talk about community helpers: mail carriers, police officers, firefighters.

Talk about what to do if your house is on fire and what not to do. Dramatize a house on fire; actors might include: firefighters, mom, dad, child, etc.

During the trip:

Talk about what firefighters wear and why. Talk about fire trucks and other equipment.

Enjoy the tour!

After the trip:

Write a thank-you letter.

Have older children draw something that is a fire hazard.

Pretend to call the fire department about a fire.

Children enjoy the thrill of sitting high up on a fire truck during a visit to the fire station.

FISHING

Before the trip:

Check out the fishing area for safety. Provide a fishing rod for each child.

Have a fishing contest at home; try to "cast" a rod in a bucket of water (use a yardstick with string and a weight attached). Cut "fish" from construction paper to stress different concepts; let children describe the fish they catch. Use:

different colors   various sizes   letters or numbers on each

Let the children cast their line; if possible, attach the "fish" to the line with a paper clip from an unseen area.

During the trip:

Talk about fishing safety, being quiet, etc. Bring a picnic lunch.

Enjoy fishing. New words: patience, bait, rod, reel.

After the trip:

Make a poster showing water animals. Use watercolors to paint fish (have the fish shape drawn; let the children paint the water, the fish, etc.)

Talk about the fish smells.

Read *Swimmy* by Leo Lionni.

FARM

Before the trip:

Arrange for convenient time to tour the farm, either an animal farm or food farm.

Talk about farms; show some photos of farm machines and discuss their uses. Read a book about a farm.

Draw some barn shapes; let the children color them. Make a farm collage from magazine pictures.

Sing "Old MacDonald."

During the trip:

Talk about the type of farm.

New words: tractor, combine, plow, cultivator.

Talk about animal care. Point out what the animals eat.

After the trip:

Tell a story with pictures on a felt board depicting how the items from a farm start out, grow, are harvested, sold to a store.

Visit a supermarket or grocery store and talk about how some of the items got there.

Plant some seeds and watch them grow. (See Chapter 23.)

On a visit to a farm the children see the cows, the milking machine, and the holding tanks of fresh milk so they learn firsthand how milk gets to the shelves of the grocery store.

is for ...

GROCERY STORE

Before the trip:

Arrange with manager for time and date to tour store.

Talk about the four food groups. Have magazine pictures of food to sort into food groups.

Pass around a grocery bag with real food; allow children to tell which food group each item belongs in. Talk about foods that do not have a group: candy, soda, etc.

Make a grocery list for children to find at the store. For example:

5 red apples	10 carrots	cheese
1 gallon milk	8 potatoes	3 oranges

During the trip:

Find the various areas: bakery goods, vegetables and fruits, meats, and dairy products. Point out the differences, for example, meats are kept cold, etc. Visit the back storage areas where the dairy products and meats are stored, where the frozen products have to be kept.

Have children select the groceries on their list and go through checkout counter to pay for them.

After the trip:

Prepare a well-balanced lunch (use some of the foods purchased).

Talk about how the food gets to grocery store.

On any field trip out-doors, the children will enjoy running, climbing, and exploring.

GARDEN

Before the trip:

Talk about where foods come from; use drawings, pictures, or sequence cards to tell the story of how a seed grows, bears fruit, and dies.

Read *The Carrot Seed* by Ruth Krauss

Discuss proper clothes for the garden.

During the trip:

Talk about the kind of garden you are visiting; what kind of plants and fruits or vegetables will grow. Talk about the stage of growth the garden is in.

Point out the various shaped leaves; touch the different textures. Taste some of the produce if ripe and edible. Enjoy the smells.

After the trip:

Tell a story letting each child tell what kind of seed he would like to be. Dramatize the story. Each child crouches down to represent seeds; the parent becomes the sun with arms encircled over head. She shines her warmth on the seeds. Then she becomes the rain with fingers "running" to represent the rain, she sprinkles each seed. Now, ever-so-slowly, the seeds begin to sprout and grow, stretching to the sky. Arms get heavy from the weight of the fruit. The parent becomes the gardener, plucking each plant's fruit. The plants then begin to wither and die, slowly falling back to the earth in peace.

Plant a variety of seeds in the sections of an egg carton and compare their rate of growth. (See Chapter 23.)

 *is for ...*

HIKE

Before the trip:

Decide on a place to hike; think about appropriate clothes for the group. (A hike can be taken to almost anywhere, although generally somewhere in a woods or forest preserve is a good choice.)

Visit the area ahead of time, if possible. Talk about where you will hike, for how long, and why you are doing this. Talk about possible dangers and how to avoid them.

Talk about whether you will want to have a snack and how to carry it.

During the trip:

Talk about how it feels to walk rather than ride.

Point out the smell of the air, the temperature, the sounds, and what they feel. Try walking slowly. Do they like a slow hike? Why? Walk quickly; what changes do they notice?

Talk about why it is easy to walk in some places and harder in others. Stop, rest, be silent, enjoy!

After the trip:

Write a group experience story about your hike; draw a picture of what they remember.

Make placemats with treasures (such as leaves, seeds, etc.); put the treasures on a piece of construction paper and cover with clear contact paper.

HISTORICAL SITE

Before the trip:

Visit the site for some background.

Talk about the historical event, person, or structure.

Read and show pictures to further enhance the children's understanding. Use grandparents' ages to explain how long ago in history ("Your grandmother was only three years old when ....").

During the trip:

Point out any printed information and mention the significance of what they are seeing.

Enjoy the outing.

After the trip:

Read about the historical site, if possible, or other stories of the history of your area.

HANDICAPPED SCHOOL

Before the trip:

Call the school well in advance to set up an appointment; discuss the types of handicaps the school works with.

Talk about handicaps; ask if they know anyone who uses a wheelchair or is blind or deaf. Talk about why some people are handicapped (birth defects, accidents, illness, etc.)

Experience some handicaps. Use sign language to tell their names or explain something. Blindfold one child at a time and have him listen to tell what you are doing: walk, tear paper, pour milk, etc.

Let children try to get around without using their legs.

During the trip:

Visit the school; discuss the need for quiet and courtesy.

Try to see various areas of the school where different projects are going on. Listen, enjoy, and learn.

After the trip:

Write a thank-you note.

Discuss the experience and how the children felt about seeing handicapped people.

Invite a handicapped person to talk with the group.

 is for ...

ICE SKATING

Before the trip:

Read a story from a Scandinavian country where the children ice skate.

Dramatize a dance on pretend skates to waltz music.

During the trip:

Rent or bring skates; if possible, have one adult for each child.

Enjoy skating.

After the trip:

Have a hot drink (apple cider or hot cocoa are nice); let the children pour and serve the adults.

 **is for ...**

JET TOUR

Before the trip:

Call airline for appointment to see if a tour can be arranged. If a special tour is not possible, take the children just for a tour of the airport.

Talk about transportation. Read about a jet ride; talk about any actual jet travel experience the children may have had.

During the trip:

Depending on the size of the airport and crowd level, your group may wish to visit the observation deck, the control tower, the weather briefing room, etc.

Point out the size of the planes. Think about how little they look in the sky. Why? (Stress good listening while the guide explains things.)

If possible to tour a real plane or go for a ride, point out:
> the cockpit controls; the rest rooms; the storage compartments; the emergency procedure cards; seat belts.

Enjoy the tour!

After the trip:

Play a control tower game. One person is the "tower"; the other children are blindfolded (for stormy, foggy weather). They must pilot their airplanes to the runway by listening to the tower. The control tower child can give directions. For example: "Take three steps forward and one step to the right. Go back five steps and turn around."

Make kites and fly them. (See Chapter 15.)

JUNK YARD

Before the trip:

Call junk yard for permission and possible tour.

Read *Regards to the Man in the Moon* by Ezia Jack Keats.

During the trip:

Talk about where all the junk comes from, whether some people might still want some things that are in the junk yard, and what they will do with the "junk."

Enjoy the tour!

After the trip:

Go on a "junk" collecting hike. Have each child bring home a "treasure" and tell why he chose it.

is for ...

KENNEL/PET STORE

Before the trip:

Arrange a convenient time for a tour.

Read *Can I Keep Him?* by Steven Kellogg or *Emmett's Pig* by Mary Stolz.

Talk about pets; how to care for them. What kind of pet would they like to have and why?

If you'll be visiting a kennel, find a book about the breeds of dogs you will see.

During the trip:

Point out the different sized cages and different types of food the animals eat.

Notice the type of equipment you would need for each type of pet—leash, dish, collar, cage, etc.

After the trip:

Let each child take a turn pretending to be a pet as the other children try to guess which one they are.

Plan a craft project related to the animals you saw. (See Chapter 15.)

is for ...

LAKE/RIVER/OCEAN/POND

Before the trip:

Talk about bodies of water. If a globe is available, show how much water is on earth. Ask the children what kinds of water they have seen. Show pictures of oceans, rivers, lakes, bays, etc.

Read *Little Toot* or *Tubby.*

Make wooden boats from wood scraps.

During the trip:

Point out the shore line. Talk about how the water moves; explore the shore. Float your boats out onto the water.

Talk about the animals that live in or near the water.

Throw pebbles into the water and talk about what happens.

After the trip:

Make a poster collage from magazine cut-outs of all the things found in, around, on, or over the lake.

The library offers the opportunity to discover what subjects are of interest to the children.

LIBRARY

Before the trip:

Talk to the Children's Librarian at your local library to arrange for a tour. Check out some library books and read them aloud. Show the children the card system or other method the library uses to keep track of their books.

With older children, obtain forms so they can fill them out and get their own library cards.

Discuss what other services your library offers: records, cassette tapes, films.

During the trip:

Have the Librarian show the children around and explain what kinds of books are in the children's section.

Let the children look around on their own. Have each select a book to check out.

If they are old enough, have them apply for their own library cards.

Look at any exhibits that are on display.

After the trip:

Read the books the children took out.

Discuss purpose of the library, how many books are there, who needs the library, etc.

Return the books when they are due; explain fines for overdue books and why these are charged.

is for ...

MUSEUM

Before the trip:

Talk about what you will be going to scc. If it is a historical museum, tell the children they will be going to a special place for people to learn about the past.

Discuss the need to be very careful of what you touch, no climbing or leaning on glass display cases, etc.

Read a story related to the exhibit you'll be seeing.

During the trip:

If it is a large museum, you may want to focus on only one or two exhibits per visit.

Enjoy the museum!

After the trip:

As a group, write an experience story about what you saw.

Let the children express their reactions in an art project.

MIME ACT

Before the trip:

Purchase tickets in advance or contact a university school of acting for permission to observe some mime.

Talk about feelings; Hap Palmer's record "Getting to Know Myself" has some good ideas.

Use examples of faces painted white for children to draw that are either happy, sad, angry, sleepy, etc.

Have children act out simple ideas without using words such as:
    brushing teeth
    walking upstairs
    swimming
    playing piano

During the trip:

Enroute, discuss proper behavior at the theater (stay seated, etc.).

Enjoy the act!

After the trip:

Paint children's faces white and have them act out nursery rhymes such as "Little Miss Muffet," "Jack and Jill," or "Humpty Dumpty."

MAGIC SHOW

Before the trip:

Read *A Special Trick* by Mercer Mayer or *The Sorcerer's Apprentice.* Talk about magic. "What is magic? If you had magic glasses, what would you do?"

Discuss proper behavior at the show.

During the trip:

Enjoy the show!

After the trip:

Practice some magic tricks. Use some clear soda and a few raisins. Put the raisins in the bottom of the glass and pour in the soda. Say: "Rise, raisins"; watch what happens. Now try the "trick" with flat soda. Ask the children why the raisins didn't rise. Use this "experiment" to talk about other science projects with magnets, sinking vs. floating objects, etc. (See Chapter 23.)

 *is for ...*

NEWSPAPER OFFICE

Before the trip:

Arrange a convenient time to visit (small newspapers may be more accommodating).

Talk about "news" and how we learn about it—television, radio, newspapers.

Be sure to have copies of the newspaper whose office you'll be visiting.

Point out parts of the paper of interest to the children—local news about their area, weather reports, etc.

Talk about how reporters find out about the news.

During the trip:

Watch the people at work and discuss what they are doing.

Observe the printing press and how fast it works.

Listen to the sounds and smell the odors.

After the trip:

Do a group newsletter; report any news about the children, the weather, book reviews; have children do some artwork. Then photocopy so each child can have a copy.

Use ink pads to make thumbprints; use stamps on the ink pad to write a message.

NATURE CENTER

Before the trip:

Talk about animals native to the area; make a list of the animals (use pictures, if possible). Put the animals into categories such as birds, reptiles, water animals, mammals.

Discuss what makes a bird a bird, or a mammal a mammal.

During the trip:

Bring a bag to collect "treasures" such as leaves, rocks, feathers.

Become detectives and search for footprints; try and describe the animal that made them.

If flowers are in bloom, take photos for the children to enjoy later.

Point out the plants. "Where is the biggest plant? The smallest? What colors are the plants and surroundings? How do the leaves feel?" (See Chapter 23.)

After the trip:

If you saw any animals, find a book that tells more about them.

Make a collage of the treasures you collected. (See Chapter 16.)

Do leaf rubbings from any leaves you found. (See Chapter 15.)

NURSING HOME

Before the trip:

Visit the facility ahead of time and determine the ability of the patients to interact with the children.

Arrange with nursing home for a convenient time and date to visit.

Talk about growing old; have children cut out pictures of
babies   children   parents   grandparents

Discuss growing older; what would make a grandparent smile?
singing   artwork   flowers   cards

Make something special to share with the patients or practice a song to sing.

During the trip:

Allow children to meet the people, perhaps sing a song or share their artwork or flowers.

After the trip:

Talk about what they experienced, and how they felt.

Make a collage of pictures showing various aged people.

Seeing animals up close at a nature center or small zoo helps children understand more about our world.

is for ...

OPTOMETRIST/OPHTHALMOLOGIST

Before the trip:

Allow plenty of time to arrange an appointment with the office.

Discuss the senses and why they are special to us. Discuss each child's eye color.

Show a picture or model of an eye (you may be able to borrow this from a local school, library, or doctor's office).

Talk about eye safety and possible dangers from the sun, sharp objects, poisons, and swimming.

Try on different pairs of glasses and tell if and how things look different.

During the trip:

Point out the appointment desk, the waiting room, the doctor's office and chair. Try sitting in the chair.

If possible, have the children take a color blindness test or simple eye test.

After the trip:

Dramatize a visit to the eye doctor

Make eyeglasses from pipe cleaners and egg cartons.

 *is for ...* **POLICE DEPARTMENT**

Before the trip:

Call local police station and arrange a date and time to visit. (Brief the person giving the tour that you may need more explanations for words the children may not understand.)

Talk about who can be a police officer. Do they have to be a certain size? strong? Are there women on the police force? How are police officers trained?

Fingerprint each child and talk about their "special" prints, discuss how fingerprints can help policemen find criminals.

Play detective; choose one child to be wanted for a crime. Let the children guess who it is by asking questions, such as, what color hair? What color eyes? Is it a boy or girl? What color clothes?

During the trip:

Point out the police uniforms. Be sure to look at a squad car.

Where are the jail cells? How can the children help the police?

After the trip:

Dramatize a child(ren) getting lost at the park, zoo, etc. Stress only going with a uniformed police officer, have them describe their mother by name. If no police officer comes, tell them to stay put and "hug a tree" or sit down until mother finds them.

Make telephones; let children practice their phone numbers. Try writing the phone numbers on cardboard, outline the numbers with glue and shake sand, oatmeal, cornmeal, etc., over the glue.

If desired, talk about avoiding strangers who might cause the child harm. Read a book such as *Who Is a Stranger and What Should I Do?* by Linda Girard.

A visit to the post office helps children realize how the mail gets to their houses every day.

POST OFFICE

Before the trip:

Write a letter as a group and walk to the mailbox to mail it.

Read *A Letter to Amy* by Ezra Jack Keats.

Make a Valentine or Get Well Card for the children to mail when they get to the post office.

During the trip:

Observe the counter area where packages and special delivery letters are picked up.

Buy stamps for the cards you brought and mail them.

Look at any stamp collector books.

If possible, have a mail carrier take the group to his station and show how he sorts his route mail.

Visit the mail bins as they come and go on and off the mail trucks.

After the trip:

Talk about how a letter travels from one city (or country) to another.

Role play mail carrier. Have one carrier, let the other children put numbers in front of them to represent addresses. Let the carrier put the correctly numbered letter at the child's "house."

Watch for the Valentines or other cards to arrive at each child's house.

PUPPET SHOW

Before the trip:

Arrange for the group to get tickets, if necessary.

Allow free play with puppets and a puppet theater.

Read a familiar tale to the children and then act it out with puppets; let the children say their parts once they are familiar with the story.

If possible, read the story that the puppet show will be based on so the children can become familiar with the characters and story line.

During the trip:

Point out what kind of puppets are being used: hand puppets, marionettes, etc.

Be quiet and courteous during the show.

During intermission, discuss what they've seen so far.

After the show:

Make puppets such as sock puppets, stick puppets, or paint faces on fingers for puppets. Have the children act out the story they saw and new stories from their own imaginations.

 *is for ...*

QUARRY

Before the trip:

Talk about the construction process; what does it take to erect a building? Ideas include: lumber, tools, earth moving machines, cement, stone

Have the children construct buildings from quart milk cartons and make a city. Try covering some with paper or, for adobe effect, mix flour, salt, and water. Log houses can be made by pasting pretzels on the cartons.

Construct a Lincoln Log, Lego, or block building.

Read *Mike Mulligan and His Steam Shovel* by Virginia Lee Burton.

During the trip:

Discuss how the stone is used in construction, how the stone is collected to be hauled, and where the stone comes from.

After the trip:

Discuss what things we use from the earth—rocks, soil/plants, jewels.

Talk about mining. Make Rock Creatures. (See Chapter 15.)

 *is for ...*

RACE

Before the trip:

Do some stretching exercises:
>touch toes without bending knees
>straddle legs and twist arms from front to back
>stand on hands and feet and jog in place

Try to run (at a jog) for a short distance; have children feel their heartbeats in their necks. Discuss how exercise makes the heart pump harder and thus get stronger.

During the trip:

Arrive early to see runners warming up. Watch the runners exercise.

Have children ask some runners why they run. If race is not too long, wait to see who wins.

After the trip:

Talk about why people run.

Why do runners need water? What kind of foods do runners eat?

Discuss winning and losing and having fun trying.

Talk about running safety tips—good shoes (tied laces), don't run while holding something, don't run in the street.

RESTAURANT

Before the trip:

Talk about the people who run a restaurant.

Have children role-play "restaurant" with each child doing his part.

Discuss the four food groups and how to order a balanced meal consisting of meat, grains, dairy, fruits, and vegetables.

Talk about restaurant manners.

During the trip:

Let children look at the menu and help them choose what to order.

Have children tell the waiter or waitress their order and talk quietly while waiting and eating. When the meal is finished, pay the waiter, waitress, or cashier.

If possible, visit the kitchen and talk to the cook

After the trip:

Ask what they enjoyed the most and the least. Have them make sample menus with pictures of food from magazines.

Plan a special snack the children can prepare, like *Everybody Helped Soup* and pretend it will be served in a restaurant. (See Chapter 17.)

 *is for ...* **SKYSCRAPER**

Before the trip:

Make a "block" city with tall buildings. If blocks fall, discuss the problems of getting a skyscraper to stay up.

Talk about big cities and all the people who work there. Talk about how the people get to the top of tall buildings.

During the trip:

Have children stand outside the skyscraper and try to see the top.

Take elevator to the top floor if possible (count the floors). Look out the windows and observe the cars, people, other buildings, etc.

After the trip:

Use rectangles pre-cut from several colors of construction paper for children to glue on a large piece of paper to create a city landscape. Add special effects with chalk, glitter, watercolors, etc.

SWIMMING POOL

Before the trip:

Talk about water and sun safety
    never swim alone
    don't run near the pool, no pushing, etc.
    don't swim immediately after eating
    if you can't swim, use a float or have a big person with you
    use lotion if you sunburn; stay in the shade a lot

Discuss bringing swimsuits and towels if you will be able to go swimming at the pool.

During the trip:

If possible to go swimming, have fun in the water. Stress respect for the water (not fear). Point out the Lifeguard and discuss some ways to help a person in the water.

Discuss why you cannot swim during a thunderstorm.

After the trip:

Make a group poster about water safety and give it to the pool as a thank-you.

Plan a science project to learn more about water. (See Chapter 23.)

 *is for ...*

TRIP TO TOWN

Before the trip:

If you live in a comparatively small town with a central business street, this trip can be great fun due to the personal attention small businesses can offer. If you live in a larger town, a shopping center will be equally interesting.

Discuss some of the things that happen in your town.

Call the shop owners and notify them of your tour date and time.

During the trip:

Have children pair up and use safe street-crossing rules. If you are going to a shopping center, practice safety in a large parking lot.

Visit several of the businesses, having children observe the purpose of each, and perhaps talk to the owner or clerk.

Observe the activity in each store for a few minutes, watching the customers select merchandise or discuss the items with a sales person.

After the trip:

Using prop boxes, let the children make-believe they are the owners of various kinds of stores. They can take turns being customers with hats, purses or wallets, etc. (See Chapter.12)

Write an experience story about your tour. If you can, make copies and send them to the businesses as a "thank-you."

THEATER

Before the trip:

Purchase tickets in advance. Try to choose a story the children are familiar with, for example, *Cinderella*.

Read the story aloud and discuss it.

Talk about the difference between actors and real people.

Talk about dressing in nice clothes to go to the play, staying in your seat, and being quiet.

During the trip:

Find your seats and look at the program (if they have one). Point out the lighting, the costumes, the music, and the props.

At the intermission, discuss what has happened so far.

Enjoy the play!

After the trip:

Dramatize *Cinderella*. Put narration on a tape recorder, allowing pauses for children to say their parts. Put on the play for the parents and brothers and sisters.

A train ride may seem routine to many adults yet it's a wonderful adventure for preschool-aged children.

TRAIN RIDE

Before the trip:

Discuss various types of transportation.

Make a train from rectangles on a white sheet of paper using buttons for wheels and cotton for smoke.

Read *The Little Engine That Could* by Watty Piper.

During the trip:

Enjoy the scenery.

Talk about the different stops along the way.

Guess where people might be going on the train.

After the trip:

Pretend to be a "human" train by taking turns being the engine and caboose.

Have the children tell a sequential story about what happened on the trip, each one taking a turn and telling what happened next. Tape-record the story and listen to it later on.

 *is for ...* **UNUSUAL PET**

Before the trip:

Arrange with owner for a good date and time to visit.

Read *Can I Keep Him?* by Steven Kellogg.

Discuss pets, their care, their cost, etc.

Read a book about the kind of pet you will be visiting and discuss with the children whether it can be handled or petted, if it is dangerous, if they must be very quiet, etc.

During the trip:

Discuss with the owner how he/she cares for his pet, feeding, watering, exercise, handling, etc. Discuss any problems he/she has encountered.

If it is possible to handle the pet have the children take turns, being very gentle and careful.

Discuss why the owner decided to get this kind of pet.

After the trip:

Read *The House on East 88th Street* by Bernard Waber.

Plan a craft project related to the kind of pet you saw.

Write a "thank-you."

 *is for ...*

VETERINARIAN

Before the trip:

Talk about animal doctors, how they are trained, what they do.

Read *Come to the Doctor, Harry* by Mary Chalmers.

Discuss how pets may get hurt or sick and what owners can do to prevent illness or accidents.

During the trip:

Observe the animals in the waiting room.

Observe the animals after seeing the veterinarian; discuss the difference.

Tour the area where surgery is performed.

Visit animals who are recovering.

After the trip:

Discuss children's feelings about visiting the doctor; compare to how the animals were behaving.

Have the children bring stuffed animals and role-play going to the vet. Take turns being the doctor, receptionist, pet owner.

Write a "thank-you" to the Veterinarian and his or her staff.

 *is for ...*

WILD FLOWER/FRUIT PICKING

Before the trip:

Talk about the beauty flowers bring to the world.

Read *Blueberries For Sal* by Robert McCloskey or *Apple Pigs* by Ruth Orback.

During the trip:

Talk about how to pick the flowers or fruit (allow enough stem to put in water-filled cup).

Collect flowers in empty spice jars or collect fruit in small container.

After the trip:

Present the flowers to someone; clean the fruit and use for a recipe or freeze for later.

Use watercolors to fill in a flower picture.

WEATHER STATION

Before the trip:

Weather Stations are sometimes located near or in an airport. Preview the one near you so you have an idea of what to expect.

Make a weather chart and discuss the weather. Have the children use simple symbols to chart the weather for a week. Talk about the seasons and the weather in each season.

Discuss why predicting the weather is important to farmers, pilots, construction workers, etc.

During the trip:

Talk to the staff about variations in the weather. Discuss dangerous weather such as tornados, hurricanes, blizzards, etc.

Observe the instruments used to predict and measure the weather. New words: meteorologist, anemometer (measures wind), atmosphere.

After the trip:

By observing the clouds, see if you can predict the weather. Discuss what clouds are made of; make a cloud chart—cumulus: use cotton balls; stratus: use grey chalk; nimbus: use cotton with black watercolor paint to darken.

 *is for ...*

X-RAY LAB

Before the trip:

Show the children a picture of a skeleton from an encyclopedia or another source. Feel your bones under your skin.

Discuss any broken bones the children have had or any time they may have needed an x-ray due to illness or an object that was swallowed or at the dentist's office.

Talk about how the x-rays help us diagnose the proper treatment.

During the trip:

Look at the x-rays. Discuss when an x-ray is necessary.

Talk to the radiologist about his or her job and training.

After the trip:

Look at pictures of skeletons again and discuss.

Draw skeletons with white chalk on black construction paper.

 *is for ...* **YOGA CLASS**

Before the trip:

Do some yoga exercises. Read *Be a Bird, Be a Tree, Be a Frog* by Rachel Carr.

Discuss how yoga makes you feel—peaceful, stretched out, relaxed.

During the trip:

Quietly observe the class.

Attempt some simple positions.

Talk to the teacher before or after the classs about yoga.

After the trip:

Review yoga positions.

Incorporate yoga exercises into daily activity plan.

Do an art project to express feelings after doing yoga exercises.

Having fun just comes naturally to these children as they prove to us that learning doesn't have to take place in a classroom.

 **is for ...** **ZOO**

Before the trip:

Use magazine pictures of zoo animals to discuss which animals are sometimes found in zoos.

Talk about the areas of the world and help the children associate an animal with each
    Europe—horses, brown bear, wild boar
    Australia—kangaroos, koalas
    Africa—lions, giraffes, elephants
    Asia—pandas, tigers
    South America—llamas, monkeys
    North America—wolves, wildcats, grizzly bears, deer
    Antarctica—polar bears, penguins

Talk about the purpose of a zoo, to preserve some animals and so people can see them.

During the trip:

Visit the animals; talk about how each animal is protected by its color, strength, speed, etc.

Point out which animals have
hooves	feathers	fur
four legs	black tongues	bright colors

Discuss whether the animals seem happy or not.

If it is a large zoo, limit the number of exhibits you visit on each trip.

Bring your lunch and enjoy a picnic.

After the trip:

Make a chart to sort the animals—use magazine pictures: birds, reptiles, fish, mammals, marsupials.

Read *If I Ran the Zoo* by Dr. Seuss.

Role-play various zoo animals.

Field Trip Planning/Report

Make copies and keep these in your group's Plan Book

Destination:

Date:

Time:

Helpers:

Food (or snacks):

Preparation:

Highlights:

Follow-up Activities:

Miscellaneous Notes:

Enjoying
the Blossoms

In Part Four of *Playful Learning*, we reaffirm our belief that a cooperative preschool-at-home can meet your child's needs while providing an enjoyable and enriching experience for both of you. You can be the one to expand your child's understanding of the world, encourage his physical capabilities, stimulate his sensory awareness, provide a challenging environment for his developing mind, and foster his need for friendship. You can do all of this by participating in your child's preschool learning experiences. We hope you'll decide to give it a try!

Bonding Again

You Can Make It Happen

I felt I already knew my daughter well, but the more we did things together in our at-home preschool, the more I got to know her in new and different ways.

DeDe Egan, mother of Candy, Crystal, and Courtney

You have come to the conclusion of *Playful Learning*. Whether you skimmed the surface glancing only at interesting pages or whether you read this book page by page from front to back makes no difference. By now you probably have some new thoughts about preschool for your child. You may be totally convinced that a cooperative preschool-at-home is right for you and your child. Or you may still have many concerns, questions, or even doubts as to your ability or desire to try an at-home preschool.

One fact remains. If you are the parent of a child between the ages of three and six, a fantastic opportunity is knocking at your door. The time is **now** for you to get involved in your child's education. Never again will you have as much time available to you from him; never again will he have such a strong desire to be with you. All too soon your baby is an independent child and, in many ways, leading a life of his own. So now is the time to seize the opportunity waiting for you.

You're still not sure? Perhaps that's because there is a big contradiction facing parents today. That is, where do you place your priorities? Do you think your child needs to be professionally "educated" or do

As a parent, you want what's best for your child in terms of emotional as well as mental development.

you believe he needs to remain at home with you to ensure an emotionally secure, happy, and socially well-adjusted human being? To put it another way, do you want to send him to a traditional preschool or do you want to keep him at home with you in a cooperative arrangement? For some, this decision is an easy one; for others it is difficult.

The Road to Success

On the one hand, society is constantly telling parents that their child must be given special opportunities to learn in order to keep up with his peers. Not only do you want him to keep up, but you would also like him to have an edge over most of them. In the 1980s and in the future, children will be exposed to more and more ideas at a younger age than ever before. By the time a child is three or four years old, he has traveled more and been exposed to more things than his parents were at that age. Society, in general, seems to continually expect more of children at increasingly younger ages. They know all the "in phrases," the names of all the rock stars and entertainers, they dress like miniature adults, and play with small versions of adult toys. Young children are aware of designer jeans, computer games, and how to place an order at a fast-food restaurant. They are expected to be mentally, physically, socially, and emotionally developed to certain levels at a certain age.

On the other hand, as parents, you want to protect your child.

Although you want him to have the kind of experiences that give him the competitive edge over others, you also want him to be secure, happy, and self-confident. You hope your child will be able to respond positively to new situations, to be happy in developing new relationships, to be socially and emotionally stable and secure.

How do you blend these two needs: the need to progress in all developmental areas and the need to be happy and secure? How can you help your child without pushing him? How can you give your child a setting for maximum learning opportunities while filling his emotional need to be with you? How do you know what is best?

These Needs Can Be Met

These two needs can be blended harmoniously in a viable alternative—a cooperative at-home preschool. A small group of children and their parents can share and learn together through playful learning.

A cooperative preschool-at-home offers your child the best of two worlds. First, it addresses the need of the young child to learn. You can direct your energies toward presenting an environment rich in stimuli for learning. Materials, projects, and activities can be aimed at the specific needs of your child. His natural desire to explore, to manipulate, to discover, along with his yearning for new ideas and his enjoyment of participating with others can be recognized, accepted, and focused upon in your cooperative at-home preschool.

In an at-home preschool, activities can be planned to meet the specific needs of your child.

Your child needs to learn at his own pace, when he is ready, without pressure to achieve or compete.

Secondly, your cooperative preschool-at-home will help prevent you from encouraging your little one to grow up too fast. Your presence— as much as he needs you to be there—allows him to adjust gradually to the separation from mother and dad. The whole academic world is introduced to him gradually with mother's or dad's involvement. As a parent, you are probably sensitive to the social pressure to see your child achieve or to perform up to expectations (yours or society's). You have learned all too well that sometimes there seems to be a race as to the biggest baby, who walked and talked the earliest, and who can perform the best. But truthfully, you do want your child to do well. You really want him to be the best he can be. You enjoy the feeling of parental accomplishment when your child reaches a goal. When he succeeds at a task or skill, you are proud of his development and feel you have done a good job in raising him.

Pressures on parents

At the same time, however, there are not-so-subtle feelings of pressure when you are asked a question about your child's development. This pressure to help your child grow up is too often transferred from society, through you, on to him. Well, you have an opportunity to halt the pressure to a certain extent. You can slow down the academic push, or at least change the emphasis or direction. You can be a vital influence in your child's first learning experience through a cooperative preschool-at-home. You can control how much he is expected to learn and how he is expected to learn it. The pressure to achieve or to perform can be almost eliminated. Rather, in a positive, non-competitive setting, learning can take place at a gradual pace.

Your involvement in your child's preschool also increases the likelihood that your child will build a sense of emotional security and trust in teachers. As his earliest learning experiences take place in a warm, caring environment, a young child comes away feeling assured that he has been nurtured in love.

As a parent of a preschool-aged child, you will be teaching many of life's lessons. Your example—your words and your actions—will be his model for learning. You can be the catalyst in his discovery process. You can be the person who guides his thoughts, his actions, and his interactions.

As Your Child Grows

You have been a vital part of your preschooler's life since his conception, birth, infancy, crawling, and toddling times. The two of you did a lot of touching in those early days. As the parent of a new baby, you held him. You touched, caressed, and kissed him. As he grew, he gradually began pulling away from you. Physically he might even struggle to get off your lap or out of your arms. He wants to get down, to move, to explore; yet he still wants you to be there. How many times does he come back for a smile, a pat, or a quick hug, and then run off again?

You have watched your preschool child develop from a helpless infant into a fairly independent child so you are the one who understands him the best.

You can share in your child's first learning experiences as he develops physically, mentally, socially, and emotionally.

Your preschooler is emotionally not too much different than your toddler. He wants his freedom to run. He wants to play and discover, yet he, too, wants to touch base with you throughout his day. Whether it is to rub a hurt, to see what you are doing, or to show you the bugs he caught or the clay dinosaur he shaped, he wants you to be a part of his growing-up world.

But a few differences are apparent when you compare the relationship you have with your three- to six-year-old to the relationship you had when he was younger. Your relationship thrived on touching, and it still does. But now you are touching each other in different ways. Though he is no longer held for many hours of the day in your arms, he still needs your attention. So he will seek it in other ways, perhaps with eye contact and conversation. His need to interact with you is shifted more to an intellectual level. You might be participating with each other in a meaningful task. His growing ability to communicate allows him to touch base with you throughout the day through conversation. He is depending upon you to be there to answer his questions and to guide his thoughts. He is growing up and growing independent. You can continue to share a special relationship with him as you guide him into independence.

At the intellectual level, you do not need to turn him over to professional teachers quite yet. You are the professional who knows him best. Parents can handle the challenges of preschool learning. You cannot prevent your little one from growing up; you cannot stop the growth process, but you can be there with him and for him. Participating in a preschool-at-home gives you the opportunity to remain involved—physically, mentally, socially, and emotionally. He can venture out gradually and still touch base with you as frequently as he needs. He can enjoy learning through playful experiences with you nearby. He can have lots of learning opportunities and he can be relaxed in a secure, happy environment at the same time. Preschool-at-home offers playful learning shared by both of you.

A Mother's View

One mother shares her thoughts about preschool-at-home: "When my daughter was born, I was overjoyed and at the same time in awe of her. She was so tiny and so totally dependent on me to meet her needs. As I cradled her warm body, I wondered how her life might be molded through my love. We touched each other's soul from the very beginning. She grew and her eyes returned my gaze especially as she nursed encircled by my arms. Soon she was able to reach out for me, and I gave her my reassuring hugs. As she crawled, she stayed within range of my shadow. Toddling a few steps, she ventured away, but kept in my sight or the range of my voice. We touched as we played—wrestling, giggling, rolling on the floor—delighting in each other's smiles and laughter.

"Then as my little one grew closer to the age of entering school, I became concerned about the separation. The preschool dilemma hung over our heads. Should I send her? Would she be able to handle a structured plan for learning and separation from her parents at the same time? Does she really need to go to preschool? The time was approaching too quickly that my little one would be leaving home, traveling by bus, to go to kindergarten. Her friends and teachers would soon be a big influence in her life.

"So for many reasons, I decided to participate in a cooperative preschool-at-home. What a wonderful experience! We had many good times together—the little adventures, the projects, the planning of many group activities. We added a whole new chapter to her childhood. It was as though we had discovered each other all over again. But this time our relationship was not just that of parent and child, but of two people who really enjoyed being together. We touched each other at the emotional, physical, and mental levels. We shared so much with the other children and their parents. Most of all, we shared so much of ourselves with each other. We have bonded again, giving us a foundation for the growing-up years.

"Several years have passed since those preschool years that we spent together. We still look into each other's eyes, hold hands, and can touch each other's soul. Our lives are richer because of the deeper bond between us. Participating in a preschool-at-home showed us the way toward playful learning, then and now."

A Lasting Gift

Being the parent of a preschool child involves an awesome commitment along with a tremendous amount of time, patience, and love. Our responsibilities to our child do not lessen even though he grows older and becomes more capable and independent. Rather our responsibilities change as our child's needs grow and change. As we make every effort to fulfill those needs as completely and naturally as we can, we have the opportunity to share in his first learning experiences. We can impart to him the knowledge we have acquired through our lifetime of experiences; we can instill in him a trust of others; we can build a foundation of a positive outlook on life, we can help him develop an insatiable desire to learn.

And when we share in our child's playful learning, the giving of ourselves is the greatest of all the gifts we have ever given him.

Appendix A

A Developmental Skills Scale

The following skills checklist, compiled from numerous sources, is intended to give parents an idea of the skills their preschoolers are working on. The skills are interrelated—building blocks for further learning. Every child is unique and will learn in his own way. The checklist provides a progress chart, a scale to use as a reference point in deciding your child's needs. You will be able to determine your own child's growth in these developmental areas and decide what needs to be emphasized during his preschool day.

Don't worry if your child seems to do better in one area and not as well in other areas—that's how children learn. We cannot force a child to learn what he is not ready to learn. We can simply expose him to the kinds of skills he needs and observe his interest level. If he gets frustrated with a new skill, encourage him to do a simpler task that he can cope with. The skill charts generally begin with simpler activities and progress to more difficult skills.

You may choose to review these when deciding what to introduce to the children in your preschool program. (See Chapter 9 for more details on planning and evaluating your preschool program.)

At a parents' get-together, each parent could be given a copy of these Development Skills and asked to think about his or her own child's progress. (Or the parents could work on these ahead of time and bring them to the meeting.) The whole group of parents can then discuss which skills the majority of the children have mastered and which ones they still need to work on, without comparing one child's progress with another's progress. For example, if most of the children seem well-prepared in Science Awareness Skills, but many still need to master Small-Muscle Coordination, the group of parents would plan future preschool sessions to include activities that develop small muscle skills. Children younger than four or five should not be expected to complete all of the skills in any of these developmental areas.

DEVELOPMENTAL SKILLS PROGRESS CHART

Big Muscle Movement

_____ I can tell you which body parts I use:

to see	to clap	to eat
to jump	to hear	to reach.

_____ I can roll a ball back and forth to a partner.

_____ I can jump with two feet together.

_____ I can identify and use my body parts:

wrists	head	neck	knees	feet	elbows
legs	shoulders	hips	ankles	arms	back.

_____ I can imitate body movements, such as, feet apart—arms over head; head down—fingers on toes, etc.

_____ I know how to move in different directions: up, down, forward, backward, sideways.

_____ I can jog in place.

_____ I can climb a horizontal ladder one foot off the ground.

_____ I can hop (land on one foot) several times using the same foot.

_____ I can leap (take a giant step through space).

_____ I can pedal a tricycle or big wheel.

_____ I can clap to a simple rhythm.

_____ I can walk, jog, or run to match a rhythmical beat.

_____ I can toss a ball with limited control.

_____ I can bounce and catch a large ball.

_____ I can balance on one foot for five seconds.

_____ I can walk forward and backward on a line (tape or chalk).

_____ I can run, jump, and hop.

_____ I am learning to skip and gallop.

_____ I can go up and down stairs using alternate feet.

_____ I can jump over a rope laid on the ground.

_____ I am learning to jump over a moving rope that is close to the floor.

Small Muscle Coordination

_____ I can pick up small things such as: rubber bands, buttons, paper clips.

_____ I can stack five to eight blocks to build a tower.

_____ I can build a block bridge when shown how.

_____ I can use my eyes to follow my thumb without moving my head.

_____ I can find likenesses and differences in objects and pictures.

_____ I can brush my teeth and comb my hair.

_____ I can wind thread onto a spool (using wrist movement).

_____ I can touch my thumb to each finger on the same hand.

_____ I can work five- to eight-piece puzzles.

_____ I can use scissors to cut straight lines.

_____ I can use scissors to cut a curved line.

_____ I can zipper, snap, and button.

_____ I am learning to tie.

_____ I can hold a pencil between my thumb and index finger when drawing.

_____ I can trace simple shapes such as: circle, cross, square.

_____ I can copy a circle and a cross; a square is more difficult but I'm getting better. (Triangles and diamonds are too hard.)

_____ I can draw a person with six body parts.

_____ I am learning to print my name using the first letter as a capital, the rest of the letters lower case.

Language and Communication

_____   I can identify and name common objects.

_____   I can say my full name.

_____   I can listen to a story without interrupting.

_____   I can use singular and plural forms of common words: one girl, two girls; one mouse, two mice, etc. (When the word changes, children have more difficulty.)

_____   I can repeat short sentences, such as: "Shut the door and lock it" or "I would like to play outside on the swingset with you."

_____   I use words that tell where:

in	on	off	up	top
under	around	bottom	away from	in front of

_____   I talk in sentences using such words as: and, if, because, etc.

_____   I am able to say most sounds correctly with the exception of some sounds, for example, sun/thun; rabbit/wabbit; yellow/lellow.

_____   I can relate experiences and express myself among friends.

_____   I can repeat a familiar nursery rhyme like "Humpty Dumpty" or "Jack and Jill."

_____   I can sing a song from memory.

_____   I can name colors: red, blue, yellow, green, black, white, purple, and orange.

_____   I can read pictures and tell a story.

_____   I can tell a story in sequence with or without pictures.

_____   I can finish sentences with opposite or rhyming words:

_____ opposite: "Fire is hot, ice is _____(cold)."

_____ rhyming: "Let's play outside where we can _____ (hide)."

_____ both: "A giraffe is tall; a mouse is _____ (small)."

_____   I can give meaningful answers when asked simple questions:

     "Why do you have to wash your hands?"

     "Why do we have clocks?"

     "What are some things found in the sky?"

Readiness for Reading

_____ I show an interest in stories and enjoy listening to them.

_____ I look at books from the front to the back cover.

_____ I am able to sequence picture cards that tell a story from left to right.

_____ I can remember from stories read aloud such things as:

the names of the characters;

what happened in the story (main idea);

the ending of the story.

_____ I can talk about how the characters feel.

_____ I can predict what would happen if the story ended differently.

_____ I am learning to recognize and name several letters or letter sounds.

_____ I can think of some simple rhyming words.

_____ I can match letters and numbers.

_____ I can recognize my own name in print.

Math Readiness

_____ I can match colors.

_____ I can grade colors by intensity.

_____ I can sort objects by colors.

_____ I can name five to eight colors.

_____ I can sort objects by size, lining up the largest to the smallest.

_____ I can match shapes.

_____ I can name some shapes:
circle   square   triangle
oval   rectangle   diamond.

_____ I can use words that describe size:
big-little   fat-thin   tall-short
more-less   high-low   long-short.

_____ I can count to ten out loud.

_____ I can name a missing object from a group of five objects which I studied for ten seconds.

_____ I can repeat a pattern of sounds or numbers, such as, "clap two quick counts, one slow" or "repeat after me: 5 7 4 2" (say at one second intervals).

_____ I am learning about the names of the days of the week.

_____ I am beginning to understand and use some time words:

morning   afternoon   nighttime
today   tomorrow   yesterday.

_____ I can count ten objects correctly.

_____ I can name the numerals from one to ten when they are out of order.

Science Awareness

_____ I can describe the weather:
sunny   rainy   cloudy   cold
hot   snowy   foggy   freezing rain.

_____ I can tell what some objects are made of:
chair   shirt   plate
shoe   book   hammers.

_____ I am using my senses to learn about likenesses and differences.

_____ I can recognize sound differences, such as, high-low; loud-soft, etc.

_____ I can tell about the four seasons.

_____ I am learning about the months of the year.

_____ I am experimenting with which objects float and sink.

_____ I am experimenting with which objects stick to a magnet.

_____ I am learning about animals:

_____ names for adult and baby animals;

_____ where animals live.

_____ I am learning how plants begin to grow from seed to fruit.

Social Growth

_____ I am able to take care of my personal needs:

_____ use the toilet;

_____ wash hands;

_____ get a drink.

_____ I am learning to share.

_____ I am learning to work cooperatively with others.

_____ I am able to keep track of my belongings.

_____ I am learning to be caring and courteous.

_____ I am learning to clean up after myself.

_____ I can almost get dressed by myself.

_____ I help with simple chores:

_____ sweep with a whiskbroom;

_____ wipe up spills;

_____ carry dishes to the sink;

_____ wipe the table.

_____ I can work alone for short periods of time without adult guidance.

_____ I am learning to follow directions.

_____ I am learning to safely cross a street.

_____ I stay with the group when on an outing; I show caution when in an unfamiliar place.

_____ I listen when others speak.

_____ I am able to think independently

_____ when working;

_____ when playing;

_____ when creating.

Emotional Growth

_____ I am learning to show self-control.

_____ I take pride in my work.

_____ I have a sense of value; I can tell good from bad.

_____ I am learning about my own feelings and how to deal with them without hurting myself or others.

_____ I am beginning to understand that other people have feelings.

Sources for the Developmental Scale

Albuquerque Public School Early Education Curriculum Guide (Ages 4-8). 725 University Blvd. SE. Albuquerque NM 87106.

Denver Developmental Screening Test (1966). Frankenburg, W. K., and J. B. Dobbs. Denver CO.

Early Childhood Individual Pupil Checklist. Valley View School District 365-U. Bolingbrook IL 60441.

Early Prevention of School Failure (Nationally validated program). K-W Curriculum Service Office. 114 N. 2nd Street, Peotone IL 60468.

How Does Your Child Hear and Talk? American Speech and Hearing Foundation. Rockville MD 20852.

Preschool Educational Attainment Scale (1966). Doll, Edgar A., and Edward L. McKnight. 2373 Chuckanut Drive Bellingham WA.

Preschool Preposition Test (1968). Aaronson, May, and Earl Schaefer. 5454 Wisconsin Avenue, Chevy Chase MD 20015.

Slosson Intelligence Test for Children and Adults. Slosson Educational Publications. 140 Pine Street, East Aurora NY 14052.

Verbal Language Developmental Scale. Mecham, Merlin J. American Guidance Service. Public Building, Circle Pines MN 55014.

Appendix B

Needs of the Young Child

EMOTIONAL

A child needs to feel secure (unthreatened).

A child needs to be with his parents.

A child needs to feel loved, capable, and worthy.

A child needs to begin to understand and label his feelings.

A child needs to begin to manage his own feelings.

SOCIAL

A child needs to have positive interactions with other children.

A child needs to learn to care about others.

A child needs to feel secure in his relationship with his parents.

A child needs to have positive interactions with other adults.

A child needs to become acquainted with people in the community (librarian, mail carrier, grocery clerk).

PHYSICAL

A child needs to explore and practice movement:

Big muscle (run, jump, climb);
Small muscle (zipper, color, cut, spoon);
Coordinate movement and sense (eye-hand, ear-hand).

A child needs to learn about his body in space:

> In relation to himself (learn to name body parts: arm, ankle, neck);
> In relation to space and time (stop, go, over, under).

A child needs to explore and use his five senses.

MENTAL

A child needs to begin labeling and ordering his sensory experiences (colors, shapes, sizes):

> Match likenesses and sort differences;
> Make comparisons (big, bigger, biggest);
> Use memory skills;
> Use patterns.

A child needs exposure to natural concepts:

> Seasons, weather;
> Animals, plants, earth.

A child needs exposure to mechanical concepts:

> Tools, scissors, hammers, pencils;
> Modes of transportation;
> Magnets, magnifying glasses.

A child needs to learn about people:

> Growth cycle (babies, children, elders);
> Handicaps;
> Other cultures;
> Occupations.

A child needs an opportunity to express himself:

> Responsible communication;
> Creative (language, art, drama);
> Imaginative play.

A child needs to learn self-care concepts:

> Health care;
> Manners;
> Getting dressed;
> Care of belongings.

A child needs to learn about holidays and special events.

Appendix C

Bibliography

Sources of Quoted Material

Beck, Joan. *How to Raise a Brighter Child.* New York: Simon & Schuster, 1975.

Bettelheim, Bruno. *The Uses of Enchantment.* New York: Random House, 1975.

Bettelheim, Bruno, and Karen Zelan. *On Learning to Read.* New York: Random House, 1982.

Bos, Bev. *Don't Move the Muffin Tins.* Roseville, California: Turn the Page Press, 1978.

Branley, Franklyn M., and Eleanor K. Vaughn. *Mickey's Magnet.* New York: Scholastic Book Services, 1956.

Briggs, Dorothy Corkille. *Your Child's Self Esteem: The Key to Life.* Garden City, New York: Doubleday & Company, 1970.

Cahill, Mary Ann. *The Heart Has Its Own Reasons.* Franklin Park, Illinois: La Leche League International, 1983.

Campbell, D. Ross. *How to Really Love Your Child.* Wheaton, Illinois: Victor Books, 1980.

Carr, Rachel. *Be a Frog, a Bird, or a Tree.* New York: Harper Colophon Books, 1973.

Dreikurs, Rudolf. *Children, the Challenge.* New York: Hawthorn Books, 1964.

Dreskin, Wendy, and William Dreskin. *The Day Care Decision: What's Best for You and Your Child.* New York: M. Evans and Co., 1983.

Elkind, David. *The Hurried Child: Growing Up Too Fast Too Soon.* Reading, Massachusetts: Addison-Wesley, 1981.

Emery, Donald G. *Teach Your Preschooler to Read.* New York: Simon and Schuster, 1975.

Faber, Adele, and Elaine Mazlish. *How to Talk So Kids Will Listen and Listen So Kids Will Talk.* New York: Avon Books, 1980.

Fiarotta, Phyllis. *Sticks and Stones and Ice Cream Cones.* New York: Workman Publishing Company, 1973.

Flint Public Library. *Ring A Ring O'Roses: Stories, Games and Fingerplays for Preschool Children.* Flint, Michigan: Flint Public Library, 1981.

Freeman, Mae. *The Real Magnet Book.* New York: Scholastic Book Services, 1967.

Glazer, Tom. *Do Your Ears Hang Low?* Garden City, New York: Doubleday, 1980.

Glazer, Tom. *Eye Winker, Tom Tinker, Chin Chopper.* Garden City, New York: Doubleday, 1973.

Gordon, Thomas. *Parent Effectiveness Training.* New York: New American Library, 1975.

Gregg, Elizabeth M., and Judith D. Knotts. *Growing Wisdom, Growing Wonder.* New York: MacMillan, 1980.

Hainstock, Elizabeth G. *Teaching Montessori in the Home: the Preschool Years.* New York: New American Library, 1968.

Holt, John. *Teach Your Own.* New York: Delacorte Press, 1981.

Honig, Alice. *Parent Involvement in Early Childhood Education.* Washington, DC: National Association for the Education of Young Children, 1975.

Hymes, James L., Jr. *The Child under Six.* Englewood Cliffs, New Jersey: Prentice-Hall, 1963.

Ilg, Frances, and Louise Bates Ames. *The Gesell Institute's Child Behavior.* New York: Harper and Row, 1955.

Jensen, Rosalie, and Deborah Spector. *Teaching Mathematics to Young Children.* Englewood Cliffs, New Jersey: Prentice-Hall, 1984.

Jones, Sandy. *Learning for Little Kids.* Boston: Houghton Mifflin, 1978.

Kaplan, Louise J. *Oneness and Separateness: From Infant to Individual.* New York: Simon and Schuster, 1978.

Katz, Pat. *Sandcastles & Snowflakes: 40 Innovative & Creative Art Activities for Children 2-7.* Walnut Creek, California: M.A.D. Publishing Company, 1980.

Kelly, Marguerite, and Elia Parsons. *The Mother's Almanac.* Garden City, New York: Doubleday, 1975.

Kenny, James, and Mary Kenny. *Whole-Life Parenting.* New York: Continuum, 1982.

Kephart, Newell. *The Slow Learner in the Classroom.* Columbus: Charles E. Merrill, 1960.

Klaus, Marshall H., and John H. Kennell. *Maternal-Infant Bonding.* St. Louis: C. V. Mosby, 1976.

La Leche League. *Whole Foods for the Whole Family.* Franklin Park, Illinois: La Leche League International, 1981.

La Leche League. *The Womanly Art of Breastfeeding.* Franklin Park, Illinois: La Leche League International, 1981.

Lansky, Vicki. *Feed Me, I'm Yours.* Wayzata, Minnesota: Meadowbrook Press, 1971.

Lowman, Kaye. *Of Cradles and Careers.* Franklin Park, Illinois: La Leche League International, 1984.

Marzollo, Jean. *Supertot: Creative Learning Activities for Children One to Three and Sympathetic Advice for Their Parents.* New York: Harper Colophon Books, 1977.

Marzollo, Jean, and Janice Lloyd. *Learning through Play.* New York: Harper and Row, 1972.

McKee, Paul. *Reading: A Program of Instruction for the Elementary School.* Boston: Houghton Mifflin, 1966.

McMahon, Peggy. *Mothering Magazine.* Summer 1982.

Montessori, Maria. *A Montessori Handbook.* New York: Capricorn Books, 1966.

Moore, Raymond, and Dorothy Moore. *Home Grown Kids.* Waco, Texas: Word Books, 1981.

Nelson, Esther L. *Dancing Games for Children of All Ages.* New York: Sterling, 1973.

Nevins, Dan. *Science Fun: Simple Experiments and Projects.* Mahwah, New Jersey: Watermill Press, 1980.

Pearce, Joseph Chilton. *Magical Child.* New York: Bantam Books, 1977.

Pine, Tillie S., and Joseph Levine. *Magnets and How to Use Them.* New York: Scholastic Book Services, 1958.

Pulaski, Mary Ann Spencer. *Your Baby's Mind and How It Grows: Piaget's Theory for Parents.* New York: Harper & Row, 1978.

Rockwell, Robert E., Elizabeth A. Sherwood, and Robert A. Williams. *Hug a Tree and Other Things to Do Outdoors with Young Children.* Mt. Ranier, Maryland: Gryphon House, 1983.

Rogers, Fred and Barry Head. *Mister Rogers Talks with Parents.* New York: Berkley Books, 1983.

Satir, Virginia. *Peoplemaking.* Palo Alto, California: Science and Behavior Books, 1972.

Sears, William. *Nighttime Parenting.* Franklin Park, Illinois: La Leche League International, 1985.

Sears, William. *Creative Parenting.* New York: Dodd, Mead, 1982.

Standing, E. M. *Maria Montessori: Her Life and Work.* New York: New American Library, 1957.

Sullivan, Molly. *Feeling Strong, Feeling Free: Movement Exploration for Young Children.* Washington, DC: National Association for the Education of Young Children, 1982.

Supraner, Robyn, and Lauren Supraner. *Plenty of Puppets to Make.* Mahwah, New Jersey: Troll Association, 1981.

Trelease, Jim. *The Read-Aloud Handbook.* New York: Viking-Penguin Books, 1982.

Walt Disney Productions. *The Mickey Mouse Make-It Book.* New York: Random House, 1974.

White, Burton L. *The First Three Years of Life.* Englewood Cliffs, New Jersey: Prentice-Hall, 1975.

White, Laurence B. *Science Toys and Tricks.* Reading, Massachusetts: Addison-Wesley, 1975.

Zaslavsky, Claudia. *Preparing Young Children for Math: A Book of Games.* New York: Schocken Books, 1979.

Zigler, Edward, and Jeanette Valentine. *Project Head Start: A Legacy of the War on Poverty.* New York: Macmillan, 1979.

Resources for Further Information about Young Children

For more background on full-time parenting

Cahill, Mary Ann. *The Heart Has Its Own Reasons.* Franklin Park, Illinois: La Leche League International, 1983.

Dreskin, Wendy, and William Dreskin. *The Day Care Decision: What's Best for You and Your Child.* New York: M. Evans & Co., 1983.

Elkind, David. *The Hurried Child: Growing Up Too Fast Too Soon.* Reading, Massachusetts: Addison-Wesley, 1981.

Green, Martin. *A Sigh of Relief: The First Aid Handbook for Childhood Emergencies.* New York: Bantam Books, 1977.

Holt, John. *Teach Your Own.* New York: Delacorte Press, 1981.

Huth, Holly Young. *Centerplay.* New York: Simon and Schuster, 1984.

Kaplan, Louise J. *Oneness and Separateness: From Infant to Individual.* New York: Simon and Schuster, 1978.

Kelly, Marguerite, and Elia Parsons. *The Mother's Almanac.* Garden City, New York: Doubleday, 1975.

Kenny, James, and Mary Kenny. *Whole-Life Parenting.* New York: Continuum, 1982.

La Leche League International. *The Womanly Art of Breastfeeding.* Franklin Park, Illinois: La Leche League International, 1987.

Lowman, Kaye. *Of Cradles and Careers.* Franklin Park, Illinois: La Leche League International, 1984.

Moore, Raymond, and Dorothy Moore. *Home Grown Kids.* Waco, Texas: Word Books, 1981.

Mothering Magazine. Santa Fe, New Mexico: Mothering Publications.

Pearce, Joseph Chilton. *Magical Child.* New York: Bantam Books, 1977.

Sullivan, S. Adams. *The Quality Time Almanac.* New York: Doubleday, 1986.

Sears, William. *Becoming a Father.* Franklin Park, Illinois: La Leche League International, 1986.

Sears, William. *Fussy Baby.* Franklin Park, Illinois: La Leche League International, 1985.

Sears, William. *Nighttime Parenting.* Franklin Park, Illinois: La Leche League International, 1985.

White, Burton L. *The First Three Years of Life.* Englewood Cliffs, New Jersey: Prentice Hall, 1975.

For more reading in the area of child development

Hymes, James L., Jr. *The Child Under Six.* Englewood Cliffs, New Jersey: Prentice-Hall, 1963.

Ilg, Frances, and Louise Bates Ames. *The Gesell Institute's Child Behavior.* New York: Harper and Row, 1955.

Pulaski, Mary Ann Spencer. *Your Baby's Mind and How It Grows: Piaget's Theory for Parents.* New York: Harper and Row, 1978.

Sears, William. *Creative Parenting.* New York: Dodd, Mead, 1982.

Sears, William. *Growing Together.* Franklin Park, Illinois: La Leche League International, 1987.

For more ideas on stimulating early learning

Beck, Joan. *How To Raise A Brighter Child.* New York: Simon and Schuster, 1975.

Broad, Laura Peabody, and Nancy Towner Butterworth. *The Playgroup Handbook.* New York: St. Martin's Press, 1974.

Dunford, Jill W. *Teach Me, Mommy.* Cincinnati, Ohio: Writers Digest Books, 1984.

Gregg, Elizabeth M., and Judith D. Knotts. *Growing Wisdom, Growing Wonder.* New York: MacMillan, 1980.

Jones, Sandy. *Learning For Little Kids.* Boston: Houghton Mifflin, 1978.

Leeper, Sarah Hammond et al. *Good Schools for Young Children.* New York: Mac Millan, 1974.

Marzolla, Jean. *Supertot.* New York: Harper Colophon Books, 1977.

Sparling, Joseph, and Isabelle Lewis. *Learning Games For the First Three Years.* New York: Berkley Books, 1979.

For information dealing with children's feelings

Briggs, Dorothy Corkille. *Your Child's Self Esteem: The Key to Life.* Garden City, New York: Doubleday, 1970.

Campbell, D. Ross. *How to Really Love Your Child.* Wheaton, Illinois: Victor Books, 1980.

Leshan, Eda. *When Your Child Drives You Crazy.* New York: St. Martin's Press, 1985.

Olshaker, Bennett. *The Child as a Work of Art.* Washington, DC: Marko Books, 1975.

Riley Sue Spayth. *How to Generate Values in Young Children.* Washington, DC: National Association for the Education of Young Children, 1984.

Rogers, Fred, and Barry Head. *Mister Rogers Talks with Parents.* New York: Berkley Books, 1983.

Satir, Virginia. *Peoplemaking.* Palo Alto, California: Science and Behavior Books, 1972.

For those interested in improving their communication abilities

Bove, Linda. *Sesame Street Sign Language Fun.* New York: Random House, 1980.

Crary, Elizabeth. *Kids Can Cooperate.* Seattle: Parenting Press, 1984.

Faber, Adele, and Elaine Mazlish. *How to Talk So Kids Will Listen and Listen So Kids Will Talk.* New York: Avon Books, 1980.

Gordon, Thomas. *Parent Effectiveness Training.* New York: New American Library, 1975.

For more information on Montessori teaching methods

Hainstock, Elizabeth. *Teaching Montessori in the Home: the Preschool Years.* New York: New American Library, 1968.

Shakesby, Paul. *Child's Work: A Learning Guide to Joyful Play.* Philadelphia: Running Press, 1974.

To learn more about the importance of play

Caney, Steven. *Playbook.* New York: Workman Publishing, 1975.

Hirsch, Elizabeth S. *The Block Book.* Washington, DC: National Association for the Education of Young Children, 1984.

Marzolla, Jean, and Janice Lloyd. *Learning through Play.* New York: Harper and Row, 1972.

Rogers, Fred, and Barry Head. *Mister Rogers' Playbook.* New York: Berkley Books, 1986.

For some creative movement ideas

Carr, Rachel. *Be a Frog, a Bird, or a Tree.* New York: Harper Colophon Books, 1973.

Sullivan, Molly. *Feeling Strong, Feeling Free: Movement Exploration For Young Children.* Washington, DC: National Association for the Education of Young Children, 1982.

To learn more about art and the preschool child

Bos, Bev. *Don't Move the Muffin Tins.* Roseville, California: Turn The Page Press, 1978.

Carson, Janet. *Tell Me About Your Picture: Art Activities to Help Children Communicate.* Englewood Cliff, New Jersey: Prentice Hall, 1984.

Katz, Pat. *Sandcastles & Snowflakes.* M.A.D. Publishing Co., 1980.

To gain more insight into reading for preschoolers

Bettelheim, Bruno, and Karen Zelan. *On Learning to Read.* New York: Random House, 1982.

Lynch-Fraser, Diane. *Getting Ready to Read.* New York: New American Library, 1985.

Smethurst, Wood. *Teaching Young Children to Read at Home.* New York: McGraw Hill, 1975.

Trelease, Jim. *The Read Aloud Handbook.* New York: Viking-Penguin Books, 1979.

To better understand science and its importance to preschoolers

Durant, Penny J., and Linda Hudson. *Cinnamon Smoke: Science Activities for Young Children.* Albuquerque: 1986.

Nevins, Dan. *Science Fun.* Mahwah, New Jersey: Watermill Press, 1980.

Rockwell, Robert E., Elizabeth A. Sherwood, and Robert A. Williams. *Hug a Tree and Other Things to Do Outdoors with Young Children.* Mt. Ranier, Maryland: Gryphon House, 1983.

White, Laurence B. *Science Toys & Tricks.* Reading, Massachusetts: Addison Wesley, 1975.

To gain more insight into mathematics for the young child

Burns, Marilyn. *The I Hate Mathematics Book.* Boston: Little, Brown & Co., 1975.

Jensen, Rosalie, and Deborah Spector. *Teaching Mathematics to Young Children.* Englewood Cliffs, New Jersey: Prentice Hall, 1984.

For more creative cooking ideas

Betty Crocker's Cookbook for Boys and Girls. New York: Golden Press, Western Publishing Company, 1975.

Jenkins, Karen S. *Kinder-Krunchies.* Available from Discovery Toys, Box 232008, Pleasant Hill, California 94523 or local sales consultant.

Jundt, Jackie, and Lucy Rumpf. *Cooking Up Learning.* Lafayette, Indiana: Growing Child Playthings, 1976. To order, send $5.00 to Lucy Rumpf, 5 Hilldale Drive, Belleville, Illinois 62223.

La Leche League International. *Whole Foods for the Whole Family.* Franklin Park, Illinois: La Leche League International, 1981.

Saltzman, Mark, Judy Garlan, and Michele Grodner. *Super Heroes Super Healthy Cookbook.* New York: Warner Books, 1981.

Veitch, Beverly, and Thelma Harms. *Cook and Learn.* Menlo Park, California: Addison-Wesley, 1981.

For more musical ideas

Beall, Pamela Conn and Susan Hagen Nipp. *Wee Sing Books.* Los Angeles, California: Price, Stern, Sloan Publishers, 1977.

Glazer, Tom. *Eye Winker, Tom Tinker, Chin Chopper.* Garden City, New York: Doubleday, 1973.

Rogers, Fred. *Mister Rogers' Song Book.* New York: Berkley Books, 1983.

Appendix D

About the Authors

Anne's Story about Preschool

I am the mother of five young children. Like you, I care very much about my children. I want them to grow up well and reach their potential. Their early experiences with structured learning were a concern to me, especially with my first daughter, Rachel. I worried, questioned, discussed, and thought some more, about whether she was ready for preschool. Many of the parents around us were sending their children to an out-of-the-home, traditional preschool. There were some very good preschools available to us.

After serious evaluation of Rachel—her needs, abilities, personality, and other factors that only a parent can know—I realized some important things. She would probably do well academically. Yet, socially, she was shy and hesitant, lacking in self-confidence. Finally I decided, with the support of my husband, that we would not send her to a traditional preschool. So instead, with the help of some neighborhood friends, I organized an informal, cooperative preschool. We met once a week for about two-and-a-half hours at a time during the year before Rachel and the others would go to kindergarten. It went well and I learned a lot about my daughter. Rachel grew and developed in many ways. Most of all, we enjoyed each other's company in this first learning environment. We had fun!

The following year, my second daughter, Laura, was four years old. Again the question of preschool came up. Again I took a good look at my daughter—her strengths, weak areas, her personality, readiness, and so on. Laura was socially confident and outgoing. Academically she was very strong. But her "effervescent" behavior would have been unac-

Anne and Jerry Engel-hardt with Rachel, Laura, Matthew, Sarah, and Luke

ceptable in a structured preschool. Again we weighed all the pros and cons about preschool, but this time I knew of our other options. The decision was much easier. I formed another at-home cooperative pre-school with four other mothers and their children. We were more or-ganized and better prepared than the first time. That year of at-home preschool was another terrific experience, one in which I felt a new level of bonding with my daughter. It was a year filled with special ex-periences for us to build upon.

It was about this time that I began to share with other mothers what I had learned about cooperative at-home preschool. Then my good friend Cheryl and I began to compare notes, discuss, and help each other with our preschool groups. There seemed to be a need for information so we decided to write a pamphlet to help other groups. Well, our pam-phlet turned into a booklet and then into a full-fledged book. We were excited about everything related to the preschool-aged child. We read and researched and attended workshops and classes to help us become better informed about our own children. This also prepared us for writ-ing some parts of our book. Our book is intended to help parents to appreciate their children, to share in their children's natural growth and development, and to enhance their relationship.

Two years later my third child, Sarah, was three years old and really ready and anxious for sociable experiences. Sarah was a happy, confident, and smart little girl. I knew she would do well and enjoy preschool. This time, however, I didn't have to worry about making a decision. Sarah would participate in our cooperative at-home preschool—there was no question about it. She could hardly wait and neither could I.

By this time I had begun to realize that a preschool experience is probably good for most three- to six-year-olds. It is probably most beneficial for its immediate value rather than for long range goals. Most of all, I realized that the alternative of participating in a cooperative at-home preschool experience offered us an opportunity to build our relationship that could happen in no other way. We were able to strengthen the parent-child bond between us. So we were a part of a playgroup when she was three years old, and a different preschool group the next year when she was four. It was everything good that we had anticipated it would be.

Well, my life has been blessed with two more children. My son Matthew will soon be three and we're planning a playgroup. I'm sure I'll be a part of a cooperative at-home preschool the next year with Matthew. And the following year, my fifth child, Luke, and I will enjoy being involved in preschool together. At this state of my mothering, it is as exciting as awaiting the birth of a baby. I can anticipate sharing a beautiful and happy experience with my little boys.

Cheryl's Story about Preschool

My experiences with playgroups and at-home preschool are unlike Anne's experience. I decided to develop an at-home preschool with my children out of a process of elimination. When Tara was about three years old, I began to look into preschools. I knew she was ready for preschool socially from watching her during our gym and swim classes in which I participated. I decided to visit some local preschools to see the children in action and to discuss the goals of the program with each of the directors. I talked to other mothers about the preschools their children were attending, and I listened to other parents share their excitement for cooperative preschools that were run by the parents themselves.

After comparing notes, looking at Tara's needs, and realizing that the preschools I had visited were doing activities that I did (or could do) at home, I decided to organize an at-home cooperative preschool for her. This preschool at-home had planned activities; we followed a simple routine, but we were flexible. We formed some good friendships between the parents and children. I really did enjoy being a part of Tara's first preschool experience. I also enjoyed my time off when she was at another parent's home.

We had decided to break for the summer and start the group again in September. During that summer, Tara begged me to allow her to go to a local preschool. Because I had previously been in touch with the school, I was able to get her enrolled. At first Tara really looked forward to going each day, but after several weeks her enthusiasm waned. She liked the teacher and the children; she seemed to enjoy the activities, but she just wanted to stay at home. I was a little afraid that if I allowed her to stay home from preschool, she would feel she could do the same when she was in kindergarten. Finally, I followed my heart and let her stay home—a decision I am still proud that we made.

In September, we reorganized our cooperative at-home preschool. This year was very special for us. Tara and I both grew. I learned of Tara's concern for other children, her joy in sharing with others. I didn't need a teacher's conference to learn about her strong points and weaknesses. I learned to respect Tara for who she was rather than what she could do.

As my son Darren approached three years of age, we decided to move across the country. Tara was ready to start kindergarten, but I wanted to participate in a cooperative at-home preschool with Darren. It was much more difficult to do this in our new community. I learned to be patient as I met others and shared my excitement for this kind of preschool. We formed a small group, but during the first year we had a constant turnover. Sometimes we had three children, then suddenly we had seven. But the children had fun, and that's what counts.

That year, I had the opportunity to co-teach in a local Montessori school. I learned about Montessori preschool firsthand. It was a good school with caring adults. I made some personal observations which eased my mind about our at-home preschool. The two-year-olds needed much adult attention and lots of holding. The three-year-olds were very social, preferring to play with one or two others. They loved to imagine and pretend; they, too, often needed recognition from an adult. The four-year-olds were more aggressive socially, forming groups of four or five friends. They didn't need as much attention from adults; they began to rely upon each other. I realized that this was only one preschool and my observations were limited to a small sample. However, this experience confirmed what I had previously read about young children.

When Darren came with me to the Montessori school, he was clingy. It was hard to share his mother with so many others. He made some friendships, but had difficulty claiming his swing on the playground when confronted by two or three other children. He wasn't as intimidated or clingy during our at-home preschool sessions. I'm sure he

would have grown more confident in a larger group if he was given some time, but it was not necessary. Our at-home cooperative preschool really took hold the next year.

Darren's year before kindergarten was great. Our preschool focused on lots of experiential opportunities. We went on a field trip every week; we went to places we never would have visited without the inspiration from one another.

Darren loved our preschool. He especially liked the art activities and craft projects. He wasn't too interested in learning about numbers or letters; he preferred listening to and acting out stories. He is especially adept at interpreting a character's feelings. I am sure that eventually the mechanics of reading and math will arouse his attention, but right now I am content to know he is pleased with himself.

Anne and I decided to write this book because we wanted to share our experiences and help you create a special relationship with your child during the preschool years. Anne made her decisions about at-home preschool almost instinctively; I made mine through trial and error. We followed two different paths but reached the same conclusion. We hope you can take what you need from PLAYFUL LEARNING and, in so doing, share a little bit of your love.

Acknowledgments

We wish to extend a special thank-you to—

Judy Torgus, our editor, who guided and corrected our toddling attempt at creating our first book;

Evelyn Anderman, who patiently and painstakingly processed our manuscript into a computer system, and Elayne Shpak, who carefully coded it for the typesetter;

La Leche League International, who gave us a foundation for nurturing relationships with our children and families;

Our parents, who instilled in us a lifelong desire to learn and a determination to experience life to its fullest;

Dede Egan and Karen Leon, our good friends, who helped spread the joy of preschooling our children;

The fine staff at the Escuela Del Sol Montessori School who helped us appreciate the natural stages of learning in young children;

The many playgroup and preschool parents who shared their children and experiences in learning through play and who expressed to us the need for a practical, hands-on book like this to use with young children.

Anne and Cheryl

About La Leche League International

La Leche League International is a nonprofit organization that offers information and encouragement to mothers who want to breastfeed their babies. La Leche League International publishes PLAYFUL LEARNING along with a variety of other books and pamphlets on breastfeeding, nutrition, and parenting.

THE WOMANLY ART OF BREASTFEEDING, now in its fourth edition, is a comprehensive guide to nursing a baby. With more than 2 million copies in print, the book has been a favorite of mothers for its practical, down-to-earth, warmly supportive approach to breastfeeding.

To order a copy of THE WOMANLY ART OF BREASTFEEDING, additional copies of PLAYFUL LEARNING, or to find out more about La Leche League International, return the coupon below to LLLI, P. O. Box 4079, Schaumburg IL 60168-4079 USA.

_____ Please send me _____ copies of PLAYFUL LEARNING: AN ALTERNATE APPROACH TO PRESCHOOL at $14.95. (Please include $4.00 for shipping and handling.)

_____ Please send me _____ copies of THE WOMANLY ART OF BREASTFEEDING, LLLI's basic how-to manual for breastfeeding mothers at $10.95. (Please include $4.00 for shipping and handling.)

_____ Please send me a FREE copy of LLLI's Catalogue.

(Please include payment with your order. IL and CA residents please include sales tax. Prices are subject to change without notice and may vary outside the USA.)

_____

Name

_____

Address

_____

State/Province   Zip/Postal Code   Country